LAND USE

McGRAW-HILL SERIES IN FOREST RESOURCES

Henry J. Vaux, Consulting Editor

*WALTER MULFORD WAS CONSULTING EDITOR OF THIS SERIES
FROM ITS INCEPTION IN 1931 UNTIL JANUARY 1, 1952.*

LAND USE

Kenneth P. Davis
Professor Emeritus of Forest Land Use
School of Forestry and Environmental Studies
Yale University

McGRAW-HILL BOOK COMPANY
New York   St. Louis   San Francisco   Auckland   Düsseldorf
Johannesburg   Kuala Lumpur   London   Mexico   Montreal   New Delhi
Panama   Paris   São Paulo   Singapore   Sydney   Tokyo   Toronto

LAND USE

1 2 3 4 5 6 7 8 9 0 D O D O 7 8 3 2 1 0 9 8 7 6

This book was set in Times Roman by National ShareGraphics, Inc.
The editors were William J. Willey and Shelly Levine Langman;
the production supervisor was Judi Allen.
R. R. Donnelley & Sons Company was printer and binder.

Library of Congress Cataloging in Publication Data

Davis, Kenneth Pickett, date
    Land Use.

    (McGraw-Hill series in forest resources)
    1. Land. I. Title.
HD111.D33   333.7   75-37593
ISBN 0-07-015534-8

*To the Yale School of Forestry
and Environmental Studies, which
made this book possible*

CONTENTS

INTRODUCTION

The purpose of this book is to increase understanding of land-use situations and problems. It is written for students and interested people generally. Because land use is broad in scope, its study is multidisciplinary; thus this book draws freely on social, biological, and physical science material.

At the outset, it is emphasized that land-use problems are people problems. They become more pressing as population and natural resource needs increase. In land use, one is consequently working with a complex and changing human-land relationship and balance, and few problems are susceptible to technological solutions only.

The scope of this book is both urban and nonurban. Although land-use situations and problems often differ widely in specifics, they all have much in common, as is emphasized in this book. Urban and nonurban areas are also deeply interdependent in land use; neither can prosper without the other. Politically, the predominantly urban vote in the United States increasingly influences and often decides the uses of nonurban lands. Some examples include agricultural and forestry land-use practices, fish and wildlife management, and mineral extraction. Similar situations exist in many other countries.

Although the author knows the United States best, his knowledge of other countries gained by study and travel strengthens the treatment of the subject. Much effort has been made to make the book as widely useful and timeless as possible.

How best to read this book will depend on the knowledge and interests of the reader. Insofar as practicable, each chapter is planned to stand alone although the chapters are grouped into three subject areas. Some readers may wish to start with Chapter 1, which gives an introduction to the peculiar importance of land, to concepts of stewardship and conservation, and to the maintenance of environmental quality regarding its use. Chapter 13 might be read early to gain a broad overview of land use. Readers might also begin with the case studies, which focus on the hard realities of particular land-use situations and should help give a better understanding of the subject material chapters.

Use of the word "principle" in this book merits some explanation. Dictionary definitions of the word give a broad range of meanings, including attitude, opinion, general rule or method for application, doctrine, general law or truth, and belief. The wide range of problems and issues encountered in the practice of land use certainly includes application of principles. However, no separate listing of land-use principles has been made. Rather, the *substance* of principles is given in the context of particular land-use situations.

The reason for this is that a principle is general, often a truism, and takes significance only in a particular context. To put it another way, there is considerable difference between discussing a matter of principle in a given situation and defining the principle itself independently of any situation. A large number of principles apply to land use because it is so deeply entrenched in human interests and feelings, but few if any are peculiar to land use. For example, the saying "the view depends on the point of view" expresses a deep truth which certainly applies to many situations other than land use.

The four case studies and concluding Chapter 13 focus on principle. Each case chapter ends with a "What has been learned" section, which identifies matters of principle although these are not formally stated. Chapter 13 emphasizes the application of principle in many different land-use contexts.

Finally, active reader participation is welcomed, as is frequently emphasized in this book. The author is keenly aware that some things were indubitably left out that might be included and that different points of view can be taken.

ACKNOWLEDGMENTS

Preparation of this book necessarily has drawn on many sources of information. I should like to acknowledge my debt to the close personal contacts with many students in the United States and other parts of the world from whom I have learned much during thirty years of teaching.

Many professional colleagues both in and out of the United States and others, whether known to me or not, have contributed in some way. This includes over a hundred professional people in ten countries who generously gave of their time and knowledge on my 1972 land-use study trip in Europe. I would like to extend particular gratitude to Henry J. Vaux, Douglas M. Knudson, and William R. Bentley.

I wish to thank the Yale School of Forestry and Environmental Studies, which gave me the opportunity to prepare this book. Also, much appreciation goes to my wife, Mary Shope Davis, and to my secretary, Anne Fletcher, who did the typing.

Kenneth P. Davis

LAND USE

PART 1, Chapters 1–5

Land and human interrelationships. Concepts of land; stewardship, conservation, and maintenance of environmental quality. Landownership, tenure, and ownership rights. Lands of many uses, reversible and irreversible. Combined uses and compatibilities both urban and nonurban. Land classifications, the basis for data collection, zoning and dominant use. Land-use controls, title ownership, and other legal controls. Police and regulatory powers, grants-in-aid, and administrative land controls.

Concepts of Land: Its Ownership and Use

As circumscribed by the earth, the area of what is considered to be land is finite and fixed in place. Land uses are subject to control by people, whose numbers are not fixed, who have many needs, and who move easily. Most of people's need for food, clothing, shelter, and energy come from the land, as do many of their needs for the amenities provided by fields, landscapes, and forests. The importance of land and the concern for its stewardship are built into people's religions.

A thesis of this book is the need to develop understanding of and respect for the land and its many natural resources; that is, to develop a land ethic which permeates thinking and engenders broad understanding. Further, it is believed that although land situations may vary widely in specifics, they share principles that can be recognized and usefully applied in practice.

One important problem common to many land-use situations is lack of adequate governance, that is, lack of sufficient authority to organize, plan, and manage. Planning, for example, may be good but fail in application for several reasons, including lack of sufficient support by concerned people, inadequate finance, or inability to revise plans to meet changing conditions. The Lake Tahoe case (Chap. 9) is an example of a long effort to establish effective governance in the Tahoe Basin, the need for which has been only partially met by establishment by the U.S. Congress of a bistate compact between Nevada and California.

Also common is the need to establish effective control over uses that may be needed to achieve successful land management. This often requires recognition of both public and private rights of ownership exercised in a desirable relationship and balance with land resources and people needs. It may also include use of legal instruments short of title ownership—as easements, leases, or land classifications such as zoning—that can be established by public authority. The basic principle here is that in unity there is strength.

To comprehend complex areas of knowledge such as land use, it is necessary to learn to recognize issues and problems that are basically similar although occurring in seemingly different contexts. Taken separately, information items can seem hopelessly complex and confusing, and one often fails to identify key issues. The capacity to recognize common denominators of integrating concepts enables one to gain an effective understanding of complex matters.

Further, if one can recognize common issues in what may seem to be dissimilar situations, then it is also possible to reverse the process and discern things that *are* significantly different, perhaps unique, and should be recognized accordingly. In land-use affairs, particular situations can vary widely, and one can be confused and ineffective in attempting to deal with a particular situation if one lacks a clear understanding of what is or is not significantly different about it.

The term land is difficult to define for much the same reasons that it is hard consistently to classify the various kinds of land. These difficulties merit emphasis from the outset. Land surfaces, depending on the definition of what should be considered as land, can be measured accurately in units of area. They also can be classified fairly readily in broad terms by geological or soil features or by climatological and related ecological-vegetative groupings. Land use, which is inevitably viewed from the human standpoint, introduces a number of classification problems because particular purposes and viewpoints must be considered. These vary widely by location, ownership, kind of use, and specific land characteristics.

Some difficulties of classifying land are illustrated by Table 1.1. Examination of the table and its footnotes reveals that the tabulation is an inconsistent mixing of some actual land uses with vegetative land-cover types. The two are difficult consistently to separate. This kind of problem can seldom be avoided as consistent data are often difficult to obtain and can be grouped in significant ways only according to a particular purpose. This

Table 1.1 Classification of Land by Major Uses and Categories in the United States (By millions of acres)

Geographic Region	Number of states	Agriculture (1)	Grassland, pasture, and range (2)	Forest (3)	Marshes, swamps, bare rocks, and tundra (4)	Special uses (5)	Urban areas (6)	Total area (7)	Percent
Northeast	11	19.7	7.1	69.5	4.9	4.8	6.2	112.2	5.9
Lake States	3	46.2	8.5	54.3	4.3	5.9	2.8	122.0	6.4
North Central	5	96.9	20.3	31.0	7.4	5.1	4.5	165.2	8.7
Northern Plains	4	100.0	80.7	5.1	1.9	2.9	3.9	194.5	10.2
Southern Plains	2	51.1	118.4	33.2	1.5	5.6	2.7	212.5	11.2
Southeast and Delta	7	40.4	22.0	135.4	6.1	8.1	4.4	216.4	11.4
Appalachian	5	29.8	10.8	74.0	2.7	4.6	2.3	124.2	6.5
Western Mountain	8	43.8	314.4	142.0	21.9	24.7	1.4	548.2	28.9
Pacific	3	26.1	54.3	96.3	12.2	11.8	3.7	204.4	10.8
Total, contiguous states	48	454.0	635.5	640.8	62.9	73.5	31.9	1,899.6	
Percent		23.9	33.5	33.7	3.3	3.9	1.7		100.0
Alaska			2.8	119.0	213.3	27.4		362.5	
Hawaii		0.4	1.2	2.0	0.4	0.1	0.1	4.2	
Total United States	50	454.4	640.5	761.8	276.6	101.0	32.0	2,266.3	
Percent		20.0	28.3	33.6	12.2	4.5	1.4		100.0

Source: Major Uses of Land and Water in the United States with Special Reference to Agriculture. U.S. Department of Agriculture. Economic Report No. 149, 1968.

Column derivations: [1]Land used for crops or in rotation; farmsteads, farm roads and lanes. [2]Nonforest pasture in farms and open and nonforested grazing land not in farms. [3]Forested land in farms and not in farms as defined by the U.S. Forest Service in its continuing inventory. [4]Areas of low agricultural value such as marshes, open swamps, bare rocks, desert, and tundra. [5]Includes rural highways, railroads, airports, national defense, flood control and industrial areas, state-owned institutions, and other miscellaneous areas. [6]Incorporated and unincorporated places of 1,000 or more population. [7]Water areas such as streams, canals less than 1/8 mile wide; lakes, reservoirs, and ponds less than 40 acres in area included in Cols. 1 to 6.

table is worthy of some attention as an excellent example of the difficulties of defining land categories for classification.

Agriculture may seem, on the face of it, to be a clearly definable land use. As stated in the footnotes of Table 1.1, the agriculture category of Col. 1 includes cropland, farmsteads, farm roads and lanes, and also some pastureland, forested areas, and small ponds. Particularly in the Western and Southern Plains regions, very large areas of land grazed by domestic stock are not included in Col. 1. Much of this land is in public ownership. It is an open question as to how much of the grassland, pasture, and range category in Col. 2 should be considered a part of agriculture as these lands are also used by wildlife, for special reservations, and for other human uses. Much of this area is in woodland cover too open and sparce to be classed as forest. From a total agricultural viewpoint, about three-fifths of the area of the forty-eight contiguous states produce crops and livestock in some degree, but much of this area cannot logically be classed as agriculture.

The forest category (Col. 2) is consistent in terms of total forest land as defined by the U.S. Forest Service. It includes potential but not necessarily actual use of the land for forestry purposes. Of the area classified as forest in Col. 3, about 500 million acres are, or are adjudged to be, capable of producing tree crops of commercial value. This includes some 296 million acres of forest land of commercial quality owned by over 3.5 million farm and other nonindustrial owners whose land-use interests vary widely. Marshes, swamps, bare rocks, and tundra included in Col. 4 are a rather miscellaneous group of lands. They are of low forest, agricultural, or urban value but often of high scenic, recreation, watershed, wildlife, and mineral values. About 75 percent of this area is in Alaska.

Urban areas are extremely important, but they are also difficult to define and classify consistently. Table 1.1 shows that about 32 million acres or 1.4 percent of United States land is in urban areas. Other estimates, including certain industrial and other areas, come to about 3 percent. It is also estimated that urban areas are increasing at the rate of about 1 million acres per year.

A broader measure of urban areas is given by recognition of metropolitan areas. These are somewhat arbitrarily defined social and economic areas that include "at least one city of fifty thousand or more, together with satellite suburbs and smaller cities, and together with economically closely integrated countryside" (Clawson, 1972). These areas make up about 10 percent of the total land area and account for about 70 percent of the total United States population. Urban-oriented voting strength consequently has much influence in the United States regarding land-use decisions. Similar situations exist in other countries.

As indicated, the special-uses category (Col. 5) is rather a catchall of several kinds of land uses difficult to identify by any consistent criterion of use or landcover. Water areas are another difficult item to classify. As stated in footnote 7, lakes, reservoirs, and ponds of less than 40 acres and streams and canals less than ⅛ mile wide are included with major land-use categories in Cols. 1 through 6. Larger water areas are not included in Table 1.1. As is brought out in Chap. 2, it is difficult to define "land," and certainly not all land is "dry."

The data of Table 1.1 illustrate in a gross way some problems of consistent land classification which are directly considered in Chap. 4. Points of emphasis are that land is highly variable in form, structure, and composition, has many present or potential uses, and can be classified in different ways depending on purpose.

HUMAN CONCEPTS OF LAND AND ITS USES

The preceding excursion into the complexities of land and its uses gives an introduction to the nature of land and the problems of identifying it. To complete this introduction, it is necessary to place human and land resources relationships in perspective by considering some important human concepts about land and its uses that have had much influence in the development of present thinking.

The Judeo-Christian tradition in the Western world gave rise to the concept that people were created separately, after other living things, and were not a part of nature. People were admonished to "be fruitful, and multiply, and replenish the earth, and subdue it." The idea that the earth and all upon it were for people has become deeply established. Recently, however, the source of authority has shifted from God to the state or "society." In any case, the notion of the supremacy of human beings has been widely used to justify conquest and exploitation of natural resources as an unquestioned human right.

In the conquest and settlement of the New World from Europe, for example, the urge to "subdue" the wilderness (and necessarily the people already on the land) and to "multiply and be fruitful" was strong indeed and frankly expressed. It is also well to recognize that the word "wilderness" meant land as something to be conquered and taken by European settlers coming to the New World. Likewise, use of terms like "undeveloped" or "developing" to characterize countries or peoples is basically an expression of a Western and relative point of view stemming from the same general concept that people are entitled to and should use land resources.

Also of biblical origin is the different and more complex notion of stewardship. This word carries the general meaning of responsibility for continuing and prudent management of something held in trust, as an agent for another, without impairment to what is being managed—and also, it is hoped, with improvement or augmentation. Stewardship also contains the idea of dominion over that which is managed and can include the concept of harmony of opinion and interests, which well describes the goal of good land use.

Another concept important in land use, as in other areas, is recognition of a concern for posterity. There is such concern, but it does not constitute a clear or consistent mandate of active responsibility. When and where a society is strongly land-based and has stable land tenure and inheritance, the idea of passing on an estate to one's heirs intact or improved is very strong and has long been so. Where this is less true, as with more mobile and urban populations as are increasingly developing, this idea is not so strong or compelling.

In times of social and technical change giving rise to uncertainty regarding the future, individuals may feel that they are doing well to support and keep their families together for a rather limited period. Certainly, people normally have strong feelings of responsibility for their children and of loyalty for their societal group or country. But how far does this extend into the future? To what extent and in what way can and actually does one generation—a very arbitrary concept—feel a direct responsibility for the next? How deeply is a person concerned about a judgment on his or her performance that may be placed by people a generation or more in the future? To put this question bluntly, there is a not too uncommon expression to the effect of "what has posterity done for me?" Even more stark is the fact that when people are pressed for survival they will destroy their natural resources to live, as history has often shown.

These are hard questions with no clear answers beyond a general judgment, which readers may question as they will, that large reliance on a posterity concept is of dubious efficacy in maintaining good land use. The same holds for expectations of religious revival. More to the point is application of good planning with built-in provisions for revision and flexibility to meet a changing future.

A more general and effective answer of how to achieve desirable use of natural resources over continuing time is given through the conservation concept. This was strongly advocated by Gifford Pinchot soon after the turn of the twentieth century (Pinchot, 1947). He proposed to give conservation a much wider and stronger meaning than its common connotation at that time—primarily to save or protect from injury or waste—expanding it to include wise use and positive management of natural resources in perpetuity. The intent was to amalgamate the concepts of stewardship, posterity, and general societal responsibility into continuing good land resource use.

The conservation movement took form in the United States in the latter part of the nineteenth century and has had much influence which extends to other countries. The breadth and often vagueness of the term "conservation" has been an advantage. Almost everyone is for conservation; it is very hard to be against it. It is also true, however, that despite much publicity, "conservation" to the average citizen in the 1970s still means essentially to protect or save from waste or injury and does not include positive emphasis on continued careful and productive management of natural resources.

Conservation as a concept and as a positive movement can arise and prosper only in an educated, organized, strong, large, and technically advanced society that is aware of the pressures of rising population on finite natural resources and land resources and also has the capacity and will to do something about them. The conservation movement did not evolve, as has sometimes been thought, out of any cumulative peasant wisdom of the ages. History does not support that idea. It is true that there are past instances of skilled and rather permanent agriculture, of stable and successful societies at different levels of culture that lived in reasonable balance with their natural resources. But a major lesson of history is that people usually do what they think they have to regarding their natural resources and will destroy them if necessary to live.

The conservation movement developed and was applied primarily in the context of open spaces and nonurban land. In that respect it is definitely limited in scope and concept. The more recent development of the highly sophisticated environmental movement with emphasis on and concern with total environmental quality is a much more comprehensive concept. It includes the earth, sea, and water as well as people in all their many interrelationships and dependencies. It is a total-ecosytem approach wherein natural resources are viewed in their entirety. They are appraised not only as sources of products that human beings and other life forms must have but also as sources of waste and pollution. The central purpose is to maintain and if possible to improve environmental quality.

The basic problem is the present fact that both population and per capita use of energy are increasing at exponential rates that cannot indefinitely continue. It is generally believed that if population could be reasonably stabilized it would be possible to deal with the energy and other resource problems and also improve or at least maintain environmental quality. It has to be taken as a commentary on the human race, able in so many respects, that seemingly it cannot control its numbers. The weight of increasing population together with rising energy needs will be emphasized in later chapters of this book.

Chapter 2

Land: Its Characteristics and Ownership

Since time immemorial land has been recognized as having special importance, properties, and value. Ownership of land and accompanying control of its many uses have always been a major cause of contention among people. This chapter presents basic characteristics of land from which stem both its uses and problems of control. An understanding of the nature of land provides perspective and gives confidence in identifying the significant characteristics of a particular parcel of land. As we have noted, the ability to recognize common problems or issues in situations that may seem to be widely different helps one recognize significant differences. This chapter will also emphasize that land-use problems derive from the basic characteristics of land in conjunction with the interests and nature of people.

WHAT IS LAND AND WHAT ARE ITS BASIC CHARACTERISTICS?

Land is surprisingly difficult to define. The common concept is some form of the idea of terra firma or "dry" land, but this is inadequate. A more comprehensive and useful definition is of legal derivation. It can be stated in different ways, but a good short definition is "any part of the earth's surface which can be owned as property, and everything annexed to it, whether by nature or by hand of man" (*The Random House Dictionary of the English Language*, 1966).

This definition points out the extremely important matter of the capacity of land for ownership. It also gives a practical basis for dealing with the difficult problems of whether water areas of various sizes and kinds should be included or excluded as land. Both water and land are a part of the earth's surface. For example, there are large and changing areas of swamps, estuaries, and tidelands where the land and the sea meet. There are also inland flood plains, streams, lakes, ponds, and other areas from very large to small that are partially or fully covered with water either seasonally or permanently in greater or less degree. The questions involving national control or ownership of sea areas are extremely complex and increasingly important. These include offshore coastal zone and territorial waters and the oil, gas, fishing, and other use rights which are claimed by countries or states. All such questions must be considered part of total landownership problems.

The legal point that things affixed by nature or by human beings to the land go with the land is also extremely important. Legally defined, permanent buildings and other structures and trees are a part of the land and are bought and sold with it unless otherwise specified and agreed. Thus, when a person buys a house the title deed specifically defines only the land area but not the structures or trees affixed to it.

Immobility

One of the most obvious and important characteristics of land is its immobility. A parcel of land remains where it is; it is a particular segment of the earth's crust and can be identified accordingly. This is the basis for establishing ownership. Location is consequently often extremely important in land use and value. Land of desired or acceptable characteristics is often in the wrong place, at least from the standpoint of its use by people. It would certainly be convenient if land suitable for urban, agricultural, and other uses could be distributed in such a way as to minimize land-use conflicts. For example, it would be good if we could avoid using limited agricultural land for urban development or, conversely, develop urban centers in wet, rough, or other disadvantageous places. But land is what and where it is, and great effort and money are often required to adapt the kind of land available to a desired use. This necessity arises from the immobility of land, and many land-use planning problems are dominated by this physical fact.

Another characteristic of land that stems from its immobility and capacity for ownership is the strategic value associated with a particular location. Control of a particular parcel of land may give control over the use of other land areas. For example, ownership of a small parcel of land in a particular area may be extremely important if single ownership of the entire area is necessary for projected business, industrial, or residential use. If public interests in the area are not sufficient to support expropriation—the taking of the land at a fair price—the owner of such a parcel may command a very high price for it. Similarly, access to streams, lakes, timber, recreation, hunting, and the like may be blocked by the owner of a strategically located parcel of land that must be crossed to get to the desired areas.

Finiteness

Within the rather narrow range of natural land accretion and land loss that geologically occurs over time, there is just so much land. Land is not reproducible. It is possible, however, to change its surface character—to level some land and to ditch, dike, dam, drain, and fill some wet or water areas to make more dry land. Much of this is being done, but it is expensive. In the Netherlands, for example, there has been large-scale reclamation of land from the sea. Cities have been built on areas having serious water-level problems, and more will probably be built. The total area of wet land on which reclamation is practicable is, however, relatively small. Further, there are many undesirable environmental consequences of wetland drainage or fill for urban or agricultural use that place sharp restrictions on the practice.

The fact that the amount of land and land-based resources is essentially finite whereas the number and needs of people are not gives increasing importance to questions of who controls the land and how it is used.

Physical and Climatic Characteristics

The importance of physical land characteristics varies greatly with location and use.

Topography Land may be flat, steep, irregular, rocky, etc. With equipment and explosives the local topography of an area can be considerably changed, but people do not level many mountains. Thus, topography controls many land uses.

Soil The character of the soil is extremely important for some uses, such as agriculture, but less so for others, such as shopping centers or industrial sites, where surface soil conditions are less limiting and often can be changed to meet needs. Soil is extremely slow to form but can be impoverished in nutrients, changed in structure, and eroded away in a relatively short time. The continued biological productivity of soil can be either increased or destroyed by use. The land surface is the base for the biota, the whole terrestrial ecosytem of living things.

Subsurface Structure and Composition   Below the surface may be rock, gravel, aggregates, sand, muck, etc. The subsurface can present problems to construction on the surface and thus limit the land's use. These subsurface materials also have influence on many surface uses.

Minerals, Oil, and Gas   The geographic distribution of these very important resources is the result of geologic processes entirely independent of human needs and convenience. Natural resources may be at, close to, or far below the surface. Bringing them to the surface consequently may be difficult, and there are often undesirable effects on the land surface.

Alternative and Combined Uses

A particular land area often can be used for several purposes, such as for building construction, agriculture, parks, or forests. Sometimes several uses can be combined (Chap. 3). The possible multiple uses of land together with its basic finite and immobile characteristics give rise to most land-use problems. A few illustrations will indicate the range of alternative and combined land-use possibilities.

For geographic reasons, buildings, towns, and cities are often located on good agricultural land—which is in short supply—even though urban use does not require land of cropland quality. Land values in the market may economically support urban uses, but from a total land resource planning standpoint such uses may be considered socially undesirable in comparison with other uses. A similar and common situation is the urban use of wetlands whose perpetuation is desirable to maintain wildlife, aquatic life, and environmental values generally. Here again, there are serious conflicts of land-use interests to resolve.

Some combination of surface and subsurface uses is often possible and desirable. For example, power and utility lines and conduits frequently can be put underground with limited damage to surface uses. Subsurface transportation, such as subways and underwater tunnels, is both common and effective. Some mineral extraction can be accomplished with limited surface disruption, as in some oil and gas fields and some deep-mine operations. Other kinds of mining, such as open-pit operations, create severe surface disruption that is difficult or impossible to prevent.

LAND TENURE—OWNERSHIP

Because land is immobile, finite, and absolutely necessary to human existence, control of land obviously is of crucial importance. It is not surprising that issues regarding land are a prime source of legal and other contention.

The basic concept of ownership is that of tenure. This means the right or capacity to have and to hold land for certain uses. Historically, the concept of tenure long preceded the idea of individual ownership. The word "tenure" means "The holding of property, especially real estate, of or by reference to a superior. Inherent in the word 'held' is the idea of exclusion, that is to set aside and keep as one's own by shutting out and excluding others. Another indispensable dimension of tenure is the period of time for which the property is held" (Harris, 1953).

Who the "superior" authority is can be a moot point. In the past, authority has been established by conquest, by might, although in Judeo-Christian areas God has frequently also been invoked as the superior authority. European conquest of the New World by the Spanish, French, and English established a new land tenure. It was at the expense of people already living there who had little or no idea of individual landownership and often no clear sense of tribal or kingdom ownership going beyond generally recognized boundaries of established occupation and control. North American Indians at land treaty meetings with white people have said: "How can we sell what belongs to the Great Spirit?"

In more recent times, law has mostly replaced might in matters of tenure. In a final showdown, however, it is essentially true that rights of tenure are no stronger than the power of sovereignty that granted them.

In English feudal times, tenure was based on the idea that all land was held by the king, as was established by William the Conqueror after the Battle of Hastings in 1066. He parceled out land to his nobles, from whom he expected loyalty and certain services in return. Similarly, the nobles granted smaller land parcels to their men. These people had tenure under the aegis of the noble but not the right to dispose of the land because it was held by a superior.

Over the course of time, this concept of tenure gave way to individual ownership, which included the right of disposal by the owner to any person by sale or other legal action. In complete terms, this concept of ownership is called "fee simple absolute," which is the highest form of tenure and normally evidenced by legal written title. This concept of landownership is dominant in Western countries. It is well to keep in mind, however, that such ownership is by no means universal. Some peoples and countries of the world do not have full individual private ownership but rather some form of limited tenure. There is even some land, notably in Antarctica, that is not owned by anybody.

Ownership as a Bundle of Rights[1]

The complete concept of fee simple absolute ownership implies that the individual owns everything on the earth surface, downward to the center of the earth, and upward to some indeterminable distance. In reality and prac-

[1] Acknowledgment is made to Harris (1953) for material used here.

tice, this is not true. It is better and much more realistic to think of ownership as a *bundle of rights,* a bundle with very different sizes, shapes, and kinds of things in it. Some of these are held by the owner and some by whoever granted the title of ownership, which brings one back to the basic concept of tenure and of the relationships of a landowner to a superior authority.

Three of these rights or powers are always reserved by this superior authority, that is, by appropriate units of government. These are:

1 The right to tax. This is a potent power that can and does influence ownership and land use in many ways depending specifically on the method and kind of taxation applied and the size of the tax.

2 The right to condemn, that is, to take title of privately held land by superior levels of government for public or quasipublic use. This is an inherent right of sovereignty in the United States (and elsewhere) regarded as implicit by retention of powers necessary to carry on essential functions of government.

3 The police power. This power is broad, important, and also extremely general. Basically it means the right of government to protect and promote public health, safety, morals, and general welfare. Applied to land use, exercise of this power can and does restrict the freedom of owners to use their land as they please. Protection from nuisance and from sanitary or safety hazards, the rights of adjoining owners, and right of police entry on land in law enforcement are a few of many public rights reserved under the police power.

Separately and collectively, these three reserved rights constitute important controls and restrictions on private land use. In addition, the public directly, but more indirectly, can influence land use through its general spending powers. The power to spend can be the power to control.

What constitutes a fourth public power, essentially implicit in the authority to grant land title, is that of escheat, of land property reverting to government ownership. The most obvious example is reversion of ownership if taxes due are not paid. For example, during the depression years of the 1930s in the United States very large areas of privately owned lands reverted to state ownership because of nonpayment of property taxes. Also, if the land is abandoned or if there is no heir, ownership reverts to the public. Basically, what the government grants can also be taken away if the terms of the grant are not fulfilled.

It is implicit to the bundle-of-rights concept of individual title ownership that these rights can be transferred. In general terms, the trend in the United States is to transfer items in this bundle from the private owner back to the public. This is done mainly through the basic and broad reserved rights of taxation, condemnation, and police power, but also in various ways through the power of public spending. Underlying this trend is the fact that legal development of private ownership concepts historically has focused on rights much more than on responsibilities of ownership. Present emphasis, in a time of strongly emerging national consciousness of environmental quality, is toward placing more emphasis on landownership responsibilities in the public interest.

The use of landownership and tenure rights often entails complex legal procedures. Owners may use or not use all their rights as they choose. They may also distribute these rights to others in various ways, such as through easements, leases, and rentals or by pledging land as security for a loan (Chap. 5). Owners may, in fact, distribute all their rights except one, that of relinquishing title to the land, as they are then no longer owners.

Exercise of Landownership Rights

Exercise of the rights of landownership are as complex as relationships between people and organizations. They occur between individual private owners, between private owners and different levels of governmental authority, and between public owners. These rights are variable and complex and are the subject of a large area of law.

It is possible, however, to give an overview that will be helpful in gaining general perspective and an understanding of land-use rights. They are here outlined by surface, subsurface, and above-surface rights. Readers should add their own illustrations, and there are many.

Surface Rights   Most land-use rights are exercised on the land surface. Strategic characteristics of the immobile nature of land have already been mentioned. Only the outline of some areas of particular interest in land use can be given. These deal particularly with, but are by no means limited to, the United States.

As a general point, legal right of landownership often does not in fact give owners actual control of all uses on the land to which they are supposedly entitled. This applies to public as well as to private owners. History is long indeed on this subject. Such uses as access to unowned land, grazing, timber cutting, hunting, and fishing have been established on both public and privately owned lands through usage and are often extremely difficult to extinguish, law or no law. Similar established-use rights and attendant ownership control problems exist in Europe and elsewhere.

These situations were common in the earlier United States history but are few now. For example, when the national forests, mostly in the West, were created by taking these areas out of the unreserved public domain, grazing by private livestock owners on these public lands was already well established without cost or public control. It has taken a long time fully to establish federal grazing control on these public lands. In the early years of the Forest Service, the policy of allowing free grazing on public land for a limited number of homestead stock, cutting of dead trees, and purchase of live timber at minimum cost for home use was adopted primarily as a means of controlling uses established by prior usage.

Access   Public and private owners have the right to control the entrance of people to their property. But they also have to establish such control by fencing, boundary posting, patrolling, oral declaration, and the like. The owner's recourse against trespass depends on what damage, inconvenience, or loss of use rights is suffered. Redress varies depending on circumstances.

Access to a property that has been uncontested by the owner for some period of time is difficult for an owner to stop. If it has been exercised by someone as necessary to reach his or her own property, such access usually cannot subsequently be legally denied. An interesting access problem is the matter of public access to public areas—such as national forests—which are open to hunting but which can be reached only through a strategically located parcel of fenced private land. If the owners claim a private road through their property, they can padlock a gate and require—or attempt to require—the hunter to join the "XYZ" hunting club for a fee essentially to obtain access to hunt on public lands. Similar problems arise in relation to access to timberlands, recreation areas, or other resources. Circumstances and legal recourse can be very complex.

Boundaries and Adverse Occupancy   Land-use controversy arising from questioned or inaccurate boundary lines or contested land titles is endless and often acrimonious. Nevertheless, some useful points can be made. Frequently there is difficulty in establishing boundaries accurately and legally—which are not necessarily the same thing. It often happens that a boundary line between two ownerships, long established by usage and often fenced and mutually accepted or at least not contested by the adjoining owners, turns out to be significantly different from what should be the true boundary line. Solution of such problems can be very difficult, both legally and practically; boundary line disputes are famous for legal complexity and strong feelings. The existence of roads and road locations of various age and use history and unclear legal status can complicate problems.

Related to boundary lines is adverse occupancy. This means, for example, occupancy by unauthorized people, often termed "squatters," who settle on land without title or other right. They may build cabins or other structures. Such occupancy can be difficult to terminate and has been a considerable problem in the United States and elsewhere. As with other land uses, uncontested use tends in time to establish rights of use.

Water   A matter of major importance and legal complexity is ownership of streams and other water areas and rights of water use. In the United

States the federal government has general control over what can be defined as navigable streams (which may in some situations be only large enough seasonally to float logs). As part of their reserved rights and regulatory powers, the states, again in general, own most natural streams and the larger water bodies. In public land surveys, permanent water control areas larger than some defined minimum size are meandered. This means that the survey goes around these larger water areas and excludes them from private ownership; thus they remain public lands. Smaller, nonmeandered water bodies accordingly are considered as "land," bottom included, and belong to whoever owns the land on which they are located. The owners can do what they please with such water bodies, including filling or draining them.

On any meandered water area, private ownership can extend only to some defined water edge. Consequently, if there is federal or state-owned land that gives land access to a lake, the water area of the lake itself is thereby open to public use. For this reason, public agencies keep, and actively seek to acquire, land to give public access to water in both streams and lakes. This is particularly important in present or potential recreation areas.

Because the public—mostly the states in the United States—controls flowing water and usually the stream bed, people often can fish in a stream going through privately owned land as long as they stay *on* the water in a boat—and usually they can walk on the stream bed, too.

Ownership of rights to *use* water can be extremely complex. In the United States there are two sharply different concepts of water rights. The first and most common, termed "riparian rights," give landowners the right to "ordinary" use of natural water adjacent to or flowing through their property. These rights apply in the Eastern United States and to some of the West. How much is "ordinary" or reasonable is debatable when supply is limited. This comes to point especially with the advent of portable power pump and pipe irrigation systems that were not envisaged when concepts of water-use rights developed.

The second concept is that of direct water-use rights. These developed in the West and date back to the California gold rush days of 1849 and specifically to placer mining, which required a diversion of running water from a stream. Such diversion right was later extended to use of water for land irrigation vital in much of the West. This use right means that landowners can legally claim a specified measured flowage of water from a certain stream whether or not the stream enters their property. The owner of a first water right can claim his or her share first, and those with a secondary right take their share next, etc. This system is obviously in direct conflict with the older riparian rights concept, and the two have been the source of much controversy and legal difficulties.

Fish and Wildlife   Control of fish and wildlife is an important land-use management problem because so many people are interested. In the

United States there is no actual ownership of fish and wildlife. The *taking* of fish and wildlife by fishing or hunting is legally controlled by the individual states except in defined private fish ponds and wildlife rearing areas. Private landowners can, for example, suffer much damage on their lands from excessive deer and elk grazing. But they can hunt only during legal game season under state license and petition for redress of damages to their property. There are many cooperative agreements between federal, state, and private authorities and interest groups relating to various kinds of private hunting clubs and other organizations. In these, the private owner's right of access, which can exclude hunters, is combined with state control over hunting, including game seasons. There are also cooperative relationships between the state fish and wildlife departments and public land management agencies which advise them on land carrying capacity in relation to current game population, such as the number and sex of deer that should be taken from a particular area during the hunting season.

Regulation of hunting and fishing varies so widely in other countries that no general characterization can be attempted here.

Owner Liability Despite having legal right to deny entry to and occupancy of their land, owners are not free from common law liability for injury and other accidents sustained by unauthorized people on their land if negligence on the owner's part can be established. For example, a person falling into an unenclosed and abandoned well, suffering injury from what can be claimed to be a hazardous road or bridge, or having an unsound tree fall on him or her may be able to claim damages from the private, state, or federal owner.

Such liability is of considerable importance in outdoor recreation and can restrict owner willingness to permit land use by nonowners. Owners of large industrial forests have, for example, found that a general open-door policy permitting public fishing, hunting, and other outdoor recreation on their lands has led to expensive lawsuits and some land misuse. This is particularly true if public use has been encouraged and visitors can claim status as a guest. Several states have passed laws limiting owner liability in such situations.

Subsurface Rights As pointed out earlier, fee simple absolute landownership including everything above, on, and below the surface is more a general concept than a reality. Subsurface mineral rights may be reserved by the public or the original owner, or they can be bought, sold, and reserved by private owners. Mining laws are extremely complex. Particularly in the Western United States, existence of a valid mineral claim can give the claimant certain peremptory authority to obtain surface rights necessary for mineral development, including reasonable land access.

Most of the present national forest lands east of the Mississippi River were either purchased by the Forest Service or obtained via land exchange procedures from lands in private ownership. This occurred mainly during the economic depression years of the 1930s and continued into the 1940s and somewhat later. At the time the lands were acquired they were considered largely submarginal for private use. Privately owned mineral rights on much of this area, coal being a large item, were not sold to the Forest Service. Under existing mining laws, control of surface disruption due to mining is difficult. The Forest Service consequently has problems exercising adequate surface land-use control. Other public agencies and private owners face similar problems.

Other major subsurface land uses involve flow resources of water, oil, and gas, which can move underground. The problem with a flow resource is not that an owner has legal ownership of what is beneath the surface of his or her land. It is that, being a flow resource, one owner can draw from another nearby with equal rights and consequently deplete his or her proper share of the resource beneath his lands.

Underground water, which can accumulate over time in some geologic strata formations, is another flow resource important in land use. Water may be drawn from underground aquifers in excess of their natural replenishment. This necessitates deeper and deeper wells requiring more energy to pump the water to the surface. Sooner or later a severe water shortage will develop unless other water sources can be developed. Water for crop irrigation is critical in such situations because this use generally requires more water per unit of area—and produces less value—than urban uses. In the southwestern United States such situations lead to difficult problems of water apportionment if additional water sources cannot be developed.

It is possible here only to mention the increasingly important, complex, and technical problems of utilization of offshore oil, mineral, and other natural resources, as well as surface fishing. These involve state, federal, and international questions of great magnitude. International high seas and rights to their use are becoming increasingly difficult to define as people turn more and more to the sea for natural resources.

Above-Surface Rights   Ownership and control of above-surface rights are increasingly raising important legal, political, and practical questions of environmental quality. Air contamination, invasion of air privacy as by airplanes, and air travel accidents are examples. Limitation of aesthetic views by undesirable or obstructing structures should also be included here. Many of these questions fall into the area of common law regarding a nuisance, i.e., something offensive, unpleasant, or obstructing owner rights of individuals. Above-surface rights are increasingly becoming the subject of laws.

Lands of Many Uses

Land characteristics and ownership, discussed in Chap. 2, give a basis for the many uses of land, the subject of this chapter. There is a wide range of uses for which land *can* can be used.

Megalopoli, cities, towns, and industrial complexes can rise on agricultural land, forested land, grassland, wetland, or even desert areas if location, topography, and human needs so indicate and necessities such as transportation and water supply can be met. Agricultural croplands, which in general require good soils, have mostly come from lands supporting vigorous natural vegetative cover. Where climate, soil, and topography were suitable, large agricultural areas in the United States have been taken from naturally forested lands. The same is true of large areas of natural grasslands. Arid lands can be (and have been) made fruitful if water can be supplied, and wetlands can be drained to support agriculture and urban development. Forested lands, which now occupy some 754 million acres or one-third of the total United States area and originally occupied much more, are an extremely versatile, stable, and self-renewable land resource capable of producing a wide range of goods and services through use. For-

21

est cover, whether naturally or artificially established, also covers large areas once cleared of forest cover for agriculture but later found submarginal for such use.

Development of transportation facilities, by water, land, and air, in about this order historically, has stimulated more than anything else the great changes in the face of America. The development of waterways, then of the railroads and great highway systems, and more recently of the system of mass transportation by air of people, mail, and high-value commodities has in increasing degree reduced the economic restrictions of geographic distance. This has at least made possible better distribution through planning of land uses.

Geography remains, however, a strong force in controlling land development and use. Mountains are where and what they are, and are not erased. The channels of most rivers are irrevocably imprinted on the land, although where and how the water is used is subject to much direction by people. Population is increasingly concentrated in metropolitan areas despite efforts to disperse it. The fact remains that population centers have developed where they have for a combination of geographic, transport, trade, and access-to-raw-material reasons that are strong and tenacious.

It is no accident that the last part of the present forty-eight contiguous United States to be traversed and known lies in the northern Rocky Mountain areas of Montana, Idaho, and Wyoming. Lewis and Clark in their expedition of 1804–1806, following the Louisiana Purchase of 1803, first discovered (from the white people's standpoint, that is) the Missouri River headwaters. They also gained substantial knowledge of the Columbia River drainage system. The land-use significance of this Rocky Mountain complex of high mountains and rivers, which offers few practicable transportation routes, is evident today by the relatively sparse settlement of the region.

REVERSIBLE AND IRREVERSIBLE USES

Because the amount of land is finite whereas the numbers of people and their many desires are not, recognition of irreversible and reversible land uses is important in land-use planning. By irreversible it is meant that application of a particular land use changes or otherwise preempts the original character of the land to such a degree that reversal to its former use or condition is impracticable if not impossible. In effect, such use is a one-way street. The time scale is important. In the context of treatment here some reasonably forseeable planning time, not geological time, is assumed.

Irreversible Uses

A classic example of very large-scale irreversible land use occurred when the Europeans by permanent settlement supplanted the native Indians of

North America. No change back to the essentially natural use of the land
was possible. Ecological advocacy of returning to "natural" land uses can
sometimes reduce in effect to an argument that the land should revert to
Indian uses.

Cities, larger towns, and industrial areas by and large are never erased
in any forseeable time although the particular kind and character of such
uses can be changed. They constitute essentially irreversible land uses in the
context used here.

Coastal and inland wetlands and other water areas are another and
very critical example. Once they are drained or filled, such areas cannot be
restored to what they were, although the subsequent use may be changed,
such as from agriculture to airports or some urban uses.

The larger river dams and reservoirs are essentially permanent. Reservoirs can in time, however, fill with sediment, which is certainly not desired
and also negates their purpose. Some other use or uses of the reservoir area
may be possible. But they will never be what they were before construction
of the dam.

Mining and related extraction from the land is, by its nature, essentially an irreversible use. Mineral ores and other mined materials are irreplace-
able. Land surface and subsurface effects of mining are many and varied.
In open-pit mining, rock and gravel quarries, and placer gold dredging,
disruption of the land surface is often extreme. It may be difficult if not
impossible to avoid disruption and restore the land to its prior use. Much,
however, can be done by careful planning of mining operation and subsequent land treatment to mitigate disruption and accomplish substantial restoration to some useful land use. For example, open-pit coal mining in the
more level lands of southern Ohio, Indiana, and Illinois is extremely disruptive of the surface soil. Depending, however, on the physical and chemical
composition of the land overlying the coal in the mined areas and also the
saving of surface soil, the land can be approximately restored and a surface
soil regime reestablished that supports good growth of trees and other cover. Recreational use of such areas has been developed, but return to its
former farm use is seldom possible. Coal mining in mountainous areas such
as eastern Kentucky offers tremendously difficult and well-known problems of achieving reasonably acceptable land restoration. Smelter fume
damage to nearby vegetation has been severe but is more subject to control
and subsequent land cover restoration. It is, however, a part of a much
more general problem of air pollution.

The use of land for the major roads, highways, and railroads of a
country is also irreversible. Their linear nature, the disruption of the soil,
and the persistence of established transportation routes makes the availability and suitability of such land for some other use extremely unlikely.

Other instances of essentially irreversible land uses could be given, but the above are indicative of this category. The point is that they are important and merit careful consideration in land-use planning. The areas involved may not be relatively large, but they can nonetheless be highly significant because of the preemptive nature of such uses and the fact that they may deeply affect other land uses. This is particularly true of transport routes which are strategically important in giving access to land.

Reversible Uses

Reversible uses include use of land in which the soil cover and landform have not been substantially changed. The land manager consequently has options in managing reversible land uses.

Agricultural cropland and improved pastures give good examples of readily reversible land uses that can be and are often applied on a planned rotation basis. Also, land used for agriculture can revert back to forest or to natural grassland cover. Large areas of marginal agricultural land have so reverted, temporarily or for long time periods.

Forested lands, which occupy very large areas, offer a number of reversible land uses. They provide an extremely persistent and durable land cover that is relatively easy to reestablish either naturally or by seeding or planting where necessary. Forests help to clean the air, build and hold soil, and produce a wide variety of goods and services. In the practice of forest management, emphasis can be on timber production, recreation, watershed protection, wildlife, or grazing, depending on purpose and land suitability.

Within urban areas a rather large degree of reversibility is physically possible but it may be highly expensive. In urban renewal, for example, a wide range of reconstruction work may be undertaken. Inadequate housing can be replaced with better and more efficient dwellings. Run-down business or factory areas may be rebuilt or put to some other use. As cities grow, age, and change in economic direction and strength, both physical and social changes may take place. Some of these, such as inner-city decline, may be both difficult and expensive to reverse.

The reason a large degree of reversibility is physically possible in urban areas is that the land functions primarily as a physical *base* and can support a wide range of urban uses. It does not *produce* products or services as do natural wetlands or agricultural uses, for example.

COMBINED USES—COMPATIBILITY

The combining of different land uses in some desirable pattern of arrangement is an old concept and is practiced in both urban and nonurban situations. Both reversible and irreversible uses are included. The reasons for seeking use combinations derive from the facts that (1) land often can have more than one use, (2) available land is often limited in a particular area,

(3) there is competition for different uses, and (4) different uses often can be combined in various ways.

The purpose of this section is first to examine the physical and biological basis for these land-use combinations and second to consider their large-scale application as a land management policy and practice. Two basic groups of land-use combinations can be recognized: first, different single uses that are spatially arranged in some desirable pattern in an area; second, physical combination of different uses on the same area. Mixtures of the two groups can, of course, also be made.

The basis for combined uses depends on the compatibilities of one kind of use with another related to the physical and biological characteristics of a particular area. The degree to which possible combined uses are applied depends on need.

Compatibility, as the term is used here, means capability of existing together in harmony, that is, in an orderly or pleasing arrangement. So understood, compatibility accurately describes the objective of good land use. It means not only a good arrangement of different uses simultaneously on the same area, where such is desired, but also a judicious spatial arrangement of separate single uses. The basic requirement is that the uses do in fact fit together in some effective and desirable arrangement.

There are an almost unlimited number of possible combinations. Given below are some of them, and the reader is welcomed to add others.

Urban Uses

The Grand Central Station complex in New York City probably exemplifies as complex and intensive multiuse of a restricted but extremely valuable area as can be found. Space below, above, and on the surface of the land is intensively used. There are several levels of railroads and subway lines below ground, the great waiting hall and other public services and shops at or near the surface level, and many offices and other uses above the general ground level.

Multiple use of buildings in urban areas is common, ranging from home offices and studios, etc., to commercial buildings in which space is rented for many dissimilar purposes. Planned developments also combine housing, commercial services, and recreation in an area.

Transport routes are combined with other land uses in various ways. Major highway routes in areas of urban concentration are often built high enough above ground to permit fairly full surface or even subsurface use by some kinds of business and industry. Underground transportation routes, particularly subways, are common, freeing the surface for other uses. Many expedients are employed to meet ever-increasing needs for motor vehicle parking space. They include single and multilevel constructions on, above, and below ground level (including some with parks on the surface), and similar construction below buildings used for other purposes. They may also include temporary use of some open-space areas for parking for athletic events and other public gatherings.

Open-space areas may be used primarily as public parks, but by use of temporary structures and facilities may also serve for major public events such as rallies and mass meetings.

The above indicates some of the combined land uses in urban areas (see also the material on zoning in Chap. 4). As a group, the uses are the result of economic compression, of strong demands pressing against a limited supply of land. The result is inevitably high cost per unit of area. Urban may seem totally different from wildland situations and in specifics this is certainly true. The basic reasons for, requirements for, and application of combined land uses are, however, much the same. The approach of looking for use compatibilities, in what may seem to be disparate situations, also illustrates the usefulness of regarding land and its capabilities as a common basis for appraising land uses. Such an approach gives understanding and confidence in dealing with a wide range of land-use problems.

Nonurban Uses

With about 90 percent of the United States occupied by nonmetropolitan lands of diverse kinds and compatibilities, there are many possibilities for combined uses in one form or another. Treatment here will focus on agricultural and forested areas, which illustrate a wide range of well-developed and large-scale applications of combined uses.

Agriculture Agriculture includes many different land uses. In general, these uses are indicated by and follow soil classifications (Chap. 4). These are mapped in considerable detail to define agricultural land capabilities.

Cropland requirements can be narrow for particular crops, but they can be broadened by modern use of fertilizers and good water control. Crop rotation is commonly practiced so that a given area may produce different crops over some planned time sequence. This could be within a single year under intensive culture or over a sequence of several years. Improved pastures are usually so used for several years but may also go into crop use if the land is suitable.

Another form of combined use through crop rotation is so-called shifting agriculture. This practice, which is crude and often very destructive, has long been widely applied on millions of acres, particularly in tropical areas of the world. It goes by many names. Essentially it means that a forested area is partially or completely cleared, usually with the aid of fire, and some kind of crop, usually annual, is planted for a short period of up to about 3 years. The process is then repeated elsewhere. This shifting agriculture is characteristically applied on land of soils, usually lateritic, of transient fertility and stability for continued agricultural use. Following this use, the area is then left to grow back to forest or brush cover as best it can. Agricultural use is repeated if and when the land recovers sufficiently. The time span between periods of crop use is highly variable—perhaps as short as a decade or several decades or perhaps an indefinite period.

This kind of agriculture was once common in the United States, particularly in the southern Appalachian Mountains, but it is nearly gone now. Rainfall in these mountains is good, and soils in this geologically old and nonglaciated area are generally fertile and often deep. But they are also subject to severe erosion on slopes.

In mixed agriculture, where a range of products is produced, such as field crops, orchard crops, and dairy or other livestock, there are more land uses and consequently more possible combinations. For example, annual crops may be produced for a time between rows in some young fruit, nut, or other orchards; livestock may feed seasonally on cropland as well as on pastures; hay or other forage production may be a part of a crop rotation schedule; seasonal grazing may be practiced in farm woodlots.

On ranches emphasizing livestock production much attention is given to pasture improvement through seeding and timing of grazing use and to production of alfalfa, clovers, and grasses for feeding. In the Western states particularly, private landownership is often only a part of the total livestock producing operation. The owner may be dependent on lease of private land, or obtain a permit for livestock grazing on public land. Western public land grazing and control is a long story that cannot be entered into here (see Chap. 7), but the basic nature of compatibilities of open-range livestock grazing with wildlife is given later in this chapter.

Compatibilities in agriculture permitting simultaneous application of two or more uses on a single land area are relatively few and not as direct as they are in urban areas. Forest and wildland areas give better illustrations of actual physical-biological combinations of uses on a single area.

Forestry and Related Wildlands Naturally forested lands, because of their self-renewing, flexible, and generally durable land cover, permit a number of combined uses.

Wildlife and Forests There are many natural compatibilities between wildlife species and forest cover. A food supply for year-round sustenance of wildlife is a basic need. As a general point, most food for wildlife has to be fairly close to the ground.

Deer, for example, are browse-, forb-, and grass-eating animals, and their food has to be within reach. Deer have a wide natural range in the United States, north and south, east and west. They are very adaptable to terrain and ground cover but basically are forest-margin animals. Forest and related woody cover is needed for protection, but most of their food is in openings, edges, and reproducing and young forest stands. There is an old saying that "deer follow the axe," and this is true. They thrive where there are new cuttings and consequently a good food supply. Mature, dense, high forest stands offer protective cover but little food.

The limiting factor, in the northern snow areas, is the lack of available late winter deer food. Food is usually plentiful during the summer and early winter. The critical time comes with deepening snow and cold in the late winter, when both the freedom of deer to range and their available food supply frequently become very restricted. During this period deer tend to congregate in small areas, often termed "yards," and are forced by hunger to eat whatever they can reach. The result is a "deer line" 7 or 8 feet above the ground. Below this, everything "chewable" has been taken, including young forest growth.

The above discussion indicates both possibilities and limitations for combined deer management and forest use. In general, deer are compatible with and prosper in a well-managed forest with emphasis on timber production, which is a major economic forest land use. A necessary proviso, however, is that the deer population be kept within the reasonable food-carrying capacity of the area. Timber harvest cuttings are normally well distributed in patches over a management unit. This creates, from a deer standpoint, a good mixture of reproducing and young stands in which herbaceous and low woody cover naturally develop, and of older stands giving protective cover. Browsing of newly established trees is sometimes a problem, but it is mainly the result of deer overpopulation.

Combining deer with timber production basically requires deciding on desired priority and then applying the knowledge and skills of management to achieve it. Very intensive timber production may support only a small deer population. If, however, there are natural intermixed areas that are not of high value for timber production, but are good for deer food production, they can be so managed and increase food supply accordingly. Also, if special attention is given to dispersing timber cutting operations and leaving areas of natural deer food production wherever reasonable, a good timber-deer combination can be supported. It is a matter of achieving a desired balance between compatible land uses.

As a more specific situation, assume that deer rather than timber production are desired as the dominating land use of a naturally forested area. This is a fact on many lands in both public and private ownership. The flexible, durable forest can be shaped to this use by emphasizing maintenance of food and cover conditions favoring wildlife. This would mean much less high forest, more openings, emphasis on woody plants other than trees, the planting of deer foods in some situations, and regulation of hunting to keep the deer population within land carrying capacity limits. Land treatment of this kind has been applied in Michigan purposefully to manage forest cover to produce more deer food in areas of winter deer concentration. Wildland management examples of this kind could be given for other game species and upland birds and nongame animals. Each has its particular ecological habitat requirements and can be either aided or hindered by changes in the forest environment whether they are caused by human beings or not.

The key point is that these ecological compatibilities do exist. Knowledge of them gives direction to management of forest cover. This is the information basis necessary for both public and private owners to adopt successful policies and concomitant land-use practices in managing forested lands to emphasize wildlife.

Outdoor Recreation and Forests   Outdoor recreation and forests naturally go together, but their relationships are complex. They are also often complicated by the deep feelings people have about forests. People in general like trees and forests. But they also many have strong, varied, and often ill-formed ideas regarding them.

As a land use, outdoor recreation can be characterized by intensive use of relatively small areas and extensive use of large areas either separately or in many combinations. For example, resorts, picnic areas, or heavily used parks in or near urban areas require relatively little space, and the recreation experience is essentially complete in the area. In contrast, automobile driving, hiking, horseback riding, stream fishing and, wildland camping also specifically utilize rather small areas, but they are dependent upon and derive their recreational value primarily from much larger associated areas of forests and other wildlands. The general setting—the existence of pleasing landscapes and views—is an essential and often major part of the recreational experience. Consequently how these ancillary areas are managed is also important and a part of outdoor recreation considered in its entirety.

In forested areas, particular attention centers on recreation in relation to timber uses. As stated above, people in general like trees and forests. Many, however, and especially those of urban orientation, understandably have aversions to and lack of understanding about the cutting of trees. This is, of course, an essential part of forest management for timber production. It is also necessary to a considerable degree in the management of naturally forested areas for recreational and wildlife uses. The controversy over timber cutting is discussed in Chap. 12. The emphasis here is on physical-ecological compatibilities of forest recreation and timber uses. These uses are not necessarily in conflict, although some adjustments of both viewpoints and land-management practices are, however, usually necessary in practice.

As a general proposition, a well-managed forest area including timber production can have both aesthetic attraction and utility. Reasonable adjustments in timber practice can meet both recreational and wildlife needs in considerable degree. In much European forestry, this is accomplished as a matter of normal practice and with general public acceptance. Concern for recreation uses does require adjustments in the conduct of cutting operations. The degree of adjustment naturally depends on circumstances. Partial cutting methods are applied where practicable, and cutting areas are dispersed where possible. Clear-cutting areas, where this method needs to be applied, should be kept reasonably small and prompt cleanup and reestablishment of forest cover emphasized.

Cost is always a consideration. There often is some economic conflict between efficiency in timber production and maintaining the inherent attractiveness of growing forests where recreation interests are also important.

Because of these conflicts, there is some tendency physically to separate such uses. However, separation is undesirable wherever it can be avoided in the interest of well-balanced management of always limited land areas. Education, understanding, and mutual tolerance is needed. In practice, combinations of reasonably compatible uses are not so difficult to work out if there is a will to do so. It is a matter of some change in viewpoints, of planning, adjustments in operating practices, good execution, and recognition of both ecological and financial consequences.

The concept of carrying capacity applied to a land area underlies most land uses, including outdoor recreation. Stated bluntly, carrying capacity means how much of what kind of use an area can sustain without significant damage. The basic ecological requirement is not to degrade the land, that is, to prevent significant soil compactment, erosion, and nutrient loss and to preserve soil quality generally. The human requirements are to give the kind of recreation experience desired. Combining these two can be difficult and often expensive.

Recreational areas in or near urban centers can be organized and managed for use by many people without undue site deterioration. But this requires money, knowledge, skill, and control of where people go in the areas; otherwise they can destroy what they came to see and use. In wetlands and some desert areas, for example, both the vegetation and the soil are sensitive and slow to recover from trampling and other disturbance by people. Such uses must be sharply limited. Similar situations also occur in intensively used parts of some national recreation areas, parks, and other public recreation areas. Wildland camping and much fishing and hunting use extensive areas, but frequently there is also undesirable concentration of use in particular places, which can damage the land and reduce the recreational experience.

Wilderness area management presents difficult land management problems. A wilderness experience should include space, solitude, primitive conditions, and personal freedom *and* responsibility.[1]

---

[1] What constitutes a wilderness experience cannot be defined because it is personal and

To quote the Wilderness Act of 1964, a wilderness is a place "where man himself is a visitor who does not remain." These conditions are more difficult to meet than might be thought as they are not directly related to total area.

For example, consider a large mountainous wilderness area of ¼ million or more acres in the United States. The Bob Marshall Wilderness (950,000 acres) in Montana is one of these. Even here meeting statutory wilderness objectives is a problem. Because of mountainous topography, the number of practicable travel routes or natural places to camp is sharply limited especially for a large party on horseback with numerous pack animals. Travel away from the relatively few trails is difficult, and few visitors can or do go far from these main routes. Wilderness regulations do not permit installation of permanent camp facilities or means of handling horses or feeding them other than by grazing on open areas. With much big game hunting in the fall, some areas get concentrated and heavy use, and they certainly show it.

These kinds of operating problems, varying in detail and intensity, are increasingly present in formally established wilderness and other wildland areas. They lead to imposition of restrictions depending on the kind of area and its use. They may include such things as prohibition of horses and use of motors on boats or canoes, a ban on the cutting of live trees or even firewood, a ban on the use of tinned foods or other nonbiodegradable packaging, limitations on the size of party and total number of people permitted in the wilderness area at one time, and restrictions on hunting. With increasing intensity of use, the trend is inevitably toward more restrictions, which is contrary to the essence of wilderness experience. There is a real management dilemma here.

The fact of the matter is that wilderness conditions as they were in truly pioneer days—and popularly are often yet thought to be—are long since gone and cannot be brought back. No longer do visitors face the responsibilities and consequences of finding their way around with poor or no trails or maps, largely sustaining themselves off the land, with little or no help in case of accident, and use of what now seems crude equipment. This is by no means intended to disparage wilderness travel—it can indeed be wonderful—but rather to recognize that the facts of land carrying capacity impose limits on the kind of recreation experience that can be expected.

The same basic problems of carrying capacity in sensitive areas apply very acutely in some desert areas. The California Desert of some 12 million acres in southern California is a prime example.

---

depends on the viewpoint, culture, understanding, need, mood, and nature of an individual. It can be experienced in areas large and small, forests and deserts, mountains and prairies. It is by no means limited to formal wilderness areas. See Chap. 7 for further treatment.

Grazing and Forests   Domestic livestock grazing and timber production are of limited compatibility as land uses. The basic reason is that grass
and trees are often vigorous competitors for the same land space and one
will dominate the other.

For example, grazing is often permitted in natural hardwood (decidu-
ous tree) areas. Particularly if the soil is of good quality, the results are
unsatisfactory unless grazing is carefully controlled as to season of year and
the number of livestock permitted in the area. Soil compactions and tree
damage—especially to young trees—may result, and grass and other low
vegetation is stimulated to the detriment of tree growth. A land-use choice
is necessary: either emphasize grazing use and retain some trees for protective livestock cover or emphasize tree growth and sharply restrict or exclude
grazing.

In the natural grassland areas of the Western states, where droughty
conditions tend to prevail, there is a delicate ecological balance to maintain
under grazing use. Overgrazing can result in loss of desirable vegetative
cover that can be both slow and difficult to restore. It is also true that there
is much natural compatibility between livestock and wildlife grazing. Livestock and wildlife often do not eat the same vegetation or use the same area
at the same time. Game usually go to the higher elevations and forested
areas during the summer and come down to the lower and more open areas
during the fall and winter. In contrast, domestic stock grazing on the open
range is largely concentrated on the lower elevations during the summer
and early fall.

In the Rocky Mountains of the West there is often a natural zone of
ecological tension between natural conifer forests and grasslands. The former extend *down* from the higher and more moist elevations. The grasslands
tend to move *upward* from the lower, drier, and often treeless valleys and
lower mountain slopes. In this intermediate or tension zone, forest and
grass cover tend to advance or recede and have for many years. Most of this
movement is due to natural wildfires, such as those started by lightning, and
to fires started by people either by intent or by accident. Some is also due
to timber cutting and livestock grazing practices. Combined use on these
middle slope areas is not generally successful as it often results in poor
productivity of both timber and grass.

Management of the piney woods in the Southern states gives a third
illustration of the general incompatibility of grazing and timber production
as land uses. Much attention, going back 20 or more years, has been given
to the development of cattle grazing in some effective combination with
timber production. By and large this has not been successful, and the reasons are different from those in either of the two preceding illustrations.

The natural grasses are mostly low in nutrition and also mainly usable
in the spring of the year. The comparatively recent and large development
of the livestock industry of the South is built on well-bred beef and milk

cattle, and hogs. This has placed emphasis on improved pastures and supplemental feeding rather than on forest grazing. Conversely, development of intensive timber production does not favor economically desirable grazing conditions. A choice of one or the other is necessary.

Water and Forests   Forests are extremely effective in watershed protection. They protect the soil and stabilize stream flow. Indeed, the maintenance of a sustained water yield from streams, lakes, and underground aquifers is of overriding importance in land use in which forests play a major role.

Attention here is on water and forest compatibilities in mountainous forested areas of the Western states. The maintenance of a good forest cover is highly compatible with and often necessary for watershed protection. Well-executed cutting for timber production is not in conflict with water yield. In fact, snow catchment, water permeation into the soil, and water yield can be increased by forest cover modification. Much research has been applied to improving the timing, amount, and quality of water yield by judicious cutting of trees and other woody vegetation.

Wildlife is compatible with water uses except when overpopulation damages vegetation and exposes the soil to erosion. Recreational land use and water are also generally compatible. Streams and lakes are, however, major recreation attractions and often require regulation to protect sensitive stream, lake, and shoreline areas from pollution and physical damage by trampling. At high mountain elevations, where vegetation grows slowly and soils are sensitive to exposure by trampling, people often must be restricted to well-constructed trails or perhaps be entirely excluded.

Grazing of domestic livestock seldom improves and is often damaging to desirable soil and watershed conditions. Overgrazing can expose the soil and cause soil compaction and erosion by trampling and removal of the natural vegetative ground cover. These undesirable effects result especially where growth is slow and the ecological margin of plant survival is narrow. Severe damage of long duration to the natural soil cover can result. For these reasons, it is often necessary to exclude grazing entirely from sensitive land areas.

APPLICATION OF COMBINED USES AS A LAND-MANAGEMENT POLICY

The preceding section gave in broad terms the ecological, physical, and practicable basis for combining different land uses through the concept of compatibility. Although a single use may be necessary on a particular area, two or more uses often can coexist simultaneously on the same area, and combinations of combined and single uses over a land area may judiciously be applied.

The purpose of this section is to extend this analysis to large-scale application of combined uses as a land-management policy. So doing requires consideration of the organizational, administrative, financial, and political problems of relating land-use capabilities and compatibilities to the needs and desires of people.

Development and Application of Multiple Uses by the U.S. Forest Service

The best example of purposeful application of combined uses on a large scale is given by the development of multiple uses by the U.S. Forest Service in the Department of Agriculture. This agency is responsible for the management of some 187 million acres of public lands in the national forests. These are distributed from Puerto Rico through the continental United States to Hawaii. These lands are of great diversity in characteristics and uses. They are also subject to the intense desires and concerns of the American people who own them. Of similar but with even a wider range of land-use problems are 470 million acres of public lands, predominantly in the Western states and Alaska (64 percent), which are administered by the Bureau of Land Management in the Department of the Interior. Treatment here will be limited to the Forest Service because it has had the longest experience in application of combined land uses. As with other public land agencies, the Service operates in full exposure to the needs, desires, and scrutiny of the American people.

Since its establishment as a land-management agency in 1905, the Forest Service has operated under the policy that all the renewable sources on the national forests were available for proper use. Its beginning is given in the famous letter of February 1, 1905, sent by Secretary of Agriculture James Wilson to the new agency in his department. His letter was also approved by President Theodore Roosevelt. Some key policy passages from the letter follow.

> All land is to be devoted to its most productive use for the permanent good of the whole people. . . .
> All the resources . . . are for use, and this use must be brought about in a thoroughly prompt and businesslike manner, under such restrictions only as will insure the permanence of these resources. . . . Where conflicting interests must be reconciled the question will always be decided from the standpoint of the greatest good of the greatest number in the long run.

From this beginning, and with additional but more specific statute directives regarding policy and administration, the Forest Service developed and operated for over a half century.

In the earlier years, attention was necessarily on first things first: to establish organization and administration of the service, to develop forest fire control, to initiate development of forest management mainly for timber, to control trespass, to establish control over grazing use which was a practice of long standing on these public lands before the advent of the Forest Service.

As a part of looking ahead to a wider range of public land-use needs on federal lands, the Forest Service in the 1920s began designating large wildland areas in the national forests for recreational use. Such areas were later codified and reclassified as "wilderness" or "wild" by the Secretary of Agriculture. Those in excess of 100,000 acres were established by the Secretary. Smaller areas down to 5,000 acres were established by the Chief of the Forest Service. All these areas were managed under the same principles and procedures.

The establishment of fifty-three of these wilderness and wild areas, plus the Boundary Waters Canoe area in Minnesota, aggregated in total over 9 million acres of national forest land and constituted the major beginning of the wilderness and related wild area reservation for public recreational uses.

Continuing and strong public interest in wilderness area establishment culminated in 1964 with the passage of the federal Wilderness Act (Public Law 85-577). The act requires thorough study, presidential recommendation, and congressional approval for either establishing or changing a wilderness area. Following passage of the act, wilderness areas previously established by the Forest Service were included in the new wilderness system, provided adjustments were made where needed to meet the requirements of the new law.

The act specified that some eighty other wildland areas, aggregating nearly 50 million acres in a number of federal ownerships, were to be examined over a 10-year period as potential additions to the wilderness system. Additional areas have been subsequently proposed for examination.

A number of these are in the Eastern United States, where very few areas clearly qualify for inclusion in the wilderness system on account of previous cutting and settlement. Wild areas are particularly needed here because of the much greater population. Also, and despite some past cutting and human habitation, there are wildland areas of great natural attraction and beauty. Considerable controversy has developed over how to meet Eastern wildland needs. It would seem that here is a situation where purism over truly "virgin" forests should give ground to a more pragmatic appraisal of what is, in fact, wild forest in relation to people needs.

Development of the wilderness movement, as briefly outlined above, is of particular land-use significance. It gives point to the increasing national need to establish a more comprehensive and clearly defined public land-management policy. The Forest Service is a case in point and is used here as a large-scale example.

Up to the midcentury point the Forest Service operated basically on the 1905 policy letter of Secretary of Agriculture Wilson to the agency. A more comprehensive policy, including status in outdoor recreation, was given by the Congress in the Multiple Use and Sustained Yield Act of 1960 (Public Law 86-517), which was passed after long hearings, much debate, and some politically necessary amendments. A similar Act for the Bureau of Land Management was passed in 1964 (Public Law 88-607).

It is worthwhile to take a good look at the significance and application of the Multiple Use Act of 1960. In the United States it is the first comprehensive public land-use management act of its kind. Its implementation well illustrates the many ramifications and problems of applying large-scale land management for a number of uses.

The act is given in two parts: policy directives and definitions. They are best presented by the act itself, as follows:

Policy Directives.
   Sec. 1. It is the policy of the Congress that the national forests are established and shall be administered for outdoor recreation, range, timber, watershed, and wildlife and fish purposes. The purposes of this Act are declared to be supplemental to, but not in derogation of, the purposes for which the national forests were established as set forth in the Act of June 4, 1897 (16 U.S.C. 475). Nothing herein shall be construed as affecting the jurisdiction or responsibilities of the several States with respect to wildlife and fish on the national forests. Nothing herein shall be construed so as to affect the use or administration of the mineral resources of national forest lands or to affect the use or administration of Federal lands not within national forest.
   Sec. 2. The Secretary of Agriculture is authorized and directed to develop and administer the renewable surface resources of the national forests for multiple use and sustained yield of the several products and services obtained therefrom. In the administration of the national forests due consideration shall be given to the relative values of the various resources in particular areas. The establishment and maintenance of areas of wilderness are consistent with the purposes and provisions of this Act.
   Sec. 3. In the effectuation of this Act the Secretary of Agriculture is authorized to cooperate with interested State and local governmental agencies and others in the development and management of the national forests.

These provisions state the policy intent of the Congress and are mandatory to the Secretary of Agriculture. They also enumerate the purposes for which the national forests are established and shall be administered. This is of major legal importance. It has been held by court decision that, although the provisions are mandatory, they are not exempt from legal review as to whether actions taken under them are in contravention of the act.

The meanings of the two key terms used in the act, "multiple use" and "sustained yield," are given in Sec. 4 as follows:

(a) "Multiple use" means: The management of all the various renewable surface resources of the national forest so that they are utilized in the combination that will best meet the needs of the American people; making the most judicious use of the land for some or all of these resources or related services over areas large enough to provide sufficient latitude for periodic adjustments in use to conform to changing needs and conditions; that some land will be used for less than all of the resources; and harmonious and coordinated management of the various resources, each with the other, without impairment of the productivity of the land, with consideration being given to the relative values of the various resources, and not necessarily the combination of uses that will give the greatest dollar return or the greatest unit output.

(b) "Sustained yield of the several products and services" means: The achievement and maintenance in perpetuity of a high-level annual or regular periodic output of the various renewable resources of the national forest without impairment of the productivity of the land.

Definitions and Meanings   Both sustained yield and multiple use express concepts that are difficult to interpret and apply. The act is more a statement of policy and meanings, of what it is about, than a true definition. In some respects the act raises about as many interpretive questions as it answers—which is often true of broad policy statements in legislative language. Both economic and biological considerations are included.

Sustained Yield   The concept of sustained yield is of major significance, but its specific meaning varies by particular land uses. It is in general a large-area concept and means that, whatever the use or uses may be or in what combination, renewable land resources must be so managed that, area by area and in total, and measured by "annual or regular periodic output," a continuing and sustainable yield is obtained without "impairment of the productivity of the land." These are important but often difficult conditions to meet.

For example, in forest management for sustained yield of timber the harvest is normally organized over rather large areas. Harvest cuttings, thinning, and regeneration of a new stand are planned sequentially to only parts of such a unit. A particular acre or other small unit cannot, for example, give a substantial timber yield each year. Different methods of forest management require different cutting schedules. Also, the total sustainable timber yield from a particular management unit may increase or diminish over time. This can be due to better knowledge of desirable and attainable management practice or because of changing combinations of land uses. The goal is not fixity in yield but rather that the land not be impaired and be under good management control. The principle of sustained yield can apply to outdoor recreation, fishing, hunting, livestock grazing, and agricultural land management generally. It can also be extended to urban situations.

Impairment is difficult to determine and measure. For example, it is very difficult to prevent *some* land impairment under domestic stock grazing on natural grasslands. Overgrazing occurred long before the Forest Service was established and is being rectified. But the wonderful Western grasslands of buffalo days can never be brought back as they once were. A variable time, value, and circumstance context has to be applied in interpretation of the word "impairment." Managed forests are not the same as entirely natural forests. Recreational use almost inevitably causes damage to soil and vegetation in areas of concentrated use. Much damage can be avoided or rectified through application of good management practices, for example, keeping people on trails in areas of sensitive vegetation, rotating campgrounds to permit their rejuvenation, or banning destructive logging methods. The measure of impairment must be related to ecological and use values over time.

Multiple Use   The term "multiple use" has been vigorously emphasized by the Forest Service. It has caught on and become a popular slogan meaning different things to different people according to their interests. It is well to take a close look at meanings and interpretations of the term. A number of them are given in the following.

1   By deliberate intent, *no* priority by particular uses is given in the act. The only criterion in this respect is that all uses will be *considered* (the key word here) without prejudice or favor. Consequently, the act gives no guide in deciding which uses should be applied and where in a particular situation. No formula can be given for choice in land uses other than fairly to consider them all. This fact opens the door wide to contention by people with particular land interests; that proper applications of multiple use means emphasis on the uses they support. The multiple-use concept consequently provides an excellent forum for appraisal of possible land uses but gives no guide to specific solutions in a particular situation.

2   How large or small can an area unit be? The act is of no help here either, but the question is important. For political reasons, the act includes the statement that "areas of wilderness are consistent with the purposes and provisions of this Act." Inasmuch as wilderness areas can include a million or more acres, and are essentially a single use for one kind of recreation insofar as any purposeful management is concerned, the area scale can be very large indeed. It would be ridiculous, for example, to divide a large tract of land into four parts, apply a different single use on each, and call it multiple use whether or not such use is necessary or the best use, all factors considered. Yet such simplistic ideas have been often advanced, and as a result almost anybody can claim "multiple use" virtue by such an approach.

3   Multiple use is a land administration *action* policy and not a static concept. Land resources are for use, and uses can change with need. It is often true that management for one use will protect another use or value in large degree with little or any special management action. For example, recreational use is of dominant importance in national parks, and its management requires much professional effort. But this use also protects wildlife and watershed valued in large degree. Under the intent of the act, in which purposeful administration is implicit, it is somewhat confusing to regard an association of uses and natural values as multiple use.

4 The act gives significant but limited guidance regarding economic policy. It states that consideration "be given to the relative values of the various resources, and not necessarily the combination of uses that will give the greatest dollar return or the greatest unit output." This introduces but gives no solutions to the difficult problems of value measurement which underlie most land resource decision making. Unfortunately, there are no simple or easy answers (see Chap. 7).

5 The act enumerates six uses on Forest Service lands which are not otherwise committed by law to limited specified uses. It consequently does not apply directly to other federal or state lands, or to various private ownerships of forest and related lands, where objectives of management may be quite different. The general principle of seeking compatible and harmonious combinations of uses certainly does, however, have general applicability under other land management objectives as emphasized previously. It does little good, however, to apply "multiple use" to all land-use situations, and too much of this has been attempted.

Combined Land Uses A broader and more fundamental general definition of the concept of combined or multiple use is needed. The following is advanced and given in three parts with bracketed commentary.

1 Lands can and do produce many goods and services, and often more than one of them can be obtained in various admixtures and combinations from a particular area of land.

[This is a broad statement of fact, a premise.]

2 Total net benefits, however measured or determined, often can be increased and perhaps maximized through some judicious combination of two or more uses on a particular area of land.

[This is the socioeconomic argument recognizing the problems of value measurement and its limitations in practice.]

3 Some compatible and harmonious combination of land uses, with flexibility for change in the future and without significant impairment of the land, is mandatory in the public interest.

[Public interest is deeply involved in land use, and this fact increasingly must be reckoned.]

Presented in these terms, it is apparent that the concept of combined uses, or the particular expression of it given in the Multiple Use Act, is a very general concept. It is not new nor limited to forest or any other kind of lands. The general principle can apply to structures, urban situations in general, multipurpose water projects, and the like.

The Multiple Problems of Applying Multiple Use   Following passage of the Multiple Use Act in 1960, the Forest Service embarked on the difficult job of applying it to the national forests. Multiple use was also publicized widely, and forest landowners large and small, public and private, were encouraged to apply the concept on their lands. The multiple-use story caught public notice. Its popularity as a catch phrase or general idea has often exceeded the understanding and application of it. It has been regarded as approaching a panacea, as being a method or a formula of some sort (which it is not), and something that will give all people what they want (which it cannot). It has been talked *about* much more than understood. Nevertheless, the general concept is powerful. It has stimulated much constructive thinking and action which has been reinforced by the rising concern over environmental quality and natural balance, of which good land use is a major part.

Following passage of the act, the Forest Service has encountered two basic but related problems in implementing multiple use on the national forests. The first is internal to the Service as an organization, and the second is external, relating to its public relationships. Analysis of each will aid in gaining general understanding of land-use application problems.

Internal Situations and Problems   The Forest Service is a very large, well-organized, strongly decentralized, mature, and dedicated organization. It can and does change to meet the times. But having many responsibilities and relationships within the federal government, to the states, to other organizations, and to the public, it cannot change rapidly. The Service has a large national research organization and extension service and long-standing and deep cooperative relationships with the states in fire control and in forest management work.

The national forest system, which is the focus of attention here, has a well-developed and decentralized line and staff organization, including strong supporting services such as finance, personnel, and legal counsel. The headquarters are in Washington, D.C. The 153 national forests are administered by several regional foresters, each having large regional responsibilities. A forest supervisor is in charge of each national forest, which is divided into several district operating units, each headed by a district ranger. This is the line organization. At each level there are supporting technical and administrative staff personnel. Also at each level, line and staff, there is much individual responsibility, as is necessary in an on-the-ground land-management organization that is continental in scope.

The Forest Service has organized the administration of the national forests primarily along functional lines, by activities. Timber management, fire control, grazing, and more recently and in increasing magnitude outdoor recreation and fish and wildlife are the major land-management functions. Wildlife and fish receive much attention from a habitat management standpoint but are under the jurisdiction of the states as regards game seasons, game limits, and issuance of hunting licenses. Watershed protection is an overriding concern but is mostly met through administration of other land uses, as has been brought out. Relatively little land management is independently and directly applied for watershed purposes only, except in municipal watersheds that include national forest lands.

This organizational sketch helps one appreciate the large administrative-personnel problems encountered in superimposing the all-encompassing concept of multiple use on a large and well-established functional organization. Introducing directions, ideas, points of view, and ways of doing things is difficult in any large organization and takes time. The Forest Service is no exception. A large and continuing job of internal education, realignment, organization, and coordination is necessary.

Following the Multiple Use Act of 1960, there was, necessarily, a period of initiation, appraisal, testing, and adjustment to apply the new act in practice. Initially, all regional foresters were required to prepare regional multiple-use guides for their regions. These were basically general policy directives by major land uses accompanied by coordinating instructions. Considerable emphasis was placed on large-scale land-use zoning by major land uses based primarily on locational and physiographical considerations. These guides followed a common pattern of purpose and policy according to broad Washington directives, but differed substantially by regions. For example, the flatlands and general situations of the lower South differ as day and night from the High Sierras of California and the Rocky Mountain West. In mountain country, the existence of strong topography and easily identified altitudinal and vegetative life zone differences and water drainages give a natural basis for large-scale land-use classification. This kind of sharp topographic differentiation does not apply in the lower South; the country, the climate, and the distribution and living conditions of people are different.

The forest supervisors of the respective regions were responsible for the implementation of these guides by their district rangers—the personnel and field organization directly on the ground. For a time, national forest multiple-use guides were also prepared for individual national forests. These were largely discontinued, placing more emphasis on the district plans, which are more definite, employ maps, etc. The recent trend is to place emphasis on planning and management by unit areas that are smaller and more homogenous than ranger districts (see Chap. 6).

Problems of coordination remain and always will. There are no formulas, and land-management problems are always changing. Land-use plans, as for timber cutting, grazing, recreation, or road development, are designed to include within them provision for coordination between different uses. Provision is also made for use of interdisciplinary study and planning teams. Supervision and inspection are given at all organizational levels.

Land management is necessarily applied in place, dealing with specific situations, area by area. Changes in land use, even if reversible, usually cannot be made quickly, and their consequences often last for years. Good land management is not cheap and by its nature is a deliberate process applied over time.

External Problems   Use of national forest lands is of concern to many organizations and individuals with both public and private interests. The Forest Service operates in full exposure to these many widely different interest groups. As a former chief once said: "If we get pressed about equally from all sides, we're probably about where we belong—right in the middle."

The Forest Service is a part of the executive branch of the federal government and consequently subject to executive directives and various other controls. It also has many relationships with other federal agencies. Like other federal bureaus, the Forest Service is subject to congressional legislation and influence, including the vital matter of appropriations, which exercise decisive administrative controls. It has long-standing and deep cooperative, financial, and administrative relationships with the states dating back to the Weeks Law of 1911 (36 Stat. 961-963).

In addition, there are an almost countless number of private organizations, groups, and individuals that are concerned with the management of the national forests and that see the Forest Service acting as steward over their lands. Other public land agencies are in a similar situation. These pressures and interests are expressed in many ways: directly, politically, and legally in the courts. Nobody, not even the Forest Service, can claim infallibility.

The problems of being responsive to public and private authorities and interests, and at the same time making their policies and actions understood, are many indeed and merit some tolerance. The Forest Service is a large organization of individuals, of people, and should not be personified and thought of as a single entity that says and does this or that.

In concluding this section, there is a large and important area of concerns that neither the Multiple Use Act nor other legislative acts clearly cover. These concerns stem from the fact that the Forest Service increasingly faces many land relationships and pressures that are not directly a part of its primary and statutory land management responsibilities. It is an old problem, now becoming more critical, and merits some attention here.

The initial forest reserve lands, primarily in the West and the nucleus of the national forests, were selected from the public domain insofar as possible to avoid inclusion of present or potential agricultural or urban lands. The same policy continued during large land acquisitions in the Eastern states, largely during the 1920–1940 period, that formed most of the present Eastern national forests. It has also guided acquisition and land exchange. The policy aim was to consolidate land holdings, sometimes scattered, to make them more manageable for national forest purposes.

Times have changed, however. Population has greatly increased, and with it many new land-use needs have developed radiating out from growing population centers. Lands once away from such uses are now increasingly in urban spheres of influence. This affects national forest land management in many ways. There is mounting land-use pressure for summer or "second" homes that tend to become permanent, outdoor recreation, subdivision developments, waste disposal projects, sewer and other utilities, water supply, roads, and school sites. These changes have important, lasting, and often irreversible impacts on adjacent or nearby national forest and other public lands. There is also need to provide areas of wildlands, open and free to the public, upon which these same spreading urban developments often depend for much of their appeal and value. Meeting these conflicting land-use needs presents difficult policy problems with no easy solution.

In addition, the nationally overriding National Environmental Policy Act of 1970 (P.L. 91-190) declares that "it is the continuing policy of the federal government to use all practicable means to create and maintain conditions under which man and nature can exist in productive and enjoyable harmony" and "to achieve a balance between population and resource use which will permit high standards of living and a wide sharing of life's amenities." These and other parts of the act have a direct bearing on national and other public land-management policies.

The Forest Service has land acquisition and exchange authorization (but limited funds), and also authority to grant special uses of various kinds. Its guiding policy, however, is to consolidate and maintain national forest area by acquisition or exchange of land parcels and not to sell lands outright or to use them extensively for uses other than stipulated in the Multiple Use Act. It has no authority to sell lands for urban or other development only because they are so needed and a good price can be received.

These pressures exist and they will increase, and there are strong differences of opinion as to solutions. Most people undoubtedly feel that the public lands are a public heritage belonging to all and that they should be maintained as such and not whittled away to meet local needs. This is countered by perfectly understandable and strong feelings by local people in an area, who can contend that nearby public lands should not be entirely sacrosanct from meeting urgent needs of a particular segment of the public.

Matters of deep public policy in land use are involved here. The inevitable development of state and national land-use planning will raise many such questions which in some respects could transcend multiple use as now practiced on the national forests. This particular situation is useful to emphasize the basic fact that land use is not static but ever-changing. The future cannot be predicted with certainty; an enlightened people will have to meet future problems as they come, building on past knowledge and experience.

Land Classifications: The Basis For Data Collection And Use

Purposeful and effective application of land management requires the collection and organization of much information regarding characteristics and use capabilities of land. This requires the establishment of classifications, which is the process of defining and grouping land information under some meaningful system of categories. The preceding chapter dealt with different kinds of land and uses; the purpose here is to give foundation for the orderly organization of needed information. Because land is fixed in place, different kinds of on-the-ground information can be shown on maps and graphs identified area by area. Demographic, climatic, and other statistical data can also be gathered and expressed in various kinds of enumerations that can be identified by areas.

Classification is consequently the basis for systematic collection and organization of information through surveys, inventories, and other data-gathering processes. The focus here is on classifications, not on data-gathering techniques and analysis methods, which are large subjects of themselves. Classifications and accompanying inventories or surveys are always conditioned by purposes, on point of view and interests. There are conse-

quently about as many different classifications possible as there are purposes.

Land classifications are presented in three groups. First are those that
deal with characteristics directly based on the land itself and not related to
particular uses. These range, from the bottom up, so to speak, from bedrock
geology to climate. They can cover systematically an entire area, be it a
specific place, an entire country, or the world. The second group are those
related in one way or another to particular kinds of land uses such as urban,
agricultural. or different uses of forested lands. Third are combinations and
adaptations of the first and second groups in which both land and use
classifications are combined in various ways for particular purposes. The
concept of combined uses in seeking harmony and balance in land use
(Chap. 3) requires such combinations. It is also recognized that classifications seldom are completely satisfactory in all aspects. Some things are
consistently difficult to define and measure. Also, constraints of data collection cost may be limiting, and purposes can be unequivocally difficult to
define.

CLASSIFICATIONS BASED ON THE LAND ONLY

Classifications based on land only, without regard to land uses, are an
essentially homogeneous group as they include items that give the land its
basic and essentially permanent characteristics. These are not people-influ-
enced in any major degree, and classifications can be applied systematically
to an entire land area.

Bedrock and Surficial Geology

Bedrock geology includes the origin, structure, and composition of rocks—
igneous, sedimentary, metamorphic, etc.—that are the parent materials occurring at the earth's surface. They are the source of mineral materials for
tills, outwash, and sedimentary deposits. The chemical and physical composition of bedrock is of large importance. The depth and structure of rock
below the immediate surface is often critical in all kinds of construction
engineering. In some situations it may be an obstacle requiring expensive
and site-destructive removal action such as blasting. It also can be an asset.
For example, rock formations furnish firm anchorage to large buildings
and, in fact, are a major factor in making the skyscraper and multilevel
subway complex of New York City possible. Rock close to the surface
limits the depth and fertility of soils and affects their drainage. The character of bedrock is a major factor in mining and drilling for water, oil, and
gas.

Surficial geology deals with such materials as unstratified glacial drift,
water-laid sediments, lake and marine deposits, deltas, and estuaries. These

deposits furnish the parent materials from which, along with organic accumulations, surface soils are formed. Their depth, composition, and structure are, as with bedrock, of great importance in land use.

Bedrock and surficial geology can be systematically classified and mapped over any land area, and such information is widely used in land-use planning.

Landforms—Geomorphology

The topography of the land—the mountains, valleys, streams, and other features created by erosion, such as plains, plateaus, and coastal flatlands—is of extreme importance. These land features change very slowly and largely determine land-use possibilities. The intensity of mapping and its accuracy depend on purpose. To determine landownership boundary lines, as for the construction of buildings, bridges, roads and highways, irrigation and drainage canals, and military purposes, high accuracy of both horizontal distances and vertical elevations is necessary.

Maps that show horizontal locations and distances only are called planimetric (i.e., related to a plane or level surface). Those that show both horizontal distances and vertical elevations are termed topographic maps. Elevations are shown by topographic lines of equal elevation called contour lines, which are measured from some base elevation, such as mean sea level. For example, the 1,000-foot contour line in upland country shows what would be the shore line if one could conceive a lake level at just 1,000 feet above sea level.

These landform maps, often also showing "culture," i.e., things like towns and highways, are prepared in various forms but all derive from horizontal and vertical measurements obtained from surveys. Aerial photographs are widely used for many mapping purposes, often in conjunction with land surveys.

Weather and Climate

The weather at the earth's surface, to which discussion is here confined, is extremely important in land use as well as for many other purposes. Climate includes a number of measurable weather conditions usually prevailing over a particular area or larger region. It can also be highly variable by place, season, and year. Climatic extremes that occur only occasionally, such as floods, hurricanes, tornadoes, or extreme temperatures, are very significant. A great deal of weather information is collected; major items measured are given below.

Precipitation, such as rain or snow; daily, seasonal, and annual averages; high and low ranges and extremes
Surface air movement (wind); direction, intensity, season, and extremes, as in hurricanes.

Air moisture content (humidity); daily range, seasonal and annual variation.

Cloudy or sunny weather; incidence by seasons

Temperatures; high, low, and average daily temperatures by seasonal averages and ranges

Air pressure; of extreme importance in weather predictions

Weather information can be presented and interpreted in many ways and for different purposes. Consideration here is limited to weather as an important, generally predictable, but variable fact of place and season that is important in land use. The treatment does not include weather prediction.

Surface weather information may be grouped or averaged to indicate the prevailing climate of an area, a region, a country, or the world as shown on atlas maps. In conjunction with topography, such maps are very valuable in large-scale land-use planning.

The same kind of information on a small-area scale is termed the microclimate. The scale may be small indeed, as applied to a house or other building. In housing and other building development on slopes and ridges, in valleys, etc., it is often advisable to make detailed study of the microclimate, especially air movements, as an aid in locating and constructing buildings to take best advantage of the site. Daily up- and down-slope and other air movements characteristic of mountain valleys are of great importance in forest fire control and have been intensively studied. So are the effects of prevailing winds on the windbreaking and related climatic influences of planted shelterbelts of varying width, height, species composition. and orientation. The microclimate above, within, and below a forest canopy of varying depth and density changes markedly, a matter of importance in forest ecology and recreation use.

On a larger scale, topographic conformation of the land markedly affects local climatic conditions. For example, a level area in a natural depression surrounded by higher country can trap or hold stagnant air. The results vary in scale from small dead-air pockets in which temperatures are abnormally low to the difficult smog-pollution situation surrounding the city of Los Angeles. Other cities, agricultural areas, etc., have similar microclimate situations caused by some combination of topographic and related air movement conditions. So-called rain shadows are caused by a high mountain range precipitating moisture and causing dry conditions on the leeward side. The Lake Tahoe area (Chap. 9) is a good example.

Soils

Soils, in general terms, are that portion of the earth's surface consisting of disintegrating rock and humus content (organic material). They are the combined result of geological parent materials, climate, topography, living

organisms, and time—a great deal of time. The processes of soil formation
are slow, but soil degradation and erosion can be rapid. Herein lies the crux
of soil-management requirements; protect and save the soil as it is most
difficult to replace.

Soil science, which is indeed a huge field, largely developed in agriculture and is farthest advanced in that area. Major study has also been given
to forest soils. Soils information is used in determining most land uses
whether urban or nonurban.

Soil classification is a most basic and also complex subject and has a
long history of development. A new and comprehensive system was adopted by the U.S. Department of Agriculture in 1960 and is followed here. This
system is based on soil properties as they occur and on soil genesis—how
soils were formed. The older system placed more emphasis on soil genesis.

The basic classification unit is the soil series,[1] which describes a generally similar group of soils in a particular place. Over 7,000 series are recognized in the United States. The name of the series in the United States is
taken from a city, river, or other name in the area in which the series is
located and described. Within a series, from one to several soil types are
also mapped, each differing in slope, drainage, depth of soil or other features, but similar in texture, profile, or fertility. Within a type, a soil phase
may be recognized based on some important deviation, such as stoniness or
chemical content, from the type norm.

An example is needed to make these relationships clear. The soil survey for Litchfield County, Connecticut, was completed in 1970 by the Soil
Conservation Service of the U.S. Department of Agriculture in cooperation
with the Connecticut Agricultural Experiment Station and the Storrs Agricultural Experiment Station (Soil Conservation Service, 1970). This bulky
publication is a part of the large and continuing job of making soil surveys
of the United States. In this report forty-six soil series, each with accompany soil mapping units, often referred to as soil types, are individually mapped in place and described. In addition, eight special disturbed situations,
including some created by people, are also described apart from the series
but included at the same level. These are borrow and fill land, alluvial land,
made land, muck-shallow, peat and muck, riverwash, rock land, and terrace
escarpment.

To give a specific example, the Stockbridge series, one of the larger in
the county, includes 14,211 acres with eleven mapping units or soil types
recognized ranging from 390 to 5,561 acres in area. Each soil type is sepa-

[1] "A group of soils that formed from a particular kind of parent material and have
genetic stratification horizons that, except for texture of the surface soil, are similar in differen-
tiating characteristics and in arrangement in profile. Among these characteristics are color,
structure, reaction, consistence and mineralogical and chemical composition" (U.S. Department of Agriculture, 1960).

rately mapped and identified on the detailed maps accompanying the county report. The series is described as follows:

> The Stockbridge series consists of well-drained, nearly level to hilly soils that developed in firm or very firm glacial till. The till was derived chiefly from Salisbury schist and limestone but, to some extent, from dolomite and quartzite. These soils occur mainly in the limestone valley in the northwestern part of the county. They also occupy small areas in the towns of Goshen and Cornwall, and in these areas they are on smooth drumlins or drumloidal hills. Permeability is moderate in the surface layer and subsoil but is slow or very slow in the substratum.
>
> A typical profile in a cultivated field has a surface layer of very dark grayish-brown loam about eight inches thick. The upper part of the subsoil is olive-brown loam, and the lower part is dark grayish-brown loam. This layer extends to a depth of about 26 inches. It is underlain by very dark grayish-brown to olive-colored loam in which dark yellowish-brown limestone ghosts are common.

A detailed description of a typical Stockbridge soil series is also given. The eleven soil types or mapping units individually recognized and mapped in the series are also described in some detail. Essentially, they vary by slope percentages, degree of erosion, and stoniness.

The above indicates the detailed description and field work entailed in soil classification and mapping. The point of emphasis here is that this work gives in-place information about soils that of itself is independent of any particular land uses, although certainly indicative of land-use potentials. It gives the basis for the extremely important, large, and growing area of interpreting soils information in the terms of particular land uses. Some of this is built into the soil type descriptions, mainly from an agricultural standpoint which, historically, has been given major attention.

Much attention and detail is given in the Litchfield report to uses of the basic soils information. This is done by interpretation of individual series and types, and by various groupings according to their capabilities for different uses. Included in considerable detail are use capabilities and characteristics for agriculture, woodland, engineering, community development (including urban), and wildlife.

Ecological-Vegetative Classifications

Ecological-vegetative classifications can be made for an area of any size as a whole. Normally, they are not related to any particular land use but are valuable in guiding uses.

These classifications can be made in many different ways but normally are designed to show, by whatever detail of grouping system used, the occurrence of natural vegetative communities—what grows where—and as such are very useful. These vegetative types are an end result. They integrate and reflect the combined effects of soils, climate, and topographic effects of altitude and aspect (north or south slopes, lowlands or uplands, etc.). A skilled ecologist can tell a great deal about the land, including considerable about its history, from the mixtures of species naturally present. These are stable and characteristic. Certain low plants, shrubs, or tree species are excellent indicators of particular habitat growing conditions and are so used.

There are no fixed systems for vegetative classifications as there are for soils. Common general groupings can be indicated, however, as given below:

Wetlands: Coastal tidelands and swamps, freshwater bogs and swamps of many kinds, periodic overflow areas, vegetative lake encroachment.

Grasslands and related vegetation: Moist and lowland areas, upland natural meadows, the large grassland areas of the West, and alpine meadows.

Woody shrubs: Lowland and upland types, the "hard" shrubby growths which are often called chaparral in the Southwest, and alpine types.

Woodlands: Large areas of pinyon pine, juniper, and other species in the Western United States occurring at different elevations and also in various mixtures with grass and shrub species.

Forests: Highly variable associations of hardwood and of coniferous trees. These occur north, south, east, and west in the United States from bottomlands to high mountains. A large number of natural ecological forest types are recognized, each with distinctive indicator species and site requirements.

Alpine boreal and tundra types: Tree and other vegetation at their climatic extremes. Includes a large number of distinctive species associations.

CLASSIFICATIONS BASED ON LAND USE

The classifications given in the preceding section are based on the land only without regard to the particular use made of it. In large degree, these give the foundation for obtaining, through application of inventories and surveys, much of the physical information needed for land-use planning. The purpose of this section is to present a group of classifications and related inventories which are focused directly on land use. Basically, they combine different kinds of information into land capability classes for different kinds of uses. The nature of the process is indicated here through some examples, and the reader is encouraged to add others.

Agriculture

Soils information is necessarily mapped in place, is descriptive of what is found in specific localities, and can be directly interpreted. However, soil series and types mapped in one place are often similar in structure and plant growth capabilities to soil series mapped under different names and located elsewhere. Groupings of soils series increasingly are made to use soils information for agriculture and many other purposes.

A major illustration, compressing and integrating a mass of information, is the eight land capability classes established by the U.S. Department of Agriculture (Soil Conservation Service, 1966) which are applicable nationwide. This is a famous classification dating back many years that has been periodically updated and revised. It is one of a number of interpretive groupings for agricultural land uses. The bulletin cited above is short, twenty one pages, and needs to be read to understand the full impact of the eight classes which are summarized directly from this publication.

LAND SUITED TO CULTIVATION AND OTHER USES

Class I—have few limitations that restrict their use. Nearly level, low erosion hazard, deep generally well-drained and easily worked soil.

Class II—have some limitations that reduce the choice of plants or require special conservation practices or both.

Class III—have severe limitations that reduce the choice of plants or require special conservation practices or both.

Class IV—have very severe limitations that restrict the choice of plant or require very careful management or both.

LAND LIMITED IN USE—GENERALLY NOT SUITED TO CULTIVATION

Class V—have little or no erosion hazard but have other limitations impractical to remove that limit their use largely to pasture, range, woodland, or wildlife food and cover.

Class VI—have severe limitations that make them generally unsuited to cultivation and limit their use largely to pasture or range, woodland, or wildlife food and cover.

Class VII—have very severe limitations that make them unsuited to cultivation and that restrict their use largely to grazing, woodland, or wildlife.

Class VIII—Soils and landforms have limitations that preclude their use for commercial plant production and restrict their use to recreation and wildlife, or water supply or to esthetic purposes.

Engineering

Soil properties are of special interest to engineers for structural reasons which are very different from agricultural needs. These needs include construction and maintenance of roads. airports, pipelines, and foundations of buildings; facilities for storing and holding water, such as dams and levees; structures for controlling erosion and drainage systems; and systems for sewage disposal. Soil surveys and related soil properties information, as obtained by the United States Department of Agriculture, are interpreted and evaluated to meet these engineering needs. Among soil properties of interest to engineers are permeability to water, soil drainage, compaction characteristics, shrink-swell characteristics, shear strength, and chemical constituents and reaction. Also important are depth to bedrock or to sand and gravel, depth to water table, and susceptibility of soils to flood erosion.

Forests

Forests cover a larger total area than agriculture or any other land-use group in the United States. Methods and techniques of classification are well developed. Some of these were indicated in Chap. 3 regarding land-use compatibilities. In this chapter they are related to ecological-vegetative classifications. Forested lands can produce a number of goods and services including timber, wildlife, grazing, outdoor recreation, and watershed protection. These lands often have soil quality and structure that are desirable for agriculture. Very large naturally forested areas have been cleared for such use and put to growing crops not endemic to the area. Lands remaining in forest cover differ from agricultural land, however, because they produce a long-lived and natural land crop. Even under intensive management, forests support tree species either natural or well adapted to the site. They consequently closely follow ecological classification criteria. In contrast, agricultural crops, except for orchard culture, are on a much shorter, commonly seasonal, time schedule and produce crops that are not natural to the site.

There are two broad kinds of classifications applied to forested areas from a productivity standpoint: (1) classifying areas by natural tree species associations called forest types and (2) classifying by site quality or growth capacity essentially measured in terms of wood volume and quality.

There are about 150 forest types in the United States, as recognized by the Society of American Foresters, ranging from mesquite and pinyon-juniper in the Southwest to highly valuable timber types. These types are defined by natural associations of key tree species, e.g., oak-hickory of the Central States, bottomland hardwoods of the lower South, Douglas-fir and associates in the Pacific Northwest. Large-area groupings of tree associations, such as southern pines and smaller subtypes, are also recognized. These classifications are analogous to those for soils, as forest types can be identified and mapped on the ground. As with any such classifications of large areas, professional opinions vary on particular definitions to use.

Site quality, the second kind of classification generally employed, is based on measurement of tree growth capacity in terms of volume and quality. Two general approaches are used.

The first and most widely used method, is based on growth measurement of trees in a forest type or a part of one. Trees are the best indicator of volume and quality growth as they integrate the combined effects of soil, climate, altitude, and aspect (e.g., north or south-facing slopes). Site quality, or site index as it is usually termed in the United States, is most commonly expressed as the average total tree height at a given age of the dominant (upper-canopy) trees on sampling areas. It has been found that height growth of these trees is strongly related to the wood-growing capacity of the site and is weakly related to the closeness together of trees (stand density). On the basis of much sample measurement and statistical correlation, growth in wood volume per acre at different stand ages can be related to the quality of the land.

The second method makes direct use of soils information and sometimes uses selected low plant species, occurring under certain kinds of undisturbed forest conditions, that are indicative of tree growth quality. Use of soils information is necessary where a forest cover is lacking or insufficient for site index measurements. A great deal of research has been done to establish soil-site relationships. Soils information and tree growth data are often used together. However, where suitable tree cover exists, site measurement derived from tree growth is usually the most accurate and is more widely used in practice.

Wildland Grazing

Livestock grazing is a large and complex subject. Treatment here is limited to the basic nature of livestock grazing as related to land classifications. It is also restricted to grazing on large, natural grassland areas primarily in the Western states. Improved pastures and general meadowland grazing are more directly related to agricultural use and are not included here.

Range management is concerned with the grazing of domestic livestock on open range lands. It is a well-developed professional field of study backed by much research emphasizing ecological relationships. It is conducted on many millions of acres of highly diverse and often semiarid lands, mainly natural grassland. Also included are brushy and other areas supporting woody vegetation and overgrazed lands that have been artificially reseeded.

The situation and problems of range management are different from those of forestry and agriculture. The basics are these:

1 The "crop" is the annual growth of grass and other low vegetation which is harvested by animals of varying eating habits and under no individual or direct control by people beyond when and where the animals range.

2 Grazing lands are ecologically fragile and certainly finite in the amount of grazing they can endure. The key land-use problems are to maintain desirable forage species and growth conditions and prevent soil compaction and erosion. The topography of the area is very important. Much ecological and soils knowledge is requisite.

Vegetative restoration and soil stabilization following improper grazing practice is slow.

3 Principal controls that can be exercised over grazing are:

a The species and number of animals that are permitted on an area during a grazing period.

b The duration and season of the grazing period. Seasonality is extremely important.

c The distribution of livestock over a grazing unit. This is also extremely important. Much depends on the kind of animals; sheep are normally under close control of a herder, horses range widely, and cattle are varied in their grazing habits and are difficult to control on the range. Distribution is effected primarily by natural barriers or fencing, location of water supply, location of salt (for cattle and horses), by herding (with sheep), or by horseback riding and/or use of jeeps or other mechanized means (with cattle).

d Standards established regarding the proper condition of the range by seasons. Principal considerations are the capacity of plant species to endure grazing, particularly as related to the seeding and growth characteristics of individual species; yearly rainfall and other climatic variations which are often large; and the need for remedial measures to restore good grazing conditions following overuse.

Classifications, and inventories based on them, are obtained primarily through the processes of range reconnaissance. These give a good illustration of land-use planning for a particular purpose, and they utilize basic soils, climate, vegetation, and related data.

Areas are mapped as to suitability for grazing by different kinds of animals as defined by predetermined standards. Soils data are used as available and applicable. The vegetative cover is sampled to determine its species composition, density, condition, and growth. Vegetation types are mapped in place much as are soil or forest types. Estimates are made of forage productivity of edible plants in volumetric terms, usually expressed as animal months of feed by particular species. This is similar to estimating the yield of hayland in tons per acre per year. Proper grazing seasons are established. Animal distribution problems are appraised, and needs for fencing, water development, and the like are estimated. The final results are maps and related data giving grazing carrying capacity based on estimates of animal months of feed available by grazing seasons or periods. The kind of livestock are also indicated together with estimates of needs for range management and development.

Treatment given here is necessarily generalized. There are many variations in classifications used and the intensity of inventories made that cannot be detailed. Grazing is an example of a very widespread land use that is difficult to control and is not generally understood by the public. It should be noted that many of the underlying principles and problems of other land uses appear although in different forms. For example, the general concepts of land productivity (carrying capacity is another way of expressing basically the same thing) apply in open-land grazing as they do in agriculture, forestry, recreation, wildlife, and to a considerable degree in urban situations.

Wildlife

Wildlife is ubiquitous and of great ecological importance because of the large niche it occupies among living things. This applies both to the number of species and to their wide distribution. As a category, wildlife includes all birds and other animals that are "living in a state of nature; not domesticated" *(Webster's New Collegiate Dictionary, 1956).* A general characteristic of wildlife is that species are primarily dependent on natural sources of food. There are few areas indeed in the United States, as elsewhere, that do not support some species of wildlife.

From a land-use standpoint, wildlife is considered as it is associated with other primary uses such as agriculture, open-land grazing, forestry, public or private parks, and residential areas. Techniques and methods of classifying wildland areas from the standpoint of wildlife suitability and productivity are well developed for many species. This is particularly true for major game species of animals and waterfowl. These techniques are similar to those applied to domestic livestock grazing on open lands previously described in Chap. 3, but specifics are different.

Wildlife as an area of concern has three major characteristics that deeply affect classifications and inventories to obtain and codify information needs.

The first is that wildlife, being essentially free-ranging by definition, is extremely difficult to control. This is hard enough for domestic livestock grazing on the open range, more so for wild animals such as deer, and far more difficult for migratory birds.

The second is the tremendous number and diversity of wildlife species and their consequent diverse habitats, feeding and breeding habits and requirements, diseases, predators, etc.

The third is the important but almost universal fact that people are interested in wildlife. These interests cover a wide spectrum from extreme concern and affection for wildlife, to highly varied hunting interests, and to dislike and fear of wildlife considered as dangerous animals, predators, pests, or poisonous creatures. Such interests and concerns permeate almost every aspect of wildlife treatment and management. These three characteristics make wildlife an extremely complex field that is ancillary to but only in part identifiable as a land use.

Outdoor Recreation

Outdoor recreation is a large and complex subject important in land use but difficult to treat because it is so intimately related to the interests of many people. The product of outdoor recreation is not directly produced *from* the land, like food, timber, or forage for livestock. It is a personal and largely individual satisfaction received by people. It is difficult indeed to measure benefits derived from relaxation, change, and refreshment of the spirit for which the land provides the necessary base (see Chap. 7).

As considered here, outdoor recreation includes not only use of land but use of streams, the smaller lakes, and other water areas closely related to the land. It also includes bird watching and noncommercial hunting and fishing, which to most people are forms of recreation.

As a land use, outdoor recreation is characterized by two major dimensions. The first is the wide range of land areas which are specifically reserved and developed for recreation as the primary and often exclusive use. These include intensively used parks and playgrounds in or near urban centers. In a wildland setting are resorts, dude ranches, wildland public parks, and campgrounds. Recreation areas are often located near water which is a major attraction to people. Of low use intensity are very large wilderness tracts that have no developed facilities. Except for wilderness areas and national parks, the key point is that the average size of recreation areas is relatively small. It is also important to recognize that, in the United States at any rate, outdoor recreation generally takes place close to home. There is a tendency in outdoor recreation literature to place attention on the use of the larger and often more remote wildland tracts in state, federal, and private ownership and give lesser emphasis to the much greater total importance of local recreation facilities.

The second dimension, and a major characteristic of outdoor recreation from a land-use standpoint, is the fact that much recreational enjoyment and experience comes from and often requires a setting of much larger areas than those that are specifically designated for recreation. The most extensive and obvious example is that of pleasing landscapes seen from public travel routes. These views are not at all limited to wildlands but include agricultural and other rural land, towns, and interesting views in general. More area-intensive recreation includes riding, walking, hiking, nature study, hunting, and fishing. Lands on which such recreational satisfaction is received are predominantly not intended for recreational use nor owned by those receiving the benefit. They include public and privately owned lands of many kinds that are owned and managed for a variety of purposes.

The fact that people get most of their recreational experience from lands they do not own merges with land aesthetics in general and becomes a matter of public policy concern. As a part of rising demand for environmental quality, people are increasingly concerned about unsightly and ecologically undesirable land uses, including junkyards, eroding fields, overlarge or badly located timber clear-cutting areas, some highway and utility construction, wetland drainage or fills, and stream pollution. Restrictions that increasingly are being placed on such land uses stem from the bundle-of-rights concept of landownership (Chap. 2). More of these rights are being appropriated in the public interest.

An important aspect of outdoor recreation is the pervading and often critical necessity of protecting the resource from the people that enjoy it. For many reasons, recreational use strongly tends to concentrate in particular areas. This can destroy the resource people came to see or use. Remedial action may require very specific and restrictive measures to preserve the soil and natural features in intensively used playgrounds and recreation areas. Similar action may be necessary to protect from damage or restore sensitive rocks, soils, vegetation, streams or lakes in large wildland recreation areas. The basic need to protect the natural resource under human use is the same everywhere; differences are only in specifics.

Much attention has been given to classification of lands for different kinds of recreational uses and to development of criteria, measures, and standards regarding their uses. Outdoor recreation is as much a sociological matter as it is a land-use matter. No general classifications and inventory approaches are possible as have been here outlined for agriculture, forests, or wildland grazing, which have measurable inputs and outputs that can be related to particular areas. Recreation classifications and related information needs consequently can be given in outline only, as specifics vary so much by situation and need. These needs fall into two general groups: those relating directly to information about the land itself and those relating to particular recreation uses.

Land Information   Outdoor recreation utilizes much of the data obtained through classifications based on the land only. These are applied in much the same general way as for agriculture, engineering, forestry, and wildland grazing. Soils and surficial geology are often extremely critical as regards drainage and capacity to sustain different kinds of uses, including roads and trails. Similarly, topography, weather, and climate are critical in site selection and in defining use possibilities. Ecological-vegetative data are likewise necessary in appraising land carrying capacity under people use and the aesthetic qualities of the site.

Recreational Uses   There is a large and well-developed body of knowledge relating to use of land and related water for outdoor recreation. It consists of the following:

1 Reconnaissance and analysis of potential recreational land uses in an area according to various classifications and standards. For example, a recreation survey of a large area, such as a national forest or a large private landownership, may be made. It could include map and on-the-ground analysis of primary topographical features relating to recreation; evaluation of lake and stream areas for swimming, boating, and fishing; survey of possible campsites as to size, location, and character; and analysis of needed access development by roads or trails to serve recreational uses. This kind of work may be done in various levels of intensity from preliminary reconnaissance to analysis and planning in depth.

2 Design and layout of recreation developments in plan implementation. A high level of professional expertise and knowledge is required here to meet the special needs of recreational uses. Many landscape architects, people especially educated in outdoor recreation, foresters, engineers, and others are employed in such work.

3 Construction of facilities, including roads and trails. This is technically demanding work requiring much specialized knowledge. For example, the design, standards, and construction of buildings and facilities for water, sewage, and garbage disposal differ from those in urban areas and offer special problems. Facilities often must be constructed and designed for seasonal use under unusual climatic conditions.

4 Operation and maintenance of facilities. This often must be done on sites distant from established habitation centers and for a transitory and usually seasonal use.

As indicated above, outdoor recreation is certainly an important land use but one that does not fit the pattern of agriculture, forestry, and wild-land grazing. Wildlife, which is land-based, and sport fishing in inland waters are basically a part of outdoor recreation but are also difficult to define as separate land uses as they are mostly related to some other use or uses. These facts in part illustrate the point that focus on the land as a common denominator gives needed unity and perspective in understanding relationships between different uses.

COMBINED-USE CLASSIFICATIONS

The purpose of this section is to consider the problems of information classifications in land-use planning for a mixture of single and combined uses. This is a more complex matter than dealing with classifications based on the land itself or on particular uses such as agriculture or forestry. It is true that information for particular uses is requisite and often applied over large areas both singly and in various groupings. But the spatial distribution and the variable and physical combinations of two or more uses create complex situations difficult to resolve. These matters will be dealt with in two parts, nonurban and urban.

Nonurban Land Uses

It should be apparent from Chap. 3 that no single classification or inventory system can possibly suffice for combined uses. This is because land uses may be combined in many different ways and often in proportions that change over time as a result of public or private decisions.

Some illustrations are necessary to clarify this matter. Forests furnish an excellent example. They are a stable, durable, diverse, and self-renewing land cover of very large areas that produce a number of goods and services often at the same time on the same area. By recognition of forest species cover types, any particular area can be mapped and identified as to its forest characteristics and use potentials. Land in federal ownership, for example, may permanently be designated for particular kinds of land uses. These may include national parks or recreation areas, natural areas which are to be completely undisturbed, federal wilderness areas, military reservations or testing areas, and such. Private owners make similar decisions as to land uses.

Such designations do not, however, answer the question of what use, or which uses in particular combinations, should be applied within much larger land areas that are not specifically designated for a particular kind of land use but that are often capable of several uses. The national forests, which operate under the general principle of multiple use, provide an excellent example. The U.S. Forest Service has not solved and cannot solve this problem of specific land-use allocations on a general basis as a result of total land area classifications. It is necessary to make specific land-use decisions, area by area, giving consideration both to land-use capabilities and to people needs. The Service must also conform to general policy guidelines given by the Congress to seek a desirable balance in the public interest—a most difficult thing to define.

To see the nature of the problem more clearly, consider timber and wildlife use in an area where the two uses are compatible within certain limits and where the product of each is desired in some combination. However the answer is determined, usually on some combination of economic and other social considerations, the fact remains that there is no formula or specific means to classify such an area for combined use or to define the particular information needed to establish the desired level and balance of combined use.

The problem comes to focus when one attempts to apply the concept of combined use to sharply different kinds of uses, unequally controllable, that do not mix evenly on the land. Wildlife and timber production are two uses that give a good example. Wildlife moves readily and is selective as to food and protective cover needs. In contrast, timber production is fixed in place although adjustments in management practice can be made as to the timing, location, and kind of timber cutting followed to favor certain wild-life species over a particular area.

But this is not all the story. In some areas a better answer, particularly applicable to some wildlife species, deer for example, is to emphasize, where practicable, timber and game uses on somewhat different but intermixed areas, each treated according to its respective capabilities and needs. This means a sort of microblending of single and combined uses on the land. This has been successfully done in forest management on state forest lands in the Lake States where deer production is a major land use and also on some game preserves. The scale and intensity of such combination obvious-ly depends on the character of the particular land concerned. Some lands are more adaptable, and in different ways, than others.

The Dominant-Use Concept A significant illustration of multiple land-use problems is given by the concept of dominant use. It is prominent-ly developed in the publication *One Third of the Nation's Forests,* the report to the President by the Public Land Law Review Commission in 1970. Application of dominant use as a basis for classifying public wildlands stimulated much public debate with political implications. These latter arose primarily from the proposal to designate by statute the classification of public lands by dominant use. Such action is in conflict with recognition of combined compatible uses given in the Multiple Use Acts for the Forest Service and the Bureau of Land Management.

The general idea and purpose of recognizing a dominant use is com-mon on both urban and nonurban lands, and on both public and private lands. On public lands it is recognized by statute. For example, there are large military reservations, atomic testing areas, national parks, fish and wildlife refuges, national recreation areas, and wilderness areas where the dominant use purpose is defined. On such areas, other uses can be and often are permitted *provided* they are compatible and also not prohibited by statute directives. Particular situations vary. For instance, timber cutting on wilderness areas established under the Wilderness Act is prohibited, where-as on wildlife refuges cutting is permitted and applied provided it enhances wildlife. The general idea in the Commission report was to classify public land areas according to their "highest and best use," permitting other uses insofar as compatible, with the accompanying idea that such uses should not interfere with the dominant use.

On the face of it, this seems a reasonable and sound policy. But the proposal engendered much controversy as it raised some problems difficult to resolve. These centered on the very large areas of federal lands adminis-tered by the Forest Service and the Bureau of Land Management under their respective Multiple Use Acts (Chap. 3).

Dominant use is a form of zoning, and its implementation would ne-cessitate such land designation. The term is not defined beyong aiming for "highest and best use," which is a difficult concept to apply. Definition would require measures of socioeconomic values which change over time and are consistently difficult to determine. No help was given on the crucial question of "how dominant is dominant?" Is it 51, 75, 90 percent, or what proportion? By whom and how would the crucial evaluations of land-use compatibilities be determined?

Political questions arose over uncertainty as to these matters of definition, interpretation, and practical application. For example, consider timber and outdoor recreation uses, each of which are supported by very strong public interests. Recreational advocates can hold that timber management is imcompatible with outdoor recreation and press for designation of very large areas for outdoor recreation as the dominant use with as little timber use as possible. Conversely, timber interests, also having influence, could press for classification of public lands for timber as the dominant use with limited interest in recreation.

This is not to imply that either recreation or timber-oriented organizations would in fact press for narrow interests. But they could. The potentials of such a situation well illustrate conditions under which controversy is born and nourished. More importantly, such classification would polarize thinking. It would lead away from a constructive and cooperative search for practicable and environmentally acceptable *combinations* of compatible uses. The same basic questions of dominance definition and compatibilities arise in urban zoning. It is impossible to zone successfully that which cannot be defined with reasonable clarity, consistency, and stability.

It seems clear that statutory application of a general dominant-use concept on either public or private lands would, although not so intended, largely negate constructive development of combined uses. The Multiple Use Act clearly recognizes single land uses, such as wilderness, and establishes no limit on the size of areas so designated. It also emphasizes compatible uses. In either case, the act emphasizes the need for seeking a good balance of uses and recognizes the necessity for on-the-ground evaluation and judgment. This need applies to both public and privately owned lands, whether urban or nonurban.

The dominant-use issue raises a very basic question. In land-use matters how far can one usefully go in attempting formally to apply zoning classifications to combined land uses? This is a difficult matter because single and combined uses work in opposite directions. Zoning tends to formalize a dominant use. Emphasis on combined uses takes the more flexible and variable approach of seeking land-use combinations where such are practicable but not denying single uses.

Classification Needs for Total Area Land-Use Planning   The importance of land-use classifications comes to particular point in land-use planning. It is increasingly being done for county, state, and regional units in the United States and elsewhere. In considering such planning, there is inevitable need to classify all land according to consistent categories which will include the total land area. There is also, as has been emphasized, a strong tendency for land-use classifications, once established, to become difficult to change. This is true worldwide. In fact almost everything about landownership moves with deliberation, as it should. A strong element of stability is surely important in land use.

Developing desirable land-use patterns is a complex matter. It must be recognized that classifications are a means, a necessary basis, for planning and do not of themselves assure good land use. The crux of the matter is to bring human needs into some desirable and enduring balance with land resources through systems of government and land-use controls judiciously applied.

The most practical approach is the pragmatic one of starting with things as they are in working toward a better total balance in land use. It is more intriguing to design the new city, community, or landscape. But this is not the norm, and the applications of this approach are not overly encouraging. Almost always, one has to start with an existing land-use situation and go on from there.

This is the approach taken in the following example, which is developed by assuming a generalized land-use situation. The purpose is to illustrate relationships of classifications to land-use planning for a generalized area.

A fairly large inland tract is assumed that includes several land uses and both private and public landownerships. People in the area are neither wealthy nor poor, and there is substantial but not strongly dominating urbanization. Geographically and economically the area is assumed to be a natural land unit and community but not necessarily a political unit such as a county.

Land groupings assumed are given below:

Urban areas   These include commercial, industrial, and residential areas and transport facilities, including an airport.

Agricultural lands—cropland and improved pastures   This is an important and well-established land use. Small to medium-large private ownerships. Agricultural land is fairly well consolidated. Some forested land is intermixed with agricultural areas.

Public ownerships   These include federal, state, county, and municipal ownerships including a good system of parks and other recreation areas. Federal land is primarily national forest and is important for water, outdoor recreation, wood, and some grazing.

Special areas   This category includes a miscellany of land uses such as state institutions, testing areas, wetlands, and some essentially unused land of low quality.

The above is deliberately generalized. The purpose is to emphasize the fact that in planning for an area as a whole, land classifications and accompanying inventories are necessary. It is not difficult to do this by landownership and use group as outlined above. This is what getting "the data," as the term is commonly used, often means.

It is another and more difficult matter to assemble land-use data applicable to the more complex job of using data integratively to meet the needs of a community. This goes beyong what can be shown on a map or be statistically summarized. Data for individual land-use units do not supply answers to many questions of balance between ownership uses.

A number of sociopolitical considerations must be considered. There can be conflicts of interest among federal, state, county, and urban units of government. Each of these has different levels and kinds of authority and objectives. Yet they all need to work together with mutual understanding. Classifications give the land information base but do not solve land-use problems.

Urban Land Uses—Zoning

Similar kinds of problems and issues arise in both urban and nonurban areas, but urban areas are more complex, intensive, and intimate socially. The value scale per unit of land area is much higher. From a land-use standpoint, urban lands are an aggregation of both single and combined uses often intensively applied in close juxtaposition. Land is predominately in private ownership. In nonurban areas public ownership is often of major importance.

Another and more fundamental difference is that on nonurban lands the major land-use purpose is to produce a crop or service from what the land itself offers, such as open space, food, timber, wildlife, water, and outdoor recreation. In contrast, land in urban use serves essentially as a physical *base* to support urban construction. The amenities of trees, grass, gardens, and open spaces are surely important, and favorable surface and subsurface soil structure and drainage are a large asset in urban development. But in major degree urban land can be made to fit the need as illustrated by the fact that major cities have been built on adverse sites such as swamps and rocky areas.

The purpose of this section is to appraise urban land-use problems primarily through the concepts and practices of zoning. The reasons for so doing are twofold. The first is that zoning, which is a classification, is a major approach to land use that has been developed and intensively applied in urban areas. In principle, the concept of zoning is not limited to urban areas, as was brought out in the discussion of dominant use, and it is being extended to county and state units. The second reason is that extension of an urban zoning approach to entire counties and larger land units brings it into direct contact, collision perhaps, with nonurban concepts and ideas about land classifications and controls. These have been developed and are applied in a different land-use context. The fact of these differences needs to be recognized and understood in appraising the present trend toward state and national land-use planning which includes both urban and nonurban lands.

What Is Zoning? The basic purpose of zoning is to delineate on the land what are considered to be noncompatible land uses. This means the establishment and mapping of land-use classifications or zones. For each zone, regulations are established by legal action stipulating the kind of land use permitted. Land zoning includes both buildings and open-space uses, such as parks. Zoning ordinances include such stipulations as building density, which may be controlled by individual lot size; height and kind of buildings permitted; use of buildings, such as for individual residences, apartments, commerce, and different kinds of industry. Aesthetic land-use considerations only can also be a valid criterion for zoning. More than one piece of land can have the same zone classification. For example, an R-2 zone defines a particular residential classification, and there could be a number of R-2 zones in a city. Establishment of zoning ordinances requires legal action by an authorized level of government. Amendments require the same procedures.

Another characteristic of zoning that relates to both establishment and amendment is that it is not retroactive. For example, if a slaughterhouse exists and is permitted in an area at the time zoning is established which would prohibit such a use, the slaughterhouse could not be condemmed and removed because it did not conform to the zoning requirement. No more slaughterhouses could be built after zoning. This use could be phased out or in some way the owner might be encouraged to sell.

A general point to be recognized about zoning is that authority affecting land use in urban areas is exercised by several governmental units other than the zoning authority. These operate at municipal, county, state, or federal levels. There are also interurban county, state, or federal compacts (such as the Tennessee Valley Authority) that bear on urban as well as nonurban land use.

Zoning originated in New York City in 1916 with "the first attempt to control land use by a municipal government" (Dilworth, 1971). The particular purpose at that time was to contain the invasion of factories into the Fifth Avenue business district and the shadowing of adjacent properties by emerging skyscrapers.

It was the work of . . .

lawyers who believed the courts could be induced to permit municipalities, by an extension of the common law nuisance doctrine, to build a comprehensive land-use regulatory scheme under the aegis of the police power. The United States Supreme Court in 1926 upheld zoning in the landmark case of *Village of Euclid v. Ambler Realty Co.* because that conservative bench regarded the intrusion of industry *and apartments* into single-family zones as cousin to a public nuisance. . . . The Court stated, "A nuisance may be merely the right thing in the wrong place, like a pig in the parlor instead of the barnyard." It concluded, "Under these circumstances, apartment houses, which in a different environment would be not only entirely unobjectionable but highly desirable, come very near to being nuisances" (Babcock, 1966, p. 4).

As indicated, the basis for zoning is the broad police power of government.

From this beginning, zoning spread rapidly in coverage and concept, being variously applied in municipalities of all sizes. There was a social need, and zoning development has been attended, as would be expected, by much uncertainty, controversy, and range in legal decisions and interpretations that cannot be reviewed here. Being social in its basic impetus as much as a land-oriented matter, zoning is not a clear concept and rather naturally collides with established legal concepts based on property ownership. Although often bitterly criticized, zoning meets a need, and its application has grown notwithstanding. The largest total success of zoning and its primary application is protection of single-family residential areas from commercial and industrial development. It has, however, developed far beyond residential-industrial issues and is as complex—and confusing—as the continuing growth of urban areas. "Zoning, including its administration and its judicial review, represents the unique American contribution to the solution of disputes over competing demands for the use of private land" (Babcock, 1966, xvi).

Zoning in Municipal Government   Zoning is a part of municipal government and by no means operates independently. By its nature it is an inseparable part of the land-use planning function, and it has been held consistently that, to have legal standing, zoning must be related to some comprehensive land-use plan. Such planning work is normally invested in what is commonly termed a planning commission or board which is a part of the executive branch of government. The planning unit may have professional staff or rely in whole or in part on planning consultants. Either way, it is usually professional planners who develop a proposed comprehensive land-use plan and draft accompanying zoning ordinances. Establishment of a zoning board or commission and adoption of zoning ordinances is a legislative function, but zoning administration is by the executive branch of government.

In addition to the planning and zoning functions there are numerous other municipal boards, commissions, authorities, etc., whose jurisdictions significantly relate to land use in one way or another. In large degree their authority also derives from exercise of the broad police powers of government. These include the following, in no order of priority:

Public health—with wide and often overriding authorities
Water department
Sewage department
Parks and recreation department
Transportation—highway department
Police and fire department
Education board—school space requirements
Board of taxation and equalization
Building codes—construction, plumbing, electrical, etc.
Special land subdivision regulation not a part of zoning as such
The city or town council

In addition to these municipal authorities, there are county authorities (not significant in New England), the superior authority of the states, and the strong influence if not direct controls exercised by the federal government. Under the Constitution of the United States, all powers not delegated to the federal government are left to the states, and these powers are very wide indeed on nonfederal lands.

To complete the staging of zoning, the *dramatis personae,* the individuals or groups primarily concerned in a test of zoning application, should be identified. These are:

The professional planners who prepare plans and draft zoning ordinances, but do not have final authority. Their social and integrative viewpoint is frequently at variance with legal and business interests.

The judge who hears a case and may be frustrated by lack of good evidence, legal foundation, or adherence to relatively clear mandates of law and consistent administrative procedures. The legal tendency at least has been to regard zoning as a property matter rather than a social matter.

The lawyers on both sides of a case who may have limited training in zoning matters and, like the judges, find it difficult to relate zoning to established legal areas.

The land developers and promoters and the investors who are in between clients, critics, and legal challenge. They can be worn out financially and otherwise by delays, unexpected requirements, and the like. The same holds true for an individual citizen seeking a building permit or a variance from a zoning regulation.

Concerned citizens, individually, collectively, and through organizations, who are for or against certain zoning restrictions or actions.

Public officials who for one reason or another have interests in the application of zoning and who also face political pressures.

Zoning Problems and Application   Governance, which means the exercise of authority and control in the act of governing, is a central problem of zoning as control of land use is a basic matter. The problems of land use are about as complex as the diverse political democracy which is the United States. Zoning has been applied primarily at the municipal level with generally limited state laws and administrative procedural guidance. There are many legal jurisdictions with different degrees of authority, sometimes overlapping. Practices, decisions, and legal or administrative precedent established in one place may not hold or apply in another. There are many examples of conflicting legal decisions made in different places.

Zoning began as a matter of recognizing a few zones, e.g., residential, commercial, and industrial. But the applications of zoning multiplied, and there may be twenty or more recognized zones, each with its definition as to kind of use and/or buildings or other construction that are permitted.

As to be expected, there is need to make more flexible or adaptive the arbitrariness and rigidity that is inherent to most zoning classifications. This is particularly true as applied to land uses, which are social matters strongly reflecting the feelings and desires of people. Many approaches have been considered to meet particular problems. Here are some that have been applied.

A variance is some change from the requirements of the zoning ordinance. It is requested on appeal from a zoning ruling. It may be granted if it can be shown that because of special conditions or unforseen circumstances, enforcement of the ordinance will result in undue hardship and that the variance will observe the spirit of the ordinance and render substantial justice. An objection to use of the variance is that it can also include favors given to special people. A more telling criticism is that it is a limited and inadequate approach to meet needs for zoning revision.

Another device is a discretionary special-use permit, which is similar to those issued for many years on the national forests. In application, a few uses are included in a district zoning ordinance that could be permitted, not as a matter of right, but at the discretion of the local zoning authority. These special permits are useful in making provision for public utility facilities or for uses that do not fit the zoning classificatiosns. As would be expected, however, special permits also can be used to recognize influence. They are also inadequate, as are variances, to meet new needs that should be met by zoning revision.

A more comprehensive concept is the so-called floating zone. For example, a zoning ordinance is passed that includes a residential zone category, the boundaries of which are not shown on any zoning map. Such an ordinance could permit one- or two- family units and buildings for multiple occupancy up to perhaps fifteen families. Such combinations individually can be permitted by amendment of the zoning map when such a zone is first established by ordinance. The idea is certainly logical in recognizing emerging situations, but can also legally be challenged as not constituting zoning.

Contract zoning is a variation on this theme in which the municipality does not preannounce its intentions. The zoning map and ordinance appear regular. "It is only when the developer seeks a change from say, Residential to Commercial (for a particular area) that he discovers that conditions will be attached by way of covenant or contract which do not appear in the text of the Commercial District" (Babcock, 1966, p. 10). A particular area is rezoned as commercial, but the net result of the covenant is that only one or two uses are actually authorized in this area.

Coming full turn in this direction is the Planned Development Unit. A model town, for example, may mix different kinds of residential units with stores and other kinds of buildings and use open space in a way that fits no usual zoning classification. Each unit development has to be considered on its merits. Shopping centers and industrial parks are in this general category.

The above review of urban zoning with its attendant problems indicates some of the complexities of urban land-use planning. These apply particularly in meeting new situation which are intensified in urban areas because of the necessity for much permanent construction. They emphasize the fact that making a plan and passing a zoning ordinance is one thing, and implementation in a changing society is another.

Urban and nonurban land-use classifications have some close similarities as well as differences. Regarding similarities, variances, special permits, floating, and contract zoning are means of achieving some flexibility in land use which is difficult under urban zoning. The same *kind* of problems arise in making harmonious combinations of forest-related land uses. These integrative problems are met on an area-by-area basis guided by rather broad land-use classifications which avoid much of the rigidity inherent in urban zoning.

Regarding major differences, urban land uses are highly concentrated and primarily constructed *on* the land and characterized by high cost and permanence. In contrast, nonurban land uses are primarily derived *from* the natural resources of the land, as in agriculture, wood production, wildlife, and recreation, and can be changed much more easily to meet human needs.

County Zoning   To broaden consideration of urban-related land-use zoning classifications, zoning by county units should be recognized. It is introduced here because it tends to be thought of, by urban interests in particular, as an extension of urban planning and zoning. It is equally logical, however, to regard it as a part of nonurban land use because by far the larger part of most county areas are not urban lands. This is where the two different points of view come together.

Whatever the viewpoint, it is clear that county unit land classification and planning is important and definitely on the increase, pressed by state directives. It is part of a general national trend toward national land-use classification and planning encompassing all land. It is at the county level, termed parishes in some of the Southern states and essentially replaced by the town unit in New England, where urban and nonurban uses most directly interact, physically come together, and often collide. The county is a legally recognized unit of state government and often has influence and control over internal municipalities. The same is true in reverse in situations where the municipalities are of dominant political importance. Counties are defined legal land units, and their areas can be added up to a state, regional, or national total. As has been emphasized, there is no clear or consistent way to separate urban and nonurban land-use interests. This becomes very clear in considering county unit planning. An illustration will be helpful.

Madera County in central California is a good example.[2] It is not a metropolitan area but is not far from the great San Francisco Bay and Los Angeles urban areas and feels urban pressures, particularly as regards recreation.

The total population is about 40,000, half of it in the county seat of Madera City. County population increased only 9.5 percent between 1953 to 1965. The county has three distinct geological features: the valley floor, which is the agricultural area; the foothill area; and the Sierra Mountains. Agriculture is the primary industry, followed by the timber industry, recreation, and some mining. The county includes the south end of Yosemite National Park; there are two large wilderness areas in and adjoining the county; and there is much national forest land in the county, including important timber-producing lands.

California state law requires each county to set up a planning commission to formulate a plan for the orderly development of the county. It establishes minimum requirements for land division ordinances, conduct of public hearings and meetings by the planning commissions, and an avenue of appeal from decisions by the planning commission.

The top governing body of the county is the board of supervisors. It appoints the planning commission, which is advisory to the board and to whom decisions of the commission may be appealed. The commission drafts policy and directs a professional staff which does the specific planning and drafting of ordinances. The board of supervisors also requests the various county departments, such as roads, health and water and sewage, to

---

[2] Acknowledgment is made to John Dozier (Dilworth, 1971) for material used here.

draft ordinances. These are related to the work of the planning commission. The board approves adoption of zoning and all other ordinances. The city of Madera also has a planning commission that works in concert with the county commission.

The Madera County zoning ordinance as approved includes zones and categories as follows:

Zone	Categories
Residential	6
Commercial	7
Industrial	2
Open space	2
Agricultural	5
Institutional	1
Quarrying and mining	1
Total	24

The ordinance also provides for planned recreation, shopping centers, and industrial parks.

This zoning ordinance, which represents much study and information from all county departments and Madera City, was approved by the board of supervisors before adoption of the comprehensive county plan. This is contrary to the usual sequence of a plan first and then zoning. The reason illustrates an interesting land-use situation.

The major land-use problem in the county was a seemingly endless number of speculative subdivisions scattered throughout the agricultural valley. The *modus operandi* was for a speculator to buy a ranch at the lowest price possible, subdivide it, typically into 1-acre lots, do a minimum amount of development without water or sewage disposal, and prepare a sales brochure complete with pictures of Yosemite and mountain lakes, etc. Many lots were purchased, but relatively few houses were built. The ranch was destroyed as an operating economic unit and as a part of the major economic base of the county. Also, the county could not stand the costs of roads, schools, police and fire protection, or water and sanitary needs had these subdivisions developed.

Controls were necessary, and the county passed ordinances relating to water, sewage, subdivisions, and agricultural zoning. These actions, the agricultural zoning in particular, brought the speculative subdivisions to a near halt. The zoning ordinance was the most effective; a variance from an agricultural to a residential zoning was hard to get.

An interesting footnote is that an attempt to establish a grazing zone in the foothill area was unacceptable to the people concerned because many owners felt that they might sometime wish to subdivide or sell areas to a developer. A residential-mountain-single-family zone was adopted instead over most of this foothill area.

No single illustration can be typical, but the Madera situation does bring out some of the workings of land-use control in the context of a county including a wide range of urban, urban-influenced, and nonurban lands. No attempt was made in this example of county planning to deal with federal lands which were organized under their own directives regarding land use. In some situations, as mentioned in Chap. 3, federal lands also are in the ambit of urban development, raising direct questions of coordination and perhaps ownership.

Chapter 5

Land-Use Controls

Treatment in this chapter is directly on methods of applying effective land-use controls. Use of land is inseparable from its control, which is a basic desire of humanity. World history is replete with examples of control established by force, by conquest, or other use of unilateral power, as by kings and dictators. This is one route, and power and influence certainly continue. Treatment here is confined to peaceful approaches under a government committed to law and order. The United States is generally assumed, but there is realization of both similarities and differences in legal structures and practices in other countries.

This chapter is divided into three general groups of land controls, each based on the kind of means employed. These are (1) land title ownership as by purchase, eminent domain, transfer, or gifts; (2) legal controls less than title ownership, including easements, various kinds of restrictive covenants and conditions, and leases; and (3) a group of controls based on public powers and influences, including the omnipresent power of taxation, police and regulatory powers, public and private grants-in-aid, intergovernmental compacts, and administrative controls.

It is stressed that no such classification of land control can constitute entirely separate compartments. There is considerable interrelatedness between different means, and they are often applied strategically in combinations. Legal aspects underlie all of them. In principle they apply to urban and nonurban lands alike. Controversy, which is inherent in land use, comes to final test in the courts, which are called upon to decide, short of force, otherwise insoluble issues.

TITLE OWNERSHIP OF LAND

The best way to control land is to own title to it free of all encumbrances. This applies in full force to public ownership, which then controls *all* the bundle of rights that go with landownership. A private owner has control over all the rights that go with his or her title. As pointed out in Chap. 1, however, the present tendency is for the private owners' bundle of rights to shrink and those controlled by higher (public) authority to increase. To give perspective on who owns land, ownership of the 1.9 billion acres in the forty-eight contiguous United States is as follows:[1]

Ownership	Percent
Federal	21
State	4
County and municipal	1
Private	74
Total	100

Although treatment in this section is on title ownership, it should be stressed that other means of land control are important, as is brought out later in this chapter.

Title ownership of land may be acquired in several ways and can be subject to a number of stipulations and agreements. As pointed out previously, owners may in one way or another assign all rights of ownership use *except that of title* as they are then no longer owners. The principal means of acquiring title ownership are given below.

Land Purchase

Lands are purchased by public and private entities or by persons at agreed-upon prices that often include financing arrangements. At the time of purchase the land is subject to whatever liens and encumbrances it may have,

---

[1] The two newest states of Hawaii and Alaska are not included as their situations are atypical. Federal and state landownership in Alaska is changing as the state exercises its option under statehood grant to select federally owned lands and also because of Indian land claims. Landownership in Hawaii is peculiar to its history.

such as unpaid taxes or assignment of rights, whether explicit by written legal agreement or implicit by established past usage. Some of these, as taxes due or terminable use leases, may be extinguished in a short time. Others having long status in time may be difficult if not impossible to extinguish. As stated previously, subsurface rights are often bought and sold separately from surface rights. Also, at or after the time of purchase, various other stipulations concerning the use of the land may be agreed upon. These are of particular importance in open-space land acquisition but may also apply in other situations. For example, a lifetime or some stipulated period of tenancy or other covenants or restrictions may be made with a previous owner or occupant (they may not be the same). Title purchase may have to include such agreements.

A common combination is purchase accompanied by a lease-back either to the previous owner or to someone else. This may be done for several reasons. In open-space reservation, a public agency may buy a farm strategically located for such use and also subject to advancing building development. By leasing, the farm is kept in operation and later may become a part of greenbelt or similar open-space use. A real estate developer may use the same procedure, but with a reverse purpose, to buy a farm for future urban development. By lease the developer hopes to keep it in farming at a lower tax rate for a period of time. States are, however, plugging this tax loophole.

More land may be purchased for public use in some situations than may be needed, either by intent or because of the size of ownership units in which land had to be acquired. Here, parcels of land may be resold to private owners although often subject to land-use stipulations.

Land may also be purchased under a legal agreement by which the total price for the property is set at the time of purchase and payments are made in specified yearly installments over some agreed-upon time period. With such an agreement, considerable saving in purchase cost is possible if land prices are rising. The seller may also have financial reasons for accepting an installment sale such as reduction in income tax.

There is also the well-known principle of strategic or preemptive purchase based on the basic land characteristic of immobility. By buying certain well-located parcels of land in a particular area, the purchaser may be in a position to control or modify land uses over the rest of the area. This tactic can be equally effective in urban-related open space and in nonurban situations. In the latter, a strategically located parcel of land could control access to timber or to wildland recreation development.

Eminent Domain

Inherent in the higher authority of government that gives land titles is its power of escheat, that is, to expropriate ownership of private land at some determined price for public welfare purposes. This power can be exercised by different levels of government depending on their jurisdictional authority. Power of eminent domain, or condemnation as it is also termed, is a primary tool used by governmental authority in acquiring land for public purposes such as for public buildings, highways, or public welfare purposes generally. Such action is taken where purchase at reasonable cost is not possible or less-than-title land-use agreements, such as rights obtained under an easement, are not considered satisfactory.

There are complexities about the exercise of the power of condemnation that come to the courts for decision. The trend is for the courts to take a liberal attitude toward use of eminent domain for the public welfare in the United States. It should also be pointed out that the power to take land gives leverage in negotiation to purchase at reasonable cost, which is preferred.

Eminent domain practices naturally differ by countries. For example, the legal basis for land condemnation or expropriation is somewhat different in the United States and Canada, adjoining countries closely similar in heritage and situation. In the United States, the basis for expropriation is in common law under its broad constitutional powers of promoting general welfare which extend to the states. Expropriation is not under statute. In Canada, which was not severed from England through revolution, public lands are under the jurisdiction of the individual Provinces and are termed Crown lands, harking back to the time when all lands were invested in the Crown. It is necessary for each Province to establish by statute its procedures governing expropriation of privately owned lands.

In general, the results are not much different in practice from those in the United States except that the authority is somewhat broader in Canada. For example, an expropriation of some 218,000 acres of privately owned forest land was recently made in the Province of New Brunswick for purposes of economic development of the Province (Davis, 1969). Title to these lands was taken from one American-owned corporation, and most of the lands were then leased by the Province to another corporation, also for forest production purposes. This would not happen in the United States, where powers of condemnation, under common law, are more narrowly construed by the courts. In this instance, there was no question about legal power to expropriate, but the question of how much was to be paid for the lands did go to the courts.

Transfer and Exchange

Transfer and exchanges of lands from one ownership to another not involving purchase are important tools in land-use control in both urban and nonurban situations. They can include public and privately owned lands. Reasons are many, including strategic and administrative purposes. There are also legal restrictions, particularly regarding public owners, depending on ownership status, public agency powers and limitations, and the particular purpose. It is impossible to include them all here.

Undoubtedly the largest administrative land transfer of all time in the United States was the transfer in 1905 of the forest reserves from the Department of the Interior to the Department of Agriculture. These lands constituted the major base for the present national forest system. This was a step of far-reaching importance in public land use and management.

Land exchange under the General Exchange Act of 1922 (42 Stat. 465, as amended) and under the Weeks Law of 1911 (36 Stat. 961–963, as amended) has been a major tool in acquisition of the national forests. It is used to consolidate land holdings for strategic reasons and to improve administration within national forest boundaries. This authorization was applied on a large scale between states and the federal government, particularly during the 1930s, when wildland prices were low and large areas reverted to the states for nonpayment of taxes. The Forest Service purchased nonreverted lands, and the states took title to the tax-forfeited lands. The two ownerships were often intermingled, particularly in the Lake States. State forest and national forest landownerships subsequently were each consolidated in some areas through mutual land exchanges, greatly improving their respective land administration.

Similar land transfers and exchanges are made by many public landowning agencies between themselves and private owners. Private owners also exchange among themselves. All these land actions are important in open-space and other land acquisition and control in both urban and wildland areas.

Donations

Private owners are often willing to donate land and other real property for public uses. The reasons involve property and income taxes paid by the owner, financial or other inability to manage a property, concern over the quality of the environment, lack of suitable heirs, family interests in a particular area, and desire to preserve areas of natural beauty and places of historical interest.

There is no set pattern or procedure for acquiring land control through donation. Attention here is on donations that require change of land title, but it is also recognized that donations also may include partial control over land use by granting specific uses, such as leases, easements, or other arrangements short of land title. Such actions may, of course, lead to future title change. Gift solicitation is an art and a personal matter. It also happens that two or more adjoining property owners may wish to act in concert.

Land donors naturally and frequently make stipulations applying to a part or all of the land given. A tenancy for life or for some stated period of time by the owner or other persons, such as valued employees, may be required, giving reserved use of some buildings and related areas. Certain existing land uses, such as for agriculture, may be permitted under lease to meet owner obligations for a time period. All or a specified part of the property may be given on condition that it be dedicated to a particular use, such as a bird sanctuary, a nature study area, or a park. A building may be permanently reserved for historical reasons.

Such listing is incomplete but makes the point that a number of land-use stipulations may be made that require legal status, recognition, and action in connection with the taking of title. These may be written into the deed or provided by terminable leases or similar covenants.

Of often overriding importance is the donor's desire for permanence of desired use. Public agencies are normally permanent, but their policies and practices may change, as may those of private corporations or trusts. (The latter may be corporations, but there can be differences in their legal structure.) It is also true that some recipients are cautious of making legal commitments in perpetuity for certain land uses. The reason is that circumstances may change and a particular land use may become undesirable or impractical. If the donor requires continuity or use, a "right of reverter" may be added providing that if the restrictions set forth in the deed are not honored, the property will automatically revert to its previous owner. A variation is a provision that the land go to a specified third party and not to the donor.

In addition to public agencies, there are a number of private corporate trusts, which also constitute a perpetuating legal "person." These accept title to lands donated for open space or other conservation purpose. Such an organization, well known in the United States, is the Nature Conservancy. This is a well-organized and well-financed, private, tax-exempt, and permanent corporate entity with much flexibility of action. It not only accepts land donations with or without restrictions but buys and sells land for conservation purposes. Having capital and freedom to act quickly, it often performs the vital function of buying lands promptly that are critically needed by a public agency and later selling them to the agency. Consequent saving in cost may be very substantial.

LEGAL CONTROLS LESS THAN TITLE OWNERSHIP

There are many legal means of achieving desired land-use controls other than by title ownership. These are presented here in three groups: (1) easements which grant specified land-use rights to other than the title owner; (2) restrictive covenants, conditions, and other limitations less than title which run over time, often without termination date; and (3) contractual leases for a definite terminable period. All these are old legal devices which are used for many purposes. Emphasis here is on their application as land-use controls in one way or another. As with title ownership, these means are used in various combinations, often in relation to title ownership and to various governmental-administrative controls.

Easements

"An easement consists in a privilege on the part of a person entitled to it to make some use of the land subject to it. It must, in some way, limit the use which the possessor (owner) of that land might otherwise make of it."[2] It is a possessory and legal right to a land use that is held by someone other than the title owner. An easement is normally a legal instrument in writing, but established and orally agreed-upon uses may assume in fact the nature of an easement. An easement runs with the land, to use a legal phrase, and hence is binding on heirs and assigns when title changes hands. An easement normally includes a reverter clause specifying that if the terms of the easement are not met, the rights so conveyed revert to the title owner.

Further, if conditions and circumstances so change that the intent and purposes of the easement no longer have relevance, the easement may be extinguished and consequently use rights granted through it revert to the title owner. This fact reflects the legal "doctrine of change," the understandable judicial dislike of perpetuating meaningless covenants. For example, a right-of-way easement for an interurban trolley line which has been permanently abandoned and the tracts taken up is extinguished. The owner of the land it traverses consequently regains full rights to the land involved in the easement.

A further manifestation of this general dislike of permanent covenants is expressed in the legal rule against perpetuities. Individuals often attempt to control things from the grave through legal instruments, and the many consequent legal complexities plague judges and administrators. It is for this general reason that, in the United States, a number of states have enacted laws limiting conservation easements to some set time period such as 30 to 60 years.

The general idea of easements is ancient. As pointed out in Chap. 2, there are always limitations to the bundle of rights constituting individual title ownership. Certain rights are also held by the higher authority granting land title. The more modern switch is that land-use rights may be granted voluntarily, as through easements, by the title owner.

It is also well to bear in mind that some land-use rights, such as rights of way, berry picking, livestock grazing, hunting and fishing, can be established by uncontested usage. In effect, such uses constitute a de facto easement without benefit of any written easement.

[2] (*American Law of Property*, 1952.)

Legal easements are of two general kinds, positive and negative. A positive easement is one that gives someone other than the title owner the right to *do* something regarding the land. A negative easement requires that the owner *not do* something regarding his or her use of the land.

Some examples will be helpful to illustrate the range and nature of these two kinds of easements. These are given here as possible approaches without regard to their frequency or whether the use rights granted might be accomplished by other means, as by leasing. Here are some examples:

Positive Easements
Rights of travel routes of various kinds across another's property; fences, paths, trails, roads, streets, and highways
Utility lines and conduits for power, water, gas, or oil above, on, or below the surface
Rights to harvest natural crops from the land; fruit or mushroom picking, grazing, or wood use; more usually handled by lease or other use contracts but can be established by easement
Access for hunting and fishing
Above-surface rights as regards airplanes; height of buildings
Subsurface rights for coal, oil, gas, or minerals; sale of these are very common and often include large areas

Negative Easements
Scenic—preservation of natural scenery, limitations on building or other land uses; to keep a farm or other area in its present use and condition
Fish and wildlife—to preserve present habitat, *not* to drain or fill, burn, dam, etc.
To conserve and protect stream and stream bank habitat, or to effect stream improvement; may or may not include the right of public access
Not to drain, fill, or otherwise change wetlands
To preserve an area, as an attractive woodland, in its natural condition
Not to permit billboards or to clear forested land

Application of Easements   Easements are a useful means of controlling certain land uses. But there are others, and easements offer no general route to gaining conservation or other land-use control objectives. A major point to keep in mind is that, being a granting of specified land-use rights that go with title ownerships, easements are a serious and rather permanent matter. They often affect the value and sale price of a property in ways that may be difficult to anticipate or evaluate. They also can affect land and income taxes and the interests of both land title and easement owners. Much depends on clear understanding by the parties involved and the legal quality of the easement document.

There has been in the United States much recent increase in the application of easements for conservation purposes. This has been primarily between private and public owners. The latter often obtain an easement as an alternative to acquiring outright ownership to accomplish conservation objectives. Such easements are largely negative in nature insofar as the owner is concerned.

Some use of easements for public purposes has been made for a considerable time. "In 1930, through the Capper-Cramton Act, Congress authorized easement acquisition along the streams and parkways of the national capital area. In the thirties, the National Park Service used scenic easements along many stretches of the Blue Ridge and Natchez Trace Parkways. But attempts were sporadic. By the late forties the device was almost forgotten" (Whyte, 1968).

Interest renewed in the 1950s and has increased since. Easements have been particularly effective in connection with construction of scenic roads and fish and game preservation. There are three general conditions for success to be met.

The first is that all parties concerned must thoroughly understand the nature and purpose of easements and believe in them and that the easement agreement be clearly and accurately executed. Both buyers and sellers are often unacquainted with and perhaps prejudiced about what can—and cannot—be done by easements. Some highway departments, for example, may be wedded to the concept that all rights of way must be purchased so that there are no questions about land control. Such a viewpoint does not engender consideration of easement possibilities. Similarly, landowners are likely not to understand easements and to be suspicious of what they may entail. For example, a landowner may assume that an easement desired to protect fish and wildlife habitat would also give rights of public entry to the land or constitute an unduly restrictive lien on the property. The care, thoroughness, and understanding reached between all parties concerned has a strong correlation with the successful use of easements.

The second condition is that, for the most part, the lands should be of relatively low market value and the easement should be essentially negative. In large degree the easement consequently requires only continuation of what the owner has been doing with the land and the situation of the landowner is little affected.

The third condition is that the rights actually needed for land-use controls can be obtained through easements for much less cost than buying all the rights and responsibilities that go with full title land ownership.

The above three conditions for successful use of land-use easements apply generally to conservation needs which do not require doing something drastic to the land. Easements would be inadequate for surface or subsurface mineral development and the building of interstate highways.

It is a mistake, however, to assume that conservation-type easements do not apply where land values are high. They do apply, and the reason is that there are high relative differences between the use values of different parcels of land. In a housing development, for example, both the desirability of sites for building and development costs often vary substantially over the tract. There is frequently a strong positive correlation between high development costs and areas that have natural scenic, conservation, and general open-space values. Some examples are poorly drained land, steep or rocky land, and some wooded areas. In such situations, easements can be an economic and also an aesthetically desirable means of preserving open-space areas. The same general principle often applies to portions of estates, historic or otherwise, or to other lands, such as along scenic highways, of open-space value that can be preserved by easements to the satisfaction of both the private owner and public interests.

In summary, easements are often a useful and relatively permanent means, selectively used, for the landowner and public interests to share the bundle of rights inherent in landownership. The landowner frequently can get more in protection than he or she gives up. Tax benefits are also a consideration. The public interest often can be served by securing the benefits it needs at less than title cost.

Conditions, Limitations, and Restrictive Covenants

Related to and often confused with easements are a group of legal conditions, limitations, and restrictive covenants that can be applied to land use. Their basic difference from easements is that they do not constitute a granting by the title owner of specified rights to land use. But they do involve a continuing "interest in the land," to use the legal phrase, and constitute long-lasting liens on land use.

Legal conditions and limitations are restrictions regarding future use of the land attached to a sale or transfer of land title. For example, an owner may sell a tract of wooded land with the express condition, written into the deed, that sale holds only *so long as no timber is cut.* This provision goes with the land, continues without time limit, and consequently applies to all future title owners. The penalty for violating this provision is not in monetary damages but in reversion of the land title to the original owner, or possibly heir, together with right of entry and without any further legal action. This can be a drastic penalty indeed!

Rather understandably on the part of courts, which do not favor perpetuities or forfeitures, "the law has not been kind to attempts to create and enforce possibilities of reverters and rights of entry for condition broken" (Brenneman, 1967). Precise and clear legal wording is important if a condition is to stand in court.

"In sum, it can be said that, selectively and knowledgeably used, these devices may in some situations serve the purposes of individuals or a conservation agency, but they must be used with care" (Brenneman, 1967).

Restrictive covenants are contractual agreements between the seller and buyer of a property in which the buyer agrees to do or not do certain stipulated things. They differ from situations previously discussed in that there is no possibility of the title reverting to the original owner because of nonperformance. Although sometimes considered as similar to easements in legal treatment, covenants do not involve partial sale of owner use rights. They differ from trusts in that no corporate entity to hold and administer the land is involved. Although a covenant may continue over a long period of time and be assigned, it is subject to the doctrine of change and may become unenforceable if the stated original purposes have so changed that the covenant is oppressive or inequitable. In the United States several states have statutes limiting covenants to some time limit, such as 30 to 60 years.

There are two kinds of covenants essentially differing only in their manner of enforcement. A common law covenant is one in which the remedy for breach is in money damages. This can entail legal complications as to determination of circumstances and amount of damage. Further, and from a land-use standpoint, monetary recompense after a breach of covenant is often not very satisfactory; the damage is done.

The other kind of covenants are in equity, legally termed "equitable servitudes," meaning that redress is in legally enforceable remedial action rather than in subsequent monetary redress. For example, an injunction may be granted before damage occurs or to stop actions in violation of the covenant. The grantor of the covenant consequently can directly influence land use and development that is not in accord with the covenant. Equity will also enforce the covenant upon the successors of either the grantor or grantee of the covenant.

"The use of equitable servitudes has grown with the growth of cities and suburban real estate developments; they have been used to preserve the character of residential neighborhoods" (Brenneman, 1967). Their use has had racial and other social overtones, which has put such covenants into some disrepute. They can be and are, however, used to serve a number of land-use purposes and constitute a useful tool. For example, a person may sell land to a developer but wish to influence how it is developed. The seller may impose on the purchaser some of his or her ideas of development, and if agreed upon, these will be stipulated by mutual covenants in the transfer deed.

As Brenneman points out, covenants also can be useful in land transfers by one incorporated conservation organization to another corporate entity. Since corporations are technically immortal "persons," the holder of the right to enforce the covenant, the grantor, becomes a continuing "watchdog" concerned with enforcing the covenant. Brenneman also emphasizes that equity covenants will not meet the hostility courts have accorded to restrictions at common law or conditions imposing forfeiture.

Leases

A lease is a contractual, legal, and enforceable agreement made between individuals or corporate entities to transfer possession or specified uses of property for a period of time, with right of reversion for nonperformance retained by the owner. It is a form of covenant. In the absence of statute to the contrary there is no limit to time duration. The terms of the lease specify the kind of and liability for the use transferred, compensation to be received by the owner on an annual or some such agreed current basis, and lease duration. A lease can be renewed at the will of the contracting parties.

Leases are exceedingly common, varied in specific detail, and relatively free of legal problems provided they are mutually understood, properly written, and for lawful purposes. One can lease, and sublease, almost anything of which one has legal control.

Leases are applied widely in land use and can include some or all use rights of property ownership except title. A lease may be a simple and straightforward agreement to lease a house and lot or to grow and harvest certain crops on farmland for specified periods. It can also be much more complex. For example, a lease agreement may cover a substantial area of forested land, and the lessee may agree to protect the land, harvest timber, and assure forest tree regeneration for 50 years. At the expiration of the period contracted the lessee must be prepared to turn the property back to the owner with a forest growing stock at least equal in volume and quality to that on the land at the beginning of the lease period. In essence, the 50-year growth of the forest has been purchased by the lease. More spectacular are 99-year leases in New York City for land on which skyscrapers have been erected; being affixed, the skyscrapers go with the land. Such leases are also renewable. In the fullness of time, however, some expiration dates have arrived raising problems and questions. These can involve heirs, divided interests of title owners, and changed conditions.

Because of their flexibility and straightforward nature, leases can often be used advantageously in land-use control in conjunction with or as an alternative to title ownership. As has been stressed, however, circumstances and needs change over time in land-use matters. There are practical as well as legal complications to long-time land-use agreements.

In some situations, the purchase of land and lease-back is an effective procedure, particularly with public agencies or private corporate entities which have long-term conservation and related interests. A lease, being both finite in its duration and renewable, has much flexibility in adjusting land use to meet owner objectives that may change with needs over time. A lease may be considered as an alternative to an easement which offers difficulties because of its binding long-term nature and possible legal complexities. Conditions and restrictive covenants can be used with easements or leases. A trust agreement can include future interests involving land-use controls. The possibilities of combining legal devices concerning ownership rights are almost endless in effecting land-use controls.

PUBLIC POWERS AND INFLUENCES

This section takes up the many ways in which public powers and influences may affect land use and control. The subject is complex, very important, and has almost endless specific applications. It must, perforce, be considered here in framework terms.

Basically, most public powers derive from constitutional or sovereign authority which is expressed through statutory enactments or embodied in common law. But they also include public administrative actions and influences that may, in practice, have many attributes of law. There is an old saying that "the law is what the administrator say it is." And there is truth to this. This de facto administrative authority can be countered only by public reaction, by protest, which in land-use controversy increasingly leads to the courts for legal adjudication and interpretation.

The development of national environmental concern in recent years has been accompanied by increasing public disposition to act. This has placed weight both on people and on their governments to perform responsibly in the public interest as regards land use as well as other matters. This trend is reflected in large and important policy changes in the scope and application of public powers. These in turn are manifested in new laws, new agencies, and governmental reorganizations. The same concerns also appear in the testing and reinterpretation of existing laws in the courts often going directly to constitutional powers. The milieu is changing and many aspects of public life with it.

Treatment is given here in five groups: (1) taxation, (2) police and regulatory powers, (3) public and private grants-in-aid, (4) intergovernmental compacts, and (5) administrative controls. This grouping is somewhat arbitrary, and necessarily so, as these groups often interrelate and defy neat compartmentalization. The aim here is to proceed in some logical sequence from the better-known and established land-use control areas of taxation and police and regulatory powers to broad governmental powers affecting land use. Nearly all include the pursuasive power to give or to withhold something, often in monetary terms.

Taxation

As has been said, the power to tax can be the power to destroy. But taxation is necessary, and it can be used as a positive means, directly or indirectly, to accomplish many desirable objectives in land use. Few landownership transfers indeed are made without attention to tax considerations by both seller and buyer. Income and property taxation are considered here.

Income Taxation   Income taxation is predominately important at the national level in the United States. It is the principal source of federal revenue. Federal income taxation was made constitutional by the Sixteenth Amendment, ratified in 1913. Many states and some municipalities also have income taxes. At the national level especially, the tax is progressive on noncorporate individuals in particular; an increasingly larger taxable income results in a proportionally larger percentage tax bite. Income is an inherently complex concept which has to be arbitrarily defined from a taxing standpoint. Ask a person what he or she "makes" in terms of "real" income and it is easy to understand why it is difficult consistently to define and interpret taxation rules and tests. By the nature of public taxation, such rules and tests must be applied to an almost endless number of different situations. Consequently and necessarily, rules and definitions have to be rather arbitrary but they are also subject to interpretation in specific situations.

Income taxation relates most directly to land-use controls in connection with transfers of land title, and particularly to different kinds of gifts or donations which are tax exempt. When a property changes hands, its value for tax purposes is normally based on fair market value at the time of transfer. The difference between this value and an applicable original cost value—often difficult to determine and subject to rules—is taxable as capital gains income, and the rate is rather high. Many charitable and other nonprofit foundations, land trusts, and other organizations are granted tax exemption from both income and land taxes. Estate and gift taxes are a part of federal and state taxation and are included here because they arise through transfer of landownership.

Eligibility for tax deductability is often a matter of prime concern to a land donor. Under certain conditions land title transfer may be spread over a period of time, such as 5 years, to reduce the capital gains tax. There is a limit to how much tax exemption can be claimed in 1 year. Easements, which constitute an interest in property rights, also can be transferred by sale or gift and may be tax deductible. Rules and regulations are as complex as property rights, and so is definition of tax exemption status.

Land Taxation   Land and other property taxes are as ancient as ownership and as complex. In older times ownership of property, and particularly of land, was a principal measure of a person's wealth and ability to pay taxes. In more recent time, property has become an increasingly inadequate measure of net income, although it remains an important measure of ability to pay taxes. Property taxation has remained the mainstay of revenue to local units of government. As would be expected, the application of land taxation is an immensely complex subject.

Treatment here is on land taxes and particularly as they are important in land use. The scope is limited to the periodic, normally annual, tax on the value of land, which is termed the ad valorem tax. In the United States, the basic legal power to levy and regulate land taxation rests with the states under their reserved powers, as recognized in the federal Constitution. Land taxes are assessed and collected by units of local government, although subject to regulation at the state level.

The basic legal premise of land taxation, as embodied in most state statutes, is that the tax be equitably levied on all. The concept of equal assessment is applied on a defined basis of value appraisal. This is related to some measure of "highest and best use," use value, or fair market value. In practice, land taxes largely are assessed and collected according to some working balance between the financial needs of local government and what the taxpayer will bear. In increasing degree, taxation is also related to some concept of desirable land use.

There are public interests in maintaining desirable land uses, but there are also counterpressures. For example, if lands presently used for agricultural or forest purposes are in the path of urban development, their market value will increase. In all likelihood, this value will exceed the present use value. Under usual assessment practices, taxes almost inevitably will also increase. As a consequence, such lands may be forced out of agriculture and forest use. Such situations are widespread and raise policy questions about land use desirable in the public interest. Because of inflation and uncertainty about the future, people increasingly look to land as a good investment. Going beyond direct urban expansion, people buy land all over the country for recreation, second homes, speculation, and other personal reasons. The result, in total, is increased land values, and the effect is felt on adjoining and nearby land as well. The inevitable result is strong pressure to increase land taxes to recognize the these higher use values (see Chap. 7 for further treatment).

These general trends are as old as the historical development of the United States—and also apply to other countries. Natural forests, grasslands, and wetlands have gone into agriculture. Agricultural lands, and these other lands, have gone into urban-related uses. Within urban areas, high-value business, industrial, and residential land uses have taken over areas of lower use value.

With the needs of increasing population pressing against a finite resource base, the effects of land taxation on land use are of rising public concern. In the United States, current land problems are due more to inefficient use, socially and generally speaking, than to a real shortage of land area. Land taxation is here approached with this general assumption. The need is to seek a more efficient use of land which can ameliorate the situation.

Some progress has been made and more can be through selective application of what is termed preferential taxation. Basically, this means tax valuation of land on its present use rather than on a market sale value. This principle has long been applied in varying degree on a practical level by local assessors who can exercise some discretion in tax assessment.

At a much broader public level, rising environmental concern has placed increasing emphasis on both the use and preservation of wetlands and privately owned forest lands. The taxation of these lands is important in maintaining what is considered to be desirable land use in the public interest.

Basically, a state has the authority to apply preferential land taxation. This does, however, require amendment of the state constitution if it includes only provision for equal assessment on a value basis. Amendment to permit preferential taxation is often difficult politically to enact for financial and procedural reasons. Assessments are made by local political taxing units which are usually hard-pressed by rising tax revenue needs. Land valuation can be very difficult to define and apply equitably. It is important also to keep in mind that the monetary tax levied is the product of the assessed land value times the tax rate, and both can vary independently.

Tax intent can be circumvented too; people are very ingenious. For example, consider a parcel of land, forest or agricultural, that is in the path of urban development and on which land values are strongly increasing or are expected to increase. The owner may keep the land in its present use or may sell it to someone else, a land developer, for example, having another and higher-value use purpose. This new owner may continue the present use by leasing the land back to the previous owner, who continues present use for the time being. In effect, the owner has a tax shelter until such time as he or she puts a changed land-use plan into effect. It is to prevent such a shelter that a roll-back clause is often included in state statutes including preferential taxation. This means that if land use changes from a lower-to a higher-value tax base and is so assessed and sold for such a use, the owner must pay the difference in additional taxes, perhaps with interest, for a specified number of years prior to the sale. In effect, the roll-back is an additional cost paid for changing from a lower to a higher land-use value.

Preferential taxation should be approached on a careful and selective basis. It is a powerful tool and can certainly help protect some lands for conservation purposes in the public interest. *How far* the public should go in instituting such land-use controls in particular situations is a social question that cannot be answered here.

Charitable, educational, religious, and similarly defined institutions do not pay property taxes. Neither do units of government. The aggregate holdings of such owners is very large and a matter of much and increasing interest to public taxing bodies. To give a large-scale example, both the Forest Service and the Bureau of Land Management manage many millions of acres of public lands from which they receive timber, grazing, and other revenues that go to the federal treasury. They also, by federal statute, make payments based on the revenues received in lieu of taxes to the counties. In some counties these payments are very substantial. But the distribution between counties is uneven both because of the different areas of public lands in the counties and the way these receipts are distributed (see Chap. 12). Much study has been given to developing a consistent and equitable system of making federal payments to counties that include federal lands which would be reasonably comparable to state land taxation practice.

Police and Regulatory Powers

Police and related public powers, implemented through laws and regulations, are both large and important. This certainly applies to the United States, on which attention is centered here, although with realization of parallels in other countries. These powers include public health, safety, morals, nuisance (which includes the right of a landowner to enjoy lawful use of his or her property), and the "general welfare," which is indeed a broad power. As a generality, these powers stipulate what one can or cannot do, but they do not include financial payment to the owner. These powers influence and control land use in many ways. In the United States these powers are left largely to the states. However, the federal government by constitutional powers to levy income and other taxes, by its spending power, and by the wide scope of the "general welfare" clause, also exercises powers that deeply affect land use.

A good example of police power use is the development and application of land-use zoning as introduced in Chap. 4. Although developed primarily on urban lands, the concept of classifying and controlling land use by zoning applies equally to nonurban land. It is applied to flood plain and wetland classifications, national and other parks, recreation areas, wilderness areas, wildlife refuges, wild or scenic rivers, national recreation areas, military areas, and other land-use designations established under federal and state authority.

The application of public regulatory powers is an exceedingly broad and important area. These powers are many and varied, and their impact on land use is often not recognized. For example, the constitutional authority of the federal government to "regulate commerce...among the several states" has basic influence on land use. It gave the United States a "Common Market" of continental scope almost from its beginning. It has enforced the free flow of agricultural, mineral, forest, ocean, and other natural resource products across the country without tariff barriers. Probably more than any other single thing, the commerce clause has made possible the development of the present United States as a nation, encouraging each state to produce what it best can. It also leaves much power of regulation to the states.

There are a maze of regulatory bodies and authorities in the United States, federal, state, and local, with respectively varied powers. It is possible here to enumerate only some of them which have impacts on land use. The reader is encouraged to add other examples.

A wide range of agricultural crop and related regulations, often accompanied by subsidies or incentive payments.

Pesticide-use regulation; affects agricultural and forest production rather deeply.

Pure food laws, which also affect agricultural production.

The establishment of new federal and state regulatory legislation and agencies concerned with the enforcement of pollution and other environmental controls. This is a wide and growing area including tax benefits, special pollution and effluent taxes; subsidies and fees to operate; difficult and expensive planning; testing and operating procedure requirements; administrative withdrawal of government-granted benefits and privileges for nonconformance with public regulations.

Some regulation of forest cutting and management practices by states which clearly have such power. Controversy in this area is old, going back over a half century and primarily centering on advocacy of federal regulation. There is renewed interest in the subject (see Chap. 12).

Public and Private Grants-in-Aid

There is a long catalog of ways in which public and private financial grants-in-aid directly affect land use.[3] In substantial degree, they are related to governmental regulatory powers. Application of better crop practices is one example. Preferential tax assessment can be regarded as a form of financial aid. It is given to continue a particular land use, such as agriculture, because this use is considered more desirable in the public interest than some other use, such as urban development.

The largest, oldest, and most far-reaching domestic grant-in-aid program in the United States is the federal-state land-grant college system of education, research, and extension. It began with the Morrill Act of June 2, 1862, which gave liberal grants of public lands, and later money from public land sales, to establish state colleges of agriculture and the mechanic arts. With direct federal and cooperative state financing, the program developed over the years into a massive program of localized action by state land-grant college units. It brought education, research, and dissemination of agricultural and mechanical knowledge by county extension units directly into application by farm people. Particularly significant is the fact the

---

[3] It is difficult consistently to distinguish between a grant-in-aid and a subsidy, which is a more general but less popular term. A public subsidy is normally a monetary grant by a unit of government for some public benefit received in return. The purpose could be to encourage agriculture, help industry, or stimulate sciences and arts. A grant-in-aid is essentially the same thing, but can include a wider range of both public and private assistance that is not necessarily in monetary terms.

program operates on a localized area-by-area basis which is consonant with the great continental land diversity of the United States.

More than anything else, this land-grant college system brought American agriculture to its present high level of productivity and efficiency. It has given this country the efficient and strong food base that has made possible the large diversion of people necessary to establish the high levels of arts, science, and technology that has been attained in the United States. Perhaps it has succeeded too well. Some negative costs must also be paid in terms of environmental detriment resulting from intensive and productive cropping practices. These negative costs will have to be met through environmental controls, which have been receiving major national attention since the latter 1960s.

Another large-scale example of public grants-in-aid that directly relates to land use is the nationwide federal-state cooperative forest management and fire control program between the Forest Service and the states. It began with the Weeks Law of 1911 and was extended by the Clarke-Mc-Nary Act of 1924 and subsequent legislation. These laws established a broad federal-state cooperative program including direct federal money, assistance, and technical aid to the states under cooperative agreements. Presently, in most situations state expenditures substantially exceed money given by the federal government. Much educational demonstration and assistance aid is given to the smaller forest landownerships. This work extends into urban areas which include much forested land. Strong state forest fire control organizations, also extending action into urbanized areas, have developed that are vital to any wildland management program. Private industrial forestry also gives much help to the smaller landowners.

Under a number of statutes and other legal provisions, the federal government gives much financial assistance to the states, and both give direct financial assistance to units of local government for the acquisition and development of parks and other open-space areas. This is usually done on a cost-sharing basis. For example, the federal government put up a part, the state another, and the local governmental unit the rest of the total cost. The aggregate of this kind of grant-in-aid assistance is very large. Such financing also entails conditions to be met in land purchase that directly control land use.

Foundations, land trusts, and other private organizations and entities also give financial assistance to open-space land acquisitions and to investigation, research, and education relating to land use. Another direct expression of land-use concern and action is through numerous national, state, or local private organizations which have particular interests in promoting, legally defending, or in other ways supporting environmental improvement, including land uses.

At the international level, federal grants-in-aid to other countries at a multibillion-dollar level should be mentioned. Much of this money is spent for improvement of land use either directly or indirectly.

Intergovernmental Compacts

For reasons of land-use development and control, often with water considerations of major importance, a number of federal-state and interstate compacts of various kinds have been developed. Because the states, historically excepting the original thirteen, were created by the federal government, it follows that legally binding interstate compacts—and this applies to all states—require consent of the Congress. This is true whether or not the federal government is directly involved—although it usually is. These intergovernmental compacts are complex and variable in purpose, form, obligations, and financing. This is a large subject and can be considered here only in terms of the nature and importance of these compacts as they relate to land use.

The largest, oldest, most comprehensive, and most widely known example of a federal-state compact in the United States is embodied in the Tennessee Valley Authority, which dates back to 1933. Its geographic scope includes most of the Tennessee River drainage. The basic aim is to develop and improve the whole economy through flood control, power and navigation development, industrialization, soil erosion control, reforestation, recreation, and better agricultural land use.

Such a proposal was made by President Franklin D. Roosevelt during his first few months in office following earlier controversy and proposals that the river system be developed as a unit. It was an economically depressed area. The Tennessee Valley Authority was created by act of Congress, May 18, 1933. This action was spurred on by the Great Depression and concurrent conservation interest of the times, plus the need for social welfare improvement. The act created a federally financed corporation "clothed with the power of government but possessed with the flexibility and initiative of a private enterprise."[4]

The story of how the TVA came to be, its economic growth, legislation, accomplishments, pros and cons, is long indeed (Smith, 1966). The TVA has been appraised, studied, and restudied at length. Termed a "noble experiment," it has not been repeated, although similar bills were subsequently introduced in the Congress to create a Missouri Valley Authority and a Columbia Valley Authority (Dana, 1956). The present significance of the TVA is that it was a precursor of large-scale regional planning and land-use development that is of growing national interest in the 1970s (see Chap. 6).

The TVA program certainly has led to large development in the river

---

[4] From a special message to the Congress by President Roosevelt giving his recommendations for a Tennessee Valley Authority.

basin area. In addition to major flood control, power, industrial, and general economic improvement, it includes a great deal of cooperative work with the concerned states in agricultural, recreational, and forest land planting and management activities. The results of these many actions are apparent on the land and in the economy of the region.

The control and use of the Colorado River is another large-scale example of federal-state and interstate actions. Needs and problems are many and difficult. They include power, conflicts between agricultural and urban water needs, flood control, and protection of the river course, which includes the world-famous Grand Canyon. Water is in limited supply in the developing region of the Southwest. There are sharp conflicts between the states over who gets how much water and the needs of urban and agricultural users. The same problems exist in many parts of the United States and are of a complexity and magnitude that necessitate large-scale planning, action, and financing. These require federal assistance and interstate agreements of a long-term and binding nature.

A specific example of an interstate compact that required the consent of Congress is that concerning the Lake Tahoe Basin. The area is divided down the middle between California and Nevada. A complex of water control, urban, recreational, and wildland interests is encountered in a single, rather fragile and beautiful area. This is the subject of Chap. 9.

In summary, intergovernmental state and federal compacts are a practical necessity in meeting large-scale water control, urban, and nonurban land-use problems. These are beyond the capacity of any single governmental entity to meet. They constitute marriages of necessity to meet situations in which nobody can go it alone and prosper. The scale of compact agreements naturally varies with need. They range from intermunicipal to international agreements.

Administrative and Land-Location Controls

In addition to land-use controls that derive from laws and their legal interpretation, two additional means of control are important but often inadequately understood. These are administrative and land-location controls.

Administrative Controls By their nature, legislative enactments give policy and purpose.[5] They also must give some latitude for administrative interpretation in application. If the interpretation is alleged to subvert legislative intent, if may be taken to court for legal adjudication. More commonly, however, the decision of the administrator is accepted.

The scope of interpretation tends to increase with the level of government. Enactments at the municipal or county level of government tend to be more specific because they are closer to the point of application. Local

---

[5] Administrative law is included here as it has force of law. See Chap. 8.

officials also tend to be more responsive to their constituents. State laws are broader because they apply to a larger area of concern. Federal statutes are still broader inasmuch as they are of national concern and apply to all or several states. There is always scope for administrative interpretation of land-use controls, and it tends to increase with the level of government.

The administration of about 187 million acres of forested and other wildlands by the U.S. Forest Service under the federal Multiple Use Act gives an example on a continental scale of land-use administration that also permits much scope for local interpretation in application. The act and its application were discussed in Chap. 3 in relation to land classifications and zoning.

As previously emphasized, the Multiple Use Act itself is a policy directive only. It requires that the national forests be administered for enumerated land uses under the concept of sustained yield. The act also requires that all uses shall be given full and impartial consideration. It is, however, silent on where and in what combination land uses should be applied. It includes the policy directive that the renewable surface resources be "utilized in the combination that will best meet the needs of the American people."

This is a broad charter indeed. It has to be such because of the extremely wide range of kinds of land and possible uses of the national forests which are to be administered in the interests of the American people. The problems of wisely making decisions to maintain the land resource base and also meet the desires of people, whose interests and needs change over time, are both apparent and difficult.

The Multiple Use Act provides a broad charter for public agency planning and administration and a public-private forum for participation in decision-making processes. The force and significance of this dual fact of authority and responsibility in controlling public land use if often overlooked and underappreciated by administrators and the public alike. The American people speak with many voices and different emphasis and through many groups and media. Desires for land use "in the public interest" depend on who is talking for what purpose. Both public agencies and voices of the public they serve are fallible.

A heavy weight of responsibility and integration rests on the public agency, the Forest Service in this instance. It normally and inevitably often finds itself in the middle of strongly differing land-use interests and cannot satisfy everybody. Urban zoning authorities encounter similar situations. Perfection is not of this world, and this is certainly true of land use. Conflicts of interest there will always be; they are inherent in a changing people-land relationship and balance over time. Mutual charity and understanding are surely requisite to mitigate destructive conflicts of public-private interests that benefit no one.

This general pattern of public-private administrative and political relationships applies to other federal landowning and management agencies such as the Bureau of Land Management, which has an even wider range of land responsibilities. The national parks, national recreation areas, wildlife refuges, and some military reservations also face similar problems, as do states and local units of government. The differences are largely in specifics. There is almost always scope for administrative interpretation and discretion, and there are always hard-to-define public interests to consider.

Land-Location Controls   Almost any substantial ownership of land, and also small but strategically located ownerships, can affect, in some degree, the use of adjoining or intermingled lands. This is because of the basic fact of land immobility and the importance of landownership. To identify the category of location controls, ownerships can include very small but strategically located land parcels; industrial areas; airports; golf courses; ski runs public or privately owned parks and other recreational areas; large private, state, or federal forest and range lands.

Land-location controls are divided here into two groups: *indirect,* where a key ownership does not require the same or similar use, and *direct,* where a key ownership does tend to enforce the same use or control another use. There may also be some other groups of land-location controls that the reader can add.

Regarding the first group, the effects of industrial areas, airports, golf courses, large parks, and related recreation areas on adjoining lands are largely indirect. A big airport, for example, certainly strongly affects but does not *require* the same use of surrounding lands. Supporting facilities nearby such as aeronautical services, motels, and meeting places develop. Other land uses both near and not so near, such as residential, are certainly affected but are not dictated by the airport land use. A large ski run or a national park likewise promotes development of ancillary services and facilities. These also often have substantial effects on private land values and consequent influence on agricultural, forest, or other nearby land uses. The point of emphasis is that a land-use pattern tends to develop around a dominant ownership use, or a grouping of several similar ownership uses as in an industrial area, that is significantly affected but not dictated by the dominant ownership use.

The second general group of locational land-use controls is characterized by the direct power either to control or to get similarity of land use within a particular area. Such ownerships do not necessarily have to be large; even a small parcel of land in a very strategic place may give much land-use control. To illustrate, the owner of a small property in a strategic urban location could, in a situation where land expropriation by public authority is not possible, either get an extremely high price for his or her property or prevent or limit other construction development. Exactly the same kind of situation can arise in wildlands where strategic landownership may control access to a lake or stream with high recreational potential or to timberlands.

The use of a substantial area may require, in greater or less degree, similar use of adjoining and especially of intermingled land. This applies to both wildland and urban areas. For example, cattle grazing on Western range lands is, by its nature, an extensive land use. Planned development of water supply and location of salt, and also stock movement by horseback or jeep, is necessary to get desired animal distribution and proper utilization of the forage resource. To be effective, such livestock control often requires natural topographical land units. If the ownership of such units is divided, there is need to combine them by lease or by range-management cooperative agreement to achieve good grazing practice over the area as a whole.

The same principle applies, although in somewhat less degree, to management for timber production. The facts of topography, log transportation routes, logging methods, and timber-growing objectives and practices collectively press toward unity of operation that is certainly complicated by divided ownership. This is especially true where private and public ownership is illogically intermingled as a result of past ownership history.

An extreme example is the checkerboard pattern of public and private landownership that still exists in the forests of the Western states. This was due to early federal grants of public lands to subsidize Western railroad construction. Alternate sections of 1 square mile were given to the railroad in broad bands along the railroad route. The Bureau of Land Management owns such lands in Oregon, greatly complicating land management by both the Bureau and private owners of alternate sections. For different reasons, the same sort of fractured ownership applies to several national forests in the Eastern states. The reason is that they had to be acquired piecemeal as lands became available for purchase.

The same basic forces that press toward consolidation of land use in a particular area apply equally in principle to urban areas. The development of urban land-use zoning (Chap. 4) is directly illustrative. Zoning is designed and applied to accomplish and to enforce unified use of land areas. The purpose is to achieve a harmonious consistency in land use between many individual ownerships in a zoned area through the application of public authority.

To put the matter in broad perspective, consider the abundant examples of undesirable results from unplanned and uncontrolled land use. Too often these are passed off under the ubiquitous term of "development," which may be due to both historic and contemporary circumstances. These results are very apparent in the so-called urban sprawl, and the same phenomena are increasingly apparent in nonurban areas. Land-hungry people with money are increasingly buying land in all sorts of parcel sizes and places for all sorts of reasons. The result can be a hodgepodge of landown-ership and land-use objectives that, once imprinted on the land by private ownership, are extremely difficult to change and put into any sensible pat-tern (see Chap. 7).

The importance of land-location controls inevitably and naturally points toward the necessity for planned land development. This is needed, on both large and small scale, to seek the best use of a limited and, relating to population, an increasingly scarce land resource.

PART 2, Chapters 6–8

People actions in land use. Planning processes; design, information needs, effective relationships between planners and those affected by planning. Value measurements, needs and methods, public and private interests. Decision-making processes; sources and flow of power, kinds of decisions.

Planning Processes

This chapter enters the arena of action in land use. It builds on the chapters of Part 1, which have given a foundation in land basics: ownership, uses, classifications, and controls. The key words of planning processes are "planning" and "plans." The word "plan" means a scheme of arrangement, action, or procedure developed to accomplish some purpose. Planning is the process by which plans are developed.

Almost everybody plans in greater or lesser degree for one purpose or another. This applies to individuals, families, and all kinds and levels of organizations, private or public. Land use, which concerns many people in many ways, includes a wide spectrum of planning and plan needs. Planning goes on and on, in land use as in every other area of life. To stop thinking, planning, and providing ahead, is to die mentally, whether individually or collectively. Without a future there is no hope or continuing purpose.

Because of the wide range of purposes and circumstances in which land-use planning is applied, the use of and emphasis on the term "planning processes" in this chapter is deliberate and important. There is no such thing as *the* planning process in land use; there are many processes differing in context, character, and purpose. Planning processes are regarded here as an extremely important part, but not the totality, of the basic goal of achieving some people-land relationship and balance of desirable land use in an area, be it individually, corporately, or by different levels of governmental units.

A workable format for treatment of the subject matter of this chapter requires the identification and characterization of different categories or aspects of planning, and the processes that go with them. The six groups presented somewhat arbitrarily here are essentially differentiated by functions of, or situations encountered in, planning and indicate the range of processes involved.

1 *Design in planning.* This includes and emphasizes the creative, innovative, artistic, and formative aspects. These are vital; good design should permeate planning.

2 *Public policy and authority in planning.* Much planning is done as a requirement of public laws, policy directives, or regulations stipulating the basic direction and content of a plan. These range in kind and specificity from local, to state, regional, and federal authority. They also include interagency or interstate compacts and other relationships.

3 *Information needs in planning.* A major aspect and foundation of planning is to obtain, analyze, and utilize a wide range of relevant information. Surveys, studies, and inventories are a necessary part of the planning process.

4 *Planner and planee relationships in planning.*[1] The extent, timing, quality, and effectiveness of the relationships between those who plan and those who are affected by plans often determine the success or failure of any plan and are a key part of the planning process. Both planners and planees have power but in varying degree and from different sources. They also both bear weight of responsibility.

5 *Continuity in planning and administration.* Plans must be updated and applied to meet changing future needs. Administration to implement planning and to carry on the operational functions is important.

6 *Planning as a profession.* Who are the planners? What education and experience are needed? What are the functions of planning consultants, consulting firms, and planning teams both within and external to the particular organization or unit of government involved.

Each of the above will be considered in this chapter. It is hoped that this structure will be useful in presenting a complex subject regarding which there are strong differences of opinion and viewpoint. It should be noted that the problems of value measurement and related decision-making processes, although recognized in this chapter, are given in Chaps. 7 and 8. The

---

[1] "Planee" is a useful term increasingly employed to indicate those concerned or affected by planning.

reason is that each of these chapters deals with large professional-technical subjects which best can be treated separately.

DESIGN IN PLANNING

The most creative and in the long run the most enduring part of any plan lies in the concepts that give it purpose and direction. Design is the best single expression of this function. The word has many meanings, most of which are applicable to some aspect of land use.[2] Design includes creativity, form, structure, purpose, organization of parts, and application of means to an end—artistry in a full sense. It includes design of structures and of land forms and their combination into a pleasing and functional whole. Design implies imagination, innovation, and the expression and integration of ideas in some harmonious fashion to a desired end.

Many if not most planners who are professionals consider themselves as artists, as designers. They do so with good reason. But their functions, in practice, are many. They may also be executors as well in the sense of an artist finishing a picture or construct, including all the painstaking detail that goes with it. More frequently, and outside the area of art, design operates in partnership with many other skills and instrumental media, all aimed at producing some harmonious and functional whole.

These many relationships are fully illustrated in land use. Functions of design, implementation, and on-going administration are, for better or worse, often widely dispersed. They are often difficult even to identify consistently. This is due primarily to the great diversity of land use, many kinds of land, great range of people interests, large values and areas, and long time spans. Land-use planning is indeed serious business because of the immobility and finiteness of available land and its natural resources, which are pressed by increasing numbers of people and their needs.

Some examples will illustrate the range and impact of the design function in land use. These will extend from the more intensive and controlled to large-scale applications. Somewhat arbitrarily, and here is where classifications become difficult, the following illustrations are given in two general groups. The first includes situations, mostly urban, in which the use of land is dominated by construction and the land primarily contributes a base or a setting. The second group emphasizes situations in which the land—its resources, natural form, character, and cover—is the dominant consideration.

Design in Building and Intensive Use of Land

Consider a larger building in an urban area. It is designed by an architect, and the quality of design is extremely important. This applies not only to

---

[2] In the 1966 unabridged Random House dictionary there are eighteen entries for the word "design" of which about fifteen can apply to some aspect of land use. The root meaning of the word is to designate or mark out.

function but to form, including relation to other buildings and landscaping possibilities. Many skills go into the construction of such a project, but design is of dominating importance.

A more complex but similar example is the construction of a group of buildings such as a center for the performing arts. A tremendous array of design, knowledge, and construction skills must be brought together in the fabrication and arrangement of structures, their siting on the land, and the treatment of open areas. Artistry in design must pervade but in concert with functionality in providing necessary supporting facilities and services.

Sharply different in form and purpose but of underlying similarity is a shopping center. It is utilitarian and must be functional, and there are many complexities in construction, organization, and operation. A large area of land is required, mostly open, for access and parking. The plan for the center must be both functional and attractive. This includes good design in the kind and placing of buildings and the utilization of the open areas.

Related to a shopping center is the development of an outdoor amusement park, which requires a substantial area to accomodate large numbers of people and to give setting for the amusement structures which are the main focus of attention. The design and location of these structures is extremely important. A major requirement is that both open space and buildings must stand up under heavy use and that maintenance costs be as low as possible. Walkways and areas where people concentrate must be designed for utility and durability. There is much scope and need for good design in use of trees, shrubs, flowers, and grass to give grace and beauty. Planned in conjunction with walkways, they are also useful in controlling the movement of people and in preventing unnecessary soil damage. The same sort of opportunities and problems apply to formal gardens, parks, large estates, and memorial areas.

Going a step further, consider a planned urban development, including the model town. Land use here requires a complex arranging and mixing of different kinds of residential and commercial construction together with emphasis on open-space amenity. Intensive planning is requisite. Good design is its distinguishing feature, and vital to success.

Strict regulation and planning is necessary to preserve historic features in the face of pressures for change. This is common in the United States but perhaps more pronounced in older countries. For example, in many European towns and cities there are strong desires, accompanied by strict regulation, to preserve old structures and also to require that remodeling or new construction conform to the older architectural style. The same principle of preservation also applies to the use of open space. The function of design here is to maintain the charm and remembrance of past time. The new is not necessarily better than the old.

Design in Extensive Land Use

Landscape architecture as a profession, and as a term stressing design, initially developed in the treatment of English country estates. The term was coined by Frederick Law Olmstead of the United States in the 1800s. It is true that the vital function of design is apparent and crucial in these places, but the concepts and need for design are not so limited. They also apply to nonurban wildlands. This section considers the application of design where the land itself is the dominant feature, with travel routes and other constructs by people performing a subordinate and facilitating function.

Parkways, scenic drives, and trails provide a means to see interesting country, including attractive rural countrysides, mountains, lakes, rivers, and seashores. All such routes can profit from application of good design in their location and construction. In the United States, as elsewhere, a number of automobile routes have been specially designed for scenic as well as transport use. The Blue Ridge Parkway Skyline Drive follows the crest of the scenic Appalachian Mountains. The Natchez Trace Highway (U.S. 40) follows the historic overland route from Nashville, Tennessee, to the Mississippi River at Memphis. The Great River Road in Wisconsin, following a part of the Mississippi River, is another example. The coastal road along much of the Pacific Coast in California and the Wilbur Cross–Merritt Parkway in Connecticut (the oldest in the United States) are other examples.

The location and construction of interstate and other U.S. highways involve a great deal of design that includes scenic and aesthetic considerations. The same applies to roads in the national parks, state parks, and the national forests. The design of traveler facilities, such as for picnic, lookout, and rest stops, must be efficient but subservient to the landscape.

Trails and walkways are often thought to be a minor form of construction with little scope for design. This is not so. In scenic areas particularly ecologically fragile ones, trail location, construction, and maintenance approach a high art. Such trails are much more expensive than commonly realized.

Municipal, county, state, and national parks in varying ways and intensities require careful design in planning. This applies not only to planning access routes but to providing necessary facilities with a minimum of detraction from, and disturbance to, the scenic qualities of landscape, mountains, streams, and lakes that people come to see.

Good design of campgrounds, cabins, and other facilities in an outdoor setting is important and also difficult. It requires special knowledge and techniques. People, unwittingly or otherwise, may destroy as well as use facilities. This is especially true when they are in an unaccustomed and often not-understood wildland environment. An unthinking or thought-to-be harmless action by one person may be multiplied by many others. This can add up to serious damage that is expensive and difficult to rectify. Design is of major importance to make needed facilities available and adequate but at the same time minimize damage. Adequate maintenance is surely important, but much damage can be prevented by skillful design.

Application of the function of design is certainly important in nonurban landscapes. Increasing public recognition that land is finite and precious should engender an ethic of respect for its care and use. Aesthetics can be combined with utility.

Well-tended and well-arranged agricultural landscapes can be attractive as well as productive and offer opportunity for design in planning. The same is true of forests. Trees are dominant, enduring, highly successful, and the most long-lived of plants. But they are also finite; trees come and go. Renewal of forests is constantly going on by natural forces, which can often be destructive and wasteful. Regeneration can also be directed by people, and the process can be disruptive and aesthetically unpleasing. Compare a forest with a field of corn, a rather tall, annual plant. After harvest and frost a cornfield is not attractive, but the time span to a new crop is short and people are accustomed to the cycle. This is not true with a forest. People often think of trees as permanent and the larger the better. Forest harvesting, for both biological and economic reasons, is done in fairly small areas at a time. The results can appear destructive, and the reestablishment of new trees normally requires several years, and many more for trees to become large. Yet much can be done by care in the size, placement, and sequence of cutting areas to ameliorate the often disruptive appearance of forest harvest. It is possible to maintain growing forests that are pleasing as well as productive. Both care in their management and public understanding are requisite (see Chap. 12).

To conclude this section, the function of design is always important and should permeate land-use planning. It is the center of creativity in the continuing search for harmony in both appearance and utility. Without consciousness of design, land-use planning becomes a soulless process, without respect for either the quality of the environment or the dignity of mankind.

PUBLIC POLICY IN PLANNING

Planning for land use is increasingly a major part of public policy. This is inevitable. As more people and their needs press against a finite land and natural resources base, public consciousness of the need to maintain environmental quality increases. Tangible expression of this concern is indicated by the fact that environmental restraints in land resource use are built into law, be it by public ordinances, rules, regulations, or statutes. This occurs at all levels of government—local, state, and federal—in the United States. The same trend is evident in other countries.

It is important to recognize that effective planning, whether public or private, implies that land-use controls are to be applied by regulation or other appropriate means which are supported by sufficient authority. In action terms, this means that certain land uses and practices are permitted under specified conditions and that other uses are not permitted. Land-use planning is a serious matter; it is done for a purpose, places lasting imprints on the land, and may affect many people.

Planning for public purposes frequently requires stipulation of requirements and restrictions which private owners would not apply in their own interest. If this were not true, there would be little reason for public action. Application of land classifications, as in urban zoning, for example, is public regulation. The point is that public policy in action may require imposition of several kinds of land-use controls whether or not they are regarded as a part of planning.

Another important point is that it is not possible consistently to separate public policy enactments applying to water, pollution, and other environmental controls from those applying to land use. There are two basic reasons. One is legal and the other is physical. Political considerations are important in both.

As regards legal aspects, it is well known that precedent established in one situation is often applied in principle to another. This is true with public enactments in the regulatory use and control of water resources. Examples are issues concerning coastal and inland waterways, lakes and shorelines, development of navigation, flood control, total river basin planning, power development, and water supplies for urban and agricultural uses. There is a long history of legal development in public legislation applying to land-use controls in the United States. The same is true, but of more recent time, as regards legislative action to require pollution and environmental controls generally.

The second and physical reason is the fact that, in the public interest, land use can only in part be separated from water and other environmental concerns. Use of land, ranging from forestry and agriculture to urban areas, affects water supply and quality. Physical structures, such as factories, are built on the land and may be a source of pollution. They also obtain their natural resources essentially from the land. There is a large degree of interrelatedness in the uses of natural resources. They deeply affect many aspects of national affairs, but the land and its control are the basic common denominator.

To demonstrate the public policy aspects of land-use planning more directly, its setting in the governmental-political structure of a country must be identified. Also, there must be recognition of the fact that there are similarities and sharp differences both within and between countries (see Chap. 11). No single unit of government can act unilaterally in land-use planning. There must be coordination of planning efforts and action between different levels and units of government. In the United States, the fifty states are political and geographic units with much authority. This applies particularly to the exercise of broad police powers remaining with the states under the Constitution. Historically, however, the states have not been strong in land-use planning despite their large authority. For political as well as financial reasons, they have tended to act in an intermediate position between the powerful federal government and in-state governments (county, municipal, and town). The tendency has been to delegate and leave land-use controls to local units of government rather than to assert regulatory power directly. The states vary greatly in size, natural resources, critical issues, and political and financial strength. The present trend, stimulated by federal financial aids and national and regional planning, is for the states to take a stronger role in land-use planning.

Within-state units of government also differ in what they do and cannot do in land-use planning and action. Their financial and natural resources, concerns, and powers are limited, and their pressures are many. Most urban governments and some counties have been active in applying land-use controls largely through zoning (Chap. 4).

The federal government of the United States is extremely powerful and has great financial resources. It is also a major landowner. Thus it has the breadth of concern, authority, and means to deal with national and regional problems that transcend state boundaries. By constitutional authority, the federal government plays a major part in interstate compacts and other interstate matters. But its influence and constitutional powers, large as they are, do not extend to direct requirement of specific land-use planning by the states. There has to be effective federal-state cooperation in land-use planning that extends from urban, county, and state action to the regional and federal level. There must be reasonable consistency in overall objectives along with latitude in implementation. This must be understood and accepted by all, with each level of government carrying its appropriate load and responsibility.

The above is a condensed statement of realities within which forward progress can be made. No person or unit of government can go it entirely alone in land-use matters, and this fact is increasingly recognized. Contention among local, state, and federal governments is endemic to a viable political democracy, but more importantly there is increasing recognition of collective responsibilities as well as authority.

Although its beginnings go back a long time, broad public concern and action in public land-use planning is relatively recent. Much of it dates from the 1960s, with increasing intensity from the beginning of the 1970s.

Terms such as "land use," "ecology," and "environmental quality" have entered the public lexicon largely since the mid-sixties. This more focused and broad concern, going beyond the earlier and more limited scope of the conservation movement, has been accompanied by legislation affecting land use at the local, state, and federal level. There is continuing search for creative, innovative, and workable design of land-use controls which will serve people needs at all levels of government.

Because of the totality of an integrated approach, federal legislation is required. At the time of writing, bills have been introduced into the Congress to establish a national land-use planning framework. It is evident that the search for acceptable and operable legislation is difficult. It will be informative briefly to consider major characteristics of the proposed legislation.

There are two general approaches. One is cooperatively to establish national land-use planning by state and subsidiary political units of government. This means development of integrated statewide plans. The other approach would focus largely on crit cal land-use problem areas. Included would be urban problems, coastal zones and estuaries, shorelands and flood plains of rivers, lakes and streams, scenic or historic areas, rare or valuable ecosytems, and major airports.

Both approaches would include large grants of federal money to states, with accompanying stipulations regarding its expenditure. These could include items such as procedures, criteria, concomitant state actions (including the critical issue of providing state matching funds), and federal technical assistance. Also of critical importance are good working relationships within and between federal and state agencies, including enforcement of legal provisions. Points of federal-state differences in interest and viewpoint center largely in particulars of the items given above.

Some comprehensive and coordinated national-state program of land-use planning must be established that will recognize and aid all levels of government. The reason is the high degree of interrelatedness and dependency that exists between levels of government. Each needs to do what it best can and must work in reasonable concert with others.

The basic pattern of such planning is federal policy, together with coordinating direction, expertise, and financial assistance, which is applied through and with the states. This general pattern is not new and exists in various forms, but it is presently piecemeal as regards land-use planning. It is necessary to recognize that planning processes, as a part of public policy, are difficult and complex to implement. Much planning is required, but it does not necessarily result in particular documentary "plans," which is a good general truth to keep in mind.

Public planning is largely regulatory in nature. It means establishing policy and the critical matters of financing, stipulation of requirements and schedules, procedural provisions for public hearings and negotiation, and enforcement by both legal means and administrative interpretation.

The design element is surely important in these matters as always, but it is often difficult to identify. At the policy formation level, design is found in the quality of ideas, in innovation and creativity, in identifying problems, and in devising solutions. It is particularly important in the writing of good legislation, which is surely a difficult matter. At the planning and implementation level, the quality of design is reflected in the creativity and skill exercised in assembling and using available information and in devising workable methods and procedures to get on with the job.

It is important to keep in mind that planning in the public interest is necessarily political in the full and proper sense of the word. It is the application of governmental power, as expressed through public authority and resources, to accomplish desired purposes in the public interest which are also open to public scrutiny. It is in these respects—not in techniques of planning, which have much commonality—that public planning processes differ sharply from planning processes in the private sector. Public authority sets the basic ground rules within which private enterprise must operate.

INFORMATION NEEDS FOR PLANNING

Planning cannot be better than the quality of ideas, experience, and information that supports it. These give the basis for successful formulation of policies and means of implementation. This applies to both public and private planning. There is something of a paradox here. Good ideas are indeed precious, and although they are seldom new in a historical sense, their particular applications and combinations can be new. Yet it can also be said with truth that ideas are a dime a dozen, meaning that ideas take on reality and value only when they can be successfully applied. It is seldom lack of ideas as such that is limiting but rather discriminating capacity to apply them.

It is common and often necessary to precede specific land-use planning with a problem analysis—with studies, inventories, sounding of public opinion, and appraisal of plan alternatives. This is often a crucial part of the total planning process. Public land-use planning enactments often include provision for inventories based on land classifications (Chap. 4) to give on-the-ground basis for action.

Planning for complex enterprises may require an immense amount of detailed information collection and analysis. Examples include large public works or highways; multi- or single-purpose water development projects involving power, irrigation and flood control, recreation, and wildlife; and large-scale urban development projects. For a large and complex undertaking it is common to make what are termed feasibility studies *before* detailed data collection and planning are undertaken. These studies focus attention on what are considered to be critical and limiting problems that must be met. Preliminary studies of a more general nature are also made to appraise data needs and collection methodology.

A further and large dimension in land-use planning, new in the United States, is that under federal environmental quality legislation proposals involving public financing and controls must include preparation of an environmental impact statement. This is public information. It is a part of the public review process and includes careful appraisal of anticipated or potential soil, air, or water pollution; biological impact, public hazards, or other effects that may be associated with the project.

Public involvement, from the local to the national level, is increasingly a large part of the planning process. The laws often require public hearings, which make information publically available for review. The public is more closely examining land use and related matters. This is most evident in public undertakings wherein citizens feel they have legitimate legal concern and judicial recognition is given to their right to have standing in court to sue. The same recognition also applies to private proposals regarding land use.

Much study and research is often needed for the preparation of legislation involving land use. Legislation based on appraisal of public needs, often drafted independently by different legislators, is subject to intensive scrutiny by legislators who represent their constituents, and by the concerned public generally. Hearings are held, and special studies also may be made. Bills are often revised and redrafted to meet the desires of different interest or political groups, are debated, and finally are voted upon. The process is often long and may extend over years, as in the development of national land-use legislation mentioned in the preceding section. Throughout, good information is requisite for sound legislation.

Because planning in land use requires a wide range of information, the means of gathering and organizing pertinent data is a major job. Multidisciplinary inventory and study groups are frequently organized representing such areas as economics, sociology, and political science; soils, ecology, and other biological fields; professional planning and landscape architecture; engineering; hydrology; agriculture; and forestry. The composition of such groups naturally depends on the particular land-use situation under consideration. They may be engaged in both devising and applying study and inventory techniques to gather needed data, or they may operate largely by assembling, organizing, and digesting available information.

In land-use planning, it is important to take a hard and discriminating look at what *are* "data"; what does the term mean and include? To use a generalized illustration, suppose a study group organized as an interdisciplinary team is charged with the job of getting "the data" for a particular land-use planning project. The assumption is often made that, since the team is interdisciplinary, the problems of obtaining information needed in planning, especially at the crucial level of decision making, are solved. This is seldom true. As stressed in Chap. 4, there are many kinds of classifications on which inventories are based. They range from those that can apply to an area as a whole without regard to a particular land use to classifications rather narrowly focused on a particular use.

There is a natural tendency for each member or part of an interdisciplinary team to get data pertinent to its field. That is, the biologist gets biological data, the hydrologist gets hydrologic data, the sociologist gets sociological data, and so on. The result can be a massive collection of perfectly sound data about different things but with little relevance or significance to decision making. Organizing this information so that it can be evaluated and applied in integrative form to meet planning needs is often difficult, but this is of crucial importance in the planning process.

There are different levels of significance and kinds of data, each depending on the use to be made of the data. There is a distinct difference between so-called basic data of the kind normally collected in subject-area inventories and studies, and the kind of information that is pertinent in making decisions in land-use planning. The difference may seem subtle and hard to grasp, but it is important. There is need from the beginning to think in terms of critical or limiting problems regarding the particular situation under study. This means delineating hard questions that have to be answered and specifying the data needed to answer them. From this viewpoint, information needs are selective and often do not follow conventional disciplinary procedures of data collection.

For example, suppose a general appraisal of a particular recreation area indicates that a key question is the carrying capacity, the ability of vegetation or trees to withstand human use. This is a matter of vegetative durability, the capacity of plants to reseed, grow, and endure under different levels of trampling. The expected season of public use is also important. A general vegetative survey might give little information directly usable on these critical questions. There is, however, considerable information available about human carrying capacity under different ecological conditions. If relevant information is available from study and experience elsewhere, perhaps an interpretive evaluation and check may be all that is necessary to arrive at the key conclusion, i.e., that people must be kept on trails. The need for a detailed field survey could be obviated.

Similarly, there may be a question about the capacity of a stream-fed water area to be biologically safe for swimming. Water tests taken at a given time not related to swimming use may indicate that the pond is safe, but the key decision may hinge on the seasonal volume of flow and its temperature in relation to the time when major swimming use is likely to occur. An evaluation may be necessary which goes beyond data collected on the site.

Surface and subsurface soil characteristics are surely important in residential building development. Basic soil survey data are valuable and give a start, but they must be interpreted from a building construction standpoint as to stability, compaction, drainage, etc. The same applies in larger scale and complexity to highway and dam construction. Soil, rock, and geological interpretation from an engineering standpoint is a large area of specialized study which must be drawn upon for answers to critical and limiting questions.

There are many examples of this kind, and readers are encouraged to add their own. The central point is that many kinds of information, often highly specialized, are needed in land-use planning. There is a constant need to take an integrative point of view in land-use information gathering, to focus on limiting factors that are important in making decisions. There is no escape from judgment. Data by themselves often do not answer questions. Data gathering is also expensive. The volume of data and the care taken in collection may have little relation to the data's usefulness. It is also true that, land use being a complex matter, economic and social information critical in planning for a particular area may be needed from sources which are far removed from the land itself. Some examples are distance and numbers of people who might visit a proposed recreation area; market information important in agricultural or forest land use; materials, transportation, and labor costs in irrigation projects.

In closing this section, recognition also should be given to large technical improvement in the collection, storage, and retrieval of data made possible by great advances in computer technology and related analytical techniques. Data banks and model building increasingly are being applied in the land-use area. However, as stressed here, the data cannot answer all questions. The mass and manipulative possibilities of data should not be confused with necessity for discrimination in the use of information which can go beyond what computers can contribute. There is danger in letting emphasis on means, important as they are, divert attention from the hard thinking that must underlie them in seeking ends. These ends are good land use, which must be achieved in the realities of actual situations on the ground.

PLANNING RELATIONSHIPS

This section deals with relationships between planners and planees. Inevitably there are differences of interest to resolve. How well these differences are understood and constructively met is of decisive importance in gaining acceptance of planning. It is better to think of a plan as an organized time schedule of actions to be taken about land use rather than to think of it as a document.

Plans that are prepared and handed down from high authority are seldom successful in operation despite good ideas and intentions. There needs to be constructive exchange of ideas and viewpoints, mutual education, understanding, and give and take during the planning process to accomplish acceptance and implementation. Without these, planning can be an expensive exercise in futility. This has often happened.

The basics of the planning process are schematically illustrated in Fig. 6.1. On the left side are the planners, representing the analysis and planning function which stems from some level of purpose and authority. On the right side are the planees, who are concerned or affected either indirectly or directly by the results of planning. The thick and rather wobbly band between them represents the varying degrees of influence between the two groups as the planning process continues. The band is not straight or even because the pathway to successful planning often is not such. At the bottom between the two sides is the hoped-for result of some plan or schedule of action that is acceptable and that can be implemented. Below and between the two sides at the bottom is an agreed-upon plan proposal. The next and crucial step is decision, or plan approval. This usually requires a higher and different level of authority than plan preparation. Following decision are plan implementation, administration, and provision for revision, which are requisite for plan continuity.

At the top of Fig. 6.1 is a sort of nimbus cloud representing power. There is no clear division of power between the two sides; both have power stemming from societal-political sources. But, as shown, planner power stems more from authority and planee power derives more from influence. Information is available to both sides of the planning equation, and there should be much in common. But because of differences in viewpoint, planee information is likely to differ in character and source.

The following summarizes the general framework within which planning is done.

Objectives—goals and needs These may be public or private and broadly social or specific by individuals or groups. Objectives set the general stage in planning, but they can change in form, direction, and intensity during the planning process and may continue to be in question during implementation and plan administration.

Information—status of knowledge The need for information has previously been stressed on the planner side, but it applies to planees as well, although points of view and interpretations are different. It is important to have effective interchange of information among all concerned if successful planning is to result.

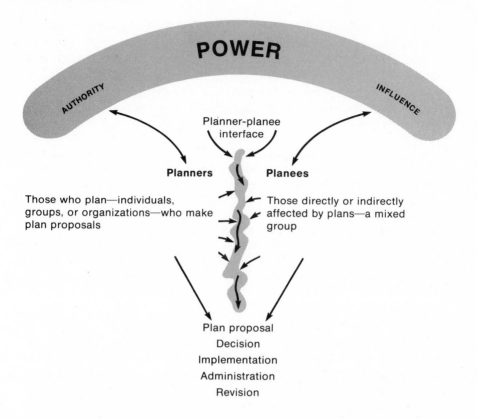

Figure 6-1   The land-use planning arena. *(From drawing by author.)*

Organizational structures The size, scope, and effectiveness of existing organizations are important to land-use planning. Organizations are needed by both sides of the planning equation, and new organizations may also be needed.

Legal framework The same basic framework of public law applies to both sides. Public agencies have authority as given to them by statutes. Private agencies likewise are subject to the existing framework of law applicable to them. Land-use planning actions by public or private individuals or organizations may be taken to the courts for legal test.

Power structure This is basically political, particularly in a political democracy like the United States. Power is the influence that can be exerted by public and private organizations and individuals in varying degree. Sources and directions of power are always to be reckoned with in planning (see Chap. 8).

The above places emphasis on the dynamics of planning, the respective powers and strengths that must be faced. Successful planning requires viable working relationships between people and organizations which often have widely differing points of view, value criteria, and kinds and degrees of influence.

Establishment of communication is a complex art and should be so recognized. A number of means are given below, but not in any sequence or priority, as these depend on the particular situation. They are presented primarily from the standpoint of the planners, who normally are the initiators in the planning process.

1 Informal, personal, individual or small-group discussions with leaders and other important people. This can be excellent, but there is danger of creating an impression that the stage is being set by the powers from above.

2 Public distribution of brochures giving statements of purpose, reasons, scope of the planning, benefits to be gained, etc. These can be effective; it is also possible to oversell and create public distrust.

3 Public hearings, which may be designed for different purposes. These are frequently required by law. A recurrent problem is to get balanced inputs from a representative sample of concerned people or interest groups. Hearings may be dominated and slanted by activist groups, pro or con.

4 Letter writing to those on selected mailing lists with or without enclosed supplemental material. This can be an effective means of informing people or organizations otherwise difficult to reach.

5 Open discussion meetings, programs, and talks. If well-organized, these can be very effective. As with item 3 above, a problem is to get balanced attendance and participation.

6 Legal public notices. These are required by law for certain public actions. Not a media for education.

7 Public media of newspapers, radio, and TV. These are effective if well done and in balance, but media are difficult to control and factional interests often can exert undue influence.

Effective use of these information-education means (except legal notices) requires experience, time, and money in substantial degree. There are also tactical and strategic problems in their use, including how fast or slow to go in seeking public support, how much and in what way to emphasize money costs and benefits, recognition of ethnic groups, occupations of concerned people, and the existence of strong factional groups or cleavages that may be significant.

The particular nature and scope of a planning project and the degree of centralized authority employed in its administration also influence the planning process.

Approaching this matter from the authoritarian end of the spectrum, there is the concept of the master plan. This derives from platonic doctrine which holds that the most able people should be fully educated and that plans prepared by them, if followed, would enable realization of the ideal society. A master plan is prepared by those who are considered to be the best informed and most capable of judging in the public interest. This approach has had considerable popularity.

The general sequence of a master plan is:

1 Statement of goals, societal needs, and far-reaching, if not ultimate, objectives
2 Detailed planning and plans backed by study and information
3 Plan implementation

This kind of approach is necessary where (1) major public interests and large resources are involved and (2) much detailed and large-scale planning is required that must be supported by strong public authority and financial strength to implement. The construction of interstate highways is a good United States example. Their construction requires tremendously complex and detailed planning and great technical skills. The socioeconomic effects of these highways are permanent and far-reaching. Large public water control projects are similar examples. Nuclear power plants, although primarily constructed by private enterprise in the United States, are deeply in the public interest. They are extremely expensive, have long life, and pose difficult residue-disposal problems. Long-range planning of great complexity is required, and there should be public participation in the process.

At the other end of the spectrum are planning situations in which total design and continuity, although desirable, are neither necessary nor attainable. However, a piecemeal or part-by-part approach in planning is possible. The term "disjointed incrementalism" has been applied to such situations which are not unusual. Long-range goals, problems, and needs must be recognized and should be supported by much information, study, and consideration of alternatives. But there is no master plan as such with a predetermined time schedule of priorities. Action is taken as it can be, with close and continuing involvement and participation by concerned people. Planning and action through consensus characterizes such processes.

There is a wide range of land-use planning situations between those requiring strong and sustained authority and those where an incremental approach is possible and may be necessary. No book such as this can detail them. The purpose here is to emphasize their existence. It is also necessary to recognize that significant political-social and often historical considerations go beyond, and often cannot clearly be separated from, what can be thought of as land use in a literal sense. A few examples will be helpful to illustrate some of the dynamics; readers are welcome to introduce their own.

Consider the city of Cincinnati. As with many of the older American metropolitan centers, the inner city was pressed by stagnation, deterioration, and business exodus to the growing periphery of the metropolitan area. The deep and in large degree irreversible events of history that gave rise to the inner city and its function have changed. What to do?

There had been much study and planning regarding solutions. Several urban renewal plans had been developed but with little result. Power and finance were lacking, and there was insufficient agreement on solutions and financing when it came to actual implementation. There was both apathy and opposition in the outer metropolitan area, where people felt that such planning would benefit the inner city and not be in their interest. There was much search for workable approaches, for fusion of interests, and for means of implementation.

A working committee was established. An open-minded, able but initially reluctant planning consultant (who had been involved in previous planning) was hired, and three planning firms were brought together. There was a long series of structured meetings with many groups, each reporting back to the working committee and to the city council. Many people were drawn into the planning process. There was a sincere attempt, through broad-based and comprehensive consultation, to combine decision-making processes with the development of planning.

Major problems and needs were systematically factored out with accompanying action alternatives. Conflicts of interest were recognized as the work progressed. Some broad city goals were very difficult to meet. The purpose was to develop a general framework for action, to recognize and do the most needed things. There was no tie to a preconceived master or general plan as such. Planning was, however, directed toward much the same ends as had been developed in previous plans. The significant difference lay in the fact that public acceptance became built in with the planning. Progress and workability were stressed. There was reasonable coordination of effort *toward* attainable and accepted goals.

In sum, progress was made. Things were done much as had been proposed in previous plans but in accomplishable segments. There was no master plan to fail.

In sharp contrast is the story of an extremely thorough land-use plan in Pennsylvania. It was prepared for an area of 37 square miles located in the outer fringe of urban expansion from the Philadelphia megalopolis and considered to be in the path of urban development. The plan was not accepted. The region is one of mixed agriculture, including considerable forest area, and has a resident population of farmers and rural residents. Most of them commute to nearby towns and larger urban areas.

The plan was developed essentially by planners from outside the study area. It was selected because it met certain planning criteria, not because it met needs expressed by the residents themselves. The purpose was to guide economic growth in a planned manner without loss in natural resources quality. The basic means was selective use of easements to control land uses in a desirable land development pattern.

Planning was supported by large grants of money from federal, state, and local governments and private foundation sources. Thorough and detailed studies were made by many consultants. The resultant plan was essentially a fusion of their technical reports into a land-use development program. Much effort went into the planning of physical developments, such as construction of a common sewage and water supply system. Detailed studies were made of measures needed to maintain stream water quality, streamside attractiveness, and general landscape quality. These needs were to be accomplished largely through use of easements and also by some zoning.

No direct study was made of the people or their reactions to different alternatives, but a long questionnaire was sent to all residents to determine their desires and goals regarding maintenance of their environment. The questionnaire dealt more with what individuals would like to have rather than what they would actually accept. The real temper of the people in the area was not sounded by the questionnaire. Also, the views of local public authorities who approved of the plan were confused with the views of private leadership and with what residents actually thought and would do when their interests were directly affected. Public meetings were held but were poorly attended. Interviewing was done during the day when people were at work, was not effective, and caused some resentment.

In summary, despite good ideas, excellent intentions, and great effort, the plan was decisively voted down by the residents when it came to the test of a secret vote. The positive relationships between planners and planees proved to be inadequate. Perhaps the major ideas could have been successful if the planning had been built from the ground up, so to speak, with strong positive rapport between the planners and those affected by the planning. This particular effort has been termed "the defeat of a perfect plan."

Similar in final result, but much different in specifics, was the fate in Connecticut of a proposed state park area, including a much-used lake. Establishment of such a state park to serve several New England towns was proposed by the local regional planning agency as a part of its regional plan.[3] The general *idea* seemed good and was initially accepted by the

[3] These towns are unique to New England and have much independence. They go back to its historical settlement in land units of around 20,000 to 30,000 acres. Agriculture and other land uses developed around a central townsite. This pattern stems from the medieval German town (Stadt), usually walled for protection in olden times, wherein agricultural people lived and went out to tend their surrounding fields. In the United States, it is the origin of the term "township" (6 miles square or 23,040 acres), credited to Thomas Jefferson for his part in

thirteen towns that were concerned. This action also came after there was considerable publicity, hearing, and discussion within the respective towns. However, as consideration of the park got down to specifics of area use—of individual town jurisdiction, administration, and intertown relationships—questions and opposition increasingly developed. Both personal and political interests were involved. The more specific the proposal became and the more it was discussed, the more questions and opposition developed. After about 6 years of consideration, the proposal was voted down. This action was not the result of a plan being handed down by the regional planning agency. There was also good publicity and information from the start. Failure in acceptance was due largely to difference among the towns, and some individuals in them, regarding jurisdiction and management of the proposed park. A large issue was the fact that most use of the park, particularly of the lake, would come from people outside the town supplying the land.

Both of these examples give point to the biblical expression about how much difference it makes as to *whose* ox is gored when one comes down to specific reactions. There is a deep planning truth here. People are what they are, and their actions are difficult to predict when their interests are directly concerned. Good ideas are not scarce. It is the gaining of their acceptance, by those directly affected, that is the crucial and most difficult part of planning processes.

In concluding this section, it is hoped that treatment given supports the fact that planning processes are indeed plural and that particulars in their execution vary widely with circumstances. An underlying common denominator or principle of planning is that, although the function of design in terms of creativity and ideas is surely of basic importance, the final test of success is acceptance by concerned people or organizations. They will have the final word. Closely related is the point that preparation of "a plan" as such is not the final objective. It is rather the establishment of planning processes that lead to constructive results over time. This leads directly to the following section on achieving continuity in planning.

CONTINUITY IN PLANNING AND ADMINISTRATION

So far, this chapter has been developed on the well-founded assumption that planning is extremely important and necessary and that the processes of its execution should lead to decision and action. This is true whether the results are embodied in a plan of some documentary form or are expressed as a sequential schedule of actions to be taken.

The final and crucial question is how the results of planning are to be

developing the rectangular public land survey system of the United States outside of the original thirteen and some of the Southeastern states.

implemented over time. This is where planning processes merge into on-going land-use administration. Plans tend to be static whereas land use cannot be, as both needs and knowledge change. This section treats problems of achieving continuity in planning, including necessary revision, so as to apply plans effectively over continuing time.

A problem to recognize at the outset derives from human nature. Planning is exacting work; it requires examination and resolution of difficult issues and must come to some conclusion. Following the development and establishment of a plan, there is a natural human tendency to relax, stop thinking, and leave the job of keeping the plan current and viable to somebody else. All of us take comfort in getting things settled and avoiding continual questioning. This human inertia coefficient applies not only to planning processes but to continuing administration as well.

Yet controversy in land use is normal. Issues and decisions often do not or cannot stay settled. Opposition to particulars of planning and plans frequently continues after the results are applied in practice. Directly or indirectly, and with varying degrees of validity, opposition may continue by organizations, groups, or individuals concerned. In the United States, court decisions have generally supported recognition of the right of concerned citizens to sue in environmental issues whether or not they are directly affected. Controversy through the courts, with injunctions, can go on for years and lead to no clear decision. Such action, and there are other forms of dissent, is often divisive and expensive. Also, organized and persistent demands for change are often successful against a much larger but unorganized majority.

These facts of human nature are important in continuity of planning and its implementation. There are no clear or easy answers, but the facts must be recognized in planning processes and implementation.

Plan Revision

A recurrent weakness of planning and plans is lack of clear provision for current or periodic revision. In the public sector, statutes prescribe the direction, structure, and public participation in the planning process. They require that planning be done with specified objectives and results. A plan of itself, however, seldom does and often cannot prescribe *how* the plan is to be revised. It is common, as in regional or national planning, to specify that a plan shall periodically be reviewed but without providing clear directives on mechanics.

A basic reason why this is so is that land-use planning is a dynamic process applied over time; situations and needs change; and one learns by experience in considerable degree. An analysis of the slow trial-and-error development of timber-management planning and plans based on long experience, in a situation where careful planning is tremendously important, is given by Davis (1966, pp. 292–297). The experience is illuminating and will be found helpful.

In the development of plans it is often impractical or even impossible to prescribe ahead what should be done other than to provide for revision. For example, regional and national land-use planning necessitates the establishment of complex federal-state financial and other relationships. Each participant has power as well as responsibility. Commitments frequently cannot be made for indefinite periods into the future. Budgets are annual, and competing financial demands have to be considered, although *authorization* for planning expenditures, as an example, may extend for a number of years and be given legislative priority. There is, consequently, a terminable aspect to public planning that is determined by the structure of a particular unit of government.

Land-use planning in the private sector is also often terminable by its nature, project by project. Consider, for example, a particular urban development, such as a housing project, a factory, or an office structure. A great deal of detailed planning is done; public interests are often strongly involved and limiting as to what can be done. Approval from several public agencies is usually required. Private individuals or groups also may enter strong objections requiring adjustment in planning. The planning process may be stormy and difficult indeed. But, once a project is approved, it can often be completed in a fairly short period of time and becomes almost irrevocably implanted on the land. Major plan revision becomes impractical; a plan has become a fixed reality.

A general principle in planning is that the frequency and importance of plan revision is related, often strongly, to the kind and degree of terminality to the planning process. If by its nature the planning process leads to a definable and finished result that requires land-use commitment for a substantial period of time, the importance of plan revision diminishes accordingly. To the extent that these conditions do not hold, as in agriculture and forestry, where land-use allocations are not permanent and can be changed, provision for periodic revision of planning becomes of major importance.

There is also a certain static quality to land-use planning processes in human affairs that needs to be recognized. Once use classifications have been made, as in zoning, where lines are drawn on a map and particular land uses allocated to designated areas, there is always difficulty in changing them. Vested interests develop. People tend to accept what is and adjust accordingly. Resistance to change often develops. Planning in land use is indeed a serious matter that justifies deliberation to establish and that often cannot be easily changed. But it is also true that use allocations cannot be all-wise. Discrimination and real wisdom is needed to know when and where not to change. No formula or pat prescription can be given, but this static nature of much land-use allocation is a general fact to keep in mind.

Governance

Closely related to planning revision, and a common weakness in planning processes, is the often inadequate provision for plan execution. Basically, this is a problem of governance (this means the function or power of governing, of establishing adequate means for planning implementation). It includes provision of adequate financing, organizational structures, delegation of authority and responsibility, qualified personnel, and often physical facilities.

For example, authority in New England towns is, by nature of their historical development, rather dispersed among town officials. In some towns major matters are still decided by the collective vote of all citizens at town meetings. A town may, for example, acquire open-space lands, yet lack consistent or continuing means to manage them for the intended purposes.

The same sort of problems apply in varying form and degree to other units of government. This problem may be critical to states which may lack either finance or existing organization to implement large-scale state-wide or regional planning. New organizational structures may have to be established and jurisdictional questions adjudicated. Financing is often a major limiting factor.

The federal government likewise has governance problems despite, or because of, its great strength and financial resources. In large-scale land-use planning there are often major issues as to which federal agency or agencies should administer planning and related policy directives. Interagency jurisdictional relationships are complex, sometimes overlapping, and competitive. There are also recurrent questions as to whether new or reorganized agencies are needed. These issues are often crucial to land-use planning processes.

In summary, governance, using the term broadly, is always an important consideration in planning processes and ultimately determine their success or failure in application.

Planning in Administration

Consideration of governance leads directly to the functions of on-going administration in land-use planning processes. These are large indeed, and the importance of administrative interpretation was stressed in Chap. 5. Planners plan in interface with those affected by the planning, and plans are developed. But their implementation is accomplished through administration, and this fact holds for both public and private organizations.

Much planning is done within an administrative organization as a normal part of its work, including that in land use. Rather commonly, however, planning is separated functionally from on-going administration through the establishment of planning teams which often include consultants.

A good illustration of complex and large-scale planning is the administration of public lands in the public interest by both state and federal agencies. Their basic objectives, functions, and responsibilities are given by statutes or policy directives from higher authority. Within this guiding framework, such agencies assume the direct responsibility for initiating land-use planning processes, including their execution. State parks, wildlife refuges, and several categories of lands administered by the National Park Service are well-known examples.

On a much larger scale are the millions of acres of lands managed in the public interest by the Bureau of Land Management and the U.S. Forest Service. Some of these lands are designated for particular uses, such as wilderness under the Wilderness Act of 1964. On most of these lands, however, particular land uses are not prescribed under the Multiple Use Acts of these agencies, which specify only that all applicable uses shall be fairly considered. Specific decisions as to their application on the land is left to the discretion of the agencies to "best meet the needs of the American people" (Chap. 3). This is a large and difficult order to meet.

As has been emphasized, the Multiple Use Act basically provides a forum within which the "mix" of particular land uses, applied singly or in combinations, has to be worked out between the planner—the government agency—and those affected or concerned, who are some segment of the public. The same need to provide effective interfaces between the two applies in full measure here.

It will be helpful here to give an illustration of how this can be done using the U.S. Forest Service as an example. It has put much effort into developing and applying planning methodology to large land areas having a number of use capabilities. It must be recognized, however, that no particular example can be all-encompassing. The Forest Service administers some 187 million acres of public lands on a continental basis. Land-use situations are extremely varied. Specifics in administrative practice also differ as they are applied by large and strongly decentralized regional field organizations.

The Eastern and Southern administrative regions of the U.S. Forest Service in 1970 jointly issued in booklet form a two-part framework for land-use planning. The first part is the *SYSTEM for Managing the National Forests in the East.* The second is the *GUIDE* which is to be prepared for each of seven subregions recognized in the Eastern national forests. This material was given wide public distribution. These two administrative regions manage some 23.6 million acres in forty-seven national forests ranging from Canada to the Gulf of Mexico. Public ownership in some of these areas is fairly well consolidated, but in others there is much admixture of privately owned lands not subject to public control.

The purpose of the *SYSTEM* and *GUIDE* was to provide a consistent basis for the application of planning processes. There have been revisions and undoubtedly there will be more. The *SYSTEM* and *GUIDE,* however, mark a step in the continuing search to develop workable procedures in applying land-use planning. Necessarily, these procedures must apply to many different kinds of lands and serve different uses.

The booklet *SYSTEM for Managing the National Forests in the East* gives governing policy in land use and also basic procedures for planning. Seven subregions are recognized, each including at least two national forests. These groupings are based on social, economic, and geographic considerations such as characterize the Lake States, Appalachian Mountains, and the Southern Coastal Plain regions. The national forests within these regional groups are well-established units and individually also separately prepare administrative and other guideline material for their forests. The most significant change made in the *SYSTEM* from previous planning practice was to subdivide national forest areas "into manageable common denominator 'units' each of which has its own specific make-up and which can logically be managed for optimum use." The intent is that a "Unit Plan" is to be prepared for each such unit. This is a marked change from previous practice of usually preparing plans by administrative ranger district units.

The first step in the planning process, as given in the *SYSTEM* booklet, is that an interdisciplinary team is established to prepare an operating *GUIDE* for each of the subregions recognized. The purpose of the *GUIDE* is to direct execution of the planning system for its subregion. It includes a listing of policy and related guidelines tailored to the particular subregion. It also includes national and regional policy direction and broad objectives for the protection and management of environmental, natural, and human resources. Provision is made for each subregion *GUIDE* to be thoroughly reviewed before issuance both within the Forest Service and by the concerned public. The interdisciplinary team also establishes the boundaries of the individual planning units within the region. The boundaries of each such unit are determined by topographical and land-use considerations using natural stream drainages as boundaries where feasible. When the *GUIDE* is approved and the unit areas are established, this interdisciplinary team disbands.

The second major step in the planning process, following issuance of a subregion *GUIDE*, is the establishment of other interdisciplinary teams by the forest supervisors to make the unit plans for their respective national forests. Preparation of these plans follows a time and procedural schedule given in the *SYSTEM*. Provision is made for review both within and without the Forest Service. The unit plans are total land-use plans which become the basis for land actions within the unit. The team also revises the unit plan as necessary. Execution of a unit plan is by the district ranger with executive support by the supervisor and regional forester. Administrative support comes from all three.

This two-part *SYSTEM* and *GUIDE* gives an illustration of a complex land-use planning process developed by an administrative organization to direct the management of very large and diverse public land areas. It is presented here becausee it is a significant proposal that merits study. It is not to be assumed that the *SYSTEM* and *GUIDE* give any final answers to planning processes and problems on national forest lands or elsewhere. The search will go on.

Some questions about the proposed system can also be raised. No such planning system can be definitive. Necessarily, there must be provision for adjustment and change to meet particular problems and needs both internal and external to the Forest Service. Provision for revision is not clear beyond the statement that unit plans will be "maintained as necessary." How well the interdisciplinary teams will work out in practice remains to be tested. They do not offer any surety of success. Interfaces with "the public" are seemingly limited to certain prescribed times in the planning schedule. These public meetings are arranged by the forest supervisor and the district ranger. They are conducted largely by the unit planning teams which are responsible for the unit plans. There is seemingly a rather sharp line here between the planning team and the district ranger and his staff. The latter are the people on the ground who work with forest users and execute the plan. But they do not seem to have much part in the planning process. This may cause difficulties in practice; there is need for exercise of judgment in plan implementation.

It also must be recognized that the Forest Service maintains comprehensive national, and in large degree a supplemental regional, handbook and manual system covering functional land use and procedural matters. These are not considered in the *SYSTEM* and *GUIDE*. These unit plans apply to fairly small areas and in total are expensive to prepare and periodically revise. Functional planning, as for recreation, wildlife, timber use, and grazing, is also done on the national forests. There can be problems in effectively integrating national forest planning and operations with these separate unit plans.

Above are the *kinds* of questions that always have to be faced in dynamic and continuing land-use management. They are not intended as criticism. No single method or approach is likely to suffice. The search for better methods and practices necessarily will continue.

PLANNING AS A PROFESSION

In concluding this chapter on planning processes it will be helpful, and add perspective, to consider planning as a professional occupation. There is certainly no question about the increasing recognition and importance of planning as a function in land use. There are many offices or other entities in both public and private organizations that are designated as planning units of one kind or another. In the public area these range from urban through regional and state levels to the federal government. The same kinds of differences in level also apply to private enterprise. Much planning is done in organizational units that are not designated by a planning label. It is also true that much planning is done by people who do not consider themselves planners by profession or occupation. There are no clear demarcations here; the term "planner" is commonly applied with little discrimination and without consistent meaning.

Who, then is a planner? It is a significant question, for the term requires some definition. As considered here, a planner is a person who by some combination of education, experience, and vocation is concerned in some directive capacity in land-use planning processes. This means work in some responsible and integrative capacity in assembling, evaluating, and applying much and varied information aimed toward some land-use purpose. Such is often, but not at all necessarily, a particular plan. Occupation of this nature seems to be the hallmark of planning as a profession and of a planner as a professional.

By this working definition, land-use planners include those occupied in a professional planning capacity whether educated as such or with a background in other academic fields such as law, architecture, engineering, forestry, economics, sociology, or biology. Individuals from these and other educational areas can, and indeed often do, operate as professional planners and are so recognized. Further, it should be clear that common usage of the term "planning teams," as often applied to an interdisciplinary group, does not mean that its members are professional planners. The purpose of such a group is to bring a range of skills and knowledge to bear on a land-use problem. Planning is a function, and those engaged in it are not necessarily planners in a professional sense.

The term "planner," and public recognition of the title, has primarily come, as would be expected, from academic preparation in this area. In the United States, such preparation historically has developed primarily in an urban context. This is evident in collegiate course preparation and in professional associations which have strong influence on the establishment of titles.

The principal professional association in the United States was founded in 1917. It was originally called the American City Planning Institute but is now the American Institute of Planners. As of 1972, it had nearly 7,000 members including about 250 members in other countries, mostly in Canada. In 1972 it recognized forty-seven colleges and universities (three in Canada) as granting degrees accredited by the institute. These degrees are in some combination of city, urban, and regional planning (which is usually connected to city or urban planning curriculums). A person may become a member of the American Institute of Planning on the basis of examination plus several combinations of accepted education requiring graduate or bachelor degrees in planning or related to planning, plus a stipulated number of years of experience including professional planning experience. Membership can also be granted without requirement of such a degree on the basis of an examination plus 8 years of planning experience. This must include at least 3 years of professional planning experience. The AIP roster indicates that its membership is primarily employed in urban areas.

Landscape architecture is a well-known profession in the United States that is directly concerned with land-use planning, and its practitioners are recognized as planners. It is a very old profession with its historical origin in the design of artistic landscapes and gardens often in relation to buildings. The scope of the profession has, however, greatly broadened. Landscape architects are employed both in and out of urban areas. They are widely employed by the Bureau of Land Management, the U.S. Forest Service, the National Park Service, and other agencies or organizations, public and private. Their work includes the location and siting of buildings, the planning of campgrounds and other recreational developments, and the enhancement of landscape quality in road and trail location and construction. Academic graduates in geography often enter similar planning work.

Planners with professional education and experience in the planning process are largely employed as consultants working both individually and in consulting firms; as city, municipal, and county planners; and in state, regional, and federal agency planning offices.

For the most part, planners are not responsible for plan implementation although they may be well informed about such and act in an advisory capacity. They are normally not land-use administrators, managers, or natural resources specialists by either education or avocation. This is an important point that bears directly on the almost chronic difficulty in land-use work of merging the planning process smoothly into effective implementation. It is largely true and inescapable that planners plan but others execute. This comment is not made in criticism but in recognition of the problems of bringing together and meshing a wide range of skills, knowledge, experience, and means into successful application of land-use planning.

Planning Areas

In concluding this section, it will be helpful to give a brief survey of planning areas involving land use with which planners are primarily concerned. Three of them can be recognized: urban, regional, and nonurban land resource management. Throughout, it should be recognized that the potent political-social influence of urban areas, where most people live, extends to the most remote of wildlands, such as specific wilderness areas established by the Congress in the United States.

The urban area is best known to the public, and planning is a vital need here. This is where planning as a profession has primarily developed and where most planners using the title work. Problems here are with the immensely complex matters of city and urban planning. This includes land development and zoning controls, utilities, transportation, the many problems that stem from population growth, the struggle to maintain reasonable aesthetics as well as necessary functions, the so-called urban sprawl, and the difficult problems of inner-city decay in some of the older metropolitan areas. It is not possible here to detail these many and complex situations.

Regional planning is a term commonly used, but it has variable meanings and there is frequent lack of understanding. It is important to recognize that what may be considered as a region from a planning standpoint often does not coincide with political units of government. In the United States, a region may be part of a state, parts of two or more states, or two or more states in their entirety. Careful discrimination is also necessary as to the point of view from which regional planning is undertaken. In major degree it is done from an urban viewpoint. This means that concern is primarily about needs and problems relating to the direction of urban-related building, power and other utilities, transportation and communication, water supply, and mineral development. As commonly used, the term often does not include planning for all land resources in a land area such as is done for agriculture or forestry and other wildland uses.

Regional situations and problems involving land use that do not fit political boundaries have long been recognized in the United States, as elsewhere, and have received much study. Concern with regional situations is increasing with the trend toward the establishment of a national framework of land-use planning under federal policy direction and financial support that is implemented through state governments. There are strong and interrelated land resource, social, and political differences between such large regions as the Northeast, Southeast, Deep South, Southwest, and Pacific Northwest, to name some. Parallels also exist in other countries. There are also socioeconomic problem areas such as parts of West Virginia, eastern Kentucky, and the Upper Peninsula of Michigan, for example.

Concern with regional and concomitant planning is of long standing in the United States. In the past, action has centered largely on water control problems which are inherently regional. They are also geographically definable by natural drainage lines that seldom coincide with political boundaries. The first and only comprehensive major river basin planning and control authority established in the United States is the Tennessee Valley Authority. Continued and intensive study, planning, and action takes place under a wide range of intergovernmental or interagency pacts, agreements, and commissions. Cooperation and joint actions of many kinds between municipalities, counties, states, and the federal government is necessary to deal with complex political, economic, and administrative land-use situations.

Regional planning is not at all limited to watersheds, as it can include almost any kind of economic-social studies and planning applied to large land areas. This work dates from and took form with the establishment of the National Resources Planning Board (NRPB) in 1933, early in the New Deal of President Franklin D. Roosevelt. This Board was largely dominated by city planners and urban-oriented planners, who constituted most of the people professionally engaged in planning. The NRPB early got into regional planning, stimulated by the river basin planning interests of the time, but its scope soon extended to city, county, state, and national planning concerns. Its activity was largely confined to data collection, study, analysis, planning, and initiation of plan proposals, including those for the post-World War II period. The NRPB had minimal implementation authority. It was abolished by the Congress in 1943 with a limiting provision that its functions could not be transferred to other federal agencies. The history of the NRPB cannot be given here, but it did a great deal of work and gave considerable impetus to large-scale planning. Regional planning, as an entity and term, got its start with the NRPB, which also accounts for its inclusion in a number of city and urban academic educational units and its general urban slant.

A major and persistent problem of regional planning is meaningful and consistent definition of regional boundaries and planning purposes. Water drainages are useful and necessary for dealing with water supply and use problems which follow identifiable geographic boundaries. But these boundaries seldom coincide with socioeconomic areas of concern. These include metropolitan, industrial, and other growth areas, and transportation problems and related land-use pressures that transcend purposeful and integrative solution by individual governmental political units.

This situation is particularly evident in so-called distressed land-use areas. For example, the eastern Kentucky situation can be analyzed in terms of demographic data, land resources and uses, transportation problems, and a wide range of socioeconomic needs. This has indeed been done in great detail and can, for the most part, be identified by a definable geographic area. But solutions to these problems can at best be found only in part within the geographic area itself. Those living in the area cannot alone solve their plight. This is because their problems are deeply related to matters of transportation, employment, manufacture, markets, natural resource use as through outdoor recreation, and financial needs whose control lies outside the area. In land-use planning no one political or geographic unit can go it alone; a broader and more integrative approach is necessary.

The same general point also applies to urban affairs. Pumping more millions of dollars into declining city centers, for example, is not likely alone to solve their basic socioeconomic ills, which largely stem from their history. Solutions must in major degree come from outside the area.

In sharp contrast is the planning situation in nonurban areas wherein the planning function is related directly to renewable natural resources growing on the land. Agriculture and forestry are large-scale and good examples. A tremendous amount of detailed and continuing land-use planning is inherent in the crop-growing process. All farmers are necessarily planners, but they do not go by that name. A massive amount of land-use planning is done through cooperative and educational assistance given by the land-grant college system, including research and well-organized extension services; by the Soil Conservation Service and the related Soil Conservation District structure; and through various crop stabilization and subsidy programs. Although much planning is done in agriculture from the local to national level, rather few people use the professional designation of planner.

The same situation also generally applies in forestry. It is an old professional area equalled by few in the necessity for long-range and detailed planning. Much of it naturally is concerned with trees which are long-lived and exceedingly diverse in their cultural needs and use capabilities. As with agriculture, however, few practicing foresters go by or use the term "planner" as a professional designation; planning is simply built into their education and calling. The same can be said for civil engineers, who do a tremendous amount of planning as an inherent part of their work. But they do it as engineers and do not generally use the planner title.

In conclusion, the question of who is a planner remains a good one that cannot be consistently answered. The basic reason is that planning in land use, as in other areas, is performed by many people, not just by planners who use the title as a professional designation. It is hoped that the treatment here will clarify this point and give better understanding of planning and planner relationships.

Chapter 7

Value Measurement

How does one determine the value of something? This basic and difficult question is considered in this chapter with application to land use. The influence of values involved, however measured and weighted, permeates land-use actions. Values are implicit in planning processes presented in the preceding chapter. Design, public policy, information needs, and planner-planee relationships are all influenced by value considerations whether explicitly recognized or not. Value considerations also extend to plan continuity. Decision-making processes given in the following chapter necessarily have a value measuremment basis. In situations wherein costs and returns are adequately measurable in money, decisions can be made on the basis of direct monetary evaluation only. In situations less clearly definable in monetary terms, subjective value judgment necessarily influences decisions.

Value measurement should be thought of as an application of concepts, methods, and techniques of economics, taken in its broad social definition as the allocation of scarce resources. Land use includes too wide a range of value measurement questions to be a separate field. It is not so regarded here although land and its uses do offer special problems that have long been recognized, as in agricultural economics.

CONCEPTS AND PRINCIPLES OF VALUATION

A working knowledge of concepts and principles of valuation is basic to an understanding of methods of value measurement.

A first essential in considering valuation is to know what the word means. The key is the word "value," which has a number of meanings that require discrimination. Dictionary definitions are the best point for beginning to recognize the many usages of the word, as follows: [1]

> Amount of a commodity, service, or medium that is equivalent to something else; a fair return in goods, services, or money.
>
> The monetary worth of something; marketable price, usually in terms of a medium of exchange.
>
> Relative worth, utility and importance, degree of excellence, status in scale of preference.
>
> A liking or regard for persons or a thing (as an heirloom).
>
> A particular quantitative determination in mathematics; the amount or extent of a specified measurement of time, space, or quantity.
>
> Something (as a principle or quality or entity) intrinsically valuable or desirable.

"Worth" is a closely related word connoting more lasting and genuine merit resting on deeper, intrinsic, and enduring qualities; of human personality or abiding worth under the tests of civilization; judicious knowledge and the dignity of individual people.

Another important word, a form of which is used in the last definition of "value" above, is "intrinsic." Key parts of its definition (from the same source) are:

> Belonging to the inmost constitution or essential nature of a thing; essential or inherent and not merely apparent, as the very essence of a thing in virtue of the metaphysical structure of the universe.
>
> Originating or due to causes or factors within a body, organ, or part.
>
> Being good of itself or irreducible; being desirable or desired for its own sake and without regard to anything else.

Although "intrinsic" is sometimes applied to land, such usage is questionable. It is difficult to think of land as having value on account of its existence only, independently of any kind of use value on account of its location (views, etc.) or more direct uses.

These definitions merit careful study as they all can apply to land use.

The above definitions of value usefully can be summed up under two general meanings. The first, often termed "value in use," expresses the utility of something, its power directly or indirectly to satisfy the needs or desires of human beings. Value in use, and land often has such values, is not necessarily dependent on either scarcity or sale value. Air, for example,

[1] *Webster's Third New International Dictionary of the English Language Unabridged,* 1961.

certainly has a large value in use but normally no market value, as so much per cubic yard or mile. This is because it is not scarce in a general sense although millions are spent to condition its quality or to control it, as in buildings. An individual may prize a certain thing highly as an heirloom even though it may have no intrinsic value and although it may have no market value.

The second general meaning of value, and the normal economic usage, is value in exchange. This means the amount of other commodities, commonly represented by money, for which a good or service can be exchanged in the open market, i.e., value as measured by market price. For something to have value in exchange, it must be measurable and have attributes of both utility and scarcity in some degree.

In land-use affairs, there are many values in use which can be measured fairly completely in market-determined monetary terms, and others which cannot. Aesthetic, sentimental, recreational, wildlife, and water values associated with land are, for example, known to be large and often of decisive importance in determining land use. But they are imperfectly and incompletely measurable in monetary terms. This fact does not lessen their importance but does make their valuation difficult. Other values, such as lumber of specified volume and grade, can be rather readily expressed in monetary-exchange terms at a given place and time. This is true even though such a value does not necessarily equate to what these products are really worth to a user in any general or even economic sense.

The degrees to which land-use values can be expressed in monetary terms at a given time and place are continuous, forming a spectrum. There are intergradations but often no clear dividing lines. For this reason it is inaccurate categorically to speak of tangible and intangible, direct or indirect, market- or non-market-determined values. Differences are often in degree or viewpoint rather than absolute.

It is a fact of life, frequently apparent in land use as elsewhere but difficult to explain, that individuals as well as organizations place different values on money in different contexts. Due to early upbringing, education or lack of it, associates, class consciousness, or ability to manage, individuals often will spend their money in ways that defy any value-in-use rationality, at least as viewed by others. They will scarcely spend money for some things, yet spend beyond their means for others. The same general phenomenon applies to businesses and to different levels of government. When one considers changing price levels owing to real or inflationary trends, political situations, and the complexities of international exchange, money loses any consistent unit meaning. Future monetary values become even more uncertain.

This point is brought in here (the reader perhaps can do a better job of explaining it) for the reason that there are strong feelings about land, which is a very basic reality. There seems to be some kind of extra and human-oriented dimension to value measurement which must be reckoned with in land use. This point will come up again later in this chapter.

Market Value

Measurement of monetary values is closely associated with the concept of a market, a mechanism for their establishment. It is consequently important to be clear on what is meant by market value. The idea of a market gives a mental image of people with something to sell, freely mingling with those interested in buying at some common meeting place more or less accessible to all. Through bargaining, prices are agreed upon and goods and money change hands. This is indeed the classical concept of a market and market price establishment. It calls attention to the basic ingredients of goods or services available for sale, some avenue or means of making them known to prospective buyers, and the element of negotiation in setting a price based on factors of supply and demand. Although in a modern technological society the processes of marketing and price determination can be exceedingly complex, the concept of a market value remains and is of basic importance in determination of monetary values.

The most direct and basic definition of market value is the maximum amount of money obtainable for a good or property under prevailing market conditions, or, more bluntly, what something can be sold for. Such a definition, however, places emphasis on the fact of sale rather than on the conditions under which it is made. Sales can be made under conditions not measuring a "fair" or "reasonable" market value. There may be fraud, lack of adequate information on the part of either buyer or seller, or undue pressure to sell at a disadvantageous time. Sales made under such circumstances, although indubitably constituting and often influencing market prices, may not be indicative of a reasonable or stable market value. A generally accepted definition expressing conditions under which a "fair" market value can be established is the price at which a property would change hands in a transaction between a willing buyer and a willing seller, neither being under compulsion to buy or sell and both being reasonably informed as to all relevant facts. It should be recognized that a market value does not necessarily reflect the value to any particular individual or organization; it is often a compromise.

In the case of real estate, the following definition is particularly significant: "The market value of a property at a designated date is that competitively established price which represents the present worth at that date of all the rights to future benefits arising from ownership, and considering its highest and best use" (Henderson, 1931). The fact that a property value is essentially a forecast of the future is emphasized by the following statement by the famous jurist Oliver Wendell Holmes:

But the value of a property at a given time depends on the relative intensity of the social desire for it at the time expressed by the value it would bring in the market. Like all values, as the word is used by the law, it depends largely on more or less certain prophecies of the future; and value is no less or real at that time if later the prophecy turns out false, than when it comes true [*Ithaca Trust Co. v. United States* 279 U.S. 151 (1929)].

Even with its weaknesses and uncertainties, the concept of a fair market value is the primary and monetary economic base for valuation and is commonly applied wherever practicable. It is integrative and reflects values considered germane at a particular place and time. As will be brought out in this chapter, existing market values, where and as best they can be determined, are the beginning point in value measurement. One can then go on with estimates of non-market-determined values.

Nature and Purposes of Valuation

Valuation is the act or procedure of estimating the value of something. Appraisal means about the same thing and the two words are often used synonymously, although appraisal is commonly applied to valuation in a specific instance. For example, one can speak properly of the valuation of land in general and the appraisal of a particular parcel of land. Similarly, watershed land values may be evaluated but the value of land involved in a particular reservoir site would be appraised. Broadly, valuation is concerned with all values whether measurable in monetary terms or not. This point will be emphasized later in this chapter through illustrations.

Valuation, being a search for value, must be broad and flexible in its application and techniques. It is not an exact science, and a practitioner should not be misled by the apparent precision of mathematical computations or the seeming finality of an appraisal from an authoritative source. Judgment is involved in valuation, and this fact should never be forgotten. The goal should be to measure within a significant level of accuracy those things that reasonably can be measured in definite terms, and with an open mind to consider and weigh, as best one can, other values that are considered to be of significant importance. There is much scope for judgment in valuation work, but it should rest on the best facts available and not be offered as a substitute for them.

In large degree, value depends on the point of view, with the corollary that value changes with the use intended. This fact cannot be overemphasized, and its weight is continually apparent in land-use affairs.

For example, consider the difference in point of view between private sellers and buyers of a particular parcel of land with or without fixed improvements that necessarily go with the land. The sellers will consider values germane to them. They may be quite conscious of what they have paid for the property, including improvements and earnings that have been made, and of sentimental or other personal attachments that may influence their ideas of value. They have a price they hope to get and a minimum under which they will not sell except under compulsion. The viewpoint of the buyers is quite different. They are not concerned with past costs, improvements, or any factors of past use except as they may affect intended future use which may be quite different from the past. They would like to buy as cheaply as possible, and they have a maximum price above which they will not go. If the sellers and buyers have a common range of acceptable price, a sale may be arranged which is a compromise between their interests. Price in a particular instance consequently does not necessarily agree with any person's estimate of value, "fair" or otherwise.

Differences in value viewpoints are particularly evident when both public and private interests are involved. This is increasingly true in the present era of environmental concern. Public actions focus strongly on land use. Inclusion of public interests broadens the range and increases the complexity of value measurement. The public has the widest range of value interests, being concerned with practically all values, directly or indirectly. This certainly applies to land use, which is a very basic matter.

Those differences between public and private points of view in value measurement come to issue in the difficult matter of what weight to place on the passage of time. Time is inexorable, and the fact of its passage can be precisely measured. But its importance cannot be, as it varies with viewpoint. That of individuals is relatively short, as is their life span; time value varies greatly by age and outlook. Corporations, trusts, and such are technically timeless. This permits a long viewpoint, but the weight they place on time depends on their particular management objectives and situation.

Public interest, as expressed through governmental structures and processes, has, at least potentially, the longest time span of interest. But it is also true that governments may come and go and policies change. Actions can be shortsighted; in democracies, governments are directed by elected officials. Nevertheless, the public, through its agencies, has the responsibility and at least the potential to take a long and broad time interest in values that affect the general welfare. In a democratic society, the general function of government is to protect common interests and to supply those services and facilities promoting public welfare that private enterprise cannot safeguard or provide. In a field so broad and so deeply affecting many interests as land use, wide differences between public and private viewpoints regarding values are both natural and to be expected.

To summarize this section, there are three underlying and closely related problems common to most appraisals as applications of value measurement.

First, the point of view, purpose, and values germane in a particular situation must be identified. This is often a difficult problem. Valuation must be for a purpose, and as has been indicated, purposes may vary widely. A key question in valuation work is *who* is to receive the value. This may make a great deal of difference in the values to be considered and in the appropriate evaluation methods to apply. Value must be appraised for a purpose and cannot be an independent or abstract entity.

Second, the appropriate methods or procedures applicable must be defined and consistently applied. *How* the valuation is to be made is often a difficult problem.

Third, the values that are considered to be involved must be measured or estimated in some meaningful way. Different *kinds* of values may be involved in the same situation or issue, making analytic comparisons difficult. Values germane in a particular situation may be known in general terms as may methods appropriate to their measurement. But successful appraisal may be prevented by inability meaningfully to measure values believed to be significant.

Interest and Investment

As everyone knows, money is a commodity, a medium of exchange. It is necessary, useful, and highly transportable. The use of money over time is worth something to the borrower as the basis for investment, and to the owner for its use. This fact is the basis for charging a rental price for the use of money over time by its owner. The rental price for money is termed interest. It is commonly stated as a percentage of the money borrowed on a yearly basis, but the actual rental period may be a small fraction of a year.

Individuals, private organizations, and governments borrow money and pay interest on it. The national debt of the United States government, on which interest is paid, is colossal and staggers the imagination. Other governmental units also borrow money and have to pay interest. Basically, interest is due to be paid only *after* a period of time as stipulated by agreement, normally a year or less. Prepaid interest, often applied on short-term loans, is interest deducted in advance at the time of loan and before it is due. Although a convenient practice, it has no economic rationale, as the user does not have the use of all the money borrowed.

As long as interest is paid when due, as in normal business practice, there can be no accumulation or compounding of principle. If interest is not paid when due, the question then arises as to whether this interest should be regarded as an accumulated bill payable and separate from principal or as an addition to the borrowed principal. If what is termed simple interest is applied, the amount of the principal remains constant, whether interest is paid when due or not. Interest is computed only on this amount.

There are many investment reasons, whether stipulated by contract or owing to other circumstances, why interest is not or cannot be paid when due but accumulates over a period of time. Land use is full of examples where the return on an investment is necessarily deferred. A good example is investment in establishing a forest stand by planting. By the deliberate nature of forest growth, little or no current income may be available for a number of years on a particular tract planted. An investment has been made on which the returns necessarily are deferred to some future time.

In such a situation the investor may quite properly take the position that interest due is capital which he or she could reinvest to earn interest. Consequently interest due *is added to the principal,* and interest is figured on an increasing total capital sum. This process of adding interest due to the initial capital is called compounding, and interest so accumulated is termed compound interest. There is no fallacy to such a process except that compounding can be carried to extremes beyond the realm of business reality. For example, the amount of a $100 loan at 8 percent per annum would amount to $108 at the end of 1 year and $222,000 at the end of 100 years!

By reversing the process, termed discounting, the present value of a promise to pay $100 at a time 100 years in the future is only 4 cents. Either of these examples may seem to be ridiculous, but it is for this very reason that commercial savings banks place a definite time limit on an inactive savings account to stop interest compounding.

To put the matter in broader terms, interest is a monetary expression of the importance of the passage of time. This is a very basic dimension in human terms and leads to the concept of time preference. Individual or organizational time preferences may vary widely and for many reasons. If there are urgent or overriding present needs, time preference is high. For example, a person with an urgent present need for food or to meet a family emergency has a high time preference that may overshadow a greater advantage in the future. This matter of time preference is of major and real consequence in land use. People living at a low subsistence level on the land often will destructively utilize their natural resources to survive. Similarly, to gain current and inevitably transitory prosperity, countries can and do exploit natural resources beyond sustainable capacity.

At the governmental level, and also taking long-time natural resource and environmental considerations into account, time preference and financial considerations become both extremely important and difficult to evaluate. National and international energy and food needs give global examples.

Generally speaking, government has concern and responsibility for social welfare both present and extending into the indefinite future. It takes great saving and investment, along with large energy requirements, to operate a technological society. Such a society has the capacity not only to utilize nonrenewable resources destructively but also to plan wisely and firmly to husband them for the future. The difficulty, even dilemma, is that in a political democracy the government is in large degree a reflection of the people who sustain it. Governments also operate on a monetary basis. Their income is derived mainly from public taxation and is expended in monetary units. Governments borrow and loan money, pay and collect interest. In this respect, government is big business but of a special kind.

Present needs are always real and pressing, whether governmental or private. The problem is how to establish a sustainable balance, to meet present needs and also plan, regulate, and finance for the future. This need comes to particular focus in land-resource management, which is basic, slow-moving, and often expensive and entails values difficult to measure. Any serious student of land use must also be a student of people, their organizations, and their behavior.

In different forms and applications these basic questions of public finance and policy enter into a number of the value measurement situations given later in this chapter.

VALUATION PROBLEMS AND APPROACHES

The preceding section has given a framework of valuation processes needed to approach actual problems of value measurement. The purpose of this section is to apply them in a wide range of valuation situations. The examples are presented in four groups. Although the items within a group may seem widely different, they have some major attribute in common.

Most of these illustrations involve land use in one way or another since so many things that people do or want ultimately, if not directly, come from the land and its many natural resources. However, some examples are drawn from other sources to round out the treatment and to emphasize the breadth of valuation approaches.

The illustrations given here deal primarily with personal and public values. These emphasize the more subjective situations requiring judgment. This is where established valuation methods, as market determination, are often not adequate. Some of the situations at first thought may seem easy to evaluate but are not. For example, it is common presupposition that the value of something is measured by what one will pay. This does indeed seem a direct, logical, and realistic approach. It is definite and economic, and money is a near-universal medium of exchange. But there are two sides to monetary transactions which apply separately and differently to buyers and sellers. For buyers to receive what they consider a benefit, they also sustain a cost. So do sellers; they too give something of value for what they receive. There is a general assumption that the cost measures the benefit, or vice versa, but this may or may not be true in terms of real gratification or satisfaction. Examples range from unwanted medical expense to cherished outdoor recreation at little or no cost to the individual. Such examples illustrate the tremendous range of benefit-cost situations to which different scales and criteria of value are applied.

Expenditures for public welfare illustrate the same kind of problem. The benefits received are difficult specifically to measure. So are the public costs, as they are derived essentially from taxation, and taxation is difficult to evaluate consistently since monetary units have different values by context and point of view.

In introducing this section, the author is acutely aware that valuation is a massive and most complex field in both practice and literature. There is disagreement between students as well as practitioners. The reader is encouraged to use this section as an exercise in value identification and measurement—to criticize, revise, add other examples, and apply different points of view. Valuation is a search for value and one that will never end.

Personal Use Values

Four items are given here that are indicative of the range in personal use value situations.

An Heirloom An heirloom, or some similar thing, has personal value to the owner but normally little actual use value. It would not have value in exchange unless it had intrinsic value (gold, precious stones, etc.) or historical interest of market value.

Household Equipment One buys new household equipment at market price. But once bought, it becomes secondhand and its resale value immediately drops, usually substantially, although value in use to the owner normally continues undiminished for considerable time. This is a very common situation. It illustrates differences in viewpoint between selling price and resale value; both may be independent of change in use value.

A Painting The value of a painting inherently is a matter of judgment. To a private owner the value is primarily one of personal possession. To a public museum a painting is essentially an item of public service value, as it is usually supported by some mixture of private endowment and public monies. There is also a highly developed commercial market structure for paintings. They are appraised and bought and sold on the market. Their valuation is based on many considerations such as age, artistic quality, reputation of the artist, current popularity of new or old art forms, and investment value. Supply and demand governs in the normal economic sense.

A Pleasing View Many people highly value a pleasing view from their home, such as a view of mountains or water, an overview of a city, an attractive open-space view in urban surroundings, or even some kind of interesting outlook from a corner apartment in the city. In varying degree, the same considerations apply to attractive places of work. These values are well recognized in real estate appraisal. But their measurement is largely a matter of judgment guided by market experience. To the owner or user such values are subjective, but they are very real as expressed in willingness to pay, which is the economic evidence of value.

Personal Experience Values

These are a group of recreation activities which cost money, result in personal enjoyment and satisfaction in one way or another, and exhibit different degrees of tangibility in value measurement.

An Evening of Bowling   With bowling, as with similar kinds of recreation, a price is paid for use of facilities. To the owner, who expects to make a profit in a competitive market, the price is the benefit. As regards the bowler, the implicit assumption is that the benefit received will at least equal cost. Just what these benefits are is less clear. People go bowling for many reasons. Some go to gain skill in the game itself, as a solitary bowler interested in practice and possibly in future competition. Others go primarily for social reasons: to meet people and to make and enjoy friends. This often includes making business-professional contacts of benefit to the individual. This simple situation illustrates the fact that human experience values received are personal and only indirectly measured by monetary cost.

A Visit to a Public Park (Near an Urban Center)   This is a more complex situation. Since the public park is publically supported, entrance is often free; if a charge is made, it is likely to be nominal. In economic terms, the land value opportunity cost of the park area is probably high. Park operating costs are also substantial although taxes are not paid. The park is owned and managed in the public interest, and its costs are not balanced against fees charged. There is no adequate way for the park administration monetarily to evaluate user benefits other than measuring the number and duration of user visits.

On the user side, benefits are social and varied. They include walking, swimming, picnicking, playing games, meeting friends, and the pleasure of seeing and identifying birds, trees, etc. Regarding costs, there may be significant expense entailed in getting to and from the park by automobile or common carrier. Heavy traffic can also cause disservices to people. In park-use analysis much attention is given to average distances traveled by visitors to a particular park as a part of evaluating needs for additional parks.

A Visit to a National Park   The national parks are managed in the public interest for the benefit and enjoyment of the people without impairment to distinctive natural features. Uses of a national park for recreational or educational purposes give added dimension to personal experience valuation. Nearly all the national parks came from federal public lands although some private land has been purchased to consolidate landownership. Consequently, there is no meaningful land investment cost. Entrance fees are nominal and do not equate to park development and management costs.

On the user side, both costs and benefits received are varied. The basic purpose of the parks is to make it possible for the public to see their outstanding natural features and at the same time to preserve them for all time. Seeing these features is a personal experience, an exhilaration of the spirit that is hard indeed to evaluate.

Actual costs are often substantial. Because most of the parks are in the Western states and far from major population centers, user travel costs are considerable. But these costs are often divided among visits to several parks, national forests, and other places. One must keep in mind that the pleasures of vacation travel itself can be regarded as much a benefit as a cost. At or near the national parks are a variety of accommodations ranging from expensive hotels to relatively inexpensive campgrounds. Within the parks, such accommodations are often operated as private concessions under park contract and close supervision, with prices often approaching fully commercial rates.

The point of emphasis here is that people visit the national parks for a variety of reasons, often intermixed with other travel purposes. This fact makes it difficult to measure costs incurred and personal values received by visitors. Many studies and estimates have indeed been made, but much uncertainty remains.

Outdoor Camping Camping, excluding back yard sleep-outs, is a generic term for a means of enjoying a wide range of outdoor activities, primarily recreational. It is a more or less economical way to go places, see and do things, and be with or visit friends in a nonurban environment. Equipment varies from expensive single-unit campers or towed trailers, to tent and related equipment transported by car, to the minimum of equipment used in backpacking. The furnishing of camping equipment is a large and growing business operated on an economic market value basis. Direct costs for furnishing such can be measured accordingly.

Provision of land space and facilities required for camping comes from both the private and the public sector. As it increasingly comes from the private sector it consequently is subject to normal economic evaluation; i.e., the camping price paid measures the cost plus profit to the supplier and the willingness of the camper to pay. It is also an important fact that private campground owners capitalize in substantial degree on the value of nearby public lands whose use is free or nearly so. On the larger public campgrounds the trend is for the charge to approach or equal that for private campgrounds.

Values to the user from camping are varied and cannot be directly measured beyond saying that, in the judgment of the user, they exceed monetary cost. Otherwise increasing numbers of people would not seek a camping experience and spend the time and money. Values can be grouped in two general categories. First is the camping experience itself. This includes getting away from home, the do-it-yourself aspects of more or less simplified living and self-reliance, and acquiring some woodsman skills. Second, camping is a convenient, inexpensive, and flexible way to travel and to do such things as swim, boat, hike, and visit national parks, national forests, and other places of interest. In this respect, camping can be largely a means to many other ends, which further complicates any direct valuation of a camping experience.

A Deer in the Woods   What is the value of a deer in wildland woods? This depends primarily on the point of view of the person who sees it. To the landowner, there is little direct cost beyond that of wildland management. The costs directly attributable to deer production are likely to be small and unidentifiable. This is particularly true on public lands.

People who see the deer may be divided into two general groups. First are people who get much pleasure in the outdoor experience of seeing deer and other wildlife in their natural habitat. This is worth a good deal to many people (including the author, who has spent much time in the woods but who has never shot nor particularly wanted to shoot a deer). The same sort of values naturally extend to seeing and learning about wildlife habitats generally. These values are difficult to define but are important and can only partially be related to or measurable by costs.

The second group are those who hunt. Here again, purposes and values are several and difficult to evaluate. But they are substantial, as evidenced by the number of hunters and often high costs of hunting. An obvious value is meat, which, properly handled, is excellent. Hunting for food was, of course, important in earlier times and still is in some parts of the world. But presently it is an expensive way to get meat, although estimates of such value are made and have some meaning depending on the particular locale.

Another value is the satisfaction of stalking and killing something, the release, perhaps, of a primal urge. This value will have to be taken for what it is worth. But it does exist, although open recognition of it is generally avoided.

Hunters also enjoy being in the woods. Hunting is often only incidental, an excuse for a trip into the woods. Hunting trips are often highly social affairs with pursuit of wildlife providing the occasion.

On the cost side, hunting is often expensive. This can be measured in terms of guns and related equipment, transportation, food and shelter, guides, game licenses, charges to hunt on private lands, getting game out of the woods, etc. The sporting-goods business is large and an indicator of hunting values. Adding up hunting costs gives some indication of values, but this indicates only what people will pay and only partially measures value to the user.

Perhaps the best way to characterize deer-hunting values to people, and this applies to many such outdoor experiences, is to say it comes in four parts: anticipation, preparation, participation (the seeing or doing), and remembrance (telling stories about it afterward). These are all important personal values which are left for the reader to evaluate.

A Wilderness Experience   Much has been written about the virtues of a "wilderness experience," but specific evaluation remains elusive. The basic reason is that the experience is subjective. For this reason there is currently much controversy and some confusion in the United States about establishment of public wilderness areas. There are many viewpoints. Politically, wilderness areas are supported by many who have no real understanding of wilderness problems or intent for personal participation.

A wilderness experience can include the opportunity to be in a truly wildland area, to see and feel the wonders and powers of living nature, to experience solitude, to contemplate, to try to sort out basic values, and to seek renewal of the spirit. These things are elusive and difficult to put into words, but there is something fundamental about wildlands that appeals to people, young or old, whether or not they have any real understanding of wildland areas. Preferably, one should travel with a partner or in a small group. Reaction to wilderness is an individual matter that depends on age and outlook. Size of the area is not controlling; one can have a wilderness feeling in a small wildland area removed from the sounds and sights of human activity. This feeling can be lessened and become outdoor sightseeing on a large horseback group trip into the back country. What constitutes a "wilderness experience" is indeed a personal, elusive, and subjective matter.

Wilderness areas are being established on a large scale on federal lands in the United States. This is done by acts of Congress designating such areas under the Wilderness Act of 1964 (P.L. 88-577).[2] What is an official wilderness area consequently becomes a matter of specific land selection which must conform to definition by law. These areas are managed by the public land agency having administrative responsibility. Selection of wilderness areas in the United States is a difficult and controversial matter as public and private viewpoints vary widely.

As would be anticipated in large wildland areas where human action (such as timber cutting) is to be suppressed and "natural" conditions main-

---

[2] Treatment here is limited, somewhat arbitrarily, to official wilderness areas. There are other public lands with similar or equal wildland values.

tained, there are difficult management problems inherent to wilderness use. These include practical questions such as the quality and amount of trails (there can be no roads); the number of people to be admitted and their distribution (users concentrate on a limited number of travel routes and camping places); whether horses should be permitted or excluded; whether or not wood can be cut or open fires built; means of disposing or removing trash; how much if any control action should be taken on natural disasters from insects, diseases, or forest fire. The key wilderness problems are managerial rather ideological.

As to valuation, wilderness areas are highly subsidized. There are no entrance fees on national forest lands although there is much public administration cost. Wilderness use in national parks is subject only to the park entrance fee. Beyond getting to and from a wilderness, which can be expensive, costs to the user are relatively low. Only backpacking equipment is necessary. This, however, eliminates people who would like to visit wilderness areas but are physically incapable of or lack the skills for such travel. Use of horses removes much of the personal fitness limitations but is expensive and requires professional outfitters. Whether hunting should be allowed is a moot question.

Users can and should get high inspirational and recreational value from a wilderness trip. But value measurement is difficult as with other largely personal and subjective experiences. It is hard to go beyond the fact of political support of wilderness areas and what visitors will pay. Basically, wilderness is a land-use value personal to an individual. Much the same value can be received on other wildlands.

Public Policy Values in Land-Use Valuation

Emphasis in this section shifts from personal and individual values to public land-use values as expressed in land-use policy actions. The two land-use illustrations given here are indicative of a wide range of situations and problems.

Coastal Wetlands   Public interest in wetlands, both coastal and inland, is deep and of long standing. Attention here is on coastal wetlands, especially tidal lands and related salt marshes. Increasing ecological-environmental concern has placed much emphasis on use of these lands, the supply is limited, and public values recognized are high and becoming higher. Both public and privately owned land-use interests are involved (Brahtz, 1972; Gosselink et al., 1973; Odum and Odum, 1972).

Principal land-use value considerations are given here in four groups.

1   Natural and self-renewable land-use values are high but are only in part recognized by the public. These wetlands provide a major segment of a complex food chain of high productivity which extends out to sea and supports much wildlife and offshore fisheries. They also give important assistance in biological disposal of waste from urbanized areas. There are substantial wildlife and recreation values as well.

2   Land development values are also high. They are directly measurable by market prices for maritime and other industry construction, agricultural uses, recreation, and housing. There is a growing trend for population to increase in coastal areas.

3   Coastal zone lands, especially wetlands, are ecologically very sensitive. Changes from natural to other land uses are essentially irreversible. It is often not unduly difficult to ditch, drain, and dam such lands, but once this is done such land is not likely to revert to its natural condition within any humanly significant period of time.

4   There is a large amount of private landownership. This raises a basic policy question as to how far the public interest, as expressed in terms of imposing regulatory controls on the use of private lands, can go without legally constituting land expropriation without fair compensation. When reasonably applied, land-use classification through zoning is a powerful tool (Chap. 4). If this is done *before* nonconforming development is undertaken, the private owner does not then have solid basis to claim injustice for not being allowed to develop land for a nonconforming but higher-value use.

As indicated above, value measurement of coastal wetlands is complex and difficult. Land values for real estate development are measured in the marketplace with a high time preference. What about values in the public interest to keep these lands in natural condition? There is a timeless yield of natural values from such lands without any development or cost. Here is where normal economic concepts of valuation, of interest accumulation and discount over time are inadequate. Time preference should be low from a public-interest standpoint, as the public can and should take a long view in such matters.

It is possible here only to indicate the basic direction and approach to answers. In a political democracy, these finally are determined by the collective judgment of people at whatever local, state, or federal level of governmental influence is involved. The "rightness" of the decision can be measured only by how fully, fairly, and honestly concerned people are informed and advised.

Farmland for Urban Development   There are recurrent problems of economic and public policy about agricultural land of varying quality being put to urban use. Agricultural lands have directly measurable market value, as does land in urban use. The question is whether to let economic forces operate or take special action in the public interest to maintain what is considered to be an adequate domestic agricultural base for food production. A penetrating analysis of this economic valuation problem is given by Peters (1970) with particular reference to Great Britain. There are several valuation approaches but no simple solutions.

Similar problems are widespread in the United States and of rising concern. Zoning increasingly is being applied but not yet generally; an instance is given in Chap. 4. Another approach is through land taxation. General practice, frequently specified in state constitutions, is to apply land taxation on an ad valorem or present-market-value basis. Lacking zoning restriction, taxes on agricultural lands under urban-use pressure tend to rise beyond the ability of a farmers to pay and they have to sell. Some states have amended their constitutions to permit tax valuation on a use, rather than on a market, basis. This helps, but recognition of both use and market value as a tax base is difficult to administer in practice without strict regulation. One reason is that an agricultural land-use rate may be claimed and used as a tax shelter with intention later to sell for urban uses. Where pressures are strong, taxation can only slow and regulate the movement of land from farm to urban use.

Public Assistance and Subsidies

A general principle of government is that it should give assistance and aid in the public interest beyond what the private sector can supply. The range of public assistance given in aids and subsidies is large, as is the literature on this subject. An indication of value measurement problems is given in the following three American-based illustrations which in principle can apply elsewhere.

Small Private Forest Landownerships   About 60 percent of the nearly 500 million acres of forested lands growing timber of commercial quality in the United States are in small and nonindustrial private ownership. Predominantly, the ownerships are less than 100 acres each. These lands are distributed widely over the United States but mainly east of the Mississippi River. In total, these lands are owned by about 4½ million people for a multitude of reasons, mostly not including any kind of purposeful forest management. Much of this land is near urban areas where the trend is toward urban-dominated uses.

Dating back to the Clarke-McNary Act of 1924, (43 Stat. 653), the federal government has worked in cooperation with the states in an increasingly large program designed to educate and assist these smaller owners to apply better forest practices. Forest industry and other private organizations also contribute substantially to the improvement of forest management practices by these small owners. Control of wildfires is also a major part of the total federal-state cooperative program.

Over the years, many millions of public money (more is spent by the states than by the federal government) has been expended in this work, which goes much beyond the original Clarke-McNary Act. The primary economic and public value justification for such assistance is the fact that these ownerships do contribute an important part of the total wood supply in the United States. It is true that emphasis in this cooperative assistance program has been to encourage timber production. But it is also true that the effects of this program are much broader. Many people increasingly have been given help and encouragement to understand and manage their forested lands for their particular interests whether or not with emphasis on wood production.

This forestry program is a good example of large-scale expenditures that have been made in the public interest but for which no specific equating of public costs with values received can be given. In final terms, validation of the program rests on the fact that it has received enough public support to indicate that it is politically favored by a sufficient segment of the public.

Grazing on Western Public Lands   Grazing on public land is very different from the preceding example and has long historical roots. It undoubtedly gives the largest United States illustration of the persistence of established land uses that tend to be claimed as rights. These were developed on large areas of Western frontier lands before there was any effective assertion of public landownership or control. In some degree, the influence of these claimed rights remains today. There are similar historical parallels in Europe (Chap. 11).

For a good many years after the great Louisiana Purchase of 1803 by the young United States, the central and northern Rocky Mountains of the West continued to be peopled by Indians—who had not been consulted about the purchase. White settlement of the West began after the California Gold Rush of 1849. One great natural resource was the grasslands, and soon the great Western livestock industry was born. "The grass was free" (Howard, 1943), and the federal land went with it. The first Texas trail herd was driven to what is now Montana in 1866. It was near the end of the 1800s before the federal government was able to establish any effective control over grazing on public lands.

The Western stockmen were initially entirely dependent, and substantially still are in some areas, on public grazing lands now administered by the Bureau of Land Management and the Forest Service. Because of this long frontier history of open range, the stockman rather naturally came to feel that they should play a large part in the management of these lands. This continues to the present time in proposals that the government should give some stockmen's associations large management control over the public lands their members graze.

On the economic side, there has been long controversy over the amount of grazing fees to be charged on public lands. For years, fees were nominal and constituted a public subsidy. There has been strong resistance to raising the fees to approach market value despite the results of long and detailed grazing value appraisals made by the public agencies. For many years the Western livestock industry had strong national political influence, but its power has decreased in recent years. A large shift of the beef-growing business to the Southeast and Middle West is probably the most important reason.

The above is an example of a large public subsidy involuntarily given over a long period to a segment of private enterprise. Because of the historical circumstances, there is no useful way to evaluate the situation in monetary terms. It must be regarded as a part of building the West.

The Civilian Conservation Corps   In sharp contrast to the preceding illustration are public aids and subsidies which combine land-use protection and improvement with social welfare objectives in the public interest. The Civilian Conservation Corps, which began in 1933 in the Great Depression of the 1930s is an outstanding example. It has continued in different forms since and remains an active concept.

Hundreds of work camps, mostly in 200-man units (although often divided into smaller working units or "spike" camps), were established in the United States. They were located primarily on federal and state lands, but some were on private lands. The purpose was to give employment, at nominal wage, to young men to do work of public value on mainly nonurban lands. This work included soil conservation and water control; construction of roads, bridges, and telephone lines; forest fire prevention (hazard reduction mainly), construction of lookout towers, and fire suppression; forest and range improvement, administrative building construction, and much outdoor recreation development. The operation and supply of the camps was handled by the Army. Both federal and state agencies directed the work program.

> When the program was at its peak in 1935 there were 52,000 enrolees in 2,652 camps, of which about half were forestry camps. Altogether, the Corps gave employment to approximately three million men at a cost of some 2 ½ billion dollars (Dana, 1956).

A general and largely urban parallel that mostly employed older people was the Works Progress Administration (WPA), which, along with other relief agencies, did many kinds of improvement and assistance work.

From a valuation standpoint, the millions of dollars spent on these programs can be estimated, but the value of these dollars in accomplishments defies specific determination. What was accomplished must be evaluated in human-social returns, in alleviation of human value erosion from unemployment, and in stimulation to the general economy. Much of what was done can be expressed in physical units, such as miles of road built, number of buildings constructed, or acres of forest land planted. The direct costs have been estimated. There is, however, no basis consistently to determine how much of the work done was "made," that is, would not have been done in normal times. This part would have to be supported by some estimate of general welfare.

VALUATION IN THE PUBLIC INTEREST

The preceding section dealt with a wide range of value measurement situations on an item-by-item basis with emphasis on personal and social aspects. The purpose was to indicate the nature, range, and scope of valuation problems, and general approaches to their measurement.

This section concerns valuation of large-scale and often highly integrative investments that deeply involve the public interest. These are dominantly but not entirely construction works. They include such things as urban redevelopment projects and dams and related structures for flood control, irrigation, and power development. There is deep public concern about both costs and benefits of such projects.

It should be emphasized that, although publically financed construction is most commonly thought of, privately financed construction is an alternative and a good one where practicable. Treatment here will focus on the more basic and recurrent valuation problems because they apply to both private and public investment. Major emphasis is, however, placed on governmental projects for the reason that they include benefits and costs that go beyond what private enterprise can undertake.

Benefit-Cost Analysis

Benefit-cost analysis has a wide range of meanings that depend on viewpoint and usage. In any context, individual, business, or public, it means that whatever are considered to be meaningful benefits and costs are considered and weighed. These can be direct or indirect, and whether amenable to specific measurement or to subjective judgment. There are no necessary restrictions inherent to the term. Benefit-cost analysis is not, except by particular definition or usage, a special valuation method or diciplinary field or study. Its roots are primarily in economics, although it also draws on other social sciences and applied fields such as business and engineering.

Costs are incurred in expectation of benefits. These can be positive or negative in the sense of preventing loss or damage. In most transactions, there is a cost and an expected return which can be expressed in monetary or other terms, depending on the circumstances. Basically, benefit-cost analysis looks at both. There is always the point-of-view question of who pays for what and who receives the benefits. Benefit-cost analysis can be applied to household management, business, and government concerns. It should be recognized, however, that major use of the term is in analysis of physical, usually long-time investments made in the public interest by governmental agencies.

At this point it is well to consider *why* benefit-cost analysis is so important and is required in public investments. Following are some major reasons.

1 Public investment necessarily operates on an economic, a monetary, base. Government collects its tax revenues in money and pays in money for salaries, wages, and goods purchased. It also borrows, pays interest, and repays debts in money. The United States, for example, has a colossal public debt on which it pays interest. Public finance in budgetary terms is also, and necessarily, conducted on a monetary base. There consequently are strong reasons to evaluate public investments in monetary terms insofar as possible.

2 Money, in terms of capital resources, is always limited in relation to the collective demands of people. There is strong competition for public projects that are claimed to be in the public interest. To guide and give basis for decisions which are political in the final analysis, a defensible, rational, and insofar as possible quantitative appraisal is needed to justify proposed projects. Benefit-cost analysis in public use is applied to give answers; it is both a planning and a decision-making necessity.

3 Large projects entailing major construction require an incredible amount of planning that may go on for years. Particularly on complex multiple projects, much evaluative comparison of alternatives must be made to arrive at, as nearly as possible, the best one. These alternatives can include no construction at all. Many costs and benefits, whether in monetary terms or not, must systematically and comparatively be considered and each given weight as equitably as possible.

4 The actual construction, including timing and coordination of many actions, often requires years and may necessitate changes, adjustments, and the meeting of contingencies that develop during the project development period. These must be foreseen insofar as possible. Risks can be estimated and allowances for uncertainty can be made through strategic and flexible planning.

5 Public understanding and support of public projects is necessary. This requires more than technical construction plans. What these plans mean in both human and physical terms must reasonably be understood and accepted by concerned people.

6 Working relationships must be established between federal, state, county, municipal, and local governments. This need complicates the planning process and requires systematic procedures to make planning information available.

7 Finally, rising national concern with the protection of environmental quality necessitates searching evaluation of both positive and negative effects of proposed projects.

The above reasons have necessitated public statement of principles, purposes, and standards to be followed in guiding application of the general benefit-cost analysis approach. In the United States, the need for written formulation of such guidelines has developed from many years of experience with large-scale federal-related public water and land resources development (U.S. Water Resources Council, 1973). These are stated in the above publication as follows:

> These principles are established for planning the use of water and related land (hereinafter referred to as water and land) resources of the United States to achieve objectives, determined cooperatively, through the coordinated actions of the Federal, State, and local governments; private enterprise and organizations; and individuals.
> The overall purpose . . . is to promote the quality of life, by reflecting society's preference for attaining the objectives defined below:
>   A. To enhance national economic development by increasing the value of the Nation's output of goods and services and improving national economic efficiency.
>   B. To enhance the quality of the environment by the management, conservation, preservation, creation, restoration or improvement of the quality of certain natural and cultural resources and ecological systems.

The standards that implement the above principles "apply to Federal participation in Federal-State cooperative planning and should also provide a useful guide to State and local planning."

A useful similar report has been published in Canada (Sewell et al., 1965). It is intended for use by both public and private organizations but does not carry governmental policy authority.

Benefit-Cost Ratios   Because benefit-cost analysis has an economic basis, a necessary initial step in making comparative project analyses is to express measurable benefits and costs in quantitative money terms. As an overall criterion, benefits should at least equal costs so that the B/C ratio is not less than 1. Following marginal analysis principles, for various levels of project development where such comparisons are possible, there is also a point where the B/C *ratio* is the highest, and another point where net benefits exceed costs by a maximum amount.

The relative significance of such comparisons depends on particular circumstances and objectives; from beginning to end the process is a weighing of alternatives. Necessarily, comparisons must be made on comparable terms. For example, maximization of net benefits does not take into account the absolute level of costs involved to produce them. To illustrate (Sewell et al., 1965), two possible alternative projects may have equal net

	Project A	Project B
Total costs	$1,000,000	$10,000,000
Total benefits	2,000,000	11,000,000
Net benefit	1,000,000	1,000,000
Benefit-cost ratio	2.0	1.1

benefits but one costs several times as much as the other: Project B obviously is not as financially productive as Projective A. Where operating costs are high in relation to investment, it is useful also to calculate a net benefit-investment ratio in addition to a benefit-cost ratio for comparative purposes. The reason is that operating costs can be set against current income, which reduces investment carrying costs.

Economic benefit-cost analysis in ratio form is useful and commonly used in making project comparisons on an economic basis. This applies especially during the planning stage when a wide range of possible alternatives is considered and weighed. It is, however, a measure of relative rather than of absolute merit. Final decisions often include other considerations which also temper judgment. A number of these are given in the following section.

Value Measurement Approaches or Considerations

The purpose here is to present a rather mixed group of items that constitute, or directly relate to, value measurement in the public interest. They apply to benefit-cost analysis at the federal level in the United States, and most of them are included in or relate to federal planning guidelines. Their use, however, is not so limited. They also apply generally to other countries and political units and to private business. Readers are welcome to add or amend according to their situations and purposes.

Viewpoints   As has been previously stated, ideas of value strongly relate to the point of view taken. This fact is of pervading importance in value measurement. The federal government, collectively, has the widest viewpoint in terms of value interest and responsibility. Many and often conflicting pressures are exerted on it. State and local government also face many interests and pressures. They are equally demanding, occur at different levels, and reflect different viewpoints. Local people affected by public construction have strong interests, individually or collectively, and press them vigorously.

In addition, there can be strong differences of professional opinion within planning groups. Opinions may differ as to relative emphasis to place on economic valuation in relation to extra-market and more social approaches; desirable project size and scope; priorities, methods, and technical feasibility. A great many viewpoints, political and individual, have to be considered and melded. This applies particularly to a large construction project which usually has important irreversible economic and environmental effects.

Time and the Interest Rate   Large water and nonurban development projects require a number of years, sometimes a decade or more, to execute. They also have an operating life that may be very long, as in dam projects. Urban renewal projects are in the same general category, as they require long and essentially irreversible land-use commitment. The rate of interest used to measure the economic importance of the passage of time consequently is of major significance. To compare different parts of multipurpose projects, which may be constructed and become operative over different periods in time, or to compare alternative projects also differing in cost and investment period, it is necessary to bring them to some common time base. Interest, the earning power of money over time, is the only means of so doing.

Determination of the rate of interest used consequently becomes a critical matter about which experts can and do disagree. After extremely thorough study, the federal interest rate in the United States was set as follows: The interest rate to be used in plan formulation and evaluation for discounting future benefits and costs, or otherwise converting benefits and costs to a common time basis, "shall be based upon the estimated average cost of Federal borrowing as determined by the Secretary of the Treasury taking into consideration the average yield during the twelve months preceding his determination on interest-bearing marketable securities of the United States with remaining periods to maturity comparable to a 50-year period of investment . . . " (U.S. Water Resources Council, 1973).

Valuation of Alternatives and Effects   It is the prime tenet in federal planning that all reasonable and viable alternatives must be considered, including the effects of no construction. The number of possible alternatives can, of course, be unduly extended; reason has to be applied. Consideration of alternatives also means that federal projects, although beneficial, will not be recommended if they would preclude alternative nonfederal projects likely to be undertaken without federal action. The test is that, if comparatively evaluated, they would contribute more effectively to federal objectives. Multipurpose projects, such as those which include water power development, flood control, irrigation, fish and wildlife, and recreation, entail extremely complex planning and value measurement problems.

Whether or not planned together, or in some sequential development pattern, projects are often interrelated in ways that can have both positive or negative effects. On the positive side, for example, a particular river dam project may stabilize seasonal water supply downstream thus increasing the effectiveness of the dam or of other water uses downstream. It may also aid in flood control if some modification in structure is made for that purpose.

There is no question that large-scale water and related land resources projects can change existing natural conditions and consequently environmental quality. The effects may be positive or negative, acceptable or not. Which they are depends on point of view and specific circumstances. Much has been written on this complex subject. Continued and often bitter controversy over the development and use of the Colorado River is a major example. Questions are involved here that transcend direct value measurement methods and require settlement by political means (Chap. 8).

Risk and Uncertainty   Risk and uncertainty are negative values which must be considered.

Risk means that the occurrence of damage is reasonably predictable. For example, the probability of destructive natural forces of fire, storm, floods, pests, aand diseases can be estimated. Likewise, engineering and operating risks generally endemic to construction can be estimated on an experience basis. Consequently, values attached to risk can be converted to an allowance factor in monetary terms. The *net* returns of a project should exclude all predictable risks either by deducting such allowances from benefits or by adding to project costs.

Uncertainty means that there is no predictable basis for estimating either beneficial or adverse effects. It may include such things as fluctuating levels in economic activity, new technology, innovations, or unforeseeable scheduling problems. Allowances for uncertainty necessarily must be based on judgment. This means that the result of a particular kind of development is considered as less certain than another but that there is no basis for calculation. Planning reports should discuss uncertainty and include strategies to meet contingencies, such as flexibility built into project designs.

Closely related to uncertainty is what is termed sensitivity analysis. This means that the sensitivity of plans to the accuracy or stability of data available should be examined, particularly as to alternative planning assumptions that might have to be changed. These would include items such as stability of prices and discount rates, and economic, demographic, or technological trends.

Extra-Market Benefits   Economic value measurement with a market basis is certainly important in benefit-cost and related analysis. It is used by government, business, and private individuals. A major reason is that almost everybody operates on a monetary exchange system. Costs tend to be measurable; a price is paid for something. Benefits also can have a monetary, a market value basis. But costs and benefits often go beyond monetary measurement. They can include values that are not, or are only partially, measurable in monetary terms. These are directly recognized in the federal guideline statement of purposes regarding water and related land resources. Extra-market benefits are also emphasized in the preceding section on valuation problems and approaches.

The collective term "extra-market benefits" is applied to this wider and more social value dimension which includes a number of value measurement approaches. Other terms used in this general area are indirect benefits, intangibles, incommensurables, evaluation by analogy, opportunity costs (using the principle of alternatives and equating benefit directly to cost), the value-added or cost-of-provision approaches, secondary benefits, imputed values, and implicit evaluation by society, as in the Netherlands, where land in the North Polders is taken from the sea and sold to farmers at about one-half the reclamation cost (See Chap. 11). A large literature concerning these extra-market benefits, including the many approaches and techniques, indicates the collective importance of the subject. Excellent literature reviews are given by Coomber and Biswas (1973), Peters (1968, 1970), Sinden (1967), and Prest and Turney (1965).

Environmental Quality Impacts Increasing public concern about maintenance of environmental quality in the use of natural resources places direct and overriding emphasis on value measurement in the public interest. The environmental movement gathered major momentum in the United States in the 1960s, has broadened to other countries, and, it is hoped, will continue with increasing strength into the future.

Passage of the National Environmental Policy Act in 1969 (P.L. 91-190) was truly landmark legislation by the U.S. Congress.

> [The Congress] declares that it is the continuing policy of the Federal government, in cooperation with state and local governments, and other concerned public and private organizations, to use all practicable means and measures, including financial and technical assistance, in a manner calculated to foster and promote the general welfare, to create and maintain conditions under which man and nature can exist in productive harmony, and fulfill the social, economic, and other requirements of present and future generations of Americans.

The Congress also "authorizes and directs" a number of other actions including:

> . . . that to the fullest extent possible . . . policies, regulations, and public laws of the United States shall be interpreted and administered in accordance with the policies set forth in this Act; . . .

[that all federal agencies apply approaches] which will insure the integrated use of the social and natural sciences; . . .

[that all federal agencies] include in every recommendation or report on proposals for legislation and other major Federal actions significantly affecting the quality of the human environment, a detailed statement by the responsible official. [This includes possible environmental impacts, alternatives, and irreversible commitments.]

[That] there is created in the Executive Office of the President a Council on Environmental Quality. [Its purpose is to act in a central and coordinating national capacity.]

In P. L. 91-224, further declaration of public policy by the Congress was given and specific provisions made for the establishment and operation of the Office of Environmental Quality to serve the Council on Environmental Quality.

By executive action, the Environmental Protection Agency was established in April 1970 to serve as the administrative agency by transferring to it functions of a number of federal agencies relating to environmental quality.

Through the above legislation and executive actions, a powerful, coordinating, and regulatory federal structure was established. It is national in scope with broad authority to promote and maintain environmental quality over land, water, and air. A primary implementation tool is the requirement that environmental impact statements be prepared for proposals affecting the quality of the environment. The coverage of this requirement is very wide. It includes federal legislation and all federal agencies; projects supported in whole or in part by federal funds including federal contracts; and grants, subsidies, leases, permits, licenses, or other entitlement for land use. These statements are submitted to the Council on Environmental Policy and are also made public.

The above constitutes value measurement of a major and publicly directed kind to *prevent* environmental damage. The basic policy assumption, enacted into federal law, is that there are important environmental values that must be protected in the public interest. No particular methodology for their measurement is established but guidelines are given. The responsibility to state and evaluate possible environmental impacts by whatever means appropriate rests directly on whoever submits a particular proposal. Neither the Council on Environmental Quality nor the Environmental Protection Agency attempts to act on or review all the numerous impact statements filed with them. The fact that they are required, must meet stated standards, and are publicly available is a powerful force to protect environmental quality. Private organizations, groups, and individuals are active in bringing pressures to safeguard environmental quality.

Public Hearings and Review Hearings and other public review of proposed projects are an important part of value measurement in the public interest. It is here that the collective judgment of people, which is important in reaching decisions, is directly expressed and a measure of its weight can be obtained. It is definitely a part of value measurement in the public interest. Federally financed projects, as in the water and land resources area, must conform to the spirit and intent of the National Environmental Policy Act of 1969, which is overriding federal law.

The purpose here is to consider the function of public hearings and review in broad terms. These include but are not limited to federally financed projects as their application is wider. This is well illustrated in Chap. 10, on the North Cascades.

Public hearings are held at publicly announced times and places following defined procedures which vary with situations. Witnesses may give oral testimony and/or present written statements. Discussion may be active and general between those holding the hearings and those making presentations or it may be limited to material presented only.

Review is primarily an interim procedure applied during the process of project development. It normally precedes completed and formal recommendation of projects for approval. Review is obtained in many ways, both formally and informally. Draft proposals or reports for parts of all of a project may be sent to or discussed with concerned people or organizations. Review, as required in federal water and land resources projects, can be at all levels. It may include governmental units concerned, nonfederal agencies both public or private, various groups within a particular organization, and within- or interagency discussions on different aspects of a project. Thorough and progressive review during the development process is an important part of project formulation.

Collectively, hearings and reviews are tremendously important both technically and politically. If there is major opposition to proposed public projects, substantial revision is indicated or the project as a whole is likely to be dropped. It is here that value measurement directly relates to decision-making processes given in the following chapter. There must be a value measurement base behind decisions.

Chapter 8

Decision-making Processes

The purpose of this chapter is to present the nature and kinds of decision-making processes with emphasis on land use. Land-use decision making includes such a wide spectrum of situations, needs, and problems that it can constitute no separate diciplinary field. No attempt here is made to define one. To be effective in land use, a practicioner needs to be a good student of the kinds of organizations and how decisions are made in them. The four cases in Chaps. 9 through 12 in substantial degree are studies of decision making in actual land-use situations.

At the outset, it will be helpful to clarify some word meanings. The key word is "decide," which has a number of meanings, including to determine or settle a question or controversy, to adjust something in dispute or doubt, and to give a judgment or come to a conclusion. There is indeed a household of decisions. The word "processes," used in the chapter title, indicates that decisions are made in many ways.

SOURCES AND FLOW OF POWER

Three key words underlie the processes of decision making: power, authority, and influence. It is well to understand them and their interrelations. First and foremost is *power,* which is defined in part as "the ability to do or act: the capability of doing or accomplishing something; the possession of control or command over others; authority; ascendency."[1] Closely related is *authority,* meaning that power is invested from some source and is exercised through individuals, groups, or organizations. The third important, but somewhat elusive, word is *influence,* meaning the "capacity or power of persons or things to produce effects on others by intangible or indirect means."[2] Influence is exerted in many ways by people or circumstances. Authority by virtue of title or position, from the head of a household to the top executive of a private organization or unit of political government, is no better than the actual power commanded. It often happens that the seat of real power does not follow organizational lines. People who have worked in organizations for any substantial length of time become aware of this significant fact.

Political Power

Political power is extremely important in land use, as in other affairs, but is so large a subject that it can be treated here in outline only.

Politics, the key word, is formally defined as the science or art of political government.[3] But the practice of politics is by no means so limited. Anyone who has had experience in group and organizational work cannot but be aware that politics permeates most human affairs. It means desire to gain control over somebody or something and hence the use of power and influence. Politics can be statesmanship, leadership, and strategy at a high level. It can also mean pressure tactics, trade-offs, deals, and intrigue. One cannot consistently relate political level to the kinds of tactics or practices employed, as the recent and voluminous Watergate and related investigations in the United States have painfully illustrated.

Governmental Agencies   Units of government, local, state, and federal, are political at the executive as well as the legislative level. Their basic power comes from their constituent electorate. Governmental departments, bureaus, or agencies are likewise, and inescapably, participants in politics. This applies externally in their relationships to the public and to other agencies, and also internally in organizational and individual rivalries.

It is popular to think that governmental agencies should adhere to their

[1] *The Random House Dictionary of the English Language,* unabridged ed., Random House, Inc., New York, 1966.
[2] Ibid.
[3] Ibid.

legislatively defined duties and be nonpolitical. This is impractical for about three major reasons.

First, legislative laws, executive directives, and such are not blueprints for action. They are framed in policy and general statements that usually leave much latitude for interpretation in administrative application.

Second, the operating agencies directly meet the public and consequently bear the initial brunt of meeting public criticism about what "the government" should or should not do.

Third, operating units of major public agencies are in frequent contact with their department heads, legislative committees, individual lawmakers, and top-level governmental executives. Their survival depends on maintaining good relationships with many people. The need for continuing appropriations is always an important consideration. Public agencies may also get executive and legislative directives that must be followed whether to their liking or not. These cannot, with propriety, be explained adversely to the public. Further, agencies in the same general area of concern, as in natural resources management, have many relationships with each other that are often competitive.

What is termed "the bureaucracy," in an unfavorable sense, often implies self-serving motives and lack of sensitivity to the public. This is in large part a public reaction to these often conflicting pressures with which public agencies must live.

Business Organizations   Most business organizations, regardless of size or kind, are concerned with politics. Large corporations are deeply and necessarily involved. Those with large regional, national, or international operations and interests are obvious examples—and they are often prominent in the newspapers. Conduct of almost any business requires politic relationships with suppliers, competitors, and customers.

Within a business organization there is also frequent contention for power and influence regarding policy, control, and personal advancement. Internal business politics is a popular employee discussion topic. Wherever there are interests there are politics.

Other Organizations   There are numerous kinds of private nonbusiness organizations, and many of them have concern about natural resources protection and management. They include professional and other societies, foundations, clubs, and citizen committees of various kinds. Many of them are active in environmental quality protection. There are a number of groups which are organized on a limited basis to achieve particular objectives only.

Many such organizations and groups exert substantial and direct political influence in land-use affairs. This is certainly true in the United States, and their influence has been strengthened since precedent has been established for the legal right of concerned citizens to sue or plead in court for injunction. This can be done against public or private organizations and/or individuals for alleged illegal action regarding environmental matters. Such action does not require that the plaintiff establish direct *personal* damage or concern.

Individuals   An individual, acting alone or in concert with others, can apply much political influence. For example, owners of urban land can exert influence on zoning authorities either to support present zoning and refuse variances they consider not to be in their interest or to grant variances that they desire. Similarly, landowners can exert influence on neighbors to stop land-use practices these owners consider inimical to their interests.

In Conclusion   The purpose of this section is to outline the nature, importance, and sources of political power in order to give a framework for approaching this complex subject. The point of emphasis is that land-use decisions of public concern basically are made through political means exerted by the collective judgment of people. In a political democracy, at any rate, there is no other way of establishing laws, rules, and regulations in the public interest.

Location and Flow of Power in Organizations

A rather common concept, particularly in formal and analytical treatment of decision making, is that those who analyze present their results to those who have decision authority. There is also a general notion that a "decision is a decision" regardless of its nature and how it was made. Such treatment unrealistically separates those who have power from those who do not. It oversimplifies the location and flow of power, influence, and actual authority in organizations.

Before considering power structure and flow in different kinds of organizations, it will be helpful to identify some important characteristics of power in relation to organizations. Five are given below.

1   Kind and degree of power concentration. Power may be concentrated in one or a few persons, a board, or an operating unit, or it may be widely dispersed through an organization.

2   Differences between nominal and actual power. Anyone who is acquainted with the operation of organizations becomes aware of the fact that actual authority often does not follow organization chart lines for a number of reasons.

3   Directions of power flow. It is normally assumed that power flows downward from higher authority. But this is by no means always the case. It can flow sideways and upward too. One department or department head may have strong influence over another of equal organizational rank for a number of reasons, including the strengh of particular individuals. A department head may in fact be more or less a captive of subordinates who can exert strong influence. Such is often true in academic organizations.

4 The level and kind of decision. This is important. Normally, or at least nominally, authority is distributed so that decisions are made at the level of those organizationally responsible. For example, operating decisions are made at the respective operating level of authority, management policy decisions at the management level, and finance decisions at the financial level. But in practice these administrative lines are often mixed because of organizational interrelationships or the influence of individuals.

5 Degree of freedom from external limitations on power. Every organization—except those of revolutionaries perhaps—has such limitations. Public organizations must operate within constitutional, legislative, and executive authority limits. Many private organizations and particularly quasi-public ones that supply public services, such as water and electricity, are subject to public regulation which limits their power.

The dynamics of power flow in practice can best be explored by examining several different kinds of organizational structures. A number of them follow in outline form. Most of them can relate to land use.

Personal and Family Decisions These include decisions involving jobs, family finance and household operation, when and whom to marry (or get unmarried from), children, etc. The nominal head of the family may or may not be the center of power. Power is frequently divided among husband, wife, and children in varying proportions. Decisions are subject to many constraints. There is usually little or no staff work beyond a family council, and there is often much uncertainty.

Individual Business Owners Individually owned businesses are characterized by concentration of power in one person with direct authority and responsibility for consequences. The head man, the owner, makes the final decisions. Authority may or may not extend to control of capital, which may be borrowed. Unilateral and arbitrary decisions are possible, and there is limited necessity for staff work. Decision authority can range from personnel to major policy decisions that may be either internal or external to the business. Incapacitation of the owner may change sharply the direction and operation of the business. It should also be recognized that, although power is centralized, the business may in fact operate with a large degree of authority delegated to employees.

Entrepreneurial Businesses Control of capital gives power. A basic and recurrent question is: Who controls the money? This entrepreneurial group is characterized by control of capital and hence concentration of decision power usually in one or a few persons. The captain of finance and industry was a frequent and rather dominant figure in the United States in past years, as exemplified by Gould, Harriman, Hill, Morgan, Carnegie, and others. This kind of business leadership is less common now but does continue.

Large Corporations   By large corporations are meant industrial giants in the United States such as General Motors, Ford, General Electric, Boeing, Du Pont, and International Business Machines. This category includes conglomerates and "big business" in general. Such units have interstate and international relationships and complex internal structures. They also have great power and in varying degree can affect federal and state politics, create markets, and affect prices.

The prime source of power in modern organizations of such kind does not rest in their size, wealth, or top executives but in what Galbraith (1967) terms the technostructure. By this is meant a cadre of educated, trained, and experienced people in the organization. Collectively, they have the technological, organizational, merchandizing, and financial expertise required to compete successfully in a highly technological era. These people function through many committees and other groups working at all levels and also between levels. Group decisions are the rule rather than those unilaterally determined by executives. This is true although decisions are usually released publicly in the name of top executives. The reality of this distribution of power and general lack of understanding by the public is evidenced by the fact that the president of one of these giant corporations could die suddenly and there would be scarcely a ripple in the stock market. It would have been quite different with some captains of industry of a half century or more ago.

The flow of *power* in such organizations is consequently diffused in actual decision making although *authority* is concentrated at the top.

Federal Agencies—The Bureaucracy   In the United States, and there are many parallels elsewhere, federal agencies are nationwide in scope and often very large indeed. They are essentially nonprofit and operate under multicontrols of Congress, both by law and by the need to seek appropriations, and of the President through executive orders and other directives. They are also subject to much political and public influence exerted by private individuals and organizations.

Because the Congress does not and cannot enact detailed administrative laws, what is known as administrative law has developed in the United States. It began in 1789 soon after establishment of the new republic. As the origin and nature of administrative law is generally not well understood, the following will give helpful background.

It was, however, with the growth of public utilities and public transportation that administrative agencies began to play a major role in American life. The passage of the Interstate Commerce Act and the establishment of the INTER-STATE COMMERCE COMMISSION in 1887 marked the start of administrative law as we know it today. The administrative process involves rule making, adjudication, investigating, supervising, prosecuting, and advising. Agencies have assumed legislative and judicial functions—the day-to-day supervision of details—for which neither Congress or the courts are adapted. This has resulted in a blurring of the traditional notion of separation of powers that is said to characterize the Federal government. . . . The principle that Congress cannot delegate its legislative powers has been circumvented by having Congress set a primary standard and allowing the agency to fill in the gaps. . . . Because of the vast range of subjects dealt with by the agencies the Federal Administrative Procedure Act was enacted in 1946 to provide uniform standards of procedure that would be common to all agencies.[4]

The application of administrative law is a practical necessity whether all people like it or not. This is a matter of point of view, and there are no simplistic answers.

Federal land-management agencies, which are of major importance in land use, normally have line-and-staff organizations and are considerably decentralized, which is necessary for operation on a national scale. The U.S. Forest Service, in the Department of Agriculture, gives a good example. Its headquarters are in Washington, DC., and it is administratively headed by a chief and his or her staff. As regards its land management operations, there are several geographic administrative regions. Each is headed by a regional forester with a staff. The national forests are distributed among the regions with each headed by a forest supervisor with a staff. The final and direct operating unit of field organization is the ranger district within a national forest. A district forest ranger is in charge and has staff assistance. Consequently, in terms of line authority, there are only two positions, the forest supervisor and the regional forester between the district forest ranger and the chief.

Anyone who has worked in such an organization for a number of years, as has the author, from district ranger to Washington office division chief, cannot help but be impressed by the complex internal flow of power and influence between government departments, bureaus, and field operating units. It goes down, up, and sideways. Line and staff functions intermix closely at all levels according to circumstances. Many internal task forces, committees, and other working groups are established for many purposes. They range from preparation of Washington-level policy and other direc-

[4] *The Columbia Encyclopedia,* 3d ed., Columbia University Press, New York and London, 1963.

tives to interdisciplinary land-use planning teams at the forest and district level.

In a number of respects, and for the same basic reasons, there is considerable similarity between large corporations and federal agencies. Both are extremely large and have wide interests, and the lines of power flow are often blurred in actual practice. A titular head of an organization can be a captive of it.

State Administrative Agencies   State administrative agencies can only be mentioned here as there are too many of them of all sizes and kinds. In general, they are similar to federal agencies. But their scope and latitude in power is more narrowly defined by state legislation, executive powers of the governor, and in some degree by federal legislation.

Commissions and Boards   Many kinds of commissions or boards have power, authority, and influence. Commission is the key word, meaning, in this context, authority granted for a particular action or function. The terms commissions and boards are often used synonymously and with some confusion. Commissions have both authority and power as in the commission form of city government adopted by many cities in the United States. The Port of New York Authority is an example of a powerful commission. It is a corporation created by joint action of two states and assigned specific powers formerly held by city government. Similarly, county commissioners are granted and assume particular powers and hence have authority in the area assigned.

There are many kinds of boards ranging from corporate or other business boards of directors to special review boards established to examine, and often to adjudicate, particular disputes or issues. Their authority and their actual power vary greatly. Large corporation boards of directors may in fact be controlled by management. Thus although their potential power is large, their actual authority could be largely nominal. This circumstance is common to many boards, emphasizing the importance of discriminating between nominal and actual authority.

Other kinds of boards, as for review and adjudication of disputes, have power to investigate, to recommend, and often to make binding decisions. However, their charter of authority is usually given to them, and their authority is consequently so circumscribed.

Universities and Foundations   There are many nonprofit organizations for different purposes. Organizationally, most foundations and many universities and colleges, particularly the private ones, are corporations. Typically, there is a governing board of directors which is appointed or elected. This body has final authority as given by public law, articles of incorporation, or such. Fund raising is often its major function.

The board, or a similar body, selects the key salaried personnel who actually operate the organization. They have much influence and in practice largely dominate. Power—policy—relationships between the board and the key personnel are variable, but operating authority is delegated by the governing board. The board usually has, however, an important ratifying function. Policy and other matters are brought before it by its operating officers for final approval. The governing board often serves a useful function in settling an issue which the chief administrator may find it expedient to pass on to the board even though he or she may have sufficient authority.

Professional, Scientific, Activist, and Religious Organizations   This is another large and highly variable group. Characteristically these organizations are not designed for profit, are mostly privately operated, are not administrative by dominant nature but have administrative problems, and generally operate considerable diffusion of power. There is usually a nonpaid governing board with a presiding officer wherein top authority technically is vested. There is also a paid staff which conducts the operating affairs of the organization.

A feature distinguishing this kind of organization from most others is that the membership, which may be large and dispersed over the country, is often collectively and individually a major force in the organization. In national or regional organizations, chapters, sections, or local groups may be organized, usually with unpaid officers. These groups are often active and influential parts of the total organization.

Power relationships among the governing body, the paid staff, and the membership—especially where there are active subsidiary chapter or section organizations—are highly variable. It is impossible to generalize except to emphasize the large differences among organizations and the diffusion of power.

In Summary   The purpose of this examination of the location and flow of power in different kinds of organizations is to give understanding of an extremely important but complex subject. There has been some orientation toward organizations important in land use, but no special category of such organizations can usefully be defined. The distinctive *kinds* of organizational structures are limited. Beyond some point, their organizational patterns become increasingly repetitive, and largely for this reason a number of important groups have not been mentioned. They include the many and often powerful trade associations and labor unions; cooperative marketing and sometimes processing associations; lobbying organizations; and administrative, recreational, and regulatory organizations operated by state and local government. Many of these organizations have interests in land use and related environmental issues. It is, in fact, heartening that they do.

PERSONAL FACTORS

The preceding section has emphasized the fact that organizations are built and operated by people. The purpose here is to present in outline form some personal factors which have a good deal to do with how decisions actually are made. This enters the complex area of interpersonal relations, and the reader is encouraged to add and amend.

1 Basic nature of the individual. This is a result of the interactions between heredity and environment that make a person what he or she is at a given time.

2 Social level, class, ambition. Some people have come up the hard way, have had to struggle and face obstacles to get ahead. Others may be more or less born to affluence and authority.

3 Personal status in the hierarchy; general place in the seniority and peer group. These reflect the amount of knowledge and experience acquired.

4 Personal aspirations. Considerations of long- and short-time advantages and liabilities in the organization. This means such things as not prejudicing one's chances for promotion, not losing influence and power by pressing too strongly for or against an issue at an unfavorable time or environment, and avoiding antagonisms.

5 Degree of personal involvement and feeling in a particular decision. How close a decision is to a person makes a difference; it can affect objectivity. Obviously, a situation involving a person's job or relationships with co-workers is different from an entirely impersonal situation.

6 Kind of decision. A decision may be about things like equipment or construction, methods and processes, or it may directly concern the job, performance, capabilities, etc. of people. Most people dislike and avoid passing judgment on others, particularly when it is adverse and the person is known to the individual giving judgment. Personnel management is a difficult art few can practice well. The most crucial test of an executive or any manager of people is often to make good personnel decisions and to know how much and when to delegate authority.

7 Strategy and trade-offs. Here one enters the political arena. In interpersonal group decision situations, one has to decide when it is politic to hold a position on a matter and when to accept compromise. For example, to accept a decision on a matter one does not consider crucial may gain support on another issue one strongly favors. The cold strategy of poker playing also enters in; one has to evaluate the strengths, weaknesses, and character of other people and organizations in the face of large uncertainty.

8 Personal situation and vulnerability. A person may have personal and financial problems regarding a husband or wife who also have careers; problems with children; parents to support; home or other investments; locale, educational, or other reasons for either wanting or not wanting transfer of work to another place. Considerations of this kind certainly can influence decisions to the advantage or detriment of both the individual and the organization.

    9   Physical and mental condition and stamina. Frequently, important decisions have to be made under stress and often with much uncertainty. Military decisions in action are an extreme example; crucial decisions in forest fire fighting with important natural resources at stake are a close civilian parallel. Political and managerial decisions, including ones affecting land use, are often made under much pressure. Physical and mental stamina and endurance can be an important asset in decision making. Some people are at their best in times of crisis; others are not. Everyone has a threshold of mental and physical endurance beyond which it is not safe to go, and it is good to know these limits.

    10   General bias or prejudice. Everybody has such in some degree. People need to be aware of their own and accurately evaluate those in others.

    11   Timing. There are times, places, and circumstances favorable or not for most things, including decisions. A person needs to judge when the time is auspicious.

DECISION MAKING IN PRACTICE

Building on the background previously given, this section directly enters the arena of decision making in practice. The center of attention is on kinds of decisions, which are illustrated by actual situations. There is indeed a household, a family, of kinds of decisions that almost everyone encounters in some degree and in one form or another. Again, readers are encouraged to add their own examples.

    Where should one start in approaching this rather elusive subject? What gives occasion to the need for making decisions? Basically, the need for decisions stems from recognition of situations that give rise to certain problems which require determinative action. Problem solving is a popular term, but it is better to place attention on circumstances behind the need for decision action.

    In the following, decisions are given by groups that more or less represent different categories. It is difficult to classify decisions as they have a persistent way of interrelating. All the groups given here can apply to land-use situations, and a number of the illustrations do. Emphasis here, however, is on the *kind* of situation involved rather than on its particular field of application. There is some virtue to this. Because land use includes such a large area of interest, placing attention on the kind of decision gives a stronger and deeper basis for recognizing land-use situations wherever they may be encountered.

Evolutionary and Sequential Decisions

Situations and policies often develop over time in a sequential and frequently unintended sort of way. There can be a continuum of events, with one decision often leading to another so that it is difficult to isolate a particular decision from a sequence of decisions. This is certainly true in natural resource affairs. A particular decision is necessarily made at a point in time, but times and circumstances change. Consequently, subsequent decisions may change the direction and intent of an initial decision. The "Great Decisions" approach, often employed in history, can be an oversimplification because it tends to overlook the causal background for a decision and the unforseen developments subsequent to a particular decision.

An excellent example of a land-use decision which had far-reaching consequences is the initial establishment of federal land reserves in 1891 out of the national domain of the United States. There had been long previous concern about the need to control better the disposal of public lands and also to retain some of these lands for public uses. This concern stemmed from great abuse and fraud in the application of public land disposal laws, policies, and practices. Perhaps the best known of these abuses are the Homestead Act of 1862 and related acts following it, and the great grants of free land to Western railroads beginning in 1850. There was also a strong conservation movement, stressing land preservation, that developed in the latter 1800s.

At any rate, a short paragraph, Sec. 24, was added by Senate conference in the closing days of the 1891 Congress to a long bill essentially of revision and procedure concerning a number of existing statutes. The act was out of Senate conference four days before final adjournment and was passed by the Senate and House without debate. It was signed by the President on March 3, 1891. It authorized the President to "set apart and reserve . . . any part of the public lands wholly or in part covered with timber or undergrowth . . . as public reservations."

It was the work of a few dedicated people and was passed by a generally ill-informed Congress. But it has had tremendous effects that could not have been foreseen or predicted. Out of it, and with much subsequent legislation, developed the present national forest system of the United States.

The great national park system had a similar origin. Following the Washburn-Langford expedition, a little-known high mountain area of about 2 million acres in what is now northwest Wyoming, by act of Congress was "dedicated and set apart as a public park or pleasure ground for the benefit and enjoyment of the people; . . . [for] preservation from injury or spoilation of all timber, mineral deposits, national curiosities, or wonders within the park, and their retention in their natural condition." The idea of the park was conceived by Nathanial P. Langford, a member of the exploration party and the first superintendent of the park. The act was signed by Ulysses S. Grant on March 1, 1872.

These two examples may seem extreme in size and importance. This is so, but magnitude is not the point here. A person also may buy a piece of land with one objective in mind and later change it to another. It is not at all unusual for a decision, or a related group of them, to have consequences that cannot be foreseen.

Levels of Decisions

Decisions differ by both their purpose and the level of authority in an organization. The general principle is that decisions should be made by those most qualified to make them. This precept may not be followed in practice because the authority of position may exert undue influence. A manager or executive may persist in making decisions that should be left to the appropriate operating level. This situation is perhaps most likely to occur in small organizations where one person has the power and attempts directly to exercise it. This is an unwise policy decision which can undermine morale and effectiveness in an organization.

A good illustration of decision related to function is given by Anthony (1965), based on much study and observation of business management. He gives a functional framework for planning and management control together with the accompanying information and kinds of decision making needed. He recognizes three major and two ancillary functional groups. The three major groups are:

> *Strategic planning* is the process of deciding on objectives of the organization, on changes in these objectives, on the resources used used to obtain these objectives, and on the policies that are to govern the acquisition, use, and disposition of these resources.
> *Management control* is the process by which managers assure that resources are obtained and used effectively and efficiently in the accomplishment of the organization's objectives.
> *Operational control* is the process of assuring that specific tasks are carried out effectively and efficiently.

The two ancillary groups are:

> *Information handling* is the process of collecting, manipulating, and transmitting information, whatever its use is to be.
> *Financial accounting* is the process of reporting financial information about the organization to the outside world.

One needs to read the book to understand the full implications of these processes in application. The point of emphasis here is that the above *are* process or functional groupings, *not* an organizational chart or hierarchy of power flow. Authority—and power—go to each group in accordance with its needs, which are different. The strategic planning process, for example, requires information from all parts of the organization. Management and operational control uses much of the same information too.

Rensis Likert (1961) came to much the same general conclusion about decision making from a psychological-sociological approach. He emphasized the establishment of effective means and practices of communication at and between different organizational levels. The purpose is to facilitate the making of decisions of different kinds through effective participation by those responsible, informed, and concerned. Decision making consequently becomes a natural concomitant of effective organizational structure, of smoothly working human relationships, and not a thing apart.

Degree of Choice or Latitude in Decisions

Many decisions are made in situations which allow limited choice or latitude in making them. Among these are what might be termed reaction decisions. These are the kind where the need for decision comes from unexpected and compelling forces outside the normal operation of the organization. The cause may be a fire or other major accident, unexpected new laws, unforeseen actions of other people or organizations, or the loss of key people in an organization. Because the cause is unexpected, and the need for action is urgent, decisions often have to be made quickly and with little latitude or choice.

Increasing public pressures from various groups and organizations concerned with preservation of environmental quality affect decisions regarding land use. New laws and regulations may leave little latitude, and moreover their interpretation in specific applications may be uncertain. Environmental protection requirements necessitate changes in operating methods, practices, and ways of doing business.

Another large and varied group of decisions with limited choice and latitude are of the ratification kind. Recommendations and proposals of various kinds come to the level of authority proper for their decision. But in fact they may have been largely predecided, leaving little choice other than to approve.

Such situations are common in professional, scientific, and social organizations with voluntary memberships. For example, a committee is appointed to study a particular situation and problem. The appointment of a committee, and especially of its leadership, is of itself an important decision as it can condition the nature and direction of the decision-making process. The chairperson of a committee or of an organization frequently can exert considerable influence although his or her direct power is limited. This influence stems from considerable power to initiate various agenda items plus personal knowledge, skill, prestige, as well as capacity to conduct meetings.

The committee makes its study and in due time presents its report and recommendations. These are normally to the person or body appointing it. If there is serious question about the report, what to do with it can be a difficult question. This is particularly true in volunteer membership organizations. If it is essentially a study report, there is less problem; the report can serve as a basis for further consideration and perhaps study. Specific recommendations are more difficult to handle. It is often politically difficult *not* to accept a committee recommendation. In perspective, committee work is often only a step in the total process of arriving at decisions. Some situations are studied and restudied by committees before final decisions are reached.

Another and closely related form of committee is the standing committee to which certain powers of review, study, and recommendation are delegated in a defined area such as membership or finance. Although such committees may not have final authority, they often wield it in practice.

The formation of a task force is a direct reversal of the standing committee approach. This is a special ad hoc group which is established to investigate a particular issue or problem and to give recommendations. Such groups are structured to assemble expertise from different parts or levels of an organization to analyze a particular question or need. Some combination of research and administrative people or an interdisciplinary technical team is often applied in land use. Final decision and implementation normally follows the task force recommendations although they are subject to review and modification by higher authority.

Related to the task force approach, but different in structure, are the methods used to conduct land-use planning by public agencies. A planning unit or office is charged by legislative, executive, or administrative action to prepare a plan within given guidelines. Statewide planning or preparation of a land-use plan for a particular part of a public land unit can be examples. Professional planners are employed. Studies are made, concerned people are consulted, and a proposed plan is prepared. It is then submitted to proper public authority and opened to public review which may be long and critical. There may be much revision before such plans are officially approved.

Strategic Decisions

Strategic decisions are those made with a larger end in view than the decision itself. The art of politics calls for strategy in decision making. It is dealt with in part in the section on sources and flow of power opening this chapter. Two widely different strategic decisions of historical significance that illustrate the principle are given here.

Marbury vs. Madison The famous *Marbury vs. Madison* case of 1803 established in principle the power of the Supreme Court to set aside laws conflicting with the Constitution (effective in 1788) for the newly established United States. The circumstances surrounding the decision give an extremely interesting illustration of principle mixed with strategic political adroitness of high order. Hendrick (1937) gives an excellent account of the political situation of the time that is drawn upon here.

Just before the Federalist (national) party was swept out of power by the elections of 1801, William Marbury, otherwise unknown to fame, was nominated by outgoing President John Adams to be justice of the peace in the District of Columbia. The nomination was signed by President Adams but was not delivered and was swept into the wastebasket by incoming President Jefferson and the Republicans or states rights advocates of the times. Marbury thought he should have the office, and suit was made to the Supreme Court, as it was a District of Columbia, not a state, matter. Chief Justice John Marshall issued a mandamus. In legal terms, this is a writ from a court directing a person to perform a specific act. It is a "rule to show cause." In this case, the "rule" was a notification to James Madison, the new Secretary of State, to appear in court and give satisfactory reasons why a mandamus should not be issued ordering delivery of the executed commission to Marbury.

"This mandamus business" became a base for bitter political issue in the press and in private argument for the next 2 years. On February 2, 1803, John Marshall gave his decision and it was a stunning surprise. President Jefferson did not need to deliver the commission to Marbury, and the Supreme Court had no intention of issuing a mandamus directing that it be done.

"And the *reason* why Marshall did not issue the second mandamus is what has made this decision immortal" (Hendrick, 1937). The mandamus had been asked for by Marbury's attorneys based on a certain section of the Judiciary Act of 1789 which gave the Supreme Court power to issue "writs of mandamus." The Supreme Court declared this to be unconstitutional because that body was not a court of "original jurisdiction" in such matters but of "appellate jurisdiction" only, to quote from the Constitution. So, for the first time, the Supreme Court declared an act of Congress to be unconstitutional. The legal basis for the decision was unassailable. The Jeffersonians had won their case so far as Marbury and "mandamus" were concerned but lost it on the major—and unexpected—point on which it was decided.

Frederick the Great and the Miller (Frank, 1942) This is an account of three interrelated and simultaneous decisions for a strategic purpose made by Frederick the Great in the latter years of his reign (1740–1786) as King of Prussia, and so at about the same time as the Marbury case. The issue involves land use.

There was a certain poor miller who could not pay his lease rent. The miller's story was that his water supply was cut off by the building of a carp pond above his mill. The builder was a relative of a person of money and influence. The case was appealed but went against the miller; there could be no further appeal, and the miller and family were to be evicted. Frederick knew of the case. The decision order, made in the name of the King, came to him and outraged his innate sense of justice. He also had a strategic purpose. He called the Lord Chancellor of Justice and three judges in to explain. The King refused the decision, and in the process he induced the Lord Chancellor, proud and with reason for the blameless conduct of his office, to resign. Frederick immediately accepted the resignation, and following their leaving his chamber, he wrote the commission of the new Lord Chancellor.

The strategic point is that Frederick had long desired preparation of a comprehensive civil code of justice for Prussia—one that would give "swift durable justice, founded on reason, right, and equity" (Frank, 1942). Some 5 years previously Frederick felt he had found the man to direct such a codification. But he could not act because he had no valid reason to remove the same Lord Chancellor who now had just "resigned." The means employed were certainly crude, but they afforded a step toward attaining a major and positive goal Frederick had in mind since becoming a young monarch some 40 years previously.

This and the Marbury decision are surely far apart in particulars. But they have in common a high level of authority, an important political goal going far beyond the immediate decision, and the seizing of what, on the face of it, might seem an unlikely opportunity to attain the goal. No inferences on means employed are made here; things are as they are by time and place.

Development and Timing of Decisions

The actual time when a particular decision is announced is important, and much is often made of the fact of final announcement. However, to gain an understanding of decision-making processes, it is equally if not more important to know how decisions develop. Behind many decisions there is a long incubation process. This begins with the recognition that something needs to be done and continues through development and often testing period to decision action.

In a family, for example, ideas, statements, concessions, or impressions often build up, often unconsciously. Some day one is called upon to decide something, and then one realizes that the decision, somewhere or somehow, seems already to have been made and all one can do is go along with it.

The same general sort of thing occurs in land-use management, business, and government. Practices develop over time. At some point a need may develop for some written guidelines or rules. What has come to be considered good practice is consequently assembled and codified for general use. When issued, it constitutes a decision. Conversely, it should be noted that attempts to prepare such guides without good pre-testing are often not successful.

Pre-testing is a frequent part of decision development. It is common practice for a proposed action to be widely circulated in draft form for review comment. This is commonly done with land-use proposals which involve many people and points of view. A number of changes in an initial proposal may result before final action is taken. In sensitive situations advance information about a proposal being considered may unofficially be "leaked" to test reaction without commitment. The term "trial balloon" is often applied to unofficial but more or less open pre-testing.

The same sort of testing may go on within a person facing a difficult decision, and it is hard to know when a conclusion is reached. An interesting example of this is given by Lincoln Steffens (1931) in his autobiography and concerns Theodore Roosevelt. Steffens once told Roosevelt that he (Roosevelt) had decided to accept nomination for governor of New York in a very complex and crucial political situation. Roosevelt was startled and said, "That's so, but how did you know it before I did?" Steffens then told Roosevelt that he had "already decided in his hips or somewhere only he didn't know it in his mind."

Political decisions are often the most complex in development. In the U.S. Congress, for example, bills may originate with the administration or in the Senate or House (Chap. 10), and development may go on for years before legislation is passed and signed by the President. The long history of framing national land-use legislation is an outstanding example that would take a book to treat.

Decisions are often made in separate increments, in steps, before final action. A good example is furnished by the Magruder Corridor issue in Montana (Chap. 12). Local opposition developed concerning land-management practices to be applied on a 173,000-acre area in the Bitterroot National Forest which had been withdrawn from previous primitive area status and opened to multiple-use management. The particular point of concern was whether, or how, timber cutting was to be permitted or conducted.

Public opposition mounted. Senators Church and Metcalf of Idaho and Montana, respectively, after failing to receive satisfaction locally or in Washington from the Forest Service, went above the agency to Secretary of Agriculture Freeman. He decided to appoint a special six-man citizens review committee, including the author, to study and report directly to him. This was the first and very important decision aimed toward definite action: a special study was to be made at a certain level and by certain people.

In considerable degree this decision set the status and general direction of the study but with no presumption about its findings. The second decision, which was the result of study and much interaction by the study team, was preparation of the team report and its recommendations. These were presented in person to the Secretary. The third decision was that made public by the Secretary, who supported the findings and recommendations of the study team and gave specific directives to the Forest Service. These constitute the official decision.

In Conclusion

This section has illustrated that there are several kinds of decisions which are made in many ways to serve different purposes. A number of the illustrations given apply to land use, and in principle all of them could. It is important to have a working understanding of different kinds of decision making and to be able to recognize and apply them in practice. It is equally important to maintain perspective regarding their place in the sequence of events. The sequence begins with recognition and appraisal of some situation or need that concerns the interest of an individual or organization. From this appraisal, present or prospective problems are identified that are considered to require decision action.

A good executive does not await problems but anticipates them insofar as possible through good administration, foresight, initiative, and planning. He or she should also stimulate others to do the same, which is probably even more important. Situations should not be allowed to build up which may require difficult decisions. This is a mark of executive incompetence. It is better to be a problem preventer than a solver.

PART 3, Chapters 9–12

Four case studies of land use in practice selected to illustrate different situations and problems. Difficult planning control problems at Lake Tahoe Basin. Controversy and decision on the use of public wildlands of the North Cascades in Washington. Reordering and consolidation of divided private landownerships in West Germany. Analysis of political controversy over clearcutting on public and privately owned forest lands in the United States. Predisposing factors, development of controversy, and results.

Lake Tahoe—Jewel
of the Sierras

This chapter presents problems, controversy, study, and action to meet a difficult land-use situation in a particular area. The setting is the Lake Tahoe Basin. It is a mountain area of outstanding scenic quality located just east of the crest of the California Sierras. It encompasses an area of 512 square miles divided between California and Nevada, of which 315 square miles are land and 197 water. The jewel in the center of the basin is beautiful Lake Tahoe of incomparable water clarity.

Increasingly difficult land-use problems have arisen in the basin stemming from urban pressures developing around the lake. These pressures are in juxtaposition to both intensive and extensive water and wildland recreational use in an ecologically fragile area. Recreation is the dominant economic interest of the basin, but it is sharply divided between outdoor and indoor kinds. The latter takes place primarily in the large gambling casinos near the lake on the Nevada, or east, side. It is only about 12 miles by air across the lower end of the lake from the Nevada Stateline casino area to the edge of the Desolation Wilderness area in the Sierras. The distance is much less from the west side of the lake. The area is readily accessible to large centers of population; San Francisco is only about 200 miles distant and is linked largely by an interstate highway.

The basic land-use problem of the Lake Tahoe Basin is how much development for what kind of people use it can endure and still essentially keep the pristine beauty of a fragile area. This is an exacting prescription to meet. There are no perfect answers; it is a problem of seeking some acceptable balance between development, which means more people use, and maintenance of the natural qualities which make the basin famous. Lake Tahoe is presented here because it illustrates a wide range of land-use problems and planning processes and the making of decisions which are both difficult and expensive to implement.

PHYSICAL LAND FEATURES

The land-use problems of the basin stem from the physical land features and use of the area and cannot be considered apart from them.

The center of attraction is the incomparable Lake Tahoe (Fig. 9.1). The natural rim level of the lake is 6,223 feet above mean sea level, but the level legally can go up to 6,229.1 feet and is controlled by a small dam on the Truckee River, its only outlet, which drains from the north into Nevada. Truckee River water is in high demand for irrigation as well as fishing. Geologically, the basin was created by a block fault which was dammed at the northern end. This accounts for the great lake depth—a maximum of 1,645 feet and an average depth of 190 feet—and its relatively flat bottom.

Figure 9-1 Lake Tahoe from Emerald Bay. *(From color picture by author.)*

There are 75 miles of shoreline. Some sixty-three watersheds, mostly small, are tributary to the lake. Lake Tahoe is a rather smooth oval oriented on a north-south axis. It is about 21 miles long and 12 miles wide, with an area of approximately 192 square miles. The conformation of the lake, with few natural irregularities, permits good natural circulation of water, which is important in maintaining its water quality. Obstructions of human origin are of water concern. Other natural lakes in the basin have a total area of about 5 square miles.

The clarity of the lake water is incredible and comparable to only two other known large lakes in the world: Crater Lake in the United States and Lake Baikal in the Soviet Union. Preservation of water purity and clarity in the lake underlies the principal land-use problems of the basin, as will be emphasized.

Topographically, the basin is bounded on the west by the crest of the Sierras and on the east by Carson Range. The higher peak elevations are around 8,500 to 9,800 feet, with Freel Peak in the Carson Range the highest at 10,681 feet. Of the 315 square miles of land in the basin, about 80 have 1 to 10 percent slope, 130 have 10 to 25 percent slope, and on 105 square miles the slopes are over 25 percent. Urban use is concentrated near the lake at elevations of not over about 300 feet above its level and on land slopes of less than 10 percent.

The soils of the area are of granitic or volcanic origin and are unstable and erosive. They are also mostly of high water permeability although some soils have a characteristic of water repellency in the presence of organic matter. These soils dominate the higher terrain. At the lower and more level areas near the lake there are alluvial and glacial overlays of the same basic origin that are also permeable and subject to erosion. Given these natural soil characteristics, and with Lake Tahoe the low center of the basin, it is apparent that soil disturbance and leaching, as from septic systems, directly affects lake water quality. Almost everything carried by water comes to the lake sooner or later (Fig. 9.2). As a result of long effort, pressed by many dedicated people and at very high cost, all sewage was treated by 1972 and the effluent pumped out of the basin. The four water treatment plants in the basin are some of the best in the country. Solid wastes are trucked out of the area. These actions are indicative of the effort and cost of maintaining Lake Tahoe water quality.

The climate of the basin is strongly influenced by its topography. Air moisture comes from the west with an annual precipitation of 50 to 60 inches near the Sierra crest. Precipitation drops sharply in a few miles to 30 inches on the west side of the lake, and to around 20 inches or less on the east side. These sharp changes in rainfall are clearly reflected in the vegetation of the basin. Most of the precipitation comes as snow mainly during December, January, and February. But because of melting temperatures and occasional torrential rains, serious flooding occurred three times in the

Figure 9-2 Severe land scarring from land development. *(From color picture by author.)*

1955–1966 period. A total annual snowfall of 15 to 18 feet is not unusual. However, because of snow settling and melting between storms, the depth of snow on the ground at any one time seldom exceeds 30 to 50 inches. With modern snow-removal equipment, access around Lake Tahoe is seldom a problem. The summers are cool with much clear weather, and the winters are seldom severe. Precipitation is lowest during July and August, and there have been years in which no precipitation has fallen at the lake from June through November.

LANDOWNERSHIP AND GOVERNANCE

Landownership

Land use of significant scale at Lake Tahoe began soon after the discovery of the great Comstock Lode (silver) in nearby Nevada in 1859. Lake Tahoe became a major supply point producing much timber along with hay and cattle. Most accessible timber was cut prior to the turn of the century, which accounts for the predominantly young pine stands now in the area. Following decline of the lode in the 1890s, Lake Tahoe became in the early 1900s a rather exclusive and summer resort serving relatively few people. By this time, the best and most of the lake shore frontage, about 80 percent, was in private ownership. This antedated establishment of the national forests which were later taken out of the remaining public domain lands. This dominantly private lake shore ownership is of large land-use significance. It accounts for the fact and problem that so little of the lake frontage, which has now become very expensive, is available for public use. There has been much recent effort to increase public landownership fronting on the lake. By 1972 it was about 33 percent (Fig. 9.3).

This general recreational-use situation largely continued until the latter 1940s. Summer visitor use increased significantly during the 1950s, augmented by the gambling casinos that came in the middle of the decade. This period marks the beginning of the present era of sharply increasing land-use pressures, public concern for the future of the Lake Tahoe area, and the necessity for intensive land-use planning and implementation.

Landownership in the Lake Tahoe Basin as of 1972 is given in Table 9.1, and its general distribution in the basin around the lake is shown in Fig. 9.4. It is important to recognize that the 122,628 acres of Lake Tahoe are public waters and technically under federal jurisdiction. The great importance of both public ownerships and interests in the basin will be brought out later.

Governance

The major problem in achieving coordinated land use and control in the Lake Tahoe Basin is its extremely divided public authority, or governance in a broad sense. To begin with, the basin is divided by the California-

Figure 9-3 Pope Beach on Forest Service land. There are nearly 2 miles of excellent public beach here, but the supply of such is sharply limited. *(From color picture by author.)*

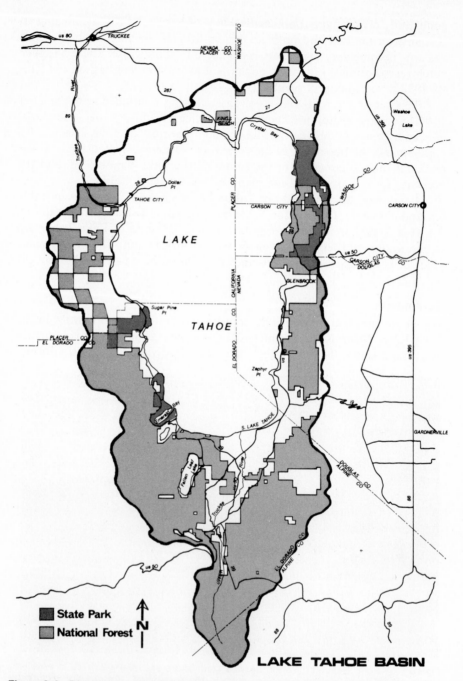

Figure 9-4 Distribution of landownership in Lake Tahoe Basin. Area in white is in private ownership. *(Courtesy of U.S. Forest Service.)*

Table 9.1   Landownership and Lake Area in the Lake Tahoe Basin

Ownership	Area in acres	Percent of total
Land		
Federal*	115,803	57.4
State		
California	3,552	1.8
Nevada	6,047	3.0
Total public	125,402	62.2
Total private	76,496	37.8
Total land area	201,898	100.0
Water area (public)		
Lake Tahoe†	122,628	
Other lakes	3,352	
Total water area	125,980	

Source: Land Resources of the Lake Tahoe Basin, Lake Tahoe Regional Planning Study, updated to July 1, 1972.

*All in three national forests except 64 acres in Placer County which are controlled by the Bureau of Reclamation.

†At legal elevation of 6,229.1 feet above mean sea level.

Nevada state line, with about 75 percent of the land and 70 percent of the surface lake area in California. Each state has sovereign powers of government. Nevada is the fastest-growing state in the United States, but it has a low population and rather limited and undeveloped natural resources. California is the third largest state and powerful in resources and population.

At the county level, there are parts of five counties in the basin all of which abut on Lake Tahoe.[1] Two are in California: El Dorado and Placer; three are in Nevada: Douglas, Carson City (formerly Ormsby), and Washoe. These counties all have major governmental responsibilities outside the basin, and none has its county seat in the basin. Carson City, the county seat closest to Lake Tahoe, is also the capital of Nevada. The one incorporated municipality in the basin, South Lake Tahoe, is in California. There are several other county-governed urban areas including Tahoe City, Kings Beach, Incline Village, and the Nevada Stateline casino area just north of South Lake Tahoe.

There were in 1967 a total of fifty-eight local governmental district and other public organizations wholly or partially in Lake Tahoe Basin. These are as follows:

[1] Technically, a small part of Alpine County is in Lake Tahoe Basin. But it is all federal land, does not front on the lake, and is not significant in basin affairs.

	Districts
11	General improvement
9	County sanitation
7	Fire protection
6	School districts
4	Soil conservation
3	County school districts
3	Public utility
2	Sewer improvement
2	Resort improvement
2	Cemeteries
1	Airport
1	Hospital
1	Joint county highway
1	California water district (El Dorado and Placer)
53	Total

	Other
3	County service areas
2	County water agencies

Adding to the complexity of many separate operating units of one kind or another, there were sixty-six domestic water supply systems, large and small, in Lake Tahoe Basin in 1971. These are in the form of municipal utilities, private water companies of many sizes and purposes, and individual systems as for resorts, a beach, a trailer park, a development unit, private estates, and recreational developments by the U.S. Forest Service and state parks.

At the state and federal level, there are a number of agencies in the basin having direct land interests. There are parts of three national forests of the U.S. Forest Service. Two of these are in California, the Eldorado and Tahoe, and their regional headquarters are in San Francisco. The third national forest, the Toiyabe, is in Nevada but has its regional office in Ogden, Utah. Together, these ownerships constitute 57.4 percent of the Lake Tahoe Basin land area. The states of California and Nevada also own increasingly important land areas.

In addition to these public agencies and landowners with direct land interests in the basin, there are in Tahoe a number of federal, California, and Nevada agencies with administrative, police, financial, and regulatory interests and authority. At the federal level, a partial listing of agencies within bureaus includes the Federal Water Quality Administration, Bureau of Outdoor Recreation, Soil Conservation Service, Corps of Engineers, Coast Guard, Bureau of Reclamation, Public Health Service, Fish and

Wildlife Service, Geological Service, Department of Housing and Urban Development, and, as has been mentioned, the U.S. Forest Service of the Department of Agriculture.

As would be expected, there are a number of private local, state, interstate, and national organizations that have an interest in Lake Tahoe Basin affairs. The two principal organizations active in the area are the Lake Tahoe Area Council and the League to Save Lake Tahoe, as will be presented later.

Another geographic fact of sociopolitical significance is that, with developable land essentially distributed in a rim around oval Lake Tahoe, there is no natural social center to the basin. To the extent there are centers, they are to the north and south, as population largely gathers around these ends of the lake. Local interests do not significantly follow either county or state lines, although these political jurisdictions are an important factor in legal governance. These circumstances contribute to lack of unity in the area and complicate planning problems. A further item is the large area of federal ownership in the basin. This is mostly national forest concentrated in the southwest part of the basin, principally in the Eldorado National Forest.

These facts of complexly divided governance and landownership are given in some detail because they are of basic and continuing importance in land-use management. They underlie the continuing search for some desirable, acceptable, and workable people-land relationship in Lake Tahoe Basin.

It can be argued, for example, with compelling validity that the presence in the basin of large-scale gambling, legal under Nevada law, is a dissonance, a nonconformity to the basic nature of the basin and that gambling should not be there. Little if any rationale can be given to this form of indoor recreation having any substantive relationship to outdoor recreation opportunities, for which the basin is justly famous. One can only say that gambling does attract more people to the area. Any virtue to this can be challenged because of the general inability of the area to provide living facilities for large numbers of people. There is also the fact that gambling facilities exist in nearby Reno and Carson City.

The same kind of argument can be advanced against encouraging nonemployment-based residents to Lake Tahoe. This is increasing because retirees and others such as writers whose place of residence need not be near their source of income desire to live there. Such desires are understandable but do raise land-use policy questions that are difficult to resolve in a political democracy.

As will be seen, land-use planning in the basin has been based on accepting permanent and transient population projections without facing such policy questions. Recently, however, determined effort has been made to do so to set upper limits in one way or another on both resident population growth and accommodations for transients. There is more flexibility in accommodating short-time visitors, many of whom do not necessarily need to stay overnight in the basin.

The physical, biological, and aesthetic qualities of the area are well known from many studies. Carrying capacities in terms of people for different kinds of land uses also can be estimated. What can be done about it will, in the final analysis, depend on the strength of governance, which must be supported by good planning and public acceptance.

DEVELOPMENT OF LAND USE AND PLANNING

It became increasingly apparent during the 1950s that rapidly increasing land use by people seriously threatened the natural qualities of Lake Tahoe Basin. Because of complexly divided governance, and the wide range of urban and nonurban land-use interests in the area, it is difficult to establish effective land-use controls in this beautiful but damageable area.

Of pragmatic necessity, land-use development projects such as power, sanitation, and construction had to proceed without any comprehensive plan. Each project required much promotion, development of organizational and financial support, and a great deal of planning. Tahoe is a story of long struggle to attain unity and some desirable people-land balance in a difficult situation.

In this respect, the area is a public laboratory for land-use studies and proposals. Seemingly, almost everyone has some ideas as to what should or should not be done, and many have expressed them vigorously. Few areas have received as much and as conflicting attention on so many different subjects. These include geology, hydrology, soils, ecology, sociology, law, political science, economics, engineering, and ethics. The number and volume of studies, publications, reports, analyses, recommendations, and hearings is truly astounding. Much of it is strongly critical, which increases the difficulty of gaining understanding and balance.

With these complementary considerations of land development and planning in mind, treatment in this section is given in two parts. The first deals with major actions taken on the land during the period of rapid population growth and land-use development from the 1950s to the mid-1960s. The second part gives the development of planning during the same period.

Land-Use Development

Land development has various connotations, but unless people are rigidly excluded from an area, there will be development if there are uses to develop. Whether this is good or bad depends on viewpoints which vary widely.

Lake Tahoe Basin is an area of extremely valuable natural resources in high demand. There has not been, nor is it likely that there can be, a specific and final prescription on numbers of people. But there are increasingly tight restrictions on what kind of and how much development will be permitted. This will limit population. Establishment of such controls is largely a policy matter that must be established by the authority of governance. This fact accounts for much of the controversial aspects of Tahoe affairs. In any event, land-use development on the ground has gone ahead; it had to with or without a comprehensive plan. Controls of increasing specificity, along with more intensive and comprehensive planning, have concomitantly developed as the need became apparent. This is not the ideal situation, but such is rare indeed in human affairs.

It will aid in understanding the problems of planning to give a brief account of some major land-use control needs that have been recognized in Lake Tahoe Basin and of actions taken to meet them.

It became apparent early that the purity of the lake water, for which Tahoe is so justly famous, was threatened by land-use development close to the shore. Sewage was a particular concern. But there were also other land uses at or near the lake shore, such as land filling, road building, grading, and other earth movement incident to construction, that induced erosion. Lakefront developments such as jetties, piers, and marinas projected into the lake. All of these, potentially, actually, and in varying degree, are injurious to lake water quality.

Regarding sewage, it is a fact that, because of soil permeability and proximity of most development to the lake, almost any effluent released will sooner or later get into the lake. This will accelerate natural eutrophication, which reduces water clarity and quality. Septic systems, which work well for the owner and were generally used, are a continuing and cumulative threat to water quality. Disposal of solid wastes by either burying or burning is also objectionable in the basin.

As a result of many studies, reports, recommendations, agitation, conferences, interagency organization, and the meeting of difficult financial problems, the construction of water treatment plants went ahead. By 1972 the use of septic systems was discontinued. All sewage was treated in some of the best treatment plants in the world, and the effluent was pumped out of the basin. Further, and although the quality of water resulting from treatment by one plant is high enough to be recycled back into a closed system where water did not return to the lake, it is also pumped out of the basin. The cost of the treatment plants was largely borne by landowner tax assessments, but public monies were also used. One has to see on the ground the problems of sewer construction, often in very rocky large-boulder glacial soils, to appreciate the magnitude and difficulty of the operation in a wildland setting. Here, earth scars are hard to heal and special construction problems are encountered. By the end of 1972 all solid wastes were trucked out of the basin and disposed of in an earth cut-and-fill procedure.

The point of emphasis here is that a massive and effective sewage and solid waste disposal program was accomplished through cooperative interagency action. This was done under difficult conditions that were imposed by the facts of divided political governance in the area. It was not done under the aegis of any master plan. One can argue that the actions taken were not soon or good enough, that the governance situation should not exist, and regarding various other "shoulds." These have been discussed at length, but nonetheless action was taken to meet the realities of the situation.

Similar actions and controls have been taken over the course of several years. They are the result of recognized pressures to act which required a number of cooperative and joint agency arrangements. Both private and public financing was necessary. The basic problem has been to cope with increasing urban and wildland-use pressures in close juxtaposition and to meet a difficult political governance situation.

It will be helpful to list some of the people and related land-use needs and problems which have arisen in the basin. All have received attention accompanied by planning.

Roads   There are six road entrances to the basin and also internal roads. Due to soil instability, rocky conditions, and dry summers, road scars show painfully and are slow to heal by any methods.

Land grading   Land movement, incident to building construction, leaves land scars difficult to heal and also affects natural water movement. Increasingly strict ordinance controls are imposed.

Land fills   Some have been made in low areas near the lake. They adversely affect aquatic life and natural water movement. Most of them should not have been permitted.

Shoreline restrictions   These are a central and sensitive need in preserving the natural beauty of Lake Tahoe. Restrictions have been inadequate, but by 1972 they had been greatly tightened by ordinances stipulating prohibitions and permit requirements.

Urban zoning and building   Construction problems are particularly difficult in the Tahoe situation. A number of urban communities have grown to sizable proportions. How much and what kind of building should be permitted is a point of concern and controversy because the amount of building basically controls the resident population of the area. Direct control of population growth is weak.

Utilities   Power and telephone lines necessary have been constructed and to high standards. These are not an apparent source of controversy.

Storm drainage   Provision for such is important and is increasingly subject to tight requirements.

Fire protection In addition to normal urban protection against fire, there is good wildland protection, much of it given by the U.S. Forest Service. There are seven organized fire protection districts in the basin.

Action has been taken more or less separately on all the above items to control development and to protect the natural qualities of Lake Tahoe Basin. Depending on viewpoint, actions may not have been either good or soon enough. There has been long and continued controversy over these matters both by people living in or closely associated with the basin and by people across the United States who are interested in the area and express themselves. It is important to recognize the duality of local and national concerns about Tahoe.

In completing this section on land-use development, it will be helpful briefly to give population estimates. These are difficult for two reasons. The first is that census problems arise because part of two states and five counties are involved. The second is that there are a large number of seasonal transients. The data given below are estimates as of 1970. The annual growth rate has been estimated as between 7 and 8 percent.

Four general groups of people can be recognized. These are:

1 Employment-based residents. This is a variable and difficult group to define. It includes both year-round residents and seasonal employees and their dependents. The number consequently changes substantially with season but is being somewhat evened out by increasing development of winter sports, primarily skiing.

2 Year-round residents who are retirees or others such as writers or artists who receive their income from outside the area. This growing group is difficult to identify but significant.

Estimates of the resident population (groups 1 and 2) range from 30,000 to 40,000, including 5,000 to 10,000 seasonally employed and 25,000 to 30,000 permanent year-round residents.

3 Seasonal visitors, including those who either own or rent housing. These are mainly families who travel by car and stay from several weeks to the entire summer. These have been estimated at about 32,000 during peak season and 7,000 or less during spring and autumn.

4 Short-term visitors, including guests at motels or hotels, campers, and single-day visitors. This is an extremely difficult group to estimate as it fluctuates widely. It is also impossible to separate outdoor recreation visitors from gambling casino customers.

A total peak-day population of around 135,000, including the resident population has been estimated.

Population projections are difficult and will not be attempted here. The resident and transient populations will certainly increase, but how much depends on general economic and other conditions outside the area and on the effect of constraints on population growth that may be imposed in the area. Some rather high projections have been made, and there is no question about a high potential. But the degree to which it may eventuate depends on planning policy backed with power to implement. This is considered later in this chapter in the section on regional planning.

Planning Development

It was early recognized that integrated and continuing planning with power to implement was needed in Lake Tahoe Basin. This was because of its great value, the sensitive and damageable character of its natural resource qualities, and the widely divided authority of governance in the basin. The three are inseparable. As brought out in the preceding section, much planning was done on a somewhat item-by-item urgency basis as need arose and action became imperative. A great deal of good work was accomplished that should be recognized. But there still remained the deeper need to integratively and with continuity the land resource management problems in the basin as a whole.

A significant beginning in this direction was the formation in 1958 of the Lake Tahoe Area Council. This is a local group, bistate in membership, and "broadly reflective of both California and Nevada interests" (Smith, 1971). It does much constructive work. Its preceding organizations were the Tahoe Improvement and Conservation Association, formed by west-side summer property owners, and the California–Nevada Lake Tahoe Association aided by Fleischman funds.

Another and continuing organization of more recent origin is the League to Save Lake Tahoe, which was formed in July 1965. It is a conservation group with membership from both in and out of the basin. It focuses on policy concerns and attempts to influence legislation. The organization has grown rapidly and is vocal and influential.

As development continued and the need for more effective basinwide planning became increasingly apparent, the Tahoe Regional Planning Commission was formed in late 1960. It had its first organization meeting in 1961. This commission grew out of the Tri-Bi Planning Directors Association composed of planners from the county jurisdictions in the two states. Actually, it was composed of two separate state groups working in concert. Membership of the commission was originally composed of two appointees from each of the three Nevada counties and three each from the two California counties, which accounts for the Tri-Bi part of the name. One of each county representative was a county commissioner. The commission was assisted by a technical advisory committee composed of the technical planning directors of each county.

In 1962 a proposal for a master plan study of Lake Tahoe Basin was developed by the commission and awarded to the consulting firm of Wilsey, Ham and Blair of California. Following about 15 months of intensive study and analysis, a master plan was prepared, and in July 1964 it was adopted by the commission as the "1980 Tahoe Regional Plan." It was then submitted to the five county governments for adoption and approval (Smith, 1971). It was never adopted by all of them, and nothing really happened. There was no stable source of staff funding, nor was there unified power of implementation. Such is the fate of many master plans. The plan did, however, collect and analyze a great deal of information, had influence, and was a significatnt step in the difficult search for action in the basin.

In December 1964, the commission, in joint meeting with the Lake Tahoe Area Council, adopted a proposal for a joint study committee to seek a more effective regional approach to meet the governance-planning needs of the Lake Tahoe Basin. The proposal was approved, concurrent legislation was passed by the respective legislatures of California and Nevada, and it was approved by the respective governors. Included in this joint legislation was a listing of twenty-two hard and searching questions about powers which should be assigned to a regional agency were it to be established. In February 1965 a 2-year study was undertaken, with funding and an adequate staff. The study committee consisted of nine members, four representing each state, and a chairperson who could be from either state.

The resultant joint study report was presented to the respective governors and legislatures of the two states in March 1967. It is an excellent and truly milestone report on Lake Tahoe Basin affairs. Besides being very informative and summing up past actions, the report has been acted upon. Its recommendations form the basis for the present governance and planning structure in the basin. This is the subject of the next section.

REGIONAL PLANNING: ISSUES AND PROBLEMS

The March 1967 report of the Lake Tahoe Joint Study Committee set the stage and pattern for seeking the present establishment of a legislative and legally supported overall regional structure of planning authority in Lake Tahoe Basin. It laid the basis for coming to grips with the divided governance problems of the Lake Tahoe Basin.

Its basic recommendation was establishment, by concurrent legislation by each state, of a "Tahoe Regional Agency possessing Region-wide and bi-state jurisdiction." The report included specific language proposed for such legislation. It was also recognized, although not explicitly stated in the report, that such legislation would constitute a bistate compact which would require consent of the Congress to make it legally binding on both states. Such action was required because Congress created the states (except for the original thirteen), and hence delegation of their sovereignty powers requires congressional approval.

Before going into this legislation and development of the present Lake

Tahoe Regional Planning Agency, it is important to recognize what a compact is and is not. To begin with, when the congress gives its consent to a compact, it does not relinquish or restrict its own powers. Neither can or does a state abrogate its respective sovereign powers other than as stipulated in the compact.

A compact is a specific and limited delegation of certain stipulated state powers as agreed upon by the respective states which also can be amended by the Congress. Final enactment is by passage of an act of Congress and signature by the President. This procedure obviously permits political consideration of what should or should not be included in the compact agreement. California and Nevada were no exceptions in writing the act for submission to the Congress. Even if it were legally possible to combine state, county, and city jurisdictions in the basin, it would be neither practicable nor desirable to do so. They exist, must be recognized, and their cooperation is necessary. Equally, it is not possible for the federal government to abrogate its substantial interests in the basin. A compact is necessarily limited in nature and is for an express purpose. It definitely cannot solve all problems; some things have to be cooperatively worked out.

These circumstances are given here because of much controversy over Lake Tahoe Basin affairs. Some workable and politically acceptable balance of effective governance had to be established, and the need for such is the continuing center of Tahoe problems.

Development of the Regional Planning Compact

To return to the sequence of events following the March 1967 report of the Tahoe Joint Study Committee, it was necessary for each state to set up interim agencies under essentially identical state laws pending the consent of Congress. The California Legislature created the California Regional Planning Agency in August 1967, and its first meeting was held in November of that year. The parallel Nevada agency act was passed in late 1968 and became effective in early 1969. These agencies, each under their respective state laws, acted *as much as possible* as if they were joined together by a binding compact. Joint agency meetings were periodically held. Each agency had a technical advisory committee to review, study, and recommend matters that should come before the monthly meetings of the respective governing bodies of two agencies.

Based on the language of the California and Nevada companion state laws, the Congress passed, with small amendment, a Senate bill which was signed by the President on December 18, 1969, as Public Law 91-148. This act was approved by the California and Nevada governors on March 17, 1970. The organization meeting of the new agency was held on March 19, 1970. Except for the enactment clause and several additions at the end added by the Congress, the language of the act is directly taken from the California and Nevada joint acts.

The principal additions made by the Congress are:

Appointment by the President of a nonvoting "representative of the United States."

Authorization by the Secretaries of the Interior and Agriculture to cooperate with the agency as being compatible with "normal duties" of their respective Departments. This gives additional federal cooperative support.

That any additional powers conferred on the agency by either state must have the consent of Congress.

That nothing in the act shall affect the powers, rights, obligations or applicability of any law or regulation of the United States regarding the region or waters of the compact area.

Except for these congressional additions, the act is, in literal fact, the consent of Congress to the bistate proposal.

Because the compact act is binding, continuing, and establishes the legal basis for planning control in the Lake Tahoe Basin, it is important to take a good look at the substance of the act. This is done here in synopsis form emphasizing policy items.

Article I Findings and Declarations of Policy "The waters of Lake Tahoe and other resources of the Lake Tahoe region are threatened with deterioration or degeneration, which may endanger the beauty and economic productivity of the region." Because of its special circumstances, the region is experiencing problems of resource use and deficiencies of environmental control. There is need to "maintain an equilibrium between the region's natural endowment and its manmade environment. . . . It is imperative that there be established an areawide planning agency with power to adopt and enforce a regional plan of resource conservation and orderly development, to exercise effective environmental controls. . . ."

Article II Definitions

Article III Organization As a political matter, the organization structure is of major importance. The Tahoe Regional Planning Agency, as created in the consent act, is governed by a ten-person voting body, five each from California and Nevada. There is also one nonvoting member representative of the United States who is appointed by the President. Six of the members are one each from the five counties (two in California and three in Nevada) and one from the city of South Lake Tahoe in California. Two are nonresidents of the basin appointed by the respective state governors, and two are the administrators of the California Resources Agency and the Nevada Department of Conservation, or their respective designees.

Thus the voting weight of the agency is six to four for the local members over the nonresidents. Some critics make much of this point, assuming that local units of government strongly favor "development," which is not necessarily true. It is likewise often assumed that interests outside the general region favor preservation or conservation. The purpose of the act certainly was for the agency to give weight to those directly responsible for and knowledgeable of Tahoe affairs. In contradistinction, some critics favor a governing body drawn primarily from members outside the basin on a more national basis. The value of this can be argued. Members serve without compensation, but their expenses are paid. Their term of office depends on their respective appointing body but shall be reviewed every 4 years. The agency appoints its executive officer.

An advisory planning commission is appointed by the agency governing body replacing the previous technical advisory committees for each state. The total membership is seventeen, including six chief planning officers of the five counties and of South Lake Tahoe, two county directors of sanitation, two county health officers, two heads (or designees) of major state health and water agencies in California and Nevada, and at least four lay members who are residents of the Tahoe region; the executive officer of the agency serves as chairperson. The commission is the working body which studies, investigates, and recommends plans, amendments, and other proposals to the governing body for action.

Every plan, ordinance, or other record of the agency that constitutes a public record under law of either state is open to inspection and copying during regular office hours.

Article IV Personnel   This covers normal qualifications and appointment and salary procedures. It also specifies that personnel standards and regulations conform insofar as possible to state civil service regulations and procedures, and that they "shall be regional and bi-state in application and effect."

Article V Planning   Reasonable and proper provisions are given for the conduct of agency affairs, including advance hearings on each plan proposed and on amendments.

The substance of the planning section is specific stipulation of the planning work to be done by the agency. This is summarized below. There are two planning requirements: an interim plan and a continuing regional plan.

Within 60 days after the formation of the agency it must recommend an interim plan, and it must adopt one in 90 days. This plan includes statement of development policies, criteria and standards for planning and development of plans or portions of plans or projects, and decisions necessary to adopt the plan on an interim basis.

Within 15 months after the formation of the agency the advisory planning commission must recommend a regional plan, and in 18 months the agency must adopt the plan, which, with the commission, it shall "continuously review and maintain."

The "plan shall include the following correlated elements:"

1 A land-use plan for integrated arrangement, location, extent, criteria, and standards for the uses of land, water, air, and other natural resources, "including, but not limited to, an indication or allocation of maximum population densities."

2 "A transportation plan for integrated development of a regional system of transportation" of all kinds.

3 "A conservation plan for the preservation, development, utilization, and management of the scenic and other natural resources within the basin . . . ."

4 "A recreation plan for the development, utilization, and management of the recreational resources of the region. . . ."

5 "A public services and facilities plan for the general location, scale and provision of public services and facilities. . . ."

It is further stated that "all provisions of the Tahoe regional general plan shall be enforced by the agency and by the states, counties and cities in the region."

The above constitute a large order to meet. It is necessary, but difficult, to factor out into separate plans the many and closely interrelated land-use considerations involved and to enforce them. The major thrust is to protect, manage, and develop the natural resources of the basin under use by people. No set limits are or can be set for "development." The agency is charged "to take account of and shall seek to harmonize the needs of the region as a whole." This leaves open the crucial question of how much is enough. It gives scope for different viewpoints and continued controversy. The basic problem is to achieve some tenable balance, recognizing realities in the basin. It is evident that everybody concerned cannot equally be satisfied.

Article VI Agency's Powers This long section is addressed to the crucial matter of agency authority. The basic pattern is that the agency, by virtue of authority given to it by the compact, establishes minimum standards through the development of implementing criteria, rules, regulations, or ordinances (nearly twenty of them named) which are binding on the existing units of government in the basin. These units continue to carry on their normal functions in the basin *provided* they at least meet the requirements set by the agency. The language of the article states and defines what the agency shall do and gives specific procedures regarding hearings, time limits, availability of records, and the like.

Means of enforcement are crucial. Remedy for noncompliance, beyond the influence of persuasion and administrative action, is through courts of competent jurisdiction. This is the same recourse as for units of local government and the states. Such actions are often slow, cumbersome, and expensive.

Because the compact states what the agency can do, it is equally important to recognize what it cannot do. Here is where political considerations, which are involved in framing almost any piece of legislation, come into play. The agency has no direct governmental authority over federal units of government nor over state or local government beyond the powers stipulated in the compact. There is an important grandfather clause too. It states that any business or recreational establishment in the basin which requires state license and was licensed back to any part of the year preceding February 5, 1968, or *is* to be constructed on land that was so zoned or designated "in a finally adopted master plan" *on the same date,* is to be recognized "as a permitted and conforming use." This naturally permits previously approved construction, including casinos and other structures.

The agency has no powers of eminent domain, taxation, or legislation. If these powers were to be granted, which would be politically impossible, they would destroy working relationships with the two states and the five counties which are only partly within the basin, and with the city of South Lake Tahoe.

Article VII Finances Before December 30 of each year the agency is to estimate its financial needs for the fiscal year starting the following July 1. Not more than $150,000 of this is apportioned to the five counties, and they are obliged to pay out of any monies available. Refusal presumably would entail state pressure or court action.

Article VIII Miscellaneous These provisions include express authorization for the U.S. Departments of the Interior and Agriculture to cooperate with the agency; this is to the advantage of the agency and Lake Tahoe Basin.

They also provide that the compact shall have no effect on the allocation or distribution of interstate waters or upon any appropriative water right. This includes the Truckee River, the use of which is important in Nevada.

Any additional powers conferred on the agency require consent of the Congress. This makes granting of additonal powers very difficult.

Finally then, after years of study, planning development, controversy, some inevitable political inter- and intrastate compromises, pre-testing experience, and much work on the part of many dedicated people in and out of Lake Tahoe Basin, a regional planning authority with basinwide powers was established. It is not perfect from all viewpoints. But it does represent what could be attained in an area and situation in which there are many and divided land-use interests.

Planning under the Regional Compact

The Tahoe Regional Planning Agency became operative by joint proclamation of the California and Nevada governors on March 17, 1970, and the agency organization meeting was held on March 19, 1970. Its path was difficult from the beginning; it was essentially a continuation of what had existed before the compact but now with legal powers of enforcement. As noted in a California newspaper:

> The agency is less than a year old yet it already has more enemies than most people acquire in a lifetime. Developers attack it for being too restrictive; conservationists attack it for being too permissive; local government leaders say it is usurping their powers; advocates of regional government say the agency is a powerless farce.

The new agency had to face immediate problems of organization, personnel, finance, and establishment of its position in the basin. Of prime urgency was the need for the advisory planning commission to prepare and recommend, and the governing body to approve, an interim plan in 90 days and a continuing regional plan in 18 months. Fortunately, there was a large amount of previous study, planning material, and cumulative experience to draw upon.

The interim plan was necessarily put together from existing materials to meet the requirement in the compact and was intended to serve as an initial operating base only. It was adopted June 19, 1970.

Legal test accompanied organization of the new agency and preparation of the interim plan. Lawsuits were filed by Placer and El Dorado Counties of California. They basically challenged the constitutionality of the former California regional planning agency and of the regional planning agency under the compact. Hardship and damage were also claimed regarding the interim plan because of insufficient public notice. None of these suits was sustained nor are they likely to be. Judicial support of the constitutional charges would, of course, have vitiated the whole concept of an integrative interstate authority with governmental power to prescribe and enforce environmental controls on land-use development in the basin.

In addition to legal challenge, and the many operating problems of establishing the new agency on a permanent basis, there was the pressing necessity to meet the requirement of preparing and adopting a regional plan in 18 months. As prescribed under the act, it is to be continuously reviewed and maintained.

An executive officer was selected who was formerly director of regional planning in the Denver area. He understood his charge to be to preserve the environment and so acted. A massive planning program was organized which assembled a large amount of environmental information based on land-use capabilities. This information was computerized and presented in a series of maps based on 22,000 ten-acre grids utilizing nearly sixty kinds of environmental information. A plan draft and the grid maps were presented at a special luncheon at the Sahara Sands Hotel in May 1971. The audience was first awed and then confused. People just did not understand. Later, as the full import and nature of the plan became understood, strong criticism developed. It was felt that the plan was impractical and unworkable, ignored property rights and contracts, and was unbalanced in not recognizing the charge in the act "to adopt and enforce a regional plan of resource conservation and orderly development."

At any rate "the lid blew off," as it has been put, and with it went the executive officer in the summer of 1971 and the plan he had directed in forming. A large expenditure in planning costs was partially lost, as was badly needed planning time.

But agency work, particularly the vital planning job, had to go ahead. There was the pressing job of preparing and approving a regional plan by 18 months after the agency's formation. A new executive officer of the agency was appointed. A member of the advisory planning commission and planning officer of Placer County, California, he was an able and experienced man in the basin and was realistic about what could and had to be done. On July 1, 1971, the governing body charged the executive officer to bring in a regional plan for consideration in 60 days. Funds were provided and a special study team was set up consisting of:

A five-member subcommittee of the commission, consisting of planning officers from the five counties and the city of South Lake Tahoe, with the executive officer, also a planning officer, serving as chairman.

Three staff members, including two professional planners and an administrative assistant

Three consultant firms

Major assistance was given by the U.S. Forest Service planning team in the basin. It had the land-use capabilities information which was assembled in the preceding agency plan. A new map was prepared following natural land lines rather than the arbitrary 10-acre grid system previously used. This capability information gives a foundation for land-use planning, but does not of itself constitute land-use zoning or a plan. Recognition of this fact strengthened the planning work and also made possible effective use of the information.

This was a most critical time for the new agency, and a crash program was necessary, but the planning deadline was met. The new plan was approved by the governing body of the agency on December 22, 1971.

"The Plan for Lake Tahoe" is a most unusual document. It consists of one large sheet of paper 22 by 33 inches. On most of one side is a large map of the basin; the rest of this side and the back carry printed matter. Accompanying this sheet, and a part of the plan, is another sheet of identical size printed on one side and entitled "Lake Tahoe Basin—Land Capabilities." This was prepared cooperatively by the Lake Tahoe Basin Planning Team of the U.S. Forest Service.

It will be helpful to summarize what is on these two big sheets; the information is condensed, informative, and to the point. It is rare indeed for a plan for so complex an area to be so brief. This was forced by the extremely short schedule and also by a strong desire to make essentials of the plan understood by the public.

The large map of the basin on the plan sheet gives basic present land-use and development information. The following areas are shown in color:

Development reserve
Recreation
Rural estates—minimum 1-acre units
Low-density residential—up to 4 dwelling units per acre
Medium-density residential—up to 8 dwelling units per acre
High-density residential—up to 15 dwelling units per acre
General commercial
Tourist commercial
Public service
General forest (by far the largest part of the basin)
Public beach
Ski areas (six)
Water transportation routes
Road transportation (seven routes of access to basin)

Text captions given alongside the map are summarized below:

The Plan for Lake Tahoe   General introduction to set the stage.
Comprehensive Land-Use Plan   Gives general guidelines and policy for the basin which are to be followed by all levels of government. These guidelines are in accordance with land-use capabilities and constraints as given on the accompanying land-capabilities sheet. Ordinances and standards have been developed further to define land capabilities more specifically.

Four major ordinances on land use were approved in early 1972 concerning land use, shoreline, subdivision, and grading. More are to be prepared.

Conservation Element   States policy and needs responding to ecological constraints of the region. Includes an estimate of 34,000 acres of unbuilt privately owned lands that should be removed by public purchase from urban development of any kind.

Transportation Element   Recommends retention of present highway levels and comprehensive study of further transportation system. Encourages more waterborne traffic across the lake.

Recreation Element   States guiding policy and direction.

Text captions on reverse side of the map are summarized below:

The Planning Process   Outlines development of planning subcommittee; nature of planning and policy as applied in the basin.

Goals and Objectives   Lists fourteen items, positive things to recognize and achieve.

Natural Resources   Describes their nature, value, status, sensitivity, and constraints needed.

The Plan   Gives overriding concepts and directives as regards land use in total perspective, recreation, and transportation.

Service Concepts   Recommends continued export of sewage and solid wastes from area; recognizes water availability as a limiting factor; supports schools, fire protection, and other urban and nonurban service needs.

Land-Use Summary and Population Estimates   Gives urban acreage data by county and use classification as shown on map. Indicates a total *possible* population of 280,000. This is *not* a goal but a planning limit only.

Implementation   States frankly that the plan as given is essentially a policy statement and that "any plan is only as good as its administration." Lists ten items including agencies, authorities, districts, public land acquisition, ordinances, programs, and development review needs that are subject to agency concern in implementing the statutory purposes of the agency.

The essence of the second large sheet is a large-scale land-capabilities map of the Lake Tahoe Basin. The map shows capability classes for land surface use. Seven general capability levels (one with three subclasses) are shown. These are derived from an integrative evaluation of tolerance for use, slope (in percent classes), relative erosion potential, runoff potential, and disturbance hazards. As stated previously, this map is a reworking of the information utilized in the ill-fated plan proposed by the former executive officer. The map and accompanying text compresses, integrates, and selectively uses a great deal of physical and biological information that determine capabilities for land use. It is readily understandable and usable by both the agency and the public. The text gives a concise and informative explanation of criteria and bases used and their significance in determining land use.

Including basic environmental protection bases, policy, and regulations, as given on these two sheets, a guiding plan that met the stipulations of the compact act was developed, and the Tahoe Regional Planning Agency got under way. The plan is supported by ordinances, much data, staff study, governance authority, and hard-earned cumulative experience gained over the years. As indicated, the plan is essentially policy, directives, and regulation to be implemented through the stipulated governing powers of the agency. This planning base is continually to be reviewed and revised.

It is a master plan, but not in the sense of being any blueprint of either environmental prescriptions or land development objectives. The estimate of 280,000 resident people, which is much misunderstood, is intended as a planning base only. It is a limit and definitely *not* a goal or objective. Physical land-use controls come through ecological-environmental constraints which directly affect permissible development.

Economic considerations are expected to be a major limitation in practice. The costs of acceptable development will be increasingly high in this beautiful but rather fragile area. They will be reflected in land, building, facility, and service costs, all of which are subject to strict land-use zoning and ordinance requirements. These restrictions will have effects on both urban and nonurban land uses. Commercial and residential building sites in urban areas that might be environmentally permissible for development are limited in area regardless of what people might want or could do without the restrictions imposed.

Public camp-ground development in nonurban areas gives a similar illustration of economic and policy limits. Land suitable for such use is limited sharply in area. Most of the land available is in national forest ownership which is oriented toward natural wildland uses. Development costs are very high in such areas. The density of use permitted per acre is low, the seasonal duration of use is short, and reasonable daily charge rates are also low. Camp grounds must be served by water, sewage, and waste disposal utilities that conform to the same standards as for other permitted uses in the basin.

A further important policy consideration is the fact that nearby and good camp-ground sites are readily available outside the basin. It is not possible here further to explore policy considerations regarding the kind and amount of camp grounds or other facilities outside the basin which might be developed and which could serve the basin. The point is that land uses of the Lake Tahoe Basin cannot be considered apart from the uses of surrounding areas.

The establishment of the Tahoe Regional Planning Agency by act of Congress, together with its initial plan and the actions taken during its first 2 years of existence, completes the Tahoe story as it can be given here. The future will undoubtedly bring new situations and problems.

WHAT HAS BEEN LEARNED FROM LAKE TAHOE?

Land-use development in Lake Tahoe Basin has had a long, difficult, and controversial history. What can be learned from the experience that has general value? This section presents a number of items, some of which may be termed principles, that are of general significance. They are given in condensed form, and the reader is welcomed to add to or amend what has been given.

Matters of governance, authority, policy, and rights of landownership are considered first, followed by planning processes and problems. The items presented are not intended to be in any particular order of importance; what is limiting or critical in one land-use situation may not be in another. It must also be recognized that there is much interrelatedness in land-use matters, making separation of items somewhat arbitrary.

Governance, Authority, Policy, and Landownership

   1 Divided authority. The overall authority of the Tahoe Regional Planning Agency is given by California and Nevada with the consent of Congress. But political governance in the basin is divided among parts of two states and five counties, and the incorporated city of South Lake Tahoe. Further jurisdictional complication is added by a number of federal agencies that have administrative responsibilities in the basin, including ownership of over half of the land area.

   2 Umbrella-type authority. It is inherently difficult to achieve necessary coordination of land-use planning and action through such an authority. The agency has been given certain stipulated powers which are applied through a number of political units of government. Implementation of such planning necessarily takes the form of policies, directives, regulations, zoning, and ordinances.

   3 Multiple interests. Whose interests are to be served? This is often a key question of land-use policy action. It is well illustrated by the Tahoe situation. In what proportion is it the interests of the "American people" at large, the general region, or the local residents? Tahoe is a focus of strong local, regional, and national interests which somehow have to be weighed and balanced. There is no formula for the "best" answer.

   4 The problem of gaining acceptance. Wherever there are conflicts, as there almost always are in land-use affairs, no decision will fully satisfy everybody. But it is necessary to attain some reasonable level of acceptance. Otherwise, there will be continuing and nonproductive controversy, perhaps obstruction, and decisions that do not hold. This is a general problem. Land use has its full share as it impinges on many different and often very strong people interests. Tahoe is an excellent example. In the long run, the success of the new basinwide planning agency will be measured by the degree of acceptance it can get and at the same time meet its responsibilities.

5   Advocacy versus responsibility. It is easier to advocate, to criticize and demand, than it is to assume responsibility. Advocacy certainly accomplishes much and is an important and necessary part of public decision-making processes. It also usually has an advantage in the public news media. This is true at Tahoe, where strong advocacy has been marked. Those on the defensive, often termed "the establishment," the vested interests, or such, say less publicly, but they frequently have an advantage in resources. There is no all-wise referee.

6   Preservation versus development. This issue underlies land-use problems in Lake Tahoe Basin. The extreme in preservation would permit minimal development and restricted land use. An extreme in development near Lake Tahoe could destroy much of the natural beauty of the basin and of the lake itself. Some reasonable balance must be found. This problem is built into the Tahoe Regional Planning Agency, which is directed by the compact law "to maintain an equilibrium between the region's natural endowment and its manmade environment; to preserve the scenic beauties and recreational opportunities of the region and to provide for and enforce orderly development."

7   Irreversible land uses. By the nature of Lake Tahoe Basin—its topography, soils, and climate—most development is irreversible. This applies especially to Lake Tahoe itself, which is the central attraction of the area. People-caused contamination of the lake, filling of marshy areas, and the building of structures along or into the lake can irreversibly change the character of the lake.

8   Rights of landownership. Ownership of Lake Tahoe Basin is divided among federal, state, and private owners, and this fact presents difficult land-use problems. Under the bistate compact, stipulated state authority is delegated to the agency, but federal authority expressly is not. A specific legal question is how far such an agency can go in placing land-use controls on present private owners through zoning, regulations, and ordinances. Carried to an extreme, such controls could constitute expropriation of property without adequate compensation.

Planning Processes and Problems

9   Plans. What is a plan? This may sound like a rhetorical question, but it is important. As emphasized in Chap. 6, the word means different things to different people and organizations. A plan also can take on many forms and have varying levels of authority. In the Tahoe case, the first regional plan of December 2, 1971, was prepared by a governing public agency acting under authority specifically given to it by state and federal law. It was certainly unusual in form, but through it the agency did exercise

its authority through policy statement, regulations, and ordinances. These are superimposed on the authority of the several nonfederal political units of government already existing in the basin. This plan is also unusual in that final authority for its approval was vested in the planning agency. This is different from a plan that must be submitted to a higher authority for approval.

10 Variables. As a general planning principle, the more variables that must be considered, the more difficult is the planning job. In the Tahoe situation, problems of land capabilities, governance, divided land-use interests, and a wide range in the kinds of land-use constraints required, constituted a difficult planning job.

11 Plan complexity. Whatever a plan may be, it has to be intelligible to those who are to use and be affected by it. This was a basic weakness of the initial and unacceptable plan prepared in early 1971. Aside from heavy emphasis on the undeniably critical ecological-environmental constraints needed in the basin, there were complex maps based on nearly sixty land-oriented variables. The text was not clearly informative as to action by the agency. The plan was not understood by those who would have to work and live with it. The initial general plan that was subsequently approved in December 1971 was direct and to the point about the agency's charge—whether everybody liked it or not.

12 Planners and planees. There must be effective interfaces between the planners and the planees. Lack of these interfaces as the planning work went along contributed substantially to the failure of the initial Tahoe plan when presented.

13 Problems of the "master plan" approach. Both the 1980 Tahoe Regional Plan prepared from 1962 to 1964, and the plan proposed in May 1971 were of this general type. Both failed but for somewhat different reasons. Regarding the "1980 Plan," there was no continuing provision for either stable staff funding or unified power of implementation. It was doomed on that account regardless of other considerations. Planning without power to execute is an expensive exercise in futility. The May 1971 plan had the compact power of law behind it but was weak on effective interfaces and was considered complicated and impractical to execute.

14 The necessity to provide for plan continuity. Failure to do this is a common weakness. In Lake Tahoe Basin it took well over a decade of interest and action by many people and organizations to build up the experience and a degree of common understanding sufficient to support establishment of a continuing regional agency with power and adequate staff. Clear provision for continuity is an inescapable prerequisite for successful planning.

15 Getting "the data." In few areas of its size have more studies been made and more data of many kinds assembled than at Tahoe. Much information is certainly needed for successful planning, but its usability, when subjected to the hard test of realities in application, may be something else. The massive data gathering behind the regional plan proposal of May 1971 is a good illustration. However good the information was technically, it did not meet the critical issues of what had to be done to support a workable plan of action.

The story of Lake Tahoe, as far as it can be given here, gives an excellent example of planning processes applied under complex and difficult conditions. Much has been accomplished and much has been learned from both successes and failures. Time goes on, and the future will bring more challenges. problems, and issues to resolve. However, a continuing basinwide authority now exists and is equipped to meet the needs of the future.

Decision in the North Cascades

The purpose of this chapter is to present decision-making processes on a large scale as applied to public land-use policy and management in the North Cascades portion of the state of Washington (Fig. 10.1). The gross area is 7 million acres of mountainous lands, much of them of outstanding scenic quality (Table 10.1). As shown, ownership is dominantly federal, 6.3 million acres or nearly 90 percent. This proportion has held for over 70 years. The rest of the area, some 728,800 acres, is in intermingled private, state, municipal, and county lands. The emphasis of this chapter is on the federal lands. Mt. Ranier National Park, established in 1899 and managed

Deep and grateful acknowledgment is made to Dr. Edward C. Crafts for major assistance in the preparation of this chapter. During the period of the major events covered here he was director of the Bureau of Outdoor Recreation, Department of the Interior, and also served as chairman of the special North Cascades Study Team. Previously, he was deputy chief of the U.S. Forest Service in the Department of Agriculture. As a career professional, he is consequently intimately informed about the North Cascades issue and played a major part in it.

Dr. Crafts not only gave me access to his personal materials but was most generous in giving me the benefit of his knowledge and experience in discussion. He has also reviewed this chapter in draft form and given valuable help. Responsibility for treatment must, however, remain with the author.

Table 10.1   Land and Water Areas by Ownership in the North Cascades Study Area

Ownership	Land area* Thousand acres	Land area* Percent	Water area† Thousand acres	Water area† Percent	Total area Thousand acres	Total area Percent
Federal						
National forest	6,067.8	86.2	6.9	21.1	6,074.7	85.9
National park	241.6	3.4	0.2	0.6	241.8	3.4
Total	6,309.4	89.6	7.1	21.7	6,316.5	89.3
Other public						
State	37.3	0.5	24.7	75.3	62.0	0.9
County	0.2	‡	0	0	0.2	‡
Municipal	51.6	0.7	0	0	51.6	0.7
Total	89.1	1.3	24.7	75.3	113.8	1.6
Total public	6,398.5	90.9	31.8	97.0	6,430.3	90.9
Total private	639.7	9.1	1.0	3.0	640.7	9.1
All ownerships	7,038.2	100.0	32.8	100.0	7,071.0	100.0

Source: North Cascades Study Team, 1965.
*Including bodies of water under 25 acres.
†Bodies of water 25 acres or larger.
‡Less than 0.05 percent.

by the National Park Service, is in the southern end of the area. The rest of the federal area is under national forest management by the U.S. Forest Service.

There has been long public controversy regarding land-use policy and management of federal lands in the North Cascades. Basically, this has centered on the degree and manner in which preservation of the outstanding natural, scenic, and recreational qualities in the area are emphasized and managed. The key questions are whether one or more new national parks, national recreation areas, or wilderness areas should be established in the area.

This situation necessarily injects questions of policy and jurisdiction between the two large federal services. Each has different statutory land-management objectives which make them competitive in situations such as this where lands of high recreational value and indubitable park quality are present. The policy of the National Park Service is that wildland areas of outstanding recreational quality and natural features are to be preserved in perpetuity for the benefit and enjoyment of the people without impairment of the resource. This is a difficult policy to apply as there is a basic conflict between preservation and use by people. The Forest Service follows a more flexible policy of a combined- or multiple-use concept of land management. This concept can and does include management of statutory national wilderness areas and national recreation areas, both of which can also be administered by the National Park Service. It also includes several classes of wildland areas with special administrative use restrictions such as primitive and limited areas.

Although the "to be or not to be" national park issue was the best known publicly, it is important to recognize that the North Cascades situation involved deeper policy and jurisdictional questions in land-use management. Both services are able and dedicated to their responsibilities. Each has a strong public image and proponents as well as detractors.

Although origins of the controversy go back a long time, some of the history must be known to understand the issues. The focus of events is, however, on the 6 years from 1963 to 1968 during which decisive study and action took place with permanent results. The chapter first presents essential information about the North Cascades and then gives the development of events through this period leading to congressional decision in 1968.

THESE ARE THE NORTH CASCADES

To understand a land-use issue, it is first necessary to know about the land from which it arises. This is particularly true of the North Cascades. The area is large, somewhat exceeding Vermont in extent, the topography is rugged, and its resources are large and varied. It must be seen to be fully appreciated. One also needs to have some knowledge of surrounding areas in the state of Washington to understand the total land situation. Perforce, treatment here will be somewhat limited in detail, but enough is given for the understanding of essentials. The report of the North Cascades Study Team in 1965 gives a thorough presentation of the area and its resources and is a key reference.

The study area, as defined by the study team, was specifically limited to federal lands within the solid boundaries shown in Fig. 10.1. As shown, the area extends on a south-north axis from a little south of Mount Ranier National Park, where it is approximately 60 miles wide, north about 175 miles to the Canadian border. The area widens, east-west, to about 100 miles over the northern half. The generally north-south Cascade Divide approximately splits the area. Most of it is 120 miles or less by air, from the large Puget Sound cities of Tacoma, Seattle, Everett, and Bellingham.

Nevertheless, at the time of the study (1963—1965) the area was surprisingly little known because of its limited public accessibility. Highways and railroads cross it east and west and only at two places in the southern half of the area. These are over the Stevens and Snoqualmie Passes, re-

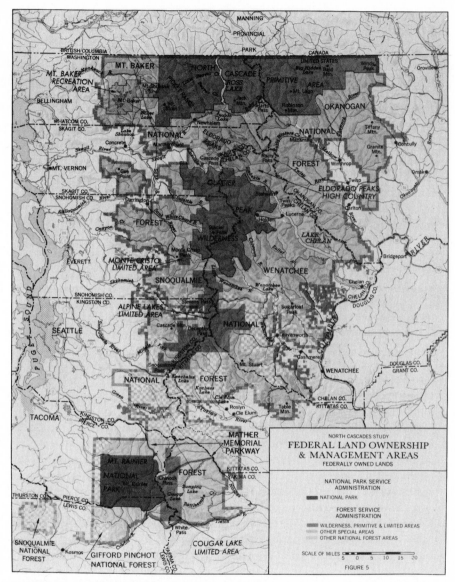

Figure 10-1   The North Cascades study area. *(From U.S. Department of the Interior and U.S. Department of Agriculture joint study report.)*

spectively, and one sees little of the country from these routes. North of Stevens Pass there are several dead-end roads that enter the area via stream drainages but give relatively limited view of the rugged mountainous terrain. There is, however, the North Cross-State Highway. At the time of the study it was constructed up the Skagit River to a little beyond Diablo Lake.

It was planned to cross the Cascade Divide and go down the Methow
River. This highway subsequently has been completed. There are only two
means of surface approach by water. The major one, and long used, is up
beautiful Lake Chelan on the east side. This narrow lake of glacial origin
penetrates some 55 miles into the heart of the North Cascades. The other,
and rather limited water access, is from Canada to the north, extending
south through Ross Lake.

Within the study area there are 288 peaks with elevations of 7,000 to
9,000 feet, and 16 above 9,000. The three highest are Mount Ranier, 14,410;
Mount Baker, 10,788; and Glacier Peak, 10,541 feet. Of particular significance at the north are Mount Shuksan and the incomparable Picket Range
close to the Canadian border. This range includes, as indicative of its rugged and spectacular nature, the high peaks from north to south of Redoubt,
Fury, Challenger, Terror, and Triumph. The Pickets were a major factor in
consideration of a national park to include them. These mountains appear
particularly high because they begin from near sea level. There are also 519
glaciers covering 97 square miles. This is about three times the glacier area
in all the rest of the United States, excluding Alaska.

Figures 10.2 to 10.6 indicate some of the outstanding topographic features of the area.

Climatically, the area is sharply split by the Cascades Divide. Moist air
coming from the western Pacific Ocean gives precipitation of from 40 to
100 inches annually on the western side. Precipitation comes as rain at the
lower elevations and mostly as snow at the higher. On the east side, precipitation drops sharply from 40 to 50 inches near the divide to 12 to 15 inches
annually at the eastern edge.

As would be expected, this precipitation pattern is markedly reflected
by the vegetation. Along the western side of the area, on the lower slopes
and to midelevations up the drainages are dense stands of Douglas-fir and
associated mesophytic species of great productivity and value. On the drier
east side, on the middle and lower slopes are ponderosa pine and mixed
conifers with some intermixed grasslands.

Between these two irregular forest belts on the western and eastern
sides of the North Cascades there is a central blunt "wedge" or core of
rugged high mountain country. This is of surpassing grandeur and wildland
scenic quality. It is widest at the Canadian border, roughly 80 miles east
and west starting with Mount Baker on the west. It tapers down to a blunt
end about 20 miles wide near Snoqualmie Pass to the south. Mount Ranier
and surrounding country further south are related but topographically
somewhat separate.

It is within this "wedge" or core part of the total study area that controversy in the North Cascades centers and always has regarding land use
management policies and jurisdiction of the Forest Service and the Nation-

Figure 10-2   Looking up the White Chuck River to Glacier Peak. *(Courtesy of U.S. Department of the Interior, National Park Service.)*

Figure 10-3 Alpine Lakes area. *(Courtesy of U.S. Department of the Interior, National Park Service.)*

al Park Service. It is important to understand this general fact from the beginning. Other wildland areas in the general North Cascades area, and indeed of the whole Northwest region of the United States, are a part of the total situation and must be recognized as such. However, the critical issues considered here are focused in this northern core part of the North Cascades. There are good reasons for this, as are itemized below regarding its status in 1963 when detailed study of the area was initiated.

1 The prime high-mountain scenic qualities of the North Cascades are mostly in this area; Mount Ranier to the south has long had national park status.

2 Because the study area was limited specifically to federal ownership, public use policy consequently could be changed by the Congress. There is no significant private land acquisition problem involved in the key study area.

3 Although there is considerable timber of commercial quality in this area, it is of relatively low value for such use due to inaccessibility. Relative recreation and scenic values are higher. Little cutting has been done.

4 Mineral resources in the North Cascades area are potentially considerable, but they are little developed in this core area. There are patented

Figure 10-4   Middle fork of Pasayten Valley. *(Courtesy of U.S. Department of the Interior, National Park Service.)*

mining claims, but the possibilities of significant detriment to the study area by mining under legal controls are considered to be small.

5   The area is of economic significance to the local counties because they receive 25 percent of national forest receipts. The *way* these receipts are distributed is important. County lines exist in national forests, and the receipts from a national forest are distributed to the counties on the basis of the percentage of each county lying within the national forest boundary. A county with a large national forest area in it consequently gets a large share of the receipts even if that area contributes little to forest receipts.

6   Hunting, primarily for goats and deer, is of considerable but not major importance in the areas which might be included in a national park.

7   This core area had been under national forest administration for many years, and was primarily but rather lightly used for recreation purposes. As shown in Fig. 10.1, large areas in it were, in 1963, classified for recreational use as follows: the Mount Baker Recreation Area, the large North Cascade Primitive Area, the limited Eldorado Peaks High country, and the Glacier Peak Wilderness. There were also limited areas to the south; the Monte Cristo Limited Area, Alpine Lakes Limited Area, and the Cougar Lakes Limited Area adjoining Mount Ranier National Park.

To summarize: the study area, being over 90 percent in federal owner-

Figure 10-5 Part of the Picket Range. *(Courtesy of U.S. Department of the Interior, National Park Service.)*

ship, was subject to congressional decision on land uses without critical land-use precommitments or large land acquisition costs to deter. The area was also little known or understood by the public at large.

THE DEVELOPMENT OF CONTROVERSY

As indicated by the foregoing, the basis for controversy over public land-use policy in the North Cascades had a long history, going back almost to the creation of the national forests and the national park system. Many studies, reports, travelogues, appraisals, and proposals about the North Cascades had been made over the years. Recurrent, and related to questions of balance in land resource uses, were proposals for establishment of additional national parks. The idea of having at least one national park in the central core area had repeatedly arisen. The overall quality of the area for such use is not debatable; differences have centered on alternatives in land-use policy and practices which differ between the National Park Service and the Forest Service. Except for Mount Ranier National Park at the southern end, the Forest Service has had the entire study area under its jurisdiction for many years. In 1963 there were parts or all of five national forests in the study area.

Figure 10-6 Marble Creek and Eldorado Peak. *(Courtesy of U.S. Department of the Interior, National Park Service.)*

As far back as 1906 the Lake Chelan region was suggested for national park status. The Mount Baker area was proposed in 1908 by the Mazamas club, a Western mountain-climbing organization. The first congressional sponsorship was during 1916 to 1919, when a number of bills for a Mount Baker National Park were introduced but with no results. A Yakima National Park was proposed in three bills in the years 1919 through 1921 but with no congressional action. The principal early report, often quoted and recommending a North Cascades National Park, was by O. A. Tomlinson and others in 1937. In 1940, a Washington state report (Washington State Planning Council, 1940) recommended that "no additional lands of the Cascade Mountains be converted into use as a national park."

So it went, back and forth, with a rising crescendo of national park advocacy on into the 1960s. An excellent and complete literature citation and a chronology of events are given in the bibliography of the North Cascades Study Team's report, 1965. A statement by the chairman of this team, Dr. Edward C. Crafts, on page 13 of the report is in point here:

> The available literature appears not to give a balanced picture of the multiple use resources of the area, their use and management. The bulk of the literature over the years has been by advocates of change, particularly those who have

favored a North Cascades Park. Their views have been repeatedly, militantly, and emotionally expressed.

In contrast, Federal administrators of the area and commercial users of the resources for the most part have been going about their business of management, administration and use, rather than defending their actions or explaining their plans.

Criticism has been freely and frequently directed at the Forest Service. Officials of that agency, as is usually the case with public servants, are necessarily restrained by their position from exercising equal freedom in their response to criticism.

It is important to recognize that park proposals have stemmed from conservationists or park advocates generally and not from states, counties, or organizations directly concerned with or responsible for land management in the Pacific Northwest.

Appointment of a Study Team

This long background of controversy in public land-use policy came to focus in the Kennedy and Johnson administrations. It was by no means limited to the North Cascades issue. Both the Department of the Interior and the Department of Agriculture were deeply concerned with large-scale public land-use management and natural resources policy matters that brought them into jurisdictional conflict.

Outdoor recreation was a matter of major concern and responsibility to both. In 1956 the National Park Service embarked on a 10 year program, "Mission 66," to strengthen critically needed national park financing and management. Shortly afterward, the Forest Service initiated a similar drive, "Operation Outdoors," to improve recreational development on the national forests, where the number of visitors greatly exceed those in the national parks. The Forest Service had strong public service reasons for wishing to strengthen national recognition of its responsibilities in outdoor recreation. This was, in fact, a major reason for its pressing for passage of the Multiple Use and Sustained Yield Act of 1960.

The two Secretaries of Agriculture and of the Interior wrote a joint letter to President Kennedy dated January 28, 1963. It is often referred to as "The Treaty of the Potomac." In it, the Secretaries stated:

> We have reached agreement on a broad range of issues which should enable our Departments to enter into "a new era of cooperation" in the management of Federal lands for outdoor recreation. . . . Neither Department will initiate unilaterally new proposals to change the status of lands under jurisdiction of the other Department.

The letter also stated that the Secretaries had agreed that:

> A joint study should be made of Federal lands in the North Cascade Moun-

tains of Washington to determine the management and administration of those lands that will best serve the public interest. . . . The study team will consist of representatives of the two Departments and will be chaired by an individual jointly selected by us.

Recommendations of the study group will be submitted to us and we in turn will make our recommendations to you.

President Kennedy replied January 31, thanking the Secretaries and saying their letter was "an excellent statement of cooperation representing a milestone in conservation progress." The only specific matter mentioned in the letter was the President's interest in the North Cascades joint study proposal.

Events moved rapidly after this exchange of correspondence. Following considerable preparatory activity, Secretaries Stewart Udall and Orville Freeman, jointly wrote on March 5 to Dr. Edward C. Crafts, then director of the Bureau of Outdoor Recreation, Department of the Interior. They appointed him chairman of the study team and named four other members, two from the Department of Agriculture—Dr. George A. Selke, consultant to the Secretary, and Arthur W. Greeley, deputy chief of the Forest Service—and two from the Department of the Interior—Dr. Owen S. Stratton,[2] consultant to the Secretary, and George B. Hartzog, Jr., director of the National Park Service.

The Secretaries also gave their charge to the study team. It was very broad. The possibility of new national park establishment was mentioned only through recognition of jurisdictional responsibilities. Some key language from the letter follows:

A joint study should be made of Federal lands . . . to determine the management and administration of those lands that will best serve the public interest.

. . . As an initial step, agreement should be reached on the specific area to be included in the study.

[The study team] should explore in an objective manner all the resource potentials of the area and the management and administration that appears to be in the public interest.

We consider this matter of high priority. . . . Facilities, files, and records of both the National Park Service and the Forest Service, as well as other facilities of the two Departments, are hereby made available to you and other members of the study team.

Your Committee should handle this assignment in the way it deems best.

Certainly there should be a review of past studies and recommendations, current use and management of the area, proposals for change, and an inventory and evaluation of all resource potentials, including a weighing of the economic and social impact of various alternatives.

Your report should include recommendations as to both management

2 Replacing Henry Caulfield, who was initially appointed.

and administration, including jurisdictional responsibility. We recognize that
there may not be unanimous agreement among the study team, although we
hope that agreement may be reached on basic facts. If there is disagreement as
to recommendations, we believe it would be appropriate for this dissent to be
shown. . . .

It would be appropriate to include in your recommendations more than
one action alternative. . . .

The Committee may, in order to evaluate public opinion and obtain views
and recommendations, find it desirable to hold public hearings.

We ask that you arrange to receive from the Governor of the State of
Washington a written statement setting forth the recommendations of the
state.

We know this is a difficult, complex, and controversial assignment.

Because of the history and complex issues involved, we are not placing a
deadline on the committee for its report. We do urge, however, that you proceed with due deliberation and haste.

With the establishment of the joint study, backed by the Secretaries of
the Interior and Agriculture and approved by the President, a major first
step in the processes of decision regarding the North Cascades was made.
Full information regarding the history, resources, and management of the
area was to be made available to the public and to the Congress, where final
decisions had to be made. Consensus by the team was not required nor
could it be. But its recommendations, with inclusion of possible differing
viewpoints by individual team members, would be documented public information. The same was true of official positions taken by the Department
of the Interior and the Department of Agriculture and presented to the
team. The bases for decision were to be made public.

THE JOINT STUDY REPORT

Following 2½ years of information collection, hearings, study, special reports, and analysis, the report of the North Cascades Study Team, *The
North Cascades* (190 pages fully illustrated), was completed in October 1965
(the printing date of the report). It was transmitted, with some later documentary additions, to the Secretaries of the Interior and Agriculture by its
chairman, Dr. Edward C. Crafts, by his letter of December 6, 1965.

Also related to the report and considered in it were six special resource
studies made by team members, six additional reports especially prepared
by others for the study team, and two state of Washington reports made in
1964. One of the latter was largely a commentary on the six special resource
studies mentioned above. The other dealt with the existing Cougar Lake
Limited Area just east of Mount Ranier National Park (Fig. 10.1). These
reports were consonant with the charge made by the two Secretaries in
establishing the joint study team to ask for recommendations from the state
of Washington.

The charge of the joint study team was thoroughly and meticulously fulfilled in this report. There "was general agreement on the facts" (chairman's transmittal letter), and the chairman also characterized it as "an extraordinary inter-departmental effort" (chairman's acknowledgement). It is truly a milestone report in North Cascades affairs and includes in one place most of the relevant information about the area. The principal questions requiring answers are briefly stated in the study report as follows:

> Among the major issues confronting the study teams were: (1) Should there be a new National Park; (2) How much Wilderness is enough; (3) How best to provide for the more conventional types of recreation desired by the great mass of people; (4) How to reconcile national and local interests when the two appear in conflict; (5) How to utilize and manage the timber resources in harmony with other multiple uses of the area; and (6) The extent to which scenic roads should be an essential ingredient in making the North Cascades available to large numbers of people.

As regards action recommendations, the report, including the important appendixes, has four important parts:

1 National Park Service agency position statement.
2 Forest Service agency position statement.
3 Team recommendations.
4 Individual statements by the four team members other than the chairman.

The National Park and Forest Service agency position statements were given to the study team before team recommendations were made. The individual statements by team members were made subsequent to the team recommendations.

Neither the agency position statements nor the views of the study team were unanimous, although there was agreement on most points. The major divergence, to be expected, was on the national park issue. There were also other differences regarding wilderness areas, national recreation areas, and other area designations. But these were susceptible to adjudication as to character, extent, location, and jurisdiction. As has been previously indicated, issues centered on the central "wedge" of the North Cascades study area.

A summary of the principal differences regarding particular designations is given below for each of the four recommendations groups. To gain a more complete understanding of the issues and the land resource situations, one needs to read the study report in full and also visit the area. Because of its complex topography and the wide ecological variation present in the North Cascades, there is much interrelatedness and interdependence between the various land area use recommendations made.

Meaningful boundaries can be drawn only from close knowledge on the ground of topography and possible land uses. Figure 10.1 should be referred to as the existing base at the time of the study and on which recommended changes are superimposed.

National Park Service Position

As regards specific and major land-use changes, the National Park Service, at the time of the study, recommended the following:

1   Establish a new Mount Baker National Park in the northwest corner of the area. It would include and enlarge the previous Mount Baker Recreation Area north to the Canadian line and east to include Mount Shuksan and the Picket Range and extend nearly to the North-south Ross Lake. It would also include the western part of the ten-existing North Cascades Primitive Area.

2   Establish a new Glacier Peak National Park essentially replacing the previous Glacier Peak Wilderness.

3   Establish essentially the balance of the present North Cascades Primitive Area as the Okanogan Wilderness.

4   Establish a new and large Eldorado-Chelan National Recreation Area essentially replacing the previous Eldorado Peaks High Country area. It would also extend southward in a wide band on the east of the proposed Glacier Peak National Park to include upper Lake Chelan.

5   Establish an Alpine Lakes–Mount Stewart Wilderness essentially replacing, with enlargement to the east, the present Alpine Lakes Limited Area.

6   Enlarge Mount Ranier National Park on the east out of the present Cougar Lake Primitive Area, which was recommended to be discontinued. A small addition to the park on the south side was also recommended.

7   Give high priority to "design and development of a system of scenic drives and parkways in the Cascades region."

Forest Service Position

Having managed the 6 million acres of federal lands in the study area for nearly 60 years and organizationally developed with the country, the Forest Service took a much different position from that of the National Park Service. It had done much land-use planning over the years and had large knowledge and experience with on-the-ground land management and administration. It had also made plans for future development. The Forest Service was, by statute, committed to multiple-use resource management, which includes wilderness, national recreation areas, and other recreation-oriented land-use classifications. Several of these were already established in the study area.

The Forest Service gave a careful but condensed statement of its present and projected plans and land-use policy for the area. Areas designated for recreation-oriented use in 1963 are shown in Fig. 10.1. As shown, predominantly recreational uses were concentrated in the central core or wedge. There was no disagreement that this was where the major issues centered. The Forest Service was, however concerned with recreation and scenic values along with other resources appraised in balance over the entire study area and including water, timber, forage, wildlife, fish, mineral, and improved road access consideration.

Essentially, the Forest Service position was a continuation and enlargement of its present land-use management designations, plans, and policies. The two major changes proposed in recreation uses were to add "some 237,000 acres to the area of dedicated Wilderness areas as well as reclassifying the 801,000-acre North Cascades Primitive area to Wilderness area status."

Team Recommendations

As indicated by the foregoing, the Department of the Interior and the Department of Agriculture were divided on the new national park issue. In an attempt to reconcile this difference and some others and to build on substantial areas of agreement, and because of personal conviction, the chairman took leadership in development of a team report somewhat between these positions but including a new national park. The proposal was carefully and thoroughly worked out and supported with stated reasons. Inasmuch as the four other team members were divided equally on the park issue and on some other points, the chairman's report became the team report. However, differing view of the other team members as they wished to express them, are published as addenda to the team report.

The chairman's twenty-one recommendations and the reasons for them cannot be given in detail here, but there was team agreement on nearly all of them. The major land-use provisions are summarized below and can generally be identified on Fig. 10.1. Again, they essentially relate to the same core area as do all other recommendations. It is recognized that a reader unacquainted with the area cannot appreciate the specific considerations of topography and resources that give basis for drawing particular boundary lines. Nevertheless, a general understanding of them is possible and gives basis for appreciation of the complexities of land-use allocation in this rugged and beautiful area.

The principal recommendations regarding specific land-use area changes are as follows:

1 Establish a North Cascades National Park of 698,000 acres to include Mount Shuksan (but excluding Mount Baker) and part of the existing North Cascade Primitive area. The park would include the Picket Range to just east of Ross Lake, extend south to the existing Glacier Peak Wilderness and south-east to the upper part of Lake Chelan and include much of the existing Eldorado Peaks High Country area.

2 Establish four new wilderness areas, a total of 720,000 acres, as
   follows:
   a Alpine Lakes—replacing, with some boundary change, the ex-
      isting limited area of the same name south of Stevens Pass
   b Enchantment—a wilderness area centered on Mount Stewart
      southeast of Alpine Lakes
   c Okanogan—replacing that part of the existing North Cascade
      Primitive Area just south of the Canadian border and beginning
      a little east of Ross Lake
   d Mount Aix—a wilderness area to the east of, but separated from,
      Mount Ranier
3 Enlarge the Glacier Peak Wilderness by 39,000 acres.
4 Enlarge Mount Ranier National Park by 7,000 acres on the south.
5 Declassify three existing limited areas—Alpine Lakes, Cougar Lake,
   and Monte Christo Peak.

Some effects of and further provisions in the team recommendations
include:

Increase by 228,000 acres the national forest lands to be placed under
normal multiple-use administration by the Forest Service.

Increase the available commercial forest land by 56,000 acres and the
volume of commercial sawtimber available to the timber industry by 1.5
billion board feet. Establish a new national park and more wilderness areas.

Provide for a 900-mile system of scenic roads and several thousand
miles of trails.

Establish a wild river in the Skagit Basin.

Statements by Team Members

After considering the recommendations proposed by the team chairman
and the agency position statements by the National Park Service and the
Forest Service, each of the four team members prepared statements on the
team chairman's proposals. The two Department of Agriculture members,
Selke and Greeley, also prepared a joint statement to summarize their views
and to make clear their position as representatives of the Department of
Agriculture. All these statements are included in the report.

The specifics of these statements cannot be given here, but they are
informative on particular issues and reflect both personal and official agency opinions.

Areas of disagreement were narrowed, clarified, and better defined.
General team agreement did emerge on several major points:

1 The Department of the Interior team members did not support the
agency recommendation for a second national park in the Glacier Peaks
area.

2   Although the team was divided 3 to 2 in favor of one national park, there was agreement as to substantially *where* it should be—in the north and west part of the central core area against the Canadian boundary. There was sharp disagreement about whether or not Mount Baker should be included.

3   There was general agreement on the Glacier Peak Wilderness and its boundaries.

4   There was interest in and support for national recreation areas but no clear consensus on locations.

5   Wilderness designation was preferred to less formal primitive or limited-use categories.

6   Although there were differences in specifics, there were no major issues that could not be resolved concerning the southern half of the study area.

7   There was general recognition that, although the entire study area and beyond had relevance, the key issues involved alternative means of protecting outstanding scenic values and providing outdoor recreation. Further, it was recognized that these questions centered in the northern core of the study area. There was unanimity that this area was most valuable for such uses. The central issue was how to allocate these land uses by categories and jurisdiction in this core area.

In Summary

The North Cascades Study Team report, the studies made in conjunction with it, the field hearings held, and a rather unprecedented joint effort by two major Departments to resolve conflicts in land use-policy constituted a major and constructive part in the process of moving toward decisions. Although the report did not necessarily change many people's opinions, and there was an increasing crescendo of public advocacy pro and con during its progress, it did give a foundation for understanding issues and a basis for formation of public opinion.

POLITICAL DECISION

Publication of the North Cascades Study Team report to the Secretaries of the Interior and Agriculture placed the decision before the President and the Congress. Congressional action is necessary to establish national parks, national recreation areas, and wilderness. Political consideration of action was held in abeyance until the study report was completed as it constituted the key public document.

Study Team Hearings

Before going into administration and congressional action, we should consider the hearings held by the study team as they are a part of the necessary process of sounding public opinion.

The study team, before preparing its report, held open public hearings in Wenatchee, Mt. Vernon, and Seattle, Washington, over a 5 day period in October 1963.

Over 300 witnesses or statements were heard or received at these hearings. The record was kept open for about a month and about 2,200 additional letters were received by the team prior to closing the record on November 15, 1963. The transcript of some 3,200 pages continues to be available at offices of the Bureau of Outdoor Recreation, National Park Service, and the Forest Service (North Cascades Study Team, 1965, p.11).

It is difficult to know, or objectively to evaluate, the backgrounds, knowledge, or motives of individuals or representatives of organizations who make statements at such hearings. This problem is evident from analysis of the hearing record. About 90 percent of the written or oral statements were made by individuals presumably speaking for themselves. The rest, some 257, were presented in the name of organizations. A wide representation of local, state, regional, and national interests were heard. Many of the same people were at all three hearings.

Of the 216 witnesses who gave oral testimony, 126 endorsed Forest Service management, whereas 87 recommended a change in policy or administration generally favoring either more Wilderness areas or a creation of a National Park. . . . Of the 2,275 statements received following the close of the hearing and before the close of the record, the ratio was about four to one in favor of establishing a National Park in the North Cascades (North Cascades Study Team, 1965, P. 82).

The 257 organizations were classified in ten groups according to their nature and included units of local and state governments, chambers of commerce, public service groups, sportsmen's groups and conservation and related groups. Of these, only the conservation and related group generally favored a national park and additional wilderness area.

Regarding the hearings as a whole, it was evident that many did not understand the management policies of either the National Park Service or the Forest Service. There was a tendency to consider national parks and wilderness areas as interchangeable, whereas management objectives differ. The latter can be administered by either organization, but in fact, most are administered by the Forest Service. In general, the more rural people with more or less direct economic or other use interests in the area favored the status quo. The conservation and related organizations, with less direct economic concern in the area, or in a position to assume responsibility for change, generally favored national parks and wilderness areas. "The center of support for a National Park was found in the urban areas and the center of opposition in the rural areas" (North Cascades Study Team, 1965, p. 85).

The hearings certainly indicated much national as well as local interest in public land-use policies in the North Cascades, whether they were understood or not. There was the usual popular tendency to try to oversimplify a complex land-use issue into the question of whether or not there should be a national park.

Before, during, and after the 2½ year study an increasing amount of material concerning the North Cascades issue was published in magazines, newspapers, and other publications. Most favored national park establishment. But the pros and cons of the arguments have already been given, and further detail probably would add little except to emphasize the existence of a wide and strong public interest in the North Cascades.

Political Action and Decision

This section gives in chronological sequence the principal events that followed completion of the North Cascades Study Team's report. They terminate with President Johnson signing, on October 2, 1968, Public Law 90-544, which established the North Cascades National Park, the Ross Lake and Lake Chelan National Recreation Areas, and the Pasayten Wilderness, and also made some changes in the boundaries of the Glacier Peak Wilderness (Fig. 10.7).

Before examining this sequence of events, it will be well to recognize some of the realities of higher-level workings in the Congress and the President's office in such matters. Such can be likened to an iceberg, as only a small part is visible to the public. The visible parts are public actions recorded in the *Congressional Record*, the *Federal Register*, reports of hearings, and other public records. The rest is action by influential people, often with no written record.

For example, a department or bureau head does not actually write many of the letters he or she signs and often does not initiate them. The joint letter that the Secretaries of the Interior and Agriculture sent to the President regarding joint policy and action on outdoor recreation matters was the subject of much discussion and informal decision. But the final draft was prepared mainly by the chairman of the study team. The joint letter sent by the two Secretaries to Dr. Crafts officially established the study team and gave policy procedural directives. The chairman, however, directly participated in the preparation of the letter, and properly so, because he was to be responsible for execution of the study. Development of official documents at higher levels of authority is frequently a complex matter. Many people and considerations are often involved and only those directly participating can know when, where, and how decisions are made and put into final form for public release.

Regarding legislative bills introduced into the Congress, what is said on the floor or given in congressional reports represents only a part of what goes on and the considerations involved.

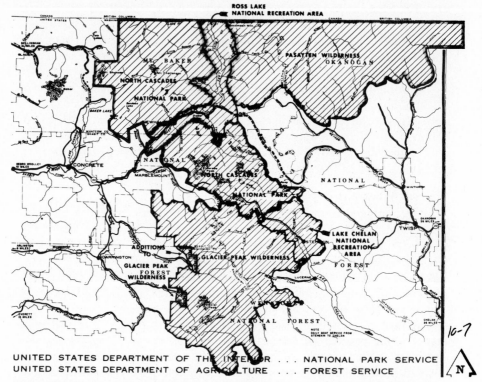

Figure 10-7 Decision in the North Cascades. Establishment by the U.S. Congress of the North Cascades National Park, the Ross Lake National Recreation Area, the Pasayten Wilderness, the Lake Chelan National Recreation Area, and the Glacier Peak Wilderness.

To return to the sequence of events regarding the joint study report, following internal departmental consideration it was publically released through a press conference jointly held by Secretaries Udall and Freeman in Seattle in January 1966. It received considerable publicity and attention.

Closely following this press conference, the Senate held field hearings on the report February 11, 1966, in Washington state. These were initiated by Senator Jackson of Washington, who was informed, concerned, determined, and influential in the North Cascades issue. Such hearing action is unusual because the Congress normally holds hearings only on proposed legislation before it, and not on administrative studies of the Executive Office.

On July 14, 1966, Governor Daniel J. Evans of Washington transmitted by letter to Senator Jackson the *North Cascades National Recreation Area; Report and Recommendations* (Evans, 1966). This report gave the results of a 3 month state study with the assistance of a high-level panel of advisors. The report did not agree with any one of the several proposals included in the joint study report but presented some new concepts. The following recommendations were made:

1 Establish a "North Cascades National Recreation Area of some 1,800,000 acres including five multiple purpose recreation areas, wilderness areas, and a wilderness-type National Park." None of these categories except wilderness officially existed.

2 By act of Congress establish a North Cascades Advisory Board consisting of the governor of Washington, the Secretary of Agriculture, the Secretary of the Interior, or their representatives.

3 That all of the North Cascades national recreation areas (item 1 above), except the wilderness-type national park, be managed by the Forest Service.

4 Complete the North Cross-State Highway (which was planned to go up the Skagit River, cross the Cascades Divide and go down the Methow River).

5 In the total North Cascades National Recreation Area establish the five following multiple-purpose recreation areas: Mount Baker, Ross Lake, Lake Chelan, Cascade River, and North Cascades Highway.

These proposals constitute the recommendations of the governor as requested by the two Secretaries in their instructions to the joint study team. None was adopted as they were in conflict with established national categories. They are given here because they are innovative, further illustrate the wide range of proposals made, and include some ideas that were acted upon.

With encouragement from the President's office, Secretaries Udall and Freeman, accompanied by Assistant Director of the Budget Philip S. Hughes, Chief of the Forest Service Edward P. Cliff, and two members of the study team, Edward C. Crafts and George B. Hartzog, made a special inspection trip to the North Cascades in the late summer of 1966. This is further evidence of the importance attached to the issue.

Legislative Action Following the 1966 on-site inspection by the two Secretaries, some high-level administration consultations were held in which two major decisions were made. The first was that a new national park be proposed to the Congress, and the second was that any national recreation areas established adjoining it be administered by the National Park Service.

Stemming from this, President Johnson's message on natural beauty to the Congress on January 30, 1967, recommended that the Ninetieth Congress establish a new national park in the North Cascades.

As is often done in matters in which the administration has strong interest, the first legislative step is to prepare a draft administration bill recommending action by the Congress. This was done within the adminis-

tration. It was transmitted to the Speaker of the House and to the President
of the Senate on March 17, 1967, through a letter from Stewart Udall,
Secretary of the Interior. It stated that the bill had been prepared in colla-
boration with the Secretary of Agriculture and had his approval. Also included, as is requisite in legislative proposals involving appropriations of
over $1 million, was an estimate of costs.

The letter further stated, "The Bureau of the Budget has advised that
this proposed legislation is in accord with the program of the President."
This statement is important as it does signify endorsement by the
President's office. Without such approval there is always the chance of
subsequent presidential veto. The wording "is in accord with" is the strong-
est endorsement one can get; it is much stronger than the wording of "no
objection" to a proposed administration bill.

The same bill was soon after introduced into the Senate and the House.
The Senate bill was S. 1321 introduced March 30, 1967, by Senator Jackson
for himself and for Senator Magnuson of Washington. The House bill was
H.R. 8970 introduced by Congressman Meeds of Washington on May 20,
1967.

These companion bills included the following key provisions as regards
land-use designations.

1 Establishment of the Ross Lake National Recreation Area to be
administered by the National Park Service. As shown in Fig. 10.7, this is
essentially a broad strip of land along both sides of the upper Skagit River
from the western national forest boundary east to Diablo Lake and power
dams, and then north up both sides the dam-impounded Ross Lake to the
Canadian boundary.

This was a new and good proposal although the general idea for such
had been previously advanced. The proposal gave this area, which is traversed by a power line, a road up to Ross Lake, and a part of the North
Cross-State Highway, a more appropriate land-use designation than national park, wilderness, or primitive area status. Another and important point,
is that establishment of the recreation area gave a proper basis for recognition of the existing power dams of the Seattle City Light and Power Co, in
the upper Skagit River. These dams created Diablo and Ross Lakes and
include a possibility of a higher dam on the latter. These land uses are
consonant with a national recreation area but not with a national park or a
wilderness area.

2 Establishment of the North Cascades National Park in two parts.
They are separated, as shown in Fig. 10.7, by the Ross Lake National
Recreation Area. The northern part included the Mount Shuksan area,
formerly a part of the Mount Baker Recreation Area, and the spectacular
Picket Range. These boundaries dealt with a point of considerable controversy because the Park Service wanted to include the Mount Baker area in
a national park. The southern part of the new park included much of the
previous Eldorado Peaks High Country area as established by the Forest

Service. It extended southeast around the Glacier Peak Wilderness to include the upper Lake Chelan area. This action also followed previous recommendation. However, by subsequent congressional amendment, this
lower part was separated and made the Lake Chelan National Recreation
Area, as shown in Fig. 10.7.

3 Establishment of the Pasayten Wilderness essentially including that
part of the previous North Cascade Primitive Area east of the Ross Lake
National Recreation Area. This was a point of previous general agreement.
Administration by the Forest Service was to continue.

4 Addition of about 10,000 acres of national forest land to the existing Glacier Peak Wilderness to deepen and round out the western boundary on the Suiattle and White Chuck Rivers. Administration by the Forest
Service was to be continued.

The proposed act also included several land acquisition, administrative, and special provisions including no change in the Forest Service formula for distribution of forest receipts to the countries. Another important
item was provision that the Picket Range and Eldorado Peaks area in the
southern part of the new national park should, within 2 years after enactment of the act, be reviewed by the Secretary of the Interior as to the
suitability or nonsuitability of any part of this area for preservation as
wilderness and so report to the President. This was another matter of considerable controversy. There was strong feeling that a part or all of this area
should be designated as wilderness.

Especially to be noted is that the administration bill placed attention
on the northern part of the inner wedge of the total study area. This is
where the key issues centered and where congressional action was required.
The administration proposal also differed substantially from proposals by
the Park Service, Washington state, the Forest Service, and the Interior and
Agriculture members of the study team. The key proposals of this bill are
similar to study team recommendations except for the creation of the Ross
Lake National Recreation Area. The administration bill provided a good
solution, and a balanced one, to a controversial problem between the Agriculture and Interior Departments.

On April 13 there was a key meeting of Governor Evans with Washington state people which included Dr. Crafts as the only administration representative. The outcome was that, although the proposed administration bill
differed sharply from the Washington recommendations, the state would
not automatically oppose it but would carefully study its provisions.

The Senate acted first on this proposed legislation, which was referred
to the Committee on Interior and Insular Affairs. In addition to the preliminary field hearings held before legislation was proposed, the Senate committee held public hearings in Washington, DC., on April 24, 1967. It also
held public hearings on the proposed legislation in Washington state: in

Seattle, May 25; Mt. Vernon, May 27; and Wenatchee, May 29. The published record of the hearings does not add in significant degree to the sampling of public opinion obtained previously by the study team or by the Senate field hearings of February 11, 1966, on the study report. The difference is that the 1967 hearings were based on introduced legislation with specific proposals. Otherwise, much the same people and interests were represented.

S.1321 was reported favorably out of the committee October 31, and, with amendments, its passage was recommended to the Senate (Senate Report 700, 90th Cong., 1st Sess., 1967). The report thoroughly reviews the North Cascades situation as regards history, existing water and uses, mining status, timber value and importance, needed private land acquisition, and other land-use values and interests.

The principal amendment made to the administration bill was to reduce the North Cascades National Park by designating the upper Lake Chelan part of it as the Lake Chelan National Recreation Area. It would be administered by the National Park Service. This was a good change, giving this area both permanent designation and needed flexibility to accomodate substantial existing recreational uses of the upper lake area. Another area amendment was to add 22,000 acres on the eastern end of the Pasayten Wilderness to improve natural boundaries. A number of water and other use rights, procedural, administrative, and minor boundary change amendments were also included which do not need to be reviewed here although they are important in specifics. These changes do, however, indicate the thoroughness of staff work and consultation that went into the Senate report. The amended bill and the Senate report were considered on the Senate floor on November 2, 1967. Senator Jackson of Washington presented and ably supported the bill. Following some discussion, the bill was passed as reported out of committee.

In the House, the administration draft of the proposed North Cascades bill was introduced on April 20, 1967, by Congressman Meeds as H.R. 8970 and referred to the Committee on Interior and Insular Affairs. Two other North Cascades bills were also introduced, H.R. 12139 by Congressman Pelly on August 7, 1967, and H.R. 16252 by Congresswoman May on March 27, 1968. Neither of these latter two bills were reported out of committee.

Public hearings were held on all three of these House bills, and S. 1321, by the Subcommittee on National Parks and Recreation as follows:

Seattle, Washington	April 19 and 20, 1968
Wenatchee, Washington	July 13, 1968
Washington, DC.	July 25 and 26, 1968
Washington, DC.	September 4, 1968

Much the same ground was gone over as in previous hearings and will not be reviewed here. There was also a field inspection by some members of the House committee.

On September 9, 1968, the House Committee on Interior and Insular Affairs favorably reported out H.R. 8970 and recommended that it be passed, as amended. The amendments were those made by the Senate on S. 1321, which were accepted, plus House specification that not more than $3,500,000 "shall be appropriated for the acquisition of lands or interest in lands." The bill was presented for debate on the House floor September 16, 1968, led by Congressman Aspinall (*Congressional Record,* pp. H. 8765–8772). The bill was debated favorably and passed.

As the final step to obtain joint approval of both houses of the Congress, S. 1321 was again briefly considered by the Senate on September 19. By motion of Senator Jackson, the House amendment setting a limit on land acquisition cost was accepted. S. 1321, as finally amended, was then sent to President Johnson for signature.

The signing of the bill was part of a historic, significant, and gala occasion in natural resources conservation for public uses. On October 2, President Johnson signed four bills creating the Redwood National Park; North Cascades National Park, together with two new national recreation areas and one wilderness in the North Cascades; the National Trails System; the National Wild and Scenic Rivers System.

All of them were the culmination of much advocacy, controversy, and inevitable compromise and adjudication worked out at the national level through the processes of decision making in a political democracy. The Redwood National Park action in particular was the result of many years of actions and often bitter controversy in a very complex, difficult situation that was poorly understood nationally. It has parallels with as well as sharp differences from the North Cascades issue. See Crafts (1971) for an informative account of the Redwood case.

The North Cascades story as developed here has focused on the main line of action in making decisions on the uses of public lands which have outstanding scenic and recreational value. Public controversy was vigorous. It should not be thought that decision was easy because no large sums of money were involved nor were there large effects on private land-use interests. There were difficult public land-use policy and jurisdictional questions to resolve. Management of the central core area, where controversy centered and decisions were made, was basically changed. Recreation and preservation were determined to be the paramount land-use management objectives.

The issues here centered on seeking permanence of land-use policy and limitation of administrative discretion. This was accomplished through congressional action, which is difficult to change. Also involved were differences of opinion in the public mind regarding the relative desirability of Forest Service versus National Park Service management of particular areas. In the discussion of hearings on the issues it was noted that people with economic or related use interests in the study area favored continuation of National Forest status which would permit more flexible land use. Dominantly urban and conservation-oriented people and organizations favored permanent national park, national recreation area, and wilderness designations. The North Cascades gives a good study of the origins, nature, and evaluation of public interest in land use.

Whether or not congressionally established wildland use units such as wilderness, national recreation areas, and national parks will in the long run necessarily result in better land use in the public interest is a debatable matter with no clear answers. Inability to change public land-use policy to meet changing conditions, which are inevitable in the people-land equation, may be desirable or not, depending on viewpoints. The public trend is to favor more land-use controls restricting development and favoring preservation of outstanding wildland areas. This is evidenced by the four bills President Johnson signed on October 2, 1968. Such decisions give the best evidence one can get as to what is collectively considered "right" in meeting particular natural resource–use problems.

WHAT CAN BE LEARNED FROM THE NORTH CASCADES?

The North Cascades case gives a good example of large-scale land-use decision making in the public interest set in a context of federal landownership and basic authority. Generally, decisions are made by people in their interests, individually or collectively, as best they can see them. Such processes are, of course, not at all limited to land-use issues, but these give excellent examples. All decisions are conditioned in greater or less degree by their specific context. Those involving land are no exception but do have peculiarities due to the nature of land. The North Cascades situation illustrates some important principles or processes regarding decisions that the reader is welcome to interpret as narrowly or broadly as may be desired. The thesis of this chapter is that a rather complex land-use situation existed which required constructive answer. Its purpose is to tell how the answer was given.

The following statements, given in no sequential order, distill out some items of general significance illustrated by the North Cascades experience. Additional points could no doubt be made, and the ones given expressed differently. As will be seen, the listing is much different from the one given for Lake Tahoe in the preceding chapter.

1 Advocacy for change has an advantage over advocacy for the status quo. It is difficult to make continuation of the status quo dramatic or popular in the general public view. In this situation, advocacy for change primarily came from urban-oriented people who individually had little to lose and expectation of something to gain. As the hearings clearly indicated, few of them had definite knowledge of either Forest Service or National Park Service land administration or of the realities of the North Cascades area.

Those with direct economic concern and knowledge of Forest Service administration generally favored continuation of the status quo. But they also had the disadvantage of being identified as representing "the interests" of timber, water and power, mining, grazing, hunting, and such. The Forest Service, which had the responsibility of administering the area for many years, was not in an effective position to present its current management and future plans. So far, it had given the central core area essentially protective and custodial treatment. Its supporters were not as effective as those advocating change. There were also those who disagreed with Forest Service practice and policy.

2   Among the general public, a trend exists toward seeking permanence in an era of changing times and deep environmental concern. There is a certain public distrust of large administrative authority, a fear of control by "the interests," etc. For example, a congressionally established wilderness is more permanent than an administratively established primitive area. Similarly, a national recreation area can be considered better than a limited-use area that is administratively established for recreational use. Along the same line, national park management is, by law, committed to a difficult dual land-use policy of preservation for public enjoyment without impairment of the resource. This directive is different from the multiple- or combined-land use approach which is statutory for the Forest Service. It is also a difficult concept for the public to understand.

Whether permanence or rigidity in land use in a changing world is desirable or not can be debated. There are no definitive answers. It should be recognized that, by and large, public agencies are responsive to public pressures. The Forest Service has wide discretionary latitude and generally does respond to it. Nevertheless, the general desire to seek permanence in land-use designations was a significant factor in the North Cascades situation.

3   Thorough and good information to guide decision making is important. This was made available to the public through *The North Cascades* study report. Related to this is action that was taken to establish effective cooperation "in the management of Federal land for outdoor recreation" by the Departments of the Interior and Agriculture. The joint study report is an outstanding example of a coordinated interdepartmental approach designed to get at the facts and assess issues independently of advocacy pressures.

Too much should not be made of the fact that study team members did not agree among themselves. This was not unexpected and almost unavoidable because of differences between agency policies as well as personal convictions. This situation forced the team chairman to develop a proposal that mediated much. It also contributed substantially to the action by the Congress. In any event, both agreement and disagreement were presented in print for all to see. The study greatly narrowed down questions at issue, and there was agreement on many points.

It should also be said that the Forest Service and National Park Service can and do work well together in the field. They certainly will need to do so in the North Cascades. This is because, by congressional decision, they must work in close concert in the same general area and help each other in administration.

4 The public was thoroughly consulted, formally and informally, locally and nationally. There were four sets of public hearings: by the study team, by the Senate on the joint study report, and later separately by the Senate and the House. In addition, concerned people were frequently consulted by the study team, members of the Congress, and the President's office.

5 Clear authority to act is important. Decision in this case was facilitated by the fact that practically all lands involved were in federal ownership over which the Congress had clear and final authority as to land-use designations. Another simplifying fact or was the existence of a consensus that outdoor recreation, wilderness use, and scenic preservation were the primary land-use considerations. The basic uses of the lands involved were not substantially changed although specific land uses and agency jurisdiction were changed.

6 Relatively few people of influence, determination, and experience are important in getting things done. This is particularly true where the issues are well defined, as in the North Cascades. The area of controversy and decision was narrowed to the central core of the study area. Here, there was little privately owned land and consequently no substantial land acquisition costs and related problems. Also, there were no major competing timber, hunting (which is not permitted in a national park), water power, mining, or grazing uses that could not be either eliminated or reasonably controlled. It would be impolitic to give names, but about a dozen people, in one way or another, were primarily responsible for carrying the North Cascades issue through to a conclusion. Not all of them were in positions of title prominence but worked behind the scenes.

7 A fair and good decision was made, taking the situation as a whole. Not everybody was pleased or could be, but nobody was seriously injured. The action taken was well designed to minimize conflict and to protect and preserve the unique scenic qualities of the area for use by people.

8 The intent of Congress in legislative matters is significant. This is important and often is not fully expressed in the specific language of legislation, as anyone with practical or legal experience in such matters well knows. No formal language can or does give all the story. In this case, much of congressional intent is to be found in Senate and House reports. It is also found in the record of hearings, in congressional debate, and in agreements and understandings existing between members of the Congress and the administration. The importance of intent also applies to other governmental agencies and to private organizations and individuals. Memories in such matters can be long. Land use, being important and often complex, gives excellent examples.

In summary, the North Cascades case illustrates means and procedures applied in arriving at land-use management decisions which are given here in a public lands context. Although the physical setting is in a large and rather remote wildland area of exceptional scenic and recreation qualities, underlying issues of principle in land use can also apply to different situations.

Chapter 11

Reordering and Consolidation of Landownership—With West German Illustrations

The purpose of this chapter is twofold. The first is to present reasons why land management problems have developed from divided ownership and different uses which require land reordering and concomitant ownership consolidation to rectify. The second purpose is to give the processes of executing land reordering in actual situations. The state of North Rhine–Westphalia, West Germany, is used to illustrate procedures applied in practice. A working knowledge of both background and application procedures is necessary to gain understanding of the detailed actions required to meet complex landownership situations.

The control of land leading to its ownership has always been regarded as a most serious and basic matter. It is the source of endless controversy and strife and a matter of worldwide concern (See Chap. 2). This has been

Grateful acknowledgment is made to the following, without whose help preparation of this chapter would not have been possible: Dr. Gerhard Naumann, Landwirtschaftskammer, Rheinland, Bonn; Dr. Hans Köpp, Institut für Forstpolitik, Universität Göttingen; and Dr. H. D. Brabänder and colleagues, Landwirtschaftkammer, Westfalen-Lippe. Dr. Brabänder is now a professor at the Universität Göttingen.

especially true since the beginning of agrarian land uses which required the establishment of ownership boundaries. Patterns of landownership and use, being slow and difficult to change, often do not keep pace with the social requirements of a developing population.

As a consequence, and increasingly evident during the latter part of the twentieth century, which has been marked by unprecedented population growth and demands for natural resources, there is a growing need to reorder, consolidate, and generally improve the existing patterns of landownership and use for the benefit of landowners and society in general.

LAND REORDERING: DEFINITIONS, PROBLEMS, AND REQUIREMENTS

Definitions and Purposes

In dealing with a large and complex subject such as land it is necessary to be clear on definitions and purposes. Landownership and use is a sensitive and complex matter. Being so, it is important *not* to think of land reordering processes as following any single procedure or pattern. Indicative of this point is the fact that there seems to be no fully meaningful or consistent English terminology regarding what is here termed land reordering. This matter of definition merits careful attention.

The German term used is *Flurbereinigung,* which has a rather wide range of meanings. It defies any direct English translation. The prefix *Flur-* has several meanings, including a piece of arable (cultivated) land, a stretch of open country, a meadow, or village lands. The following part, *bereinigen* (verb form), is closely related to the English "amend" and "emend", which to free from defects, correct, put right, improve, alter, change for the better. The German term is also related to the English "order," which has many meanings, including the idea of harmonious arrangement and proper or satisfactory condition. A related and more general term is *Raumordnung,* which means the ordering of space, or room. This is more of a regional planning term that is applied to complex and integrative urban and nonurban land use on large areas. The meanings above indicate the range of land-use actions of which *Flurbereinigung* is a part.

The word "consolidation" is rather commonly used in the United States as an equivalent term. But it is neither a good translation of the German word nor indicative of its meaning in practice. Consolidation has a more limited dictionary meaning: to bring together (separate parts) into a whole; to unite, make firm, combine. Consolidation is a good land-use term applicable to a situation where an owner buys additional land belonging to several others to assemble a larger and more workable single ownership. Consolidation could also mean or imply expropriation of small private parcels of land necessary to establish control of an area for public uses.

In this chapter, the term "reordering" is used as it points in the right direction and gives latitude for specific procedures and applications which can and do vary widely in particular situations. These may include:

1 Equivalent reallotment of badly fractured landownerships in an area to essentially the same number of owners but combined in fewer, larger, and more efficiently operable land units. This is the most common action and is applied in both agriculture and forestry.
2 Some changes in land use that may result from the establishment of larger land units and changing economic opportunities.
3 Improvement of general landscape quality including recreation and amenities.
4 Better design of transport facilities (may include highways).
5 Improvement of utilities, drainage, and water control generally.
6 Socioeconomic gains resulting from such things as having fewer and more viable agricultural or forestry land units to give better economic balance with increasing industrial and urban development.

As indicated above, the general concept and purpose of land reordering is broad and variable and can take many different forms to meet particular purposes. In basic procedures, however, specific applications do have much in common. Land reordering is a part of the broader processes of regional land-use planning. This should be kept in mind and is emphasized later in this chapter.

Land Reordering Related to the History and Political Structure of a Country

To understand the landownership structure of a modern country that creates the need for land reordering it is necessary to know how the country came to be as it is. Basically, the inescapable heritage of the past meets the future through the medium of the present. The historical-political development of land use in a country defines its present status and gives the base for future development. A few illustrations will give perspective to the basic forces that currently give rise to the need for land reordering.

Usually following an initial period of family or tribal land claims, land-use rights of many present countries went through a time when land was controlled by a conqueror, a king, and his satellites (See Chap. 2). Individual private landownerships developed later with the trend of government toward a political democracy.

European countries have developed more or less following this historical pattern. One has only to trace the historical development of their land-use rights and titles to appreciate these basic facts of landownership. With the large increase of private landownership, most large estates or other such holdings have been subdivided into smaller parcels of land although public, communal, and large private ownerships remain.

Land is in short supply in Europe, and there is no frontier of new lands. Continued subdivision of private ownerships over the years, primarily by inheritance, has resulted in the fractioning of landownerships into incredibly small units. Because land is basic and tenaciously held, remedies to the fractioning of landownership must be deliberate, carefully planned, and executed with public participation and assistance. Application of a laissez faire, or "let be," concept of a free economic market is not sufficient.

The history of land development in the United States illustrates the consequences, on a continental scale, of public policy encouraging unrestricted private landownership. Supplanting the native Indians, Europeans, who wanted to own land, settled this country. Following the American Revolution of 1776, and to a considerable degree previously, the country followed a general policy of encouraging private landownership. In the beginning large areas of land were taken by European conquest. After formation of the new republic, land acquisition continued by purchase—the great Louisiana Purchase—by negotiation and some military action with European powers, and by further conquest from the American Indians. America did not follow the European history of land control initially established by sovereignty. Almost from the beginning of its history, private individuals could acquire and hold land. This is what European settlers were largely denied at home and came to the New World to get.

The policy of encouraging private landownership, with continental space for expansion, was particularly evident in the rapid Western settlement of the country. The passage of the federal Homestead Act in 1862 is a major illustration of large-scale disposal of public lands. The government gave 160 acres of land directly to private citizens following a stiuplated peiod of residence and development of the land. There were also other public land disposal laws, including large grants to aid the building of the Western railroads. Much public land was also sold outright to private owners. Land disposal was essentially unplanned. There was neither adequate knowledge nor means to prevent undesirable consequences.

The effects of millions of acres of public lands going into private ownership in a rapidly expanding new country were both positive and negative. Such a policy was at that time considered necessary and undoubtedly it was. There was no real alternative if the country was to be rapidly settled and "developed," but great natural resources were exploited in the process, often recklessly and unwisely. These negative consequences have a direct bearing on subsequent land reordering, which in American was primarily consolidation of land into larger and more viable ownerships.

Millions of acres of forested land were cleared. The assumption was that these lands were destined for agriculture or urban uses, and large areas were so used. Land being abundant and cheap, forested lands were cut for the merchantable timber that was on them and simply left—for repeated fires in many cases.

Major personal hardship, controversy, public assistance, and cost has accompanied these public land disposal policies which were applied across the country to the Pacific. In subsequent years, thousands of farms too small for economic operation have been purchased by other farmers to make larger and more viable operating units. Cutover or cleared forest lands have been bought by private timber companies and by public agencies. For example, nearly all the present 23.6 million acres of national forest land in the Eastern United States (including the Lake states and South) were purchased from private owners. Other large areas in private ownership, primarily in the northern portions of the Lake states, were acquired by the states because of nonpayment of taxes and resultant reversion of title to the state.

Similar examples of landownership and use problems could be given from different parts of the world. Perhaps enough is given, however, to support the fact that present-day problems requiring land reordering largely derive from past history of a country, become critical due to present situations, and are difficult and expensive to resolve.

Requirements for Successful Land Reordering

The long and varied development of land-use ownership and patterns around the world preclude any uniform procedural statement of how to accomplish needed land reordering. It is possible, however, to give a list of requirements for its successful application. Five are given below.

1 There must be real and generally recognized need. This is certainly so in a well-developed political democracy, as is assumed here. Land reordering is slow, complex, and expensive; realizable and commensurate benefits must be obtained from the process.

2 An advanced, informed, concerned, and reasonable government with both authority and means to do its needed part is requisite. This work patently cannot be left to the free working of private economics and action, as was the situation during the frontier period of the United States.

3 There must be a reasonable stable and strong national economic situation. Public assistance of various kinds, usually including subsidy, is needed in substantial amount. Landownership evokes strong feelings in people; in times of stress or uncertainty they cling to the land whether rationally or not. Confidence in the stability of the country is requisite.

4 Sound and workable legal and administrative procedures are required that are consonant with the particular structure of a country and that are consistently applied. Land reordering is a complex, detailed, and technical process. General policy dictums do not suffice.

5 There must be an adequate level of technical and professional knowledge, and a cadre of informed and capable personnel in public service who can apply land reordering effectively and fairly.

AGRICULTURAL AND FOREST LANDOWNERSHIP IN WEST GERMANY

Transition is made at this point from general consideration of land reordering to its application in West Germany. Although many countries have similar land problems involving need for land reordering, they differ in specifics due to their past history and present land-use situation. Further, land being fixed in place by its inherent nature, it is necessary to consider the particulars of each situation.

The Federal Republic of West Germany, a country of about 91 million acres and a population of about 60 million, gives an excellent example of current action in land reordering. The country has made strong recovery since World War II with increasing industrialization and consequent concentration of population in urban areas. However, almost two-thirds of the country consists of mountains or highlands which impose limitations on the kinds of urban and nonurban land uses applicable.

Agriculture and forestry remain of major national importance and certainly so in terms of land areas so used. The current classifaction of land use in the country is summarized in Table 11.1. As shown, agriculture and forestry make up nearly 86 percent of the total land area, and there is little unusable land. There is a close on-the-ground relationship between forest and much of the grassland which is used for both hay and grazing. Historically, much forest land has also been grazed, and some still is; long-estab-

Table 11.1   Land-Use Classification of the Federal Republic of Germany

Land use	Area (in thousands)		Percent
	Hectares	Acres*	
Farmland			
Arable (cultivated)	7,609.0	18,794	30.7
Garden, vineyard, etc.	564.1	1,393	2.3
Grassland	5,806.0	14,434	23.5
Other farm	54.4	134	0.2
Total farmland	14,033.5	34,755	56.7
Forest	7,183.5	17,743	29.0
Buildings, streets, railways (including urban)	2,295.3	5,669	9.3
Waste (barren, bogs, etc.)	812.5	2,007	3.3
Water	423.8	1,047	1.7
Total	24,748.6	61,221	100.0

Source: Forestry and Forest Products Division of the Federal Ministry of Food, Agriculture and Forestry, *Forestry and Wood Economy in the Federal Republic of Germany,* 1967.
   *Converted at ratio of 1 hectare = 2.47 acres.

lished forest grazing rights persist in some areas. There has also been shifting back and forth between grassland and forest use as land of the same soil quality often can be used for either. At present, the trend is for the more marginal grassland areas to be planted to forest use. Farmland (including grassland) is predominantly in private ownership. Regarding ownership of the forest area, about 31 percent is state and federal (less than 2 percent of the latter), 25 percent is held by corporations (corporation and communal ownerships are classed as public) and the rest, or about 44 percent, is in private ownership. Public forest land is well consolidated, and there is little intermingling with private forest lands.

The long and often turbulent history of what is now West Germany as regards the development of private landownership cannot be reviewed here although some knowledge of it is helpful fully to understand the present situation. See Müller (1964) for a good account. But the results are apparent on present landownership maps. Figures 11.1 to 11.3 illustrate a range of situations both before and after land reordering. As shown, private landownership can become incredibly subdivided. This is largely the result of repeated land subdivision through inheritance by several children. This is in contrast to primogeniture, whereby all land passes to the eldest child, or more frequently to the eldest son if there are sons. One has to visit such areas, ownership map in hand, to appreciate the situation. Ownerships may be of strips not over 10 feet wide and in the tenths of acres. These occur in both farm and forest areas. In urban areas one is accustomed to expect land subdivision into small ownership units.

Not only are individual land parcels often very small, but the total ownership by a single owner is often too little for effective economic operation even though much land is leased. The situation is further exacerbated by the fact that some land parcels are owned by individuals living in urban areas who have no direct interest in operating the land but who cling to ownership for a number of reasons, including the common desire of people to own land.

Much of this situation grew out of a practice of long history, rather prevalent in West Germany, whereby farmers lived in small towns with their livestock. They worked their fields from there in land parcels which tended to get smaller and smaller for the reasons given above. This practice goes back many years to the time when protection by walled towns was needed. This pattern of landownership and use makes fascinating land and town mosaics for visitors to see, but it is not conducive to efficient farming, especially with the widespread advent of power machinery which economically has become necessary. It is equally if not more inefficient to manage forest land in narrow strips which may be subject to windthrow. Farm and

Figure 11-1 Landscape near Münster, West Germany, showing harmonious ordering of transportation and predominantly agricultural land use.

forest labor is becoming increasingly scarce and expensive due to employment competition from urban areas. As they often say in Germany, the girls
are increasingly less inclined to marry farmers.

The development of the European Common Market, in which West
Germany is a major participant, placed increasing pressure on individual
countries competitively to do what they best can. This makes inefficiency of
production within countries less tolerable. Agricultural, forest, and other
products are in direct competition with those from other countries.

The Federal Republic of Germany is a parliamentary democracy in
which there are eight *Lands* or provinces, which are equivalent to states in
the United States and will hereafter be so termed. There are also three city
states of equal political level with the land states: Hamburg, Bremen, and
West Berlin. Collectively, the eleven units are termed *Laender,* or states.

Within the land states are regions, or *Regierungsbezirke.* These units do
not have law-making or parliamentary powers but serve a function of supplying civil servants and expertise. They also have authority and administrative power in land-use planning, in the distribution of subsidies, and in
land reordering.

Also within the land states are political units, the *Kreis,* which in general are comparable to counties in the United States. There are, however, two
different governmental structures in a *Kreis* but of equal political level. The
larger cities and their environs, which are geographically in a *Kreis,* have
separate and independent government much as in the United States. The
smaller cities and towns and more rural areas in a *Kreis* also have separate
units of government much as in the United States. Some larger cities are
also a land *Kreis;* much history is involved here.

Of particular importance in land use is the fact that the states, city
states, regions, and *Kreis* have a large degree of autonomy. In fact, a visitor
from outside the country who is concerned with land use will hear little
about the federal government but much about the states and their subdivisions. Due to long political history behind the formation of the present
states, which are the outgrowth of many formerly independent principali-
ties, kingdoms, and such units, the states have much individuality in laws
and practices regarding land-use control. For this reason, it is impossible to
speak of West Germany as doing this or that in land use except in terms of
broad policy.

Also by long development, there is a complex structure of land-use
controls, practices, and public aids and subsidies of various kinds which
apply to agricultural and forest lands as well as urban areas. Historically
and at present, much privately owned forest land is a part of a farm unit;
this is particularly true in upland and mountainous areas.

(a)

Figure 11-2 Land reordering in a town and rural area, Düsseldorf region, West Germany. *(a)* Before reordering; *(b)* after reordering. Note the major rearrangement of roads and highways. Residential, business, work, and public-use areas have been consolidated through rezoning. Small rural-agricultural landownerships have also been reordered through consolidation.

LAND REORDERING IN NORTH RHINE–WESTPHALIA

A specific illustration of executing a land reordering project is necessary to give understanding of the procedure and also of public land-use controls and assistance which constitute a major part of the total process.

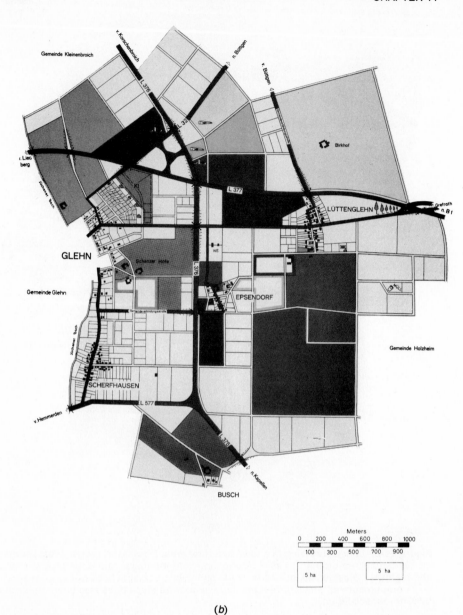

(b)

Figure 11-2 *Continued*

The Situation

The West German state of North Rhine–Westphalia is an area of 8.4 million acres, including the heavily industrialized Ruhr area of the lower Rhine

(a)

Figure 11-3 Primarily agricultureal land reordering in the Netherlands. (a) Before reordering; (b) after reordering.

adjoining the Netherlands. The population is about 16.8 million or 1,280 per square mile, the most dense of any land state in West Germany. Despite this high population density, there are 5.2 million acres in agricultural lands and 2 million acres in forest lands. Together they constitute 86 percent of the total state area, of which agriculture accounts for 62 percent and forests make up 24 percent.

In relation to the high population of the state these nonurban lands are of great importance not only for food, forest products, and transportation

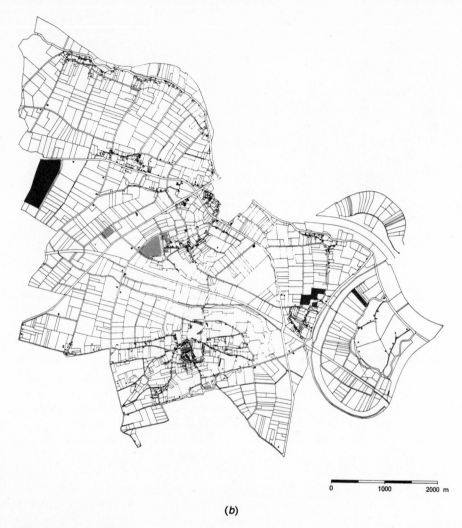

0   1000   2000 m

(b)

Figure 11-3 *Continued*

routes, but for water, recreation, and related amenities needed by urban
people. These lands are all within easy travel distance from urban centers.
All land is important in a highly developed area such as North Rhine–
Westphalia, and there is much public interest and concern about the management of these nonurban lands as their good use is vital to the social and
economic well-being of the state as a whole.

The focus of this example of land reordering is on agricultural and
forested lands. Although emphasis is on the latter, the processes are basically the same on both. Land reordering was, in fact, first developed to deal

with landownership problems on farms. Forested lands are closely related to and are a part of many farm units. Land of marginal value for hay or pasture use is often more valuable for forest use. There is a current trend for lands to be reforested as a part of the farm unit.

Trees being a land crop of long duration, either forest planting of grassland or the taking of land out of forest use is an important decision that is of both private and public concern. Further, the value of forested land necessarily must be determined at a specific time in land reordering. For example, forest land can be an area recently planted, an established but immature young stand, or a mature forest stand of high timber value in addition to its bare land value. This range of land values presents difficult valuation problems that are not encountered on other land. Landscape quality, recreational use, and soil protection values must also be considered. For these reasons, forestry gives an added dimension to the application of land reordering procedures.

Basic authority for *Flurbereinigung,* including procedures for such land reordering, comes from federal law. Its procedural specificity is rather unusual as federal law normally establishes policy direction and framework within which the states have much latitude in implementation. It is an early law of the present Federal Republic which was established in 1949.

Procedures in Land Reordering

A number of steps are necessary to accomplish land reordering. As nearly as possible they will be given here in sequential order. Emphasis will be placed on privately owned lands because here is where the major problems lie.

To begin with, there must be a real need for land reordering that is recognized by the owners as well as by public authorities. To the extent private owners are able or willing to buy, sell, and lease voluntarily among themselves and achieve desirable results, no special land reordering procedures may be necessary. But such actions are seldom adequate. Also, public approval is required if there is a change in land use, as from forest to agricultural use and especially to urban use. The situation considered here is the normal one which private owners cannot meet among themselves. Basic steps in the reordering process follow:

Legal Establishment of a reordering Unit   This is the first, direct, and crucial action step. It results from recognition of private and public need. Much study and discussion among private owners and public officials concerned is commonly necessary to establish the boundaries of a particular land unit. Under the authority of the national *Flurbereinigung* act, the state can declare that land reordering be carried out in a particular area if it decides that the situation warrants such action. The state exerts this power in special cases only. Consent of at least a majority of the landowners is the usual situation and is assumed in this case. *All* landowners in the area, including corporate, communal, church, and association ownerships must be participants in the reordering process. Other people or groups in or near the area who are financially or otherwise directly concerned are co-participants. It is not necessary that they be landowners. Legal establishment is necessary as many owners in the unit may not be in accord with the proposal but must participate nevertheless. Without this public authority little land reordering would be accomplished. It is basic public policy that there be no land expropriation and also that as nearly as possible, each owner has the same total land value after reordering as before. This does not necessarily mean the same land area.

Owner and Land Identification Concurrently with the first step, all owners, lessors, and others directly concerned in a proposed unit must be identified and informed. It is no small job to identify and make contact with all these people. Landownership titles, existing leases, and land unit boundaries must likewise be identified. The detailed and expensive work of landownership area and value analysis obviously cannot be undertaken until such groundwork has been accomplished.

Soil Analysis and Classification Following legal establishment of a unit, detailed study and classification by soil classes is made of all land by individual ownership parcels. Initially, this is done on an agricultrual basis by classifying all land as potentially plowland or pastureland. This classification is applied on both agricultural and forested land. It is expressed as an aggregate number of "points" for each owner based on the basic soil value of his or her land. One reason for this procedure goes back to a federal act of 1935 which applies to agricultural land only and is followed in this step. Another reason is that both agricultural and forested land is often included in the same reordering unit and a uniform soil classification is considered necessary. There are 100 soil classes but they are compressed to about ten for this reordering work. The classes include consideration of soil origin, profile, and climate.

Appraisal of Land-Use Needs Following soil classification, a detailed appraisal is made of land-use development needs. These include roads, water, drainage, possible new homesites, and other needs for good land management. Consideration is also given to meet public interests which can include appraisal of landscape quality, recreation, and related amenity concerns. Costs of such appraisal are mostly met by public money. Roads are of major importance because one major objective of land reordering is to give needed access to all land units. Previously, this was frequently lacking.

Partial Payment of Area Development Needs   As determined by the appraisal of land-use needs (step 4), each owner gives up some of his or her share of points (step 3) to meet costs of needed area development. In effect, this is a common levy made to meet these area costs.

Forest Inventory   A detailed inventory is made on forested lands including tree species and wood volumes, degree of forest stocking (how fully the land is utilized) and its ratio to potential or full tree stocking, timber quality, and the composition of the forest by tree species (whether pure or mixed in some proportion). All this information is put on maps. All timber cutting is stopped during the inventory process and until completion of the land reordering project.

Timber Value Appraisal   Using the inventory information, the value of the standing timber is appraised. Fair timber market values are used, and values of forest stands of different ages are brought to the present time by discounting methods. For example, the value of a stand now 25 years old that would normally be harvested at age 60 would be estimated by discounting 35 years at some reasonable and accepted interest rate to equate to the present age of 25 years. Much effort is made to achieve comparability in valuation. Because trees take a long time to reach economic maturity, forest stands require different valuation methods than do yearly harvested agricultural crops. This valuation process is necessary because forest and agricultural land values must be put on a common valuation basis in land reordering. A particular reason is that agricultural landowners may want to put some lower-value agricultrual land parcels into forest production. The process could work the other way as well, with land being taken out of forest use at the time of forest crop maturity.

The Reallocation Process   The actual land reallocation comes after large amount of preparatory work. As stated earlier, the objective is to give each owner equal value in relation to the land he or she originally owned, *and* to reorder the land into more efficiently manageable units. With the complex pattern of existing ownerships this is a difficult and complex task, the solution of a sort of super jigsaw puzzle. Knowledge, judgment, and patience are necessary. Almost everything possible is considered, including crop value, soil value, present timber value, topography, access roads needed, and drainage needs. Individual owner interests and desires are considered and met insofar as possible. No distinctions are made as to whether the owner lives on the land, is an absentee owner, or leases rather than manages the land. Absentee owners and others, are encouraged to sell during the allocation process as this reduces land reordering problems. No owner is forced to sell, but since an owner may be allocated a land parcel that he or she does not desire, the pressure to accept fair value for one's present property can be rather strong.

Reordering requires a great deal of conference and negotiation in addition to inventory and other fact-finding work. The work is conducted by informed and expert people in public service who are assigned to a particular unit. It is not done by consultants. Public legal hearings and court action may be necessary to adjudicate disputes. Rearrangement of landownership is very serious business indeed.

Value Adjustments   No allocation process such as this can be perfect. Some terminal financial balancing-out of land values is often necessary to give owners their fair share. Value differences are settled in money over a period of time. Settlement values of up to 20 percent may be paid or received depending on whether the allocation process resulted in an owner receiving more or less than his or her share.

Owner Payment for the Reordering Work   Owners share in the reordering cost. They usually pay between 10 and 40 percent of direct land-imporovement costs, with public agencies paying the rest. If an expressway or some such expensive public project is involved, the owner might pay no more than 5 percent.

Physical Construction and Land Record Updating   In addition to the land reallocation process, there may be a large job of road building, drainage installation, and other physical development accompanying a land reordering project. Landownership and other public records must also be changed, payments due collected, and a variety of administrative detail attended to. Subsequent land use is subject to existing laws, public land-use controls and related restrictions, and public assistance.

Land Reordering Costs

In concluding this procedural section, the author is keenly aware of the difficulty of giving a feeling for the need, complexity, and human and physical realities of land reordering. The process deeply and lastingly affects people, both individually and collectively. It is consequently difficult to identify and evaluate all the costs and benefits of such work.

Land reordering work is indeed expensive when all costs, direct and indirect, are included. There are the direct costs of execution, designing and installing better drainage systems, building needed access roads, and moving or rebuilding structures. There are also many indirect costs, incurred by state, region, county, and local publicly employed people, which are difficult to measure but certainly substantial. These include costs of much planning, identifying and contacting landowners and other concerned people,

organizing and conducting many meetings, changing landownership records, conducting legal hearings, and taking other court actions as may be
needed. A good many different professional people are involved.

In summary, the cost of land reordering is high, as indicated above,
with the landowners paying a relatively small part. In total, the work can
cost as much or more than the current market value of the land itself (but
not including standing timber values). In addition, there is substantial public subsidy, particularly in agriculture. In fact, these subsidies are one reason why private owners are interested in land reordering. The total process
may require 10 years or more to complete. The deliberate nature of the
processes illustrates the significance of the five requirements for successful
land reordering that were given earlier.

ILLUSTRATIONS OF LAND REORDERING AS A PART OF
LARGER REGIONAL PLANNING

The procedures given in the preceding section give some understanding of
the detail and specificity necessary to execute a particular land reordering
project. There are also more complex situations which require an integration of several different kinds of land reordering actions to resolve. A narra-
tive account of specific land-use actions taken in two actual situations will
be helpful.

A Farmland, Highway, and Railroad Situation

A lowland area, predominantly farmland but with some forest land, lies
near Münster. The fields are fertile and level but require drainage. After
land reordering, the fields are larger and in units that are efficient to work
with power equipment. Much drainage work was done; there are new, better, deeper, and fewer drainage ditches. In one area, the lower part of a
small stream connecting to field drainage ditches was moved about a quarter of a mile. The stream was reconnected to new ditches and to a new
outlet into a barge canal. At this entrance a special and expensive masonry
water riffle and catchment basin was built to slow water movement so that
sediment would be deposited before the water entered the canal. The accumulated sediment is periodically removed.

Good, new, and better-located farm roads were built. They have a
surface width of a little over 10 feet and a 6 ½-foot center strip that is
asphalt paved. The roadway is wellgraded and drained; previous roads
were poorly drained and often very muddy. There were fewer and better
farm building units with good road access to them. In several instances
buildings were moved to or rebuilt on a new site.

Concurrent with and related to the farmland reordering work there
was also considerable highway building in the area. This included an ex-

pressway and a major state highway which required connections between them and to other roads. It was also necessary to solve a somewhat difficult problem of providing access to a large private estate which was otherwise blocked by the highway construction.

A major railroad line traversed the area, and there were three open railroad crossings fairly close together which necessitated employment of three railroad watchmen. Train speeds were reduced through the area because of these open crossings. The railroad was willing to pay for a single-lane overpass bridge. This necessitated road construction to connect the three previous crossing roads to the single crossing. There was also a fairly large town nearby whose residents previously had to take a rather circuitous route to get to Münster, their major shopping center. The overpass, together with the new connecting roads, would be a shorter and better route. Consequently, pressure was put on the railroad to build a two-lane overpass; this would be instead of the single lane that would normally be built for local farm traffic. After considerable negotiation, the railroad agreed to this arrangement.

The Bigge See Area

The Bigge See area is about 40 miles south of Dortmund and about 50 miles east of Cologne, both big industrial cities. It is a most attractive and heavily used recreation area and provides seasonal hunting. The topography is a rolling upland which is fairly mountainous. The landscape is also partially people-made, as will be brought out.

To begin with, a large lake is the result of a dam built in a valley to store water for the great lower Rhine industrial and densely populated area to the west. Since it is a water storage lake, its level varies seasonally within upper and lower limits. However, by some good engineering, a hydroelectric plant has been built to utilize power generated from a stable low water level. The present lake is very scenic and adds to the general area. There is fishing, and a fine beach was recently constructed with visitor facilities. All this construction work was carefully designed for aesthetics as well as for utilitarian uses, fits the landscape, and was meticulously completed with good tree and shrub plantings.

Two major problems were created by the lake storage and water power project. Because of the lake, the railroad that follows the valley had to be relocated for several miles, which involved construction of a long and very expensive tunnel.

The other and even more difficult matter was the fact that the portion of the valley covered by the new lake previously supported a town of about 2,000 people and included considerable good agricultural land. It was necessary for the public to buy all the lands affected by the water impoundment. This included more land than was submerged because access to some land was cut off. To replace the town submerged by the lake, a new town was built on a nearby site. Agricultural lands also had to be bought near the new town to replace those now under the lake. Building the new town and buying agricultural land was a complex job. Long, expensive, and careful planning, including *much* negotiation and adjudication with the people affected, was necessary.

The new town is well laid out, attractive, and well accepted by the people. The resettlement job was handled carefully, fairly, and in thorough detail. The process was executed on a replacement basis, almost piece by piece. Existing residences, businesses, and other buildings in the old town were appraised on a liberal present-value basis, and each owner was credited accordingly. A good townsite was acquired, and the new town was carefully planned with business and residential areas along with good roads and streets. Necessary utilities of power, water, sanitation, and communication were provided. Each owner could select a building site in the new town subject to reasonable limits. Also, each owner could have a new building at a cost equivalent to his or her previous one in the valley. If people wanted something more expensive, they had to pay the additional cost. One can imagine the complex and interesting times planners and builders had with homemakers, professional people, and others in selecting the site and in building the new homes, stores, etc. The new town should prosper as it is well located in an intensively used recreational area.

In Summary

The two examples given above illustrate the fact that land reordering in a given area can merge with and become a part of the broader and more general concerns of regional planning. The land-use changes made in both of these examples constitute in substantial degree a reshaping of the landscape. These examples also indicate the complexity of integrated land-use planning and the necessity for authority and public assistance, including subsidy, to implement action.

WHAT CAN BE LEARNED FROM THE LAND REORDERING ILLUSTRATIONS

This chapter is sharply different from the previous case chapters, which emphasized planning and establishment of public land-use controls and large-scale land-use management policy decisions by public authority. This chapter centers on the difficult and complex procedural problems of executing needed land reordering in a well-developed country. What can be learned from this chapter relates to this framework of reference.

1 The social and political history of a country shapes its present land-

use problems and the attitudes of people about land. How landownership and uses developed in the past strongly influences what can be done in the present and in the future.

2 There are certain rather basic requirements for successful land reordering. There must be (1) a real and recognized need; (2) an advanced, informed, and reasonable government with both means and authority to act; (3) a reasonably stable and strong national economic situation, including an established structure of public assistance in financial aids and subsidies; (4) sound and workable laws and administrative procedures that are consonant with the particular structure of a country; and (5) an adequate level of technical and professional knowledge and an available supply of informed and capable personnel in public service.

3 Laws alone are not sufficient. It is necessary that there be application of good judgment, discrimination, discretion, and willingness to negotiate in particular situations.

4 There must be a generally favorable attitude of people toward, and acceptance of, necessary public authority. This is not to imply that everyone must like authority, but necessity for it and its application must be recognized. More specifically, the land reordering process cannot be successful if it is unduly beset with controversy and appeals to the courts.

5 There often is a separation between gathering and analyzing information and making proposals, and the subsequent hard realities of decision, implementation, and continuity necessary to make planning a reality. The emphasis of this chapter is on this subsequent part, on what it takes to get things done on the ground in an actual situation.

6 Land reordering to meet particular land needs merges with and becomes a part of the broader and more general concerns of regional planning.

Chapter 12

To Cut A Tree—The
Anatomy of a Controversy

This chapter analyzes why and how a significant national land-use controversy developed in the United States and examines its consequences. The
focus is on methods applied—clearcutting in this case—to harvest and re-
generate a forest area. The controversy began in the middle 1960s. Initially,
it centered on national forests, but it later extended to industrial forest
lands. It started in a few areas but developed to national proportions of
importance in forest land-use practice and policy. Basically, it was a part of
the awakening concern over environmental quality that developed strongly
during the same general time and that has become a national movement, it
is hoped of continuing momentum.

The sequence of treatment begins with predisposing factors that made
the controversy possible. There always have to be such, and they often have
deeper roots than is commonly realized. Next in the sequence come the
triggers, the particular events that set the controversy in motion. These are
followed by a discussion of its national development and results and consequences. The previous chapters on Lake Tahoe and the North Cascades
also deal with land-use problems and controversy, but they differ sharply in

that they focus on seeking answers to difficult land-use decision and governance problems in two particular geographic areas. In this chapter, although the issues were first rather narrowly focussed in particular areas, they broadened to include national land-use policy and practice issues.

PREDISPOSING FACTORS

No large controversy can develop in land-use matters without the existence of predisposing factors of substance to sustain it; that is, the climate has to be favorable. In the clearcutting situation, there were a number of such predisposing factors, many with a long history. They are given here in condensed form:

1   The time was right. The conservation and associated preservation movement that developed in the latter 1800s focused strongly on public land-use policy. The movement was responsible for the establishment of the large forest reserves, primarily in the West, around the turn of the century. Out of these developed the national forest system and the Forest Service. This movement coalesced with and became a part of the much broader and more sophisticated development of concern over environmental quality that took form in the 1960s and intensified in the 1970s. Forested lands, with which the United States is so richly endowed, have always been an important part of public concern over natural resources management.

2   People like trees. This is a significant fact of perhaps dim and evolutionary origin. Because of the relatively short human life span, people tend to think of trees as permanent rather than as the very successful, abundant, and relatively long-lived superplants which they are. Trees, like other plants, come and go in the course of time. A forest tends to be thought of as something permanent and unchanging, whereas it is constantly changing owing to forces of nature if not of people. Despite much educational effort, there is general lack of public recognition that trees and forests can be managed by people. People can improve upon natural processes which are often crude and wasteful. In fact, what is "natural" is very difficult to define.

Also, people often do not relate forests to the many products that come from trees, such as wood, paper, chemicals, and other derived products which are used in great quantities in daily living.

3   Population is increasingly concentrated in urban areas, and urban voting power over land-use policy decisions increases accordingly. Urban people keenly feel the pressures of restricted living space, and they increasingly feel forested areas should be kept available for outdoor recreation, wildlife, and other natural land uses. This is a perfectly understandable feeling. However, this combined with a

general lack of understanding about trees and forest management provides the basis for easily aroused distrust of timber-cutting practices.

4 Memories of past destructive forest-cutting practices remain and can be inflamed. The United States was and is bountifully supplied with forested lands which support prodigious volumes of good timber. In the earlier years of settlement, timber was superabundant and cheap. Forests were also an obstacle in the path of development which required the clearing of forested lands for agriculture and settlement. The burning of trees by settlers in land clearing was once regarded as an encouraging indication of progress. Early cutting practices were destructive, and they were accompanied by wildfires which for many years ran rampant. These wildfires resulted in forest destruction much beyond the needs of settlement.

In the public mind forest devastation has been and can be linked to timber-cutting practices. There is an unclear distinction in popular understanding between uncontrolled cutting—taking trees that are considered merchantable from the forest and leaving the rest—and clearcutting of a particular area as a part of forest renewal applied under planned, controlled, and productive forest management practice (Davis, 1971). Given this situation, it is easy to arouse public opposition to almost any kind of cutting other than the ubiquitous "selective cutting" which sounds good but has no consistent professional meaning.

5 To the general public, clearcutting, which requires the harvesting of all trees from a particular area, *looks* like forest destruction. And it is, but it is also a prelude to forest renewal. People easily can be led to believe that clearcutting is only destruction and consequently bad forest practice. The concepts of organized forest management to achieve continued and sustained yield from the forest are not easily explained to the public.

Also, clearcutting is often highly visible to the public. This is particularly true in mountainous areas, especially in the coniferous forests of the West, where new trees established after cutting may require a number of years to show. Clearcutting can be an aesthetic affront to people, which is a large factor in public opinion; people do like trees and forests and do not like to see them cut down in swaths.

6 There is a large and increasing demand for wood in the United States. It is needed, despite more recycling of forest products, to supply these same urban-oriented people whose population is increasing. These needs place pressures on national and other forest areas to produce more timber. People most certainly want more wood products, but they also want outdoor recreation, wildlife, and other amenities of the forest. They often do not relate wood with these other forest values and face the fact that forested areas are not

unlimited. It should be recognized that clearcutting, properly applied, is not only efficient in wood production but ecologically necessary to maintain some forest types.

7 Federal forest landownerships are large. In the national forests some 92 million acres of forested lands are classified as commercial, that is, are capable of producing timber of commercial quality. These lands belong to the American people. Under the Multiple Use Act they are to be managed in the people's interests, which are numerous and often conflicting (Chap. 3). Public agencies are always open targets for advocacy by particular interests. They tread a difficult path between interest groups and also have constraints in defending themselves.

8 Concomitant to the above is an easily inflamed public idea that the Forest Service, being the largest public commercial forest landowner, is a captive of big business—the timber industry specifically—which is also susceptible to public attack. It is true that in some areas, in the West especially, the timber industry is substantially dependent on public timber supplies. The Forest Service sells timber as stumpage, i.e., standing timber in the forest, and is in constant controversy with the timber industry to enforce federal timber-cutting regulations and land-use policies. These policies include increasing cutting restrictions and also withdrawal from cutting of large areas supporting timber of commercial value for wilderness and general outdoor recreation use, fish and wildlife, and for other environmental protection purposes.

9 There is an understandable desire on the part of the Forest Service, pressed as it is by the public demands for more wood, to increase forest productivity on large forested areas currently unproductive from a timber growth standpoint. These areas occur in both the Eastern and Western United States. It must also be recognized that practically all national forest lands east of the Mississippi River, and also substantial areas in the West, are lands that in about the last half century were cutover by, and subsequently purchased from, private owners. These lands were mostly in poor condition when acquired. People forget, if indeed they ever knew, these facts of existing forest conditions and the long job of forest rehabilitation that has been undertaken by the Forest Service.

10 There has long been a popular urge to reorganize federal bureaus. This was given recent impetus in the Nixon administration. Many reorganization studies have been made, and all have dealt prominently with natural resources management agencies. In the 1930s, under the administration of Franklin D. Roosevelt, the Forest Service was almost transferred from the Department of Agriculture to the Department of the Interior, which was to have been reorganized as the Department of Natural Resources. Such action would have put the Forest Service, National Park Service, Fish and Wildlife Service, and the Bureau of Outdoor Recreation in the same depart-

ment. The various reasons given for such a grouping include reducing the independence of the Forest Service and making it more amenable to natural resources conservation interests.

These general ideas of reorganization have been around for a long time, rightly or wrongly, depending on one's viewpoint. The significant point for this chapter is that the clearcutting issue was intended by some as a means to limit the Forest Service and achieve departmental reorganization.

11 As brought out in the Lake Tahoe and North Cascades chapters, advocacy in environmental matters, particularly during the initial crest of the movement, is strong and entails little responsibility. The attacker has an initial advantage in such matters.

12 There is the unquestionable fact that the Forest Service was vulnerable on several counts, as follows:

a It had, in recent years, greatly accelerated the application of clearcutting on the national forests as part of a general policy to produce more timber for the nation's needs. Clearcutting is a systematic practice easily reduced to procedures. It is normally prompt in results and is effective in reestablishing good growing forest cover. It was applied both on unmanaged natural stands and on previously cutover stands which were not in a good condition for growth. To some degree clearcutting had become a habit, an established practice. It was applied, with accompanying roads, to overly large areas and on soils and slopes where the practice was open to criticism on ecological, wildlife, and aesthetic grounds.

b The Forest Service is a mature, large, and able organization of continental dimensions that is well established, successful, and with reason proud of its accomplishments. Such organizations are always open to attack; some people always want to pull down the leaders.

c Although the Forest Service led in the wilderness movement and, as brought out in Chap. 3, had pressed for the Multiple Use Act to give the Service a broad statutory mandate to consider all resources without bias, it was also accused of being bureaucratic, unresponsive, and timber-oriented by conservationists, ecologists, and others who were riding on the crest of the rising environmental movement. There is truth to these accusations in instances, but the degree depends on particular viewpoints. Because of the large scope of its land-use responsibilities, the Forest Service is continually pressed by different interest groups. It also had some internal problems in applying its multiple-use mandate in practice.

The preceding indicates the complex of predisposing factors, many of them more or less interrelated and with long background, that underlie the clearcutting controversy and that made its development possible. To repeat, the time was right. The 1960s were a period of ferment and change, and as the environmental movement developed, it took different forms and directions. Controversy, although it can be abrasive and wasteful, is also an inherent and needed part of such a movement.

THE TRIGGERS—HOW IT HAPPENED

Given the predisposing factors outlined above, only the place, situation, and opportunity—the triggers—are needed to set a controversy in motion. These were provided.

The clearcutting issue took form in three areas: Wyoming, West Virginia, and the Bitterroot Valley in Montana. All concern national forest lands. Of these, the Bitterroot Valley situation was the first to develop. It was probably the most significant and had the most build-up. For these reasons it will be given particular attention but with recognition that other areas are also important and differ mainly in specifics. It should also be emphasized, as stated previously in this chapter, that clearcutting had come to be fairly widely applied on the national forests. It was also much applied on privately owned land, especially in the Pacific Northwest and in the South.

Clearcutting Controversy in the Bitterroots

The beautiful mountain-enclosed Bitterroot Valley located in southwestern Montana is about 100 miles long and 30 miles wide and is drained by the Bitterroot River. Its western boundary is the Bitterroot Range, with high points up to 8,000 and 9,000 feet. This divide is the boundary between Montana and the northern Idaho Panhandle. The valley, historically at least, is predominantly agricultural and is nationally known as the source of the McIntosh apple.

The lower slopes and valley bottom are in private ownership. The upper slopes and mountaintops on both sides are in rather solid national forest ownership. These lands are administered by the Bitterroot National Forest, which has a net area of about 1,240,000 acres. The southwestern part of the forest extends west over the Bitterroot Mountains divide and is a part of the big Selway-Bitterroot Wilderness. Nearly half of the total forest area is designated as wilderness, primitive area, and game preserve land. All the Salmon River Breaks Primitive Area (which probably will become formal wilderness), which includes about 217,000 acres, is in the forest. As indicated, much of the Bitterroot National Forest is dedicated to wildland uses. The rest of it is available for recreational uses as well as for timber production.

Since about 1960 clearcutting had been fairly widely applied on national forest lands. Most of this practice had been in the Western states.

There had been considerable objection, largely local, to such cutting in several places. The Bitterroot Valley was one of them, and it was the first to achieve national visibility. The beginning was the Magruder Corridor issue.

The Magruder Corridor Issue—An Opener   When the boundaries of the Selway-Bitterroot Wilderness were formally established in 1963, following public hearings and much study, what is known as the Magruder Corridor, a wildland area of about 173,000 acres to the south of it and in the Bitterroot National Forest, was not included. It was taken out of a previous primitive area classification, under which it had received custodial and protective management only, and put under general national forest administration, which could include timber cutting. There were four reasons for withdrawal of the corridor. The first is that the area is traversed east-west by the Darby–Elk City road, which follows one of the few passable routes between Montana and northern Idaho. The second is that the area was a natural entry route to the Selway-Bitterroot Wilderness to the north and to the Salmon River Primitive Area to the south. Third, the corridor had long been used locally for hunting, fishing, and general outdoor recreation. Fourth, the area had a substantial volume of commercial timber, although no cutting had been done there. Much of the timber was, however, of marginal economic value from the standpoint of continuing forest management.

Following reclassification of the corridor, the Forest Service proceeded to apply normal multiple-use management, which included road location for logging in a part of the corridor. There was much objection to timber cutting, which to the public meant clearcutting.

Gaining no satisfaction from the local forest administration, critics went to the regional and then to the national level of the Forest Service, but again without obtaining answers satisfactory to them. Finally at the congressional level, Senators Church and Metcalf, of Idaho and Montana, respectively, took the matter to the Secretary of Agriculture, Orville L. Freeman. The Secretary took the unusual step of appointing, on September 6, 1966, a special six-member citizens review committee "to review on a broad basis the Forest Service plans for the management of the Magruder Corridor" [1] and to report its findings to the Secretary. The author, a native of Montana, was a member of this committee.

A thorough field study was made, including holding public meeting in Missoula, Montana, and Boise and Grangeville in Idaho. From the start, questions and criticisms centered on proposed timber cutting in the area and the road building proposed to implement it. There was strong objection

[1] Public statement by Secretary Freeman on the report of the review committee, June 1, 1967.

to scarring this wildland area with visible clearcuttings and with expensive and hard-to-maintain roads.

In its report to the Secretary, the review committee did not ban timber cutting but recommended that it be deferred until some rather hard conditions were met. In summary, these were that more specific and comprehensive evaluation be made of timber-management values and potentials; that action be taken to prevent significant erosion and stream sedimentation from road construction at justifiable cost; that the scenic aspects of present cutting methods be given further evaluation to determine where cutting reasonably could be compatible with the high aesthetic values of the area.

The inadequacy of multiple land-use planning, as applied in this area, was that each use was considered more or less separately and without evaluating uses in relation to each other and to the primary values of the planning area as a whole. In this case, these were largely recreational.

The committee report was presented to Secretary Freeman on April 17, 1967. On June 1 he supported the recommendations of the committee in a press release and a public statement giving his directions to the Forest Service. The committee report and the Secretary's statement were given wide distribution, particularly by conservation organizations that considered it a victory. The report was regarded as careful and fair, and it drew no major criticisms from forest industry people.

The Magruder Corridor issue was significant on several counts. It was one of the first controversies over federal timber-cutting policy and practice to receive attention at a national level. It delineated some weaknesses of Forest Service multiple-use planning as practiced in a particular situation but applicable elsewhere. It gave conservation-minded people in the Bitterroot practice and confidence that their influence could be felt. It was an opener, as it were, to militant advocacy against clearcutting in particular. As will later be seen, it spread into broader forest policy issues.

How Did the Controversy Develop?   Given a predisposing situation, how did the Bitterroot clearcutting controversy develop? The situation itself was not designed. It grew out of a number of favoring circumstances, as previously outlined. But action to capitalize on this situation, to develop it locally, and to expand it to a national issue requires planning and organization. Such things are not spontaneous. How did it come about?

To answer this question, one must first identify the concerned people and organizations that were active in the Bitterroot at the time the controversy developed. These include the following, given in no particular order.

1   A federal research laboratory in the valley at Hamilton, the principal town. Initially a spotted fever laboratory, it now does other scientific research. The staff and families are a highly educated group. A number of

them are strongly conservation-minded and free to pursue this interest. There are also an increasing number of out-of-state people resident in the valley, mostly retirees.

2 A former forest supervisor of the Bitterroot National Forest who lived in the valley. He was outspoken in criticism of current national forest administration in the area and particularly of clearcutting. He was well known in Montana and politically active. He played the part of the forester carrying on the precepts of the early leader of the Forest Service Gifford Pinchot, which he felt had been betrayed. There was also an articulate former forest ranger in the valley at odds with the Forest Service.

3 A state writer on the *Daily Missoulian,* principal newspaper in western Montana. An able, ambitious, and vigorous man with environmental interests, he was given a free hand. The newspaper is one of a chain with outside policy direction.

4 Senator Lee Metcalf, junior Senator from Montana, whose home is in the Bitterroot and who has strong conservation interests.

5 Some local ranchers and other people in the Bitterroot who felt that clearcutting was adverse to their interests. Reasons included were that clearcutting caused erosion, streamflow instability, and damage to wildlife, was aesthetically objectional, and was contrary to "sustained-yield forestry." Many of these people were poorly informed.

6 The leadership of the School of Forestry at the University of Montana. This group had a strong conservation-environmental orientation and was also critical of the Forest Service.

7 A forest industry that was neither disposed nor in a position to take an active part in such a controversy. The same was generally true of the public at large in western Montana. The Forest Service is the major landowner in the region; there always were criticisms of the Service, but general public relations were good.

8 Continued application of clearcutting by the Forest Service in Montana. It was done in the ponderosa pine and the Douglas-fir forest types, but particularly in stands of mature lodgepole pine. Such treatment is especially effective in the regeneration and management of this species. The practice of clearcutting is also subject to economic question when it is applied in areas of relatively low timber productivity, of which there are many in Montana.

9 The strong interest of some national conservation organizations, particularly the Sierra Club, in the Bitterroot situation.

The major source of written material in the controversy was a series of stories published in the *Daily Missoulian,* mostly from about November 1967 well into 1970. They dealt critically with the pros and cons of clearcutting in the Bitterroot. Most of them were in the form of interviews conducted and written by the state writer of the *Missoulian* (item 3 above). These interviews were with people of knowledge, influence, and opinion in the Bitterroot and included ranchers, forest industry people, members of the

Forest Service in both administration and research, and a few outside people. This material was put in book form (Burk, 1970) together with a digest of findings from a Forest Service investigative team that will be mentioned later. These feature stories were also distributed outside the state and gained wide readership. Different sides of the clearcutting–timber-management issue were given, but the tone and treatment in net effect were sharply critical of Forest Service timber-management policy and practice.

This journalistic enterprise certainly brought clearcutting and related issues to national attention. As stated in the publisher's acknowledgment to Burk's book:

> It would be an understatement to say that the articles attracted nation-wide attention, for they have served as a focal point for coast-to-coast concern of forest management practices in the United States.

The general policy and strategic intent of the materials included in this book are indicated in its epilogue:

> If the people of the Bitterroot and Montana and this nation truly want good resource management they must speak out and demand it.
>
> Do we care enough to commit ourselves to provide those within the Forest Service who want to do a good job of resource management with the public backing they deserve. Richly deserve, for there are many dedicated individuals in the Forest Service—admittedly outside the power structure—who want to do right.
>
> The Bitterroot controversy is but the beginning. The issue is out now. It's public. And there's no backing away from what we have brought before us. We must insist that where practices are admittedly poor they be improved. And we must insist that where they are fair they must be made better.
>
> That means that we, individually, must scrutinize and critically evaluate this land that is ours . . . and be heard in support of good management techniques. We must offset those who bring pressure to bear for the manipulation of these forests for the single benefit of some one special interest group.

The above is an attractive and stirring call to the colors. An undefined "we" is in fact a special-interest group. It represents the "good" and militantly goes out against other interests that by the same logic are not good. Such is the name of the game in public advocacy; it is inevitably polarizing. It can admit of little or no compromise, whereas in reality there has to be some adjudication and balancing in land-use affairs such as these. The above-quoted statements also clearly indicate the desire to extend the controversy nationally and to divide people in the Forest Service by placing blame on its leaders for what is claimed to be erring policy.

A second significant item was the release in April 1970 of the Forest Service task force appraisal report, *Management Practices on the Bitterroot National Forest* (U.S. Forest Service Task Force, 1970). This report of 100 pages was the result of a thorough investigation conducted over nearly a year by a special Forest Service team with a specific charge to study and report the situation as they saw it. It is an informative, comprehensive, and careful report directly considering and evaluating the principal questions about timber management and related questions and giving recommendations. As mentioned previously, a digest of some of its findings is included in the Burk book. This report is the best source of solid information. As such, it was used to support controversy. Being prepared by the Forest Service, it also was questioned on the grounds that no organization can fairly investigate itself.

A third item in the Montana sequence of events, was release of the University of Montana Select Committee report, or more commonly termed the Bolle report. The circumstances are briefly these. On December 2, 1969, Senator Lee Metcalf of Montana wrote to Dean Arnold W. Bolle of the Montana School of Forestry saying, "I believe a study of Forest Service policy in the Bitterroot by an outside professional group would be beneficial to the Montana Congressional delegation and to the entire Congress. . . . I hope appropriate faculty members at the University of Montana will participate."

Such a study was made, and the report was released with a public press statement by Senator Metcalf in Washington on November 18, 1970. The report was also inserted into the *Congressional Record* at that time.

The general nature and tone of the report are given in its "Statement of Findings." Some items from it are given below.

> Multiple use management, in fact, does not exist as the governing principle on the Bitterroot National Forest.
>
> Quality timber management and harvest practices are missing. Consideration of recreation, watershed, wildlife and grazing appear as afterthoughts.
>
> The management sequence of clearcutting-terracing cannot be justified as an investment for producing timber on the BNF. . . . The practice of terracing should be stopped.
>
> A clear distinction should be made between timber *management* and timber *mining*. Timber management, i.e. continuous production of timber crops, is rational only on highly productive sites, where an appropriate rate of return on invested capital can be expected. All other timber cutting activities must be considered as timber mining.
>
> We find the bureaucratic line structure as it operates archaic, undesirable and subject to change.
>
> The Forest Service as an effective and efficient bureaucracy needs to be reconstructed so that substantial, responsible, local public participation in the processes of policy formation and decision-making can *naturally* take place.

The report had the benefit of the Forest Service task force report as an information base but went on from there. It gives no real information of its own and makes sweeping and unsupported statements. It was designed for a general public audience. Being provocative and coming from a university source, it had wide distribution and substantial influence on what was by then becoming a truly national issue with large ramifications. The report received much and severe criticism from professional foresters and others, but this had little effect in the total picture.

The Wyoming and Monongahela Situations

Arising independently and at about the same time, similar questions concerning the application of clearcutting to national forest lands arose in Wyoming and West Virginia. Along with Montana, they were significant focal points in the development of the clearcutting issue which, as previously seen, extended to larger questions of federal land-management policy.

Wyoming   The clearcutting issue that developed in Wyoming, the state south of Montana, is essentially a parallel to the Montana issue. It arose for much the same predisposing reasons. The state is large, 62.7 million acres in area, and has a relatively small population of about 311,000 people. Approximately 9.7 million acres are national forest. Outdoor recreation, including Yellowstone National Park, and livestock production are of major economic importance in the state. There is a large dude ranch and visitor outfitting business. Fish and wildlife management and watershed protection are of much interest and concern.

As regards the national forest area, timber production is of limited and largely local importance. Fairly large-scale timber cutting in the national forests developed in the late 1950s and early 1960s as part of a general policy to make forested lands more productive by converting old and deteriorating natural forests to vigorous and growing young ones. This had general public support, at least in principle, and substantial areas of lodgepole pine and some spruce forests were clearcut. Timber-processing plants were built, and an economic business was stimulated. Then, a public reaction set in.

> By about 1965, the apparently unforeseen visual impacts of clearcut timber harvesting reached the public. The result was organized opposition. The belief became widespread that continued harvesting of timber in the high altitude forests of Wyoming would have serious adverse effects on soil, water, fish and wildlife, and landscape values. The belief took on special currency with the rapidly increasing public attention to environmental quality during the late 1960s (Wyoming Joint Forest Study Team, 1971).

The senior Senator from Wyoming, Gale McGee, was deeply interested in conservation affairs, including forestry, and was actively concerned over this clearcutting situation. His chief advisor on conservation matters, Mike Leon, was also deeply concerned. He is a university graduate in sociology with much successful newspaper and other journalistic experience.

Beginning in 1968 the Senator received complaints about clearcutting and toured the Bridger National Forest to see for himself as did Leon. The senator twice wrote to the Secretary of Agriculture asking for a blue ribbon commission to investigate the situation in Wyoming. He spoke in the Congress and also questioned Forest Service officials in Washington but did not receive answers from them satisfactory to him. He. also requested, on June 4, 1970, the chairman of the Council on Environmental Quality "to evaluate the timber management practices of the United States Forest Service with particular attention to the policy of clearcutting" (*The Case for a Blue Ribbon Commission on Timber Management in the National Forests,* n.d.). The senator also kept in touch with the Montana situation and in the summer of 1971 made an inspection tour in the Bitterroot which was publicized in the *Daily Missoulian.*

Also being concerned about clearcutting practices in Wyoming and expressed public concern, the Forest Service appointed in mid-1970 a six-man study team to investigate and report. The team had professional qualifications in both research and administration, including timber management, forest insect and disease research, landscape architecture, wildlife, hydrology, range management, and multiple-use planning. Its report was released in 1971. In making its analysis the team stated:

> We relied on two principal sources of information. One was a combination of field examination, review of pertinent plans and policies, and gathering of statements from employees at Regional, Forest, and Ranger District levels. The other was verbal and written communication with individuals who spoke as representatives of a wide variety of organizations, companies, and local governments, and who also expressed their own strictly personal viewpoints (Wyoming Joint Forest Study Team, 1971).

The printed report of eighty-one pages is thorough, frank, and informative. It is also directly critical of much current practice and makes many constructive and corrective recommendations. Remedial action on the ground had also been taken concomitant with the study. Regardless of its quality, the report suffered from the handicap, exploited by critics who wanted drastic changes, that it was an in-service report and therefore subject to bias. Also, by this time lines had hardened and controversy had developed to a point where what might be considered as palliatives were no longer acceptable. More sweeping changes were demanded.

The Monongahela National Forest   The situation on the Monongahela National Forest in West Virginia developed quite independently of action in Montana and Wyoming, but for basically the same reasons, namely, criticisms of rather large-scale application of clearcutting. The general situation is described in the report by a special review committee of the Forest Service in 1970:

The controversy over clearcutting practices on the Monongahela National Forest did not derive from a vacuum. It started with a major change by the Forest Service in the system of forest management. It grew when the technical correctness of this change was questioned by a few laymen largely on the basis of a deeply-held belief (derived in part from earlier Forest Service teaching) that clearcutting is a destructive practice. The controversy enlarged, fueled by mistakes, fanned by distrust, and heated by emotions. All involved to a degree are responsible for its development; all must help find a solution (U.S. Forest Service Special Review Committee, 1970).

The Monongahela National Forest of 947,200 acres follows the Appalachian Mountains in West Virginia. It touches Maryland on the north and borders on Virginia along its southeastern side. The forests are practically all of numerous hardwood species, very different from the fewer species occurring in Western conifers. They are complex in structure and difficult to manage. Beginning in about the 1920s, the lands in the present Monongahela National Forest were purchased from private owners. Before purchase, these lands had been for years subject to unrestrained exploitive cutting and forest fire. They were in poor condition. Names such as "The Great Brush Patch" or "Burn" had been attached to them. A long protection and rebuilding job by the Forest Service was necessary. In the latter 1960s recreation use had increased to upward of a million recreation days a year and the forest value of timber cut to about $750,000 annually.

It was with this background of forest land acquisition and development that timber harvest by clearcutting was initiated in the middle 1960s on some areas, but not generally. This was a major change in cutting practice. Previous cutting was mainly selective, which develops forests of generally mixed tree ages. In contrast, clearcutting produces dominantly even-aged stands, area by area, as cutting is done. People did not understand this change in cutting practice; it looked like forest destruction to them. In a literal sense this is true at the time of cutting, although good hardwood species normally reproduce promptly, abundantly, and well following such cutting. It seemed to many people like a reversion to destructive timber-cutting practices of the past, which in fact it was not.

Criticism developed from hunters, fishermen, recreationists, and conservation-minded people generally. Protest reached the legislative level. In 1964 the West Virginia Legislature passed a resolution calling for a study "of the current management practices being carried out in the Monongahela National Forest."[2] Another similar resolution was passed in 1967 asking for a legislative committee of five members each from the House and the Senate. A report was made, but the 1968 Legislature did not adopt it. A third resolution was passed in 1967 for a legislative investigative commis-

[2] West Virginia House of Delegates Resolution No. 5, Feb. 15, 1964.

sion. The issue also received attention from U.S. Senators Robert C. Byrd and Jennings Randolph, both of whom met with Forest Service officials. Stemming from this general concern the Forest Service made a study of the situation (U.S. Forest Service Special Review Committee, 1970).

The Case for a Blue Ribbon Commission on Timber Management in the National Forests

To complete this analysis of how the clearcutting issue grew to national proportions, mention should be made of the publication entitled *The Case for a Blue Ribbon Commission on Timber Management in the National Forests* (n.d.). This publication is rather a conglomerate in content. It does, however, represent in a sense a culmination of several more or less local developments, as have been sketched above, that grew into an attempt to achieve recognition of national proportions.

The report was released in late 1970 as a joint publication of the Rocky Mountain Chapter of the Sierra Club and the Western Regional Office of the Wilderness Society. The influence of the national Sierra Club, which had been active in this issue, clearly shows here along with other forest-preservation activists. Also significant was continuing effort to pit wilderness-preservation interests against forest-management practice. This was done through emphasis on clearcutting.

The report is a direct attack on the leadership, direction, and credibility of the Forest Service and asked for its thorough investigation. The report is written by ten people, including representation from both Montana and Wyoming, and has been widely circulated.

The general nature and direction of the report is best illustrated by its table of contents.

Introduction. By Gale McGee, senior U.S. Senator from Wyoming.
Part I. What Is the Problem; the Holiday Is Over. By Mike Leon, conservation adivsor to Senator McGee.
Part II. When the Forest Service Began; Historical Perspective. By G. M. Brandborg, from the Bitterroot in Montana.
Part III. The Present Bureaucracy. This is a long section by five authors and ranges from public concern and agency response to castigation of present forestry school education.
Part IV. A Jolt Is Necessary; the Legal Dilemma of the Forest Service. By H. Anthony Ruckel, an attorney engaged by the Sierra Club.
Part V. Tomorrow Belongs to the Public; Why the Status of American Forestry Must Change. By Gordon Robinson, a consulting forester engaged by the Sierra Club.

Developing out of the sequence of actions given above, and focusing on three areas of particular significance, a national controversy of many ramifications and wide importance arose. The purpose of this section has been to trace the triggers that set it off; This is a feature that is common to most controversy development: given favorable predisposing causes— which were present in this situation—focal points develop somewhere, often fortuitously in part, and then spread.

NATIONAL DEVELOPMENT—ACTION AND REACTION

The clearcutting controversy came when the time was right. It caught on with the general public and then spread and deepened on a number of fronts. It was supported by a number of the basic predisposing factors given at the beginning of this chapter. Their importance will become increasingly apparent to the reader later in this chapter. The controversy was fueled by the zeal of the developing environmental movement. Advocacy was strong, and restraints were few. It was popular to attack, and vested interests were suspect.

Perforce, the national development of this issue will be treated in broad terms: (1) the spread to other areas from the initial points of focus, (2) the popular front as expressed through the press and news media, (3) congressional action, and (4) the most constructive part but slower to develop, actions taken to meet the issues by government agencies, forestry organizations, and many individuals.

Spread to Other Areas

Controversy about clearcutting was easiest to generate where public interests in forest land uses and public landownership were high and where economic and private interests in wood production and forest landownership were relatively low. The initial three focal points of controversy given above all fit this prescription.

There are two major forest areas of the United States in which clearcutting had been well-developed and widely applied but where major controversy did not develop. These are given below. It should also be recognized that there are many different forest types in the United States in which clearcutting has a place along with other forest harvest and regeneration methods.

The first area of major significance in the widening of the clearcutting issue was the Pacific Northwest. Here, it centered on old-growth stands of the Douglas-fir forest type which are dense and of high volume and value. Public ownership is extensive, and there is a large wood-using industry of major economic importance. It is also substantially dependent on buying stumpage (standing timber) from federal ownerships under the jurisdiction of both the Forest Service and the Bureau of Land Management.

After about a quarter century of trial-and-error experience and much research with partial harvest cutting methods, application of clearcutting in some form has been found to be the most effective way of harvesting and regenerating most of these old-growth stands. (Old growth here means several hundred years.) In many situations there are no practicable alternatives if commercial cutting is to be done. Once old-growth stands are replaced by young and growing forests, a wider range of forest management practices can be applied.

Responsive action to criticism of clearcutting on public lands, and to a considerable degree on industry lands, took the form of modification of cutting practice as regards the size and location of areas, application of more ecological selectivity in cutting methods where others reasonably could be applied, and avoidance of clearcutting as a standard practice, which can become a habit. On Forest Service lands, attention was also given to preservation of areas, including old-growth stands, through wilderness or other recreational land-use designations. The North Cascades situation described in Chap. 10 is an example of such action on public lands.

The other area where clearcutting has long been a major forest practice is in the lower South of the United States. The forest situation here is sharply different from that in the Pacific Northwest, and indeed from that in the rest of the country. Concern about clearcutting practice developed later in the South than elsewhere and took on a more local pattern of ecological concern. There are at least three major reasons for this that are listed briefly below as they bear on the general anatomy of controversy.

1 In the South forested lands are predominantly in private ownership, mostly small. Ownership of the 198.8 million acres in the South is as follows: 5.3 percent national forests, 3.5 percent in other public ownership, 17.9 percent industrial, and 73.3 percent in other private ownerships, mostly small. There is consequently no politically vulnerable and dominating large public landownership agency to hold accountable.

2 The production of forest products, including the giant pulp and paper industry, is a major economic resource of the South. It is a primary means through which the South has gained a substantial and well-recognized measure of economic equality with the North. This means that state and national legislators from this region are not likely to engage in political attack on forest practices.

3 Particularly in the piney woods area of the lower South, the original forests have long since been cut over and new young forests are dominant. The South is now in what is termed the Third Forest, which consists mainly of planted trees. Much planting has been done on land abandoned for agricultural use and often seriously eroded. This has been done with strong public support. In Georgia, for example, the banks have donated a planting machine to every county. Clearcutting is followed by some seeding but mostly by planting with increasing use of genetically improved stock. The regeneration period following cutting is short, results are good, and the new trees show plainly within 3 or 4 years after cutting. The piney woods country is flat or rolling; clearcutting is not conspicuous as in mountainous areas so there is less aesthetic affront to the general public. People in general are used to this kind of cutting.

Considerable concern about clearcutting has, however, developed in the South. It has been directed to the forest industry because it is of dominant importance and gets most of its wood from small private owners. It has focused on a number of questions: the shape and location of clearcuts; effects on stream and land drainage, including skidding, roading, and drainage ditching; use of prescribed burning; possible soil and erosion damage; effects on wildlife, including hunting and fishing; effects on outdoor recreation; aesthetic considerations; and use of other cutting methods where desirable and practicable. Modifications in forest practice are recommended, but no attack on clearcutting as such has developed. It is too much a bread-and-butter matter, it is generally accepted, and where well-applied it has been neither destructive nor seriously objectionable. Industry has been responsive to public criticism.

The Popular Front

As stated previously, the clearcutting issue caught on in the public mind and became a vehicle for other and deeper issues and forest-management questions. Clearcutting received much attention in national and local newspapers, magazines, and other public media. Mostly, the media were sharply critical. The environmental movement was at high tide. Ecologists, conservationists, and others responded to a receptive but generally uninformed audience. Advocacy, criticism, and extremism were popular, and they make news. Rebuttal of specific allegations was made by public and private agencies, professional forestry organizations, and informed individuals, but in such matters the attackers always have the initial advantage and defenders get less news attention no matter how accurate their story.

Forests offer a good medium for controversy for several reasons. The first is that people are interested in and do like trees. They also think of trees as permanent rather than as very successful plants which live and die. Second, although people need and use wood in large quantities, as in building, paper, and many other uses, they do not relate these products to their forest source. Third, people do not understand or have much interest in methods of forest management. Timber cutting is equated with forest exploitation and is seen as the antithesis of conservation.

The above reasons and more were exploited in the clearcutting controversy and related criticism of public agencies and "the industry." It is easy

to make inaccurate, misleading, and insufficiently discriminating statements about forest management. Foresters have done so along with others.

A few examples will be useful to illustrate the general nature of some
allegations made.

Allegation	Answer
Clearcutting violates the principle of sustained yield.	There is no necessary or direct relationship whatever. Forests can be cut for a time beyond their sustained-growth capacity by any harvesting method. Cut patently cannot exceed growth indefinitely.
Clearcutting violates the principle of multiple use.	There is no necessary conflict. Multiple use seeks a combination of compatible and desired land uses though not applied on every acre. The problem is to achieve harmony and balance in practice, and there are no fixed or simple answers.
"Selective cutting" is a general alternative to clearcutting and is more desirable.	"Selective cutting" has no clear forestry definition or usage. It implies maintaining uneven-aged forests by making periodic partial harvest cuttings, mostly of the larger trees. This is inapplicable to many forest types for both ecological and economic reasons. Where alternative cutting methods are feasible, choice depends mostly on purpose.
Clearcutting is undesirable because it has adverse effects on wildlife, soil structure, fertility, and water.	No single answer can be given. Clearcutting can have both positive and negative effects. This depends on how and where it is applied, the adverse soil effects in question, and the viewpoint taken. Roads, which accompany most timber cutting, can and often do cause more damage to soil and water drainage than does the cutting operation itself, regardless of the particular method applied. Wildlife generally thrives under clearcutting provided the areas cut are not too large.
Clearcutting is forest destruction.	Literally, at the time of forest removal, it is. Properly done, and accompanied by good cleanup and planting or seeding, it is forest renewal akin to nature's methods but more prompt and effective.

Congressional Action

As would be expected, the Congress has had a long and deep interest in
forestry matters, and this included the clearcutting issue. By the end of 1975
it had not, however, passed legislation directly bearing on clearcutting, and
such action does not appear likely.

On April 17, 1970, the Subcommittee on Interior and Related Agencies of the Senate Committee on Appropriations held hearings on the clearcutting issue but not on legislation. Most of the witnesses were critical, as would be expected from the fact that the hearings were held in response to vigorously expressed public criticism. In April, May, and June 1971, hearings were also held before the Senate Subcommittee on Public Lands of the Committee on Interior and Insular Affairs. These were mainly concerned with clearcutting by the Forest Service. As before, the witnesses were strongly pro and con. Those on the critical side presented the many allegations about soil damage and nutrient loss, violation of the Multiple Use Act, dominance of timber use in relation to other "conservation" land uses. The value and uses of clearcutting, which were recognized, were also defended along with the need for better and more scientific information.

On April 20, Senator McGee, for himself and others introduced a bill (S. 1592, 92d Cong., 1st Sess.) "to establish a commission to study the practice of clearcutting of timber resources of the United States on federal lands." An identical bill, H.R. 14354, was introduced into the House by Congressman D. M. Fraser for himself and Congressman J. D. Dow on April 13. In summary, these bills provided for an "Interdisciplinary Clearcutting Study Commission" of twelve members, appointed by the Senate and the House, to study and report to the Congress in 18 months. Members could be either in the Congress or outside of it. An authorization of $2,500,000 was recommended (only in the Senate bill) to carry out the provisions of the act. Neither bill was passed. It will be recalled that advocacy of such a commission was a major purpose of the publication *The Case for a Blue Ribbon Commission on Timber Management on the National Forests.*

In these bills provision was also made that during the commission study and for a maximum of 2 years after it, no clearcutting on federal lands would be permitted, constituting a blanket moratorium. This matter of a moratorium was considered at the Senate hearings of April 1970 and April, May, and June 1971. An unsuccessful attempt was also made to get such action by presidential order. A moratorium would be a drastic, not to say irresponsible, action, because of the many existing timber sale contracts that would be broken if the act was applied literally. It would also constitute a negative decision before a clear basis was established. Further, it would be difficult to define the conditions for lifting the moratorium once it was imposed. This matter is mentioned here because it indicates the degree to which the argument against clearcutting could be carried. A similar bill, without a moratorium, was introduced into the House in the summer of 1972 but was not passed.

In 1971, a Senate bill was introduced that directly concerned clearcutting but also went much further. It was S. 1734 introduced by Senator

Metcalf, and on May 5 it was referred for consideration to the Committee on Interior and Insular Affairs.[3] It has often been termed the Sierra Club bill and had its strong support. It was a very strong regulatory and planning bill that would apply to both privately owned and federal forest lands. Responsibility for administration was to be placed with the Secretary of Agriculture. He would work through the states regarding enforcement on privately owned lands. The bill is long and comprehensive and cannot be reviewed in detail here. Some items are briefly discussed below.

Clearcutting, though not actually prohibited, was sharply limited by two provisions. One, under the heading of "sound forest practice," in addition to a number of ecological and environmental integrity requirements, stipulated "limitation of clear cuts to small openings." The other provision was of a regulatory nature. It placed a limitation on federal lands by requiring that before any clearcutting, specific showing be made that it constitutes "sound forest practice" and that all "feasible and prudent alternatives" have been considered.

The bill gives provisions and time limits for planning on both public and private lands. These include stipulations on availability of proposed plans for public review and hearings, approval of plans by the Secretary, and legal methods of enforcement with strong penalties for plan violation. Special provisions are given for employee protection for informing regarding alleged violations of the act.[4]

A somewhat related bill (S. 350) was introduced into the Senate on January 27, 1971, by Senator Mark Hatfield of Oregon and was also referred to the Committee on Interior and Insular Affairs. It applied to privately owned forest lands only. It focused on a forestry incentive and assistance program with federal grants and was not a regulatory bill. Joint hearings were held in 1971 on the Metcalf and Hatfield bills in July, August, and September in Atlanta, Georgia; Portland, Oregon; and Syracuse, New York, respectively. The hearings were well attended with vigorous expression of pro and con opinions.

The Metcalf bill, S. 1734, was not passed, and passage of legislation of this nature does not seem likely. It is presented here because it seems to

---

[3] An identical bill, H.R. 7383, was introduced in the House by Congressman Dingell for himself and others on April 7, 1971.

[4] Section 208(a) reads as follows:

No person shall discharge or in any other way discriminate against any employee of any timber harvesting operation or any authorized representative thereof by reason of the fact that such employee or representative (1) has notified the Secretary or his authorized representative of any alleged violation, (2) has filed, instituted, or caused to be filed or instituted any proceeding under this Act, or (3) has testified or is about to testify in any proceeding resulting from the administration or enforcement of the provisions of this Act.

Detailed procedures are also given for action to support an employee who informs.

mark the high tide of public criticism of clearcutting and demands for federal forest practice regulation.

Looking at the matter clinically, it would seem that the clearcutting controversy crested at about this time but without action being taken as critics requested. There seem to be three general reasons why such action was not taken. The first is that the controversy had a shallow base in general public support. Although much public attention was generated, it was difficult to sustain it for lack of solid substance. The excesses of advocacy and claims, characteristic of any such movement, also contributed to its decline in effectiveness.

A second factor is that public rebuttal, although slower in developing, as is usually the case, increased in strength and had a cumulative effect.

A third and more basic reason is the simple fact that no widespread, quick, or easy solutions to forest land-management problems, by either legislative or administrative means, are possible. This fact is generally recognized by the Congress, which dealt with forest land-management affairs for a long time. American forests are continental in extent, complex, and also predominantly (nearly 75 percent) privately owned. Attempts to regulate forest cutting practices through national legislation have been made for over 50 years. They have not been successful. A major reason is that about 60 percent of the total forested area capable of commercial forest production is under nonindustrial private ownership. There are about 3 ½ million of these private owners, mostly with small acreage, and their purposes of management are legion. As a practical matter, cutting regulation would be exceedingly difficult to apply, aside from lacking general public support.

Reactions and Consequences

As is usual in public controversy, the advocates of change had the initial advantage in the clearcutting controversy. Not only a particular practice but forest land-management practices and policies in general were vigorously challenged. This challenge caused much and serious reassessment and rethinking by public agencies and certainly by the Forest Service, forest industry, professional foresters in general, and many other concerned people. Action *was* taken to improve timber-cutting practices to correct misapprehensions and erroneous statements and to give the public a better understanding of forest management generally. Misapplications of clearcutting were not denied or defended, but the need for well-applied clearcutting *was* vigorously defended.

The most important and constructive aspect of the whole clearcutting issue was that much good did result, and this is the point that must be kept in mind. Change often does require advocacy and pressures that may be painful in the process. Much of the positive results are internal in changing people's minds and attitudes.

It is ironical but perhaps not unusual that the Forest Service found itself in the middle of this forest land-use controversy. It has long supported wilderness and other forest-preservation policy and asked for the Multiple Use Act in 1960 to give it a clear statutory directive, hitherto lacking, to fully consider all possible public forest land uses. Balance never comes easy and did not here, but it must be sought both internally in the administrative operation of a very large agency, and externally in satisfying the wide range of public interests in national forests lands. In the clearcutting controversy the Forest Service not only had its forest-management decisions challenged but its credibility and leadership questioned. In the early 1960s no one could have predicted the extent and power of the environmental movement that formed during this decade. The Forest Service was inevitably deeply involved and should be, as were many other public and private organizations in sensitive positions of action and responsibility.

The Forest Service responded constructively in many ways to the clearcutting controversy, both internally and externally. Much effort is being placed on improving land-use planning methods and standards and getting effective public participation in land-use decisions. Timber management and other practices are critically examined. Good land management is not cheap, and better funding is needed to support it on public lands. The Forest Service and other public and private land-management agencies are attempting through many means to meet in constructive fashion the pressures and responsibilities placed upon them.

The above is about as far as delineation of the causes, development, and consequences of a land-use controversy, can usefully be carried in this book. The purpose is to focus attention on what is in total a very large, sensitive, and complex issue of national proportions. Much had to be left out, as readers with special knowledge and interests will recognize.

WHAT HAS BEEN LEARNED FROM THE CLEARCUTTING CONTROVERSY?

The subject material of this chapter is sharply different from that of the Lake Tahoe and North Cascades cases, Chaps. 9 and 10. All three involve controversy, but it is well to recognize some significant differences in the context of controversy.

At Lake Tahoe the primary problems arose from the need to establish effective governance in a situation where it was badly divided. The Congress was deeply involved but could act only to the extent of giving authority for a legal framework *for* decision—the Consent of Congress Act. The specific decisions were necessarily left to a regional planning agency which worked with and through local government and other agencies. In the North Cascades, the problem was essentially one of reaching a decision regarding land-use policy and agency jurisdiction on federal lands in a particular area for which the Congress and the President had authority. In this chapter the focus is on controversy itself. It arose in several separate places and grew to national proportions but resulted in no specific and comprehensive decisions.

What can be learned from the clearcutting controversy that is of general significance? It is apparent here, as elsewhere in this book, that matters of principle deriving from land-use situations are not limited to them but go beyond to people—the ever-changing people-land relationship and balance. It is also true that little in principle is peculiar either to the clearcutting issue or to land-use issues in general. A number of items are given here, but no particular priority is intended.

1 For a public controversy to develop, there must be predisposing factors and a favorable climate, both of which almost always have deep roots in the past. This fact is clearly evident in the clearcutting issue. There were a number of predisposing factors, some seemingly unrelated but nonetheless germane, that had years of background. Controversy always starts from something, and usually much more is behind it than commonly recognized. In this case, there were a number of predisposing factors that were a part of, and were given momentum and form by, the wide public concern over environmental quality that so strongly developed in the 1960s.

2 There must also be "detonators," or specific causes that arise at focal points. These seldom can be deliberately prearranged, but occur by chance in a particular time and place. A situation develops, and some people see the opportunity offered and act on it.

3 Determined, able, and motivated people are necessary to develop and maintain a controversy. Only a relatively few are necessary, and this fact was clearly evident in the clearcutting controversy. Many people questioned the large-scale application of the cutting practice, but a relatively few set in motion a controversy that gained national attention in the public news media. There was both strength and weakness. The strength was that with focused leadership the issue caught on, capitalizing on a receptive but generally uninformed public feeling. The weakness was that public comprehension was decidedly limited, the scope for action was fairly narrow, and a few people could not sustain the controversy.

4 The above leads to a more general point. Complex issues or questions which rest on a favorable and popular climate can be oversimplified and generate much heat, but they cannot be sustained unless it is possible to carry them to some direct and clear decision. Otherwise, the heat tends to dissipate rather rapidly, as any practitioner of politics knows. This was evident in the clearcutting case, which revealed the tremendous complexity of environmental problems. Clearcutting is a necessary and effective method that is applied around the world to harvest and reestablish new forests. Only particular applications, not the method itself, can be attacked, and this was the basic situation in this case. The method can be both overused and misapplied, but there is no consistent way to separate these from acceptable applications because of differing points of view. Because of the continental extent and complexity of American forests, owned not only by the public but by several million private owners, large and small, there are no simple administrative or legislative ways to regulate clearcutting. Its abolition or arbitrary regulation would be akin to banning a valuable drug because it can be misapplied.

5   Public controversy is a rough game, but in a political democracy like the United States it seems a necessary means for change, and much good comes out of it. This was certainly true in the clearcutting case. Controversy forced hard scrutiny not only of clearcutting but of forest-management practices generally. Abuses and poor practices were exposed, with corrective action resulting. Also exposed were many exaggerations and misstatements. But most important there was undoubtedly improvement in public understanding. Controversy can bring enlightenment as well as change.

6   In land-use affairs, which touch many interests, it is often difficult clearly to separate a particular issue from several interrelated factors which often are not apparent or generally understood. This was surely true in this case. As pointed out at the beginning of this chapter there were a number of predisposing factors that made possible an attack on the practices of clearcutting. But they also applied to some larger and deeper issues of practice and policy. There was conflict between the more directly measurable economics of forest use for wood production and the rising tide of urban-dominated desires for amenities, aesthetics, and outdoor recreation and environmental concern for the preservation and wise use of renewable natural resources.

7   Related to the above is the fact that, in seeking change through advocacy, a popular issue can be used as a means to gain larger objectives. Opportunism is important in political action.

8   Land-use issues often do not remain settled, particularly where there is strong and organized advocacy that is often persistent and unyielding. The Magruder Corridor issue is a good example. A great deal of study was given to the withdrawal of the area from its earlier primitive-area status at the time the large Selway-Bitterroot Wilderness was established in 1963. Long hearings were held, and opinions were strongly presented on both sides. The corridor lies between two of the largest wilderness areas of the country and, being traversed by a road, it serves as a useful means of access to them. Nonetheless, wilderness-preservationist groups continue active pressure to put the corridor into formal wilderness (Norton, 1972).

Chapter 13

Land Use in Review

The purpose of this chapter is to bring together recurrent problems, issues, practices, and concepts about land use that apply matters of principle. It is not a summary of preceding chapters but is based upon and draws from them. The chapter is structured around eight subjects, each of which presents a particular aspect of land use in practice. Reality is accepted as the final test.

The hope is that such treatment will stimulate thought and emphasize the fact that, despite the complexities of land use, there are unifying common denominators, or matters of principle, which are useful to recognize and apply in practice.

CONCEPTS OF LAND USE

Land use can be characterized as a constantly changing people-land relationship and balance. The implications of this statement are outlined below and give foundation for analysis of particular land-use situations and problems.

People are present in growing numbers and with increasing needs and desires. They can move readily from place to place if there is desire and opportunity, but they also cling strongly to their home place and stubbornly resist forced resettlement, as history has shown. People are, directly or indirectly, dependent on land for the many goods and resources it provides.

In sharp contrast, the amount of land is finite and fixed in place. Natural resources to supply people needs are basically limited. This is particularly true of the nonrenewable resources such as minerals, oil, and coal. But there are limits to the available supply of renewable natural resources which are increasingly becoming critical.

The many, close, and changing people-land relationships stem from a number of causal factors. These include the facts of population growth and the distribution of people within and among countries; changing attitudes of people about land and about their social interrelationships; political changes within and among countries that have many current implications; present, developing, and potential technology which applies to both energy sources and food supply.

In major degree, the practice of land use is a continuing search for some acceptable balance to this changing but inescapable people-land relationship. By their nature, balances are always unstable. Landownership and land use evoke strong human feelings. There is much scope for differing attitudes which depend on the viewpoint taken. Controversy is inherent in the practice of land use. This fact should be accepted along with its corollary that every effort should be made to make controversy constructive. As pointed out in this book and in the case chapters particularly, controversy, although it can be demanding and abrasive on occasion, also challenges and focuses issues. It can and should lead to better understanding and positive results.

The balance of this chapter builds on the implications of this inescapable people-land balance by presenting a number of recurrent situations, problems, and issues encountered in the practice of land use.

PEOPLE-LAND RELATIONSHIPS AND BALANCE

Each of the eight subjects in this section focus on an aspect of land use in practice. The grouping is necessarily somewhat arbitrary and results in some repetition as there is much interrelatedness in land-use affairs. The author is aware that other people could group some items differently, and readers are encouraged to make their own combinations. The subject material is condensed to emphasize substance and matters of principle so as to give an overview of land-use issues and problems of general significance.

Permanence versus Change

Land itself is permanent, but its uses can be changed. There are strongly divided opinions on the desirability of permanence versus change. People in general tend to favor permanence in land use, particularly in times of change and uncertainty. This is currently true with increasing environmental concern and recognition of limited natural resources. This rather general truth is reflected in public policy questions regarding the degree of rigidity or flexibility desirable in land use. For example, there is strong public pressure in the United States to establish more special-use areas such as wilderness. In contrast, the statutory Multiple Use Act establishes a policy of flexibility in land use to meet changing needs.

Point of view, collectively or individually, has strong influence. This fact was strongly evident in the North Cascades situation (Chap. 10). Those with direct concern and knowledge of the area favored the status quo to which they were accustomed. In contrast, the more numerous, more distant, and urban-oriented people strongly favored change to establish large and permanent recreational land-use designations. In this particular situation, they had something to gain and nothing to lose.

Some land-use issues or disputes do not remain settled despite careful study and attempts at arbitration. There have been many such disputes between individuals, groups, or countries. An illustration given in this book is the Magruder Corridor issue. After careful study, made by a special Citizens Review Committee appointed by the Secretary of Agriculture, a particular wildland area in western Montana was withdrawn from a primitive-area classification and put under general national forest administration with seeming approval of concerned people. Nonetheless, there is continuing pressure to put the corridor into formal wilderness.

Related to the above, but expressed more directly in principle form, is the need to reduce conflict in decisions or agreements insofar as possible by deliberate design. As applied to land use, this means inclusion of options or alternatives for future change in a land agreement so to leave as few opportunities as possible for controversy.

Decision Making

Decisions in land use are primarily made through the collective judgment of concerned people, and this is especially true in a political democracy. This principle, or truth, applies generally, including private groups, businesses, and other organizations and public agencies at local, state, and federal levels.

Three aspects of decision-making processes are given below.

Level of Decision As a general principle, decisions should be made by those the most responsible, able, and qualified to make them. This can and should hold for all levels of decision making. Throughout, the goal is to make fair decisions that endure.

For example, suppose that some individuals have a problem or dispute of some kind regarding boundaries, access to land, or joint uses. Unless the problem is handled fairly, and with true agreement by those concerned. decisions made will not hold and may exacerbate the situation. At the community level, issues involve more people and are also more complex. The same principle applies to increasingly higher levels including towns and cities, counties, states, and the federal government. Recourse to the courts for decision is available throughout. Procedures at each level should be consonant with the situation and need.

Kinds of Decisions   There is an extremely wide range in the kinds of decisions to serve different purposes, as is emphasized in Chap. 8. They may be procedural, sequential (in that one decision leads to another), policy, or strategic. Value measurement of some kind enters into most kinds of decisions.

The application of benefit-cost analysis is in point here. This procedure opens the door to direct consideration and comparison of all values whether expressed in monetary units or not. Such analysis influences the kind of decisions by giving them a broad base and preventing a limited approach. See Chap. 7 for seven reasons why the benefit-cost approach is important.

The ability to recognize the commonality of decision-making processes in situations that seem to be widely different gives understanding and strength to deal with a wide range of land-use problems.

Quality of Decisions   It is important to consider the quality of a decision being made. This includes fairness, operability, and, in many situations, capacity to meet changing situations.

In the North Cascades, for example (Chap. 10), a good decision on public land use was made based on much study and public hearings. The decision was final as it was made by the President's office and the Congress, who had full authority to act in the public interest. There were strong differences in opinion by concerned people and public agencies. The decision was designed to minimize future conflict, and no interests were seriously hurt.

In contrast, the establishment of the bistate Tahoe Regional Planning Agency with the consent of Congress created an umbrella-type of authority over the badly divided governance of Lake Tahoe Basin. It includes two states, five counties, and an incorporated municipality, and involves a number of state and federal land-use interests and responsibilities. The agency was a significant step forward in achieving better governance over the beautiful but rather fragile basin. But its authority is necessarily limited. Controversy over land-use management of the basin does and will continue. Nevertheless, establishment of the agency was a good decision because it provided a strong and workable base for coordinated planning in the future.

Development and Timing of Decisions   Many decisions undergo a long period of incubation before they are actually made. Decision making can be an incremental or step-by-step process. Situations, problems, and needs arise that require some decision.

In legislative bodies, for example, legislation grows out of needs and pressures exerted by constituents. These develop into introduced bills which frequently undergo hearings and amendment, which often continues for a long time before any final action is taken. Many land-use regulatory bills introduced in the U.S. Congress give excellent examples.

Pre-testing is not unusual in decision making and is a sound principle to follow where practicable. A draft of proposed action is circulated for review comment. This is commonly done by public agencies regarding land-use proposals which involve many people and points of view. A number of changes may be made before action is taken, and the quality and acceptance of the decision is improved as a consequence.

The timing of a decision may be important. As a major land-use example, the act of March 3, 1891, included a provision to authorize the President to reserve public forest lands from sale. This action was the work of a few dedicated conservationists at a time when wholesale disposal of public lands was rampant.

Another aspect of timing is anticipating the need for decision and to taking steps either to avoid its necessity or to institute action to prepare a good decision. A good executive does not await problems but anticipates them as much as possible through good administration, foresight, initiative, and planning.

A further attribute of a good decision is that it is amenable to amendment to meet changed needs. Such flexibility often can be built into the wording of a regulation, legislative enactment, or administrative directive.

Land Classifications

Because there are many different kinds of land and possible land uses, it is necessary to identify and classify land according to its characteristics and use potentials. A principle here is that one cannot classify what cannot be consistently and meaningfully identified. A broader but related principle is that almost everything about land—its ownership, control, and major changes in its use—moves with deliberation. A strong element of stability in land use is important. Classifications give the basis for the systematic gathering of information that is necessary in land use.

As presented in Chap. 4, there are a number of different kinds of land classifications that are applied for different purposes: (1) classifications based on the land only, which include bedrock and surficial geology, weather and climate, and soils; (2) classifications based directly on land use such as agriculture, forestry, and outdoor recreation; (3) use classifications applied in the zoning of urban land and the related dominant-use concept applied to nonurban lands.

All these classifications are important in land use, and a practitioner should be prepared to apply them as needed in particular situations. It should also be emphasized, as a general fact, that classifications once applied are difficult to change.

There is a basic difference between urban and nonurban uses of land that should be recognized as it affects viewpoints about land management. On nonurban lands the major land-use purpose is to *produce* a crop or a service *from* the land. In contrast, the land in urban areas serves essentially as a physical *base* to support urban construction and related amenities. No major product is taken from the land itself.

It will be useful to examine relationships and differences among three different land-use classifications.

The first is urban land zoning. It is establishment of a classification system that is designed to separate what are considered to be noncompatible land uses, e.g., residential, commercial, and industrial. A number of zones are defined and mapped to meet the range of urban land-use needs. Some flexibility is provided by exceptions permitting uses that are not established for a particular zone.

The second is the concept of dominant use which was developed and emphasized in the publication *One Third of the Nation's Land.* This is the report of the Public Land Law Review Commission given to the President of the United States in 1970. Dominant use is a form of zoning. The general *idea* of recognizing a dominant use is common on both urban and nonurban lands. In this publication it meant that public lands should be classified by dominant use whether it be military, fish and wildlife refuges, wood production, etc. Dominant use was not defined beyond the objective of achieving the "highest and best use," which is difficult to define. There was no clarity as to what constituted "dominant"; 51 percent or what? Uses other than dominant uses were permitted provided they were compatible and not prohibited.

The third is the concept and application of multiple use. The Multiple Use Act is a law prescribing a flexible policy and is not a classification system per se. Basically, multiple use requires that all permitted forest and range land resource uses be equally and fairly considered in the public interest and that compatible uses be managed in harmonious combinations on particular areas. In effect, the policy of multiple use provides a flexible basis for the application of specified land-use classifications on particular areas.

These three examples illustrate different approaches to the application of the general principle of classifications in land use. Zoning is necessary, direct, effective, and administratively operable in urban land use, for which it was developed. It has need for and provides flexibility to meet particular situations. The use of variances, contract zoning, and planned development units are examples. The concept of multiple use is designed for large-scale management of public lands which have a wide range of possible land uses that, inescapably, must be applied in various combinations. The dominant-use proposal met strong and wide public opposition basically because it was considered an unclear and inoperable approach to the management of public lands.

Collectively, these examples lead to a general principle that land-use classifications must be specifically and realistically designed to meet particular needs. Urban zoning is designed for, necessary for, and effective in meeting urban problems, but is not practicable for application to nonurban land use. The basic reason is that in the latter the product or what is managed comes *from* the land—water, wood, recreation, etc.—whereas in urban zoning it is control of what is placed *on* the land itself that is sought through zoning. Discerning specificity is necessary in land-use control and management.

Land-Use Controls

The purpose of this section is to review in terms of principle a group of ways by which controls or influences over land uses are exercised in practice. Basically, they derive from the nature of land and its ownership as given in Chaps. 1 and 2. Legal and administrative power is presented in Chap. 5.

One Land Use Affects Another It is well-known truism that one land use in an area may strongly affect and sometimes control another. The effects may be positive or negative. A few examples follow.

Establishment of an airport certainly affects nearby land areas both negatively and positively. A nearby residential area, subject to noise and possible hazard, is negatively affected, and this is reflected in reduced land values. On the other side of the coin, services, and businesses related or not to airport needs may develop near airports and increase land values.

In an entirely different situation, an influx of retirement or summer homes, and recreational business generally, into a well-established agricultural area has changed or virtually destroyed the agricultural economy of an area and consequently its food production. It is also well known that the construction of interstate highways has deeply affected the local economy, especially near interchanges.

Land-Location Controls Another and major control, which stems directly from the immobility of land, is the importance of land-location controls. In urban building, for example, it is normally necessary to gain complete ownership of the entire area required for construction. Without public power of condemnation, it may be necessary to pay a very high price to gain ownership of a particular parcel of land, perhaps very small, that is included in the development area. In cities one often sees a small separate building that rather obviously should be a part of a much larger and newer building adjoining. Because of cost, or perhaps for some other reason, the land supporting the small building was not purchased.

The same general principle also applies to strategic location of nonurban lands. It is not uncommon, for example, for a person to own a small piece of land that controls access to lands he or she does not own. Again, a high price may be paid to gain such access.

The Plight of Distressed Regions   A recurrent socioeconomic principle of land use is that a distressed and declining region seldom can restore itself. The same principle applies to declining city centers. Causes of the situation are often studied at length. But remedies must largely come from sources outside the area. The underlying reasons are that the basic causes for decline usually have developed over a long period of time and the distressed area has fallen behind in development. It is difficult to remedy such a situation.

In the United States, for example, eastern Kentucky has long had social problems that stem from its topography, history of settlement, and exploitive land use. Much study has been made and assistance given, but solving problems is slow and difficult work. The same general situation exists in the Upper Peninsula of Michigan and some other regions.

Land Consolidation and Reordering   Land, especially for agricultural uses, has often become divided into ownerships too small to manage economically. This problem is prevalent in Europe and elsewhere (see Chap. 11).

From its beginning, the United States followed a general policy of encouraging private landownership of initially public lands. Lacking land-use planning controls, much land was subdivided into ownerships too small to support a family unit. Through the workings of a free economy, a major part of this land subsequently was consolidated into larger and economically manageable units.

In European countries, having a different history, this laissez faire solution could not work. Through inheritance, rural landownership has often become divided into incredibly small units. Remedy of this situation has necessitated major public assistance to reorder fractured ownerships into units of economic size. The cost of this work can be measured by the fact that the complete job of land reordering in West Germany can equal the market value of the land. See Chap. 11, for the requirements of successful land reordering and for procedures followed to reorder an area in West Germany.

A principle underlying reordering is that the public should pay for public benefits. In the West German situation a strong public incentive was the advent of the European Common Market. This requires that each member country meet competition from other countries without tariff barriers. There were consequently strong policy as well as economic reasons for the country to maintain a competitive position in supplying national food needs.

Public Influences and Controls In a political democracy such as the United States, land-use controls are applied through different levels of government. Land-use needs and problems are many and deeply interrelated, and no political unit can go it alone. This applies from communities to the federal government. Public aid and assistance are needed at all levels.

A general principle of public policy is that the public should pay commensurably for benefits in the public interest. The corollary of this principle is that some form of controls, in the form of laws, directives, regulations and such, must accompany public expenditures. Otherwise, public agencies would be open to criticism for spending public funds derived from taxation without proper accountability. Public money is given for a purpose. Obvious as the above may seem, there is need clearly to recognize the necessarily two-way nature of public assistance.

As is well known, there is continuing need for public aids of many kinds and combinations. These include cost sharing and subsidies, many uses of public lands, free assistance given by public personnel, flood controls, expenditures for transportation needs such as roads and railroads, and a large volume of free publications on many subjects of public interest. Land-use interests are included in all of them.

Several large-scale examples of public assistance and accompanying influence are given in this book. They are summarized below as an indication of the kinds of public assistance given.

The Tennessee Valley Authority was the first (1933) and so far is the only comprehensive and major river basin planning and control authority established in the United States. Large public subsidy and public agency assistance have been given.

The federal-state land-grant college system of education, research, and extension began with the Morrill Act of 1862. It is cooperatively funded largely by the federal government and the states.

The federal-state cooperative forest-management and fire control program of the U.S. Forest Service and the states began with the Weeks Law of 1921 and was extended by the Clarke-McNary Act of 1924 and subsequent legislation. It is financed by the states and federal government, with the former paying the larger amount.

The Civilian Conservation Corps was one of the federal agencies established in 1933 during the Great Depression. It was financed primarily by the federal government but with substantial state cooperation.

Grazing on Western public lands was one consequence of rapid Western expansion of land use and settlement in the United States during the 1800s. Widespread private livestock grazing developed on public lands before public controls could be established. The result was a de facto subsidy to the developing Western livestock industry.

A large number of public land-management agencies provide much public recreation and other wildland services at low or no cost. These include the National Park Service, Fish and Wildlife Service, Bureau of Land Management, Forest Service, and agencies within all fifty states.

The above examples illustrate only part of one sector of the total scope of public services and benefits. Land use, in one way or another, enters into all of them, and it is impractical to draw consistent distinctions in application of underlying principle.

Compatible And Combined Uses

Land has many potential uses. Some uses are essentially permanent, and others permit change. There is constant need to achieve some desirable balance in the inescapable people-land relationship. A number of land-use concepts are given here that relate to this underlying problem of seeking balance of compatible uses. They apply to both private and public landownership.

Irreversible and Reversible Uses   Because it is desirable to maintain option for change, essentially irreversible land-use proposals should receive very close scrutiny and be avoided wherever possible. Some are necessary, but some are not. There is range for strong differences in viewpoint.

Changes from one urban land use to another are often made, and so such uses are reversible to some degree. But a change from urban to some nonurban use such as agriculture or forestry is not practicable. Highways, railroads, and power lines and dams are essentially irreversible land uses, although much can be done to avoid land disruption by careful location and construction. A land use that has distinctly limited option for reversibility is, for example, mining for coal, iron, and other minerals.

Natural coastal and inland wetlands are of particular environmental concern because change to another use is often relatively easy and profitable but ecologically irreversible. The concern about such a change in land use lies in the fact that there is a large and timeless yield of natural values from such lands in the public interest that transcends what can be measured by conventional economic methods.

In situations such as the above, the underlying principle is that land-use value decisions, in the final analysis, are made by the collective judgment of people. The corollary to this is the need to inform people about the costs, values, and consequences of irreversible land uses so as to improve the quality of decisions made.

Compatibilities in Land Use   The concept of compatibility, the capability of existing together in harmony, certainly applies to land use. It means not only a good arrangement of different uses on the same area but a judicious and harmonious spatial arrangement of separate single uses. The term well describes the objectives of good land use. Many compatible combinations are possible in practice and include both urban and nonurban land uses.

Compatibilities and limitations differ depending on the kind of land uses involved. For example, a positive and direct people use of an extensive wilderness area for recreation should not, with reasonable limitations, reduce either the natural watershed or wildlife values of the area. These natural values are also uses and so regarded. In this sense, a particular use of land by people may, in effect, protect a natural use.

Another kind of compatibility is the capability of one to coexist with another with some adjustment of both but with little detriment to either. The result is a total net gain in use value. For example, wildlife and timber production have much natural compatibility. Timber cutting creates open spaces which increase available wildlife food on or near the ground, where it is most needed. An old saying in Michigan is that "deer follow the axe," and they do, as cutover areas attest.

Similar kinds of compatibilities also exist in urban areas involving uses on, below, and above ground level. A common characteristic of combined uses in both urban and nonurban areas is that they require much knowledge and skill to plan and administer. A further point is the value of learning to recognize and apply land-use compatibilities in what may seem to be disparate situations. This is an application of the strength-of-unity principle emphasized in Chap. 1.

Underlying the application of compatibilities in land use is the concept of carrying capacity, that is, the ecological and physical limits to how much of what kind of use an area can accommodate without significant loss or damage. To determine carrying capacity requires much technical and professional knowledge that is applicable to a wide range of situations.

The concept of carrying capacity applies to both urban and nonurban land uses. For example, in urban areas it affects street and highway design and construction, building height and density, stadium capacity, and socially acceptable low-cost housing. In nonurban areas it determines such things as livestock or game permitted on an area, concentration of people in recreation areas, and agricultural practices.

Sustained Yield   The application of the principle of sustained yield means that, whatever the land use or combination of uses may be, a continuing flow of goods and services can be obtained without impairment of the productibity of the land. This does not require that the flow necessarily remain constant over time or that the composition of the yield remain the same. As applied in management for timber production, the annual cut for a particular management unit may vary from year to year. Reasons could include a change in market demand, ecological or environmental considerations, a change in the merchantability of particular sizes and species of trees, or a change of management policy in the intensity of management practice desired to meet economic purposes.

The principle of sustained yield, or continuity in a general sense, is important and applies generally. For example, it applies to fish and wildlife management, livestock or other production from a farm unit, and factory production.

Planning and Plans

The purpose of this section is to present a number of problems, varied needs, and matters of recurrent principle about planning and plans as applied in land use. These are grouped under four topics: design, information needs, planning processes and plans, and plan revision and continuity.

Design   In the long run the most creative and enduring part of any plan lies in the quality of the concepts that give it purpose and direction. Design is the best single term to express this function. It includes creativity, form, structure, purpose, organization of parts, and application of means to an end. It is artistry in a broad sense. Design implies imagination, innovation, and the integration of ideas in some harmonious fashion to meet a desired end. It should permeate land-use planning and be applied in partnership with other needed skills and areas of knowledge.

Functions of design in land use can be illustrated in two general groups as follows:

1 Design in intensive use of land. This could include design and siting of residences, public buildings, shopping centers, amusement parks, and a model town.
2 Design in extensive land use. In principle, the basics of design are the same as in intensive land use but the problems and techniques of application differ. Three general examples follow.
   a Parkways and scenic drives which provide a means to see interesting country. Much careful and skillful design is required in their construction.
   b Trails and walkways. In ecologically fragile areas particularly, the construction of such trails approaches a high art. People must be able to see the natural resources but also be prevented from damaging them.
   c Municipal, county, state, and national parks. All these require careful design in planning that is applied in many ways.

Information Needs   Land-use planning requires a large amount of many different kinds of information. Obtaining and analyzing it can constitute a major part of the total job. Information can be grouped into two general categories. The first is the expression of needs and opinions obtained directly from people. The second is a wide range of ecological, social and physical data collected in useful form.

A general principle of economy in information gathering is the need to identify and obtain information on critical or controlling problems. These may include the political climate. Focusing on needs can save both time and money. Information obtained en masse can be impressive in bulk, but it may not give answer to key questions.

The use of interdisciplinary study teams is common and has both strength and weakness. The strength lies in the collective skills of a group of people representing different areas of knowledge working together on a particular project. The weakness can be the natural tendency for each person to gather information in his or her particular field of competence and not work effectively together on hard analysis of critical and limiting problems which lead to decision making.

An important group of information-gathering procedures include feasibility studies, preplanning, and problem analysis. Their purpose is to obtain, in advance of detailed data gathering and planning, an overall appraisal of the scope and practicability of executing a particular project. Thorough consideration of possible alternatives is an important part of preplanning. See Chap. 7 for treatment of project valuation in the public interest which is in point here.

Planning Processes and Plans   For effective planning in land use to take place, there must be good interrelationships between those who plan and those who are affected. Lacking these, there will not be mutual understanding nor successful planning. Both the planners and the planees have power, but it comes from somewhat different sociopolitical sources. On the planner side, power comes mainly from authority—by delegation—whereas on the planee side, it stems more from political influence.

Planning processes differ with the purpose of the plan and the planning approaches followed. On the authoritarian end of the spectrum there is the concept of the so-called master plan. This means that a plan is prepared by those adjudged to be the best qualified and capable of judging in the public interest—but not without consultation with the public. This kind of approach is necessary where large public interests and resources are involved. Much detailed planning is required which is supported by strong public authority and financial strength. The construction of interstate highways or development of large irrigation and hydroelectric projects are examples.

At the other end of the spectrum is what has been called "disjointed incrementalism." This part-by-part planning approach may be necessitated by lack of finance and sufficient agreement to implement a complete plan. Instead, agreed-upon projects that are consonant with total planning objectives are undertaken as they can be financed.

Another not infrequent planning situation is that what initially may seem to be a good land-use proposal may break down as its implications become better understood.

Plan Revision and Continuity   Plans tend to be static, whereas land use cannot be as both needs and knowledge change. Two characteristics of human nature tend to operate in different directions in maintaining plan continuity. The first is that people desire to get things settled, to accept what is, and to avoid continual questioning. The second is that people are often not satisfied by a planning decision and continue to press for revision and change. As is well known, controversy can go on for years. Both of these human attributes are good; they give dimension to a changing people-land relationship and balance. There are no clear or easy answers, but these human trends must be recognized in revision and continuity of plans.

Controversy in Land Use

The purpose of this section is to give in summary and generally sequential order a number of matters of principle commonly involved in land-use controversy. The author is aware that they could be presented in different ways, and the reader is encouraged to make amendments and additions. An effective practitioner in land use should be a student of controversy.

Controversy is inevitable in land use. It is inherent in an ever-changing people-land relationship and balance in the use of natural resources. As emphasized frequently in this book, people hold strong interests in and opinions about land and its uses. Accompanying advocacy can be a rough, hard, and sometimes destructive matter. Three case studies in this book, Chaps. 9, 10, and 12, are in large degree studies of controversy leading to decision. Controversy also enters indirectly or directly into several other chapters.

Predisposing Factors   For a land-use controversy to develop and be sustained, there must be a number of predisposing factors that often go back in time for their genesis. Situations, circumstances, problems, and issues develop in a cumulative sort of way and coalesce. A good example of this phenomenon is given in some detail in the opening of Chap. 12 on the clearcutting controversy. Basically, the time has to be right.

Clear and Actionable Issues   For a controversy to develop successfully, there must be clear, definable, and actionable issues on which public attention can be focused. To gain and hold public attention, complex issues must be simplified to something that is readily understandable.

In the North Cascades (Chap. 10) the basic issue was clear. There was strong public desire to establish permanent emphasis on public recreation in managing an area of outstanding scenic excellence. Decisive action could be taken because the area was in public ownership. The basic principle of actionability also applies in land reordering, but the situation in Chap. 11 was not a controversy in the usual sense of the term although there were many problems to resolve. There was pressing need, in both the public and the private interest, to reorder and consolidate badly divided private landownerships into larger and economically viable units. There was strong public authority which was supported with much public assistance.

At Lake Tahoe (Chap. 9) there was and remains much controversy. The continuing problem is fractured governance in the basin that cannot be changed. But an overall authority was provided by the formation of the Tahoe Regional Planning Agency. Regarding the clearcutting controversy given in Chap. 12, the issue was popular and clear enough. But definitive action could not be taken because only *applications* of a common and accepted forest-management practice, not the practice itself, could be attacked. The base of the controversy was weak in this respect.

Triggers   Given a propitious situation and base, there need to be particular causes, or triggers, to set a controversy in motion. These may be planned but can also be more or less fortuitous. This phenomenon was evident in the clearcutting controversy. Focal points of controversy in West Virginia, Montana, and Wyoming developed independently and were coalesced into a national controversy by well-organized design.

Leadership   Given a favorable situation and cause, determined and able leadership is necessary to give particular point and direction to a controversy. This is almost always true. It is also true that rather few such people are necessary, as the history of controversy amply attests. Unity and strong leadership are needed to capitalize on a favorable situation, but without the capacity to maintain general public interest, comprehension, and support, a few people cannot sustain a public controversy to conclusion. A strong public front is needed, and this is different from having a few leaders with a large personal following.

Information Needs and Viewpoints   If one accepts the principle that land-use decisions are, for the most part at any rate, made by the collective judgment of people, it follows that people should be adequately informed. An analysis of the various means of so doing is beyond the scope of treatment here, but some general points can be made.

It is important to distinguish between controversy and advocacy, as the words are often confused. Controversy means only that there is a dispute, a difference of opinion, about some question. Advocacy means taking sides; an advocate is one who espouses or defends a cause by argument, a pleader. In the North Cascades much effort was made by the public agencies con cerned to give solid information as presented in the joint study report. Differences in viewpoint were also included in the report. At the public hearings private people and organizations were free to, and did, advocate their point of view. The collective judgment of people consequently could be made on a broad base.

Tactics and Motives in Controversy   Advocacy in popular issue can be a tactical maneuver. A principle here is to strike at vulnerable places to gain larger ends. The clearcutting issue in Chap. 11 gives an illustration. Behind the immediate issue of clearcutting there were recurrent questions about the economic use of public forest land for timber production balanced against the importance of outdoor recreation, wildlife, and forest aesthetics generally. A larger purpose, which seldom surfaced in this issue, was to reduce the independence and power of the Forest Service by transferring it from the Department of Agriculture to the Department of the Interior. In one form or another this goal goes back many years and has been a recurrent item in the many studies of and recommendations for reorganization of the executive branch.

Responsibility and Accountability   People in general wish to keep what they have and at the same time seek more, for a net gain in their interest. This situation is common in land use and is an important factor in weighing differences in viewpoints.

Regarding urban-oriented interests, there is, for example, a strong tendency to favor more wildland preservation in terms of wilderness, national parks, and national recreation areas on public lands. This is perfectly understandable from their point of view as they have something to gain and little to lose. But this desire can also run counter to the interests of nonurban people who may desire more economic use of wildlands. As always, there is the need to attain some acceptable balance.

A principle of responsibility and accountability is involved in controversy. The attackers usually have an initial advantage in land-use controversy as to demand is relatively easy. But advocates usually cannot assume responsibility for the actions they propose because they are not directly accountable. What is termed sometimes disparagingly, "the establishment" has to accept accountability. It is well to keep in mind that the advocate asks, but it is primarily the people in positions of public or private responsibility who have to take land-use actions and largely assume responsibility for their consequences.

Environmental Quality in Land Use

The purpose of this concluding section is to bring together some problems, concepts, and other matters of principle that are important in achieving a desirable and sustainable level of environmental quality in land use. This goal applies to both urban and nonurban land uses although the measures

of accomplishment may differ. Some European comparisons are included
to give added perspective.

What Is "Natural"?   The question of what is "natural" arises in many
land-use contexts, and its implications are closely related to measures of
environmental quality. People tend to accept what they are accustomed to
and often consider it natural.

To give an illustration, in an attractive forest area people regard trees
as natural and desirable for aesthetic reasons, and they are not concerned
whether the trees are, in fact, of natural origin. Now assume that a sample
of these same people visited a forest which recently had suffered severe
damage by natural agents such as storm, fire, insects, or disease. The result
would be anything but attractive, and the reaction of these people would be
strongly negative. People in general are not accustomed to the natural processes of forest growth and renewal.

On a much larger area and time scale, and a reversal of the above
illustration, the essentially treeless mountains of the lake country of northern England are justly cherished, and have so been back to Queen
Elizabeth's time, for their beauty. But, ecologically, their present condition
is the result of centuries of people-directed sheep grazing and land clearing
with some burning that destroyed an earlier natural tree cover. The same
kind of history and result applies to the large treeless areas in Scotland,
Ireland, and elsewhere in the world.

The point in common between these examples is that people strongly
tend to equate what is "natural" in vegetative land cover with what is
considered as aesthetically desirable. Consequently there is no consistent
relationship to what is ecologically natural.

Quality of Design in Large-Scale Land Use

The aesthetic quality of land use can be substantially increased on a large
scale and at reasonable cost through careful design in planning. Application
of the nature park concept, which is very popular in Europe, gives an excellent example. The basic idea is to maintain, and to enhance as practicable,
the aesthetic quality of a naturally attractive area and at the same time
continue existing land uses. Land is in short supply in Europe and must be
put to good use. There is limited opportunity to establish large national
parks, wilderness, or other such areas solely for recreational uses, as is done
in the United States.

The Harz Mountains Nature Park of northern West Germany is a
good example. It is a large and extremely attractive area that is well developed and heavily used for outdoor recreation. It also supports agriculture
and some small industry, and the extensive forest areas are well managed
for wood production. By law, the area has been established as a nature

park. What this means essentially is that present uses may be continued, although some nonconforming uses may be phased out. But further development for industrial use is prohibited as are other uses that are considered incompatible to the area. The nature park concept is widely applied in a number of European countries, but the specifics differ. English countrysides have, for instance, long been famous for their beauty. This is not a happenstance but the result of much attention and care without any general law.

The nature park concept illustrates a flexible approach to the larger need to build environmental quality by design into land-use management generally. To do so requires continuing rapport between private and public interests at all levels of government and so establish and maintain a desirable people-land relationship and balance.

Bibliography: Group 1

Chapters 1 to 5 and 13: Land Characteristics, Uses, Classifications, Ownership, and Control

American Law of Property, 1952. A. J. Casner (ed.). Little, Brown and Company, Boston.

Babcock, Richard F., 1966. *The Zoning Game: Municipal Practices and Principles.* The University of Wisconsin Press, Madison; Milwaukee; London. 2d printing, 1969.

Behan, R. W., and R. M. Weddle (eds.), 1971. *Ecology, Economics, Environment.* University of Montana Press, Missoula.

Black, John, 1970. *The Dominion of Man.* University Press, Edinburgh; Aldine Publishing Company, Chicago.

Brenneman, R. L., 1967. *Private Approaches to the Preservation of Open Land.* The Conservation and Research Foundation, Connecticut College, New London, CT. 133 pp.

Brockman, C. F., and L. C. Merriam, Jr., 1973. *Recreational Use of Wild Lands.* McGraw-Hill Book Company, New York. 329 pp.

Buckman, H. O., and N. C. Brady, 1969. *The Nature and Properties of Soils,* 7th ed. The Macmillan Company, New York. 653 pp.

Burch, W. R., Jr., 1971. *Daydreams and Nightmares: A Sociological Essay on the American Environment.* Harper & Row, Publishers, Incorporated, New York. 175 pp.

Carbonnier, Charles, et al., 1971. *Definition of Forest Land and Methods of Land and Site Classification.* International Union of Forest Research Organizations. Department of Forest Yield Research, Royal College of Forestry, Stockholm, Sweden.

Commonèr, Barry, 1971. *The Closing Circle; Nature, Man and Technology.* Alfred A. Knopf, Inc., New York. 326 pp.

Clawson, Marion, 1964. *Man and Land in the United States.* University of Nebraska Press, Lincoln. 178 pp.

———, 1968. *Policy Directions for U.S. Agriculture: Long Range Choices in Farming and Rural Living.* The Johns Hopkins Press, Baltimore. 398 pp.

———, 1972. *America's Land and Its Uses.* Resources for the Future, Inc. The Johns Hopkins Press, Baltimore and London.

———, and Peter Hall, 1973. *Planning and Urban Growth: An Anglo-American Comparison.* Resources for the Future, Inc. The Johns Hopkins Press, Baltimore and London. 300 pp.

———, R. B. Held, and C. H. Stoddard, 1960. *Land for the Future.* The Johns Hopkins Press, Baltimore. 570 pp.

———, and C. L. Stewart, 1965. *Land Use Information.* Resources for the Future, Inc. The Johns Hopkins Press, Baltimore. 402 pp.

Davis, K. P., 1969. "What Multiple Land Use and for Whom?" *Journal of Forestry,* **67**:718–721.

———, 1969. *Valuation of the Nashwaak Timberlands.* Oxford Paper Co. 96pp.

———, et al., 1970. *Federal Public Land Laws and Policies Relating to Multiple Use of Public Lands.* PB 194419. A study prepared for the Public Land Law Review Commission. Reproduced by the Clearinghouse for Federal Scientific and Technical Information, Springfield, VA. 110 pp.

Dasmann, R. F., 1965. *The Destruction of California.* The Macmillan Company, New York.

———, 1959. *Environmental Conservation,* 2d ed., 1968. John Wiley & Sons, Inc., New York. 375 pp.

Delafons, John, 1969. *Land Use Controls in the United States States,* 2d ed. The M.I.T. Press, Cambridge, MA, and London. 203 pp.

Detwyler, T. R. (ed.), 1972. *Urbanization and Environment: The Physical Geography of the City.* Ten chapters by ten authors. Duxbury Press, Duxbury, MA.

Dilworth, J. R., 1971. *Land Use Planning and Zoning.* Department of Printing, Oregon State University, Corvallis. 95 pp.

Duerr, W. A. (ed.), 1973. *Timber: Problems, Prospects, Policies.* The Iowa State University Press, Ames. 260 pp.

Dunham, Allison, 1966. *Preservation of Open Space Areas: A Study of the Non-governmental Role.* Welfare Council of Metropolitan Chicago, Publication 1014.

Eiseley, Loren, 1970. *The Invisible Pyramid.* Charles Scribner's Sons, New York.

Environmental Studies Board, 1972. *Institutional Arrangements for International En-*

vironmental Cooperation: A Report to the Department of State. National Academy of Sciences, Washington, DC.

Firey, W. I., 1960. *Man, Land, and Mind: A Theory of Resource Use.* The Free Press of Glencoe, IL, 256 pp.

Fleming, Donald, 1972. *Roots of the New Conservation Movement.* Perspectives in American history. Charles Warren Center for Studies in American History. Harvard University Press, Cambridge, MA.

Fraser, Don Lee, 1967. "Achieving Public Acceptance of Multiple Use." *Proceedings, 58th Annual Meeting of Western Forestry and Conservation Association,* Portland, OR.

Garvey, Gerald, 1972. *Energy, Ecology, Economy.* A project of the Center of Environmental Studies, Princeton University. W. W. Norton and Company, Inc., New York.

Gillette, Elizabeth R. (ed.), 1972. *Action for Wilderness.* Sierra Club Battlebook Series, 7. San Francisco. 222 pp.

Glackmeyer Subcommittee, Northern Region Land-Use Planning Committee, 1960. *A Multiple Land-use Plan for the Glackmeyer Development Area.* Ontario Department of Lands and Forests. 210 pp. with 11 maps.

Golembiewski, R. T., Frank Gibson, and G. Y. Cornog (eds.), 1966. *Public Administration Readings in Institutions, Processes, Behavior.* Political Science Series. Rand McNally, Chicago. 498 pp.

Gould, E. M., 1969. "Whatever became of the Invisible Hand?" *Forest History* **12**(4):7–9.

Graham, E. H., 1944. *Natural Principles of Land Use.* Oxford University Press, London and New York. 274 pp.

Gray, O. S., 1970. *Cases and Materials on Environmental Law.* Washington Bureau of National Affairs. 1252 pp.

Hady, T. F., and T. F. Stinson, 1967. *Taxation of Farmland on the Rural-Urban Fringe; a Summary of State Preferential Assessment Activity.* U.S. Department of Agriculture, Economic Research Service, Agricultural Economic Report 119.

Harper, V. L., 1973. "The National Forest Multiple Use Act of 1960. Excerpts from an Oral History." *Journal of Forestry,* **71**(4):203–205.

Harris, Marshall, 1953. *Origin of the Land Tenure System in the United States.* Iowa State College Press, Ames. 445 pp.

Held, R. B., and Marion Clawson, 1965. *Soil Conservation in Perspective.* Resources for the Future, Inc. The Johns Hopkins Press, Baltimore. 344 pp, illus.

Helfrich, H. W., Jr. (ed.), 1970. *The Environmental Crisis: Man's Struggle to Live with Himself.* Twelve contributors. Yale University Press, New Haven, CO.

Huntley, J. R., 1972. *Man's Environment and the Atlantic Alliance,* 2d ed. NATO Information Service, 1110 Brussels, Belgium.

Jarrett, Henry (ed.), 1958. *Perspectives on Conservation: Essays on America's Natural Resources.* Twenty-two separate papers. The Johns Hopkins Press, Baltimore. 260 pp.

Judson, Sheldon, 1968. "Erosion of the Land—Or What's Happening to Our Continents?" *American Scientist,* **56**(4):356–374.

Keser, N., 1970. *A Mapping and Interpretation System for the Forested Land of British Columbia—First Approximation.* British Columbia Forest Service, Report 54, Department of Lands, Forests, and Water Resources.

Klingebeil, A. A., and P. H. Montgomery, 1966. *Land Capability Classification.* Soil Conservation Service, U.S. Department of Agriculture Handbook 210. 21 pp.

Legget, R. F., 1973. *Cities and Geology.* McGraw-Hill Book Company, New York. 624 pp.

Little, C. E., 1968. *Challenge of the Land.* Open Space Action Institute, Inc., New York. 151 pp.

Litton, R. B., Jr., 1968. *Forest Landscape Descriptions and Inventories—A Basis for Land Planning and Design.* U.S. Forest Service Research Paper PSW-49.

Macon, J. W., H. H. Webster, and R. L. Hilliker, 1970. "For more Effective Links between Resource Management and Research." *Journal of Forestry,* **67**:170–174.

McClellan, G. S. (ed.), 1971. *Land Use in the United States; Exploitation or Conservation.* The Reference Shelf, vol. 43, no. 2. The H. W. Wilson Company, New York.

Meadows, D. H., D. L. Meadows, Jorgen Renders, W. W. Behrens III, 1972. *The Limits to Growth.* A Potomac Associates Book, Universe Books, New York.

Mergen, Francois (ed.), 1970. *Man and His Environment: The Ecological Limits of Optimism.* With R. S. Miller, G. M. Woodwell, W. R. Burch, P. A. Jordan, and R. L. Means. Yale University, School of Forestry Bulletin 76.

Merriam, L. C., and R. B. Ammons, 1968. "Wilderness Users and Management in Three Montana Areas." *Journal of Forestry,* **66**:390–395.

Millman, Roger, 1972. "Mosaic of Scottish Land Borders." *The Geographical Magazine,* **44**(10):699–704.

Murphy, E. F., 1967. *Governing Nature.* Problems of American Society. Quadrangle Books, Inc., Chicago. 333 pp.

Murray, L. A., 1968. *Land Trusts.* Open Space Action Institute, New York.

National Academy of Sciences, 1969. *Program for Outdoor Recreation Research,* National Academy of Sciences Publication 1727.

Natural Resources Council of America, H. K. Pyles, Coordinator, 1970. *What's Ahead for Our Public Lands?* Natural Resources Council of America, 709 Wire Building, Washington, DC.

Northeast Regional Resource Economics Committee, 1967. *Preserving Open Space in Expanding Urban Areas.* Bulletin 567, Massachusetts Agricultural Experiment Station, Amherst, MA.

North Central Land Tenure Research Seminar, 1963. *Land Use Controls.* Department of Agricultural Economics, University of Illinois, Special Publication 7.

O'Callaghan, J. A., 1967. "The Mining Law and Multiple Use." *Natural Resources Journal,* **7**(2):242–251.

Open Space Action Committee, 1967. *Proceedings, First Professional Level Conference on Open Space Preservation Methods, May 21-22, 1967.* Open Space Action Committee, New York.

Open Space Institute, 1965. *Stewardship; Modern Methods of Land Preservation Used by "Good Steward" Land Owners.* Open Space Action Committee, New York.

Parsons, K. H., R. J. Penn, and P. M. Raup (eds.), 1956. *Land Tenure: Proceedings of International Conference on Land Tenure and Related Problems.* University of Wisconsin Press, Madison. 739 pp.

Pinchot, Gifford, 1947. *Breaking New Ground.* Harcourt, Brace and Company, Inc., New York.

President's Advisory Panel on Timber and the Environment, 1973. *Report.* U.S. Government Printing Office, Washington, DC. 541 pp.

Public Land Law Review Commission, 1970. *One Third of the Nation's Land.* U.S. Government Printing Office, Washington, DC. 342 pp.

Recreation Symposium, 1971. Sponsored by New York State University College of Forestry, U.S.D.A. Forest Service, et al. Held at College of Forestry, Syracuse, NY, Oct. 12–14, 1971. Proceedings prepared by Northeastern Forest Experiment Station, U.S. Forest Service. 211 pp.

Ridd, M. K., 1965. *Area-oriented Multiple Use Analysis.* U.S. Forest Service, Intermountain Forest and Range Experiment Station, Ogden, UT. 14 pp., illus.

Sax, Joseph L., 1964. "Takings and the Police Power." *Yale Law Journal* **74**:36–76.

Scheffey, A. J. W., 1969. *Conservation Commissions in Massachusetts.* With supplemental report on the emergence of conservation commissions in six other northeastern states, by W. J. Duddleson. The Conservation Foundation, Washington, DC.

"Scenic Easements in Action," 1966. *Proceedings of conference, Dec. 16–17, 1966.* University of Wisconsin Law School, Madison.

Sears, P. B., 1966. *The Living Landscape.* Basic Books, Inc., Publishers, New York. 199 pp.

Shomon, J. J., 1971. *Open Land for Urban America; Acquisition, Safekeeping, and Use.* The Johns Hopkins Press, Baltimore. 171 pp., illus.

Simonson, R. W., 1962. "Soil Classification in the United States." *Science,* **137**:117–126.

Smith, F. E., 1966. *The Politics of Conservation.* Pantheon Books, Random House, Inc., New York. 338 pp.

————, U.S. Department of Agriculture, in cooperation with Connecticut Agricultural Experiment Station and Storrs Agricultural Experiment Station, 1970. *Soil Survey, Litchfield County, Conn.*

Soil Conservation Society of America, 1973. *National Land Use Policy; Objectives, Components, Implementation.* Soil Conservation Society of America, Ankeny, OH.

Stacer, T. C., 1967. "The Case of Timber Trespass." *Journal of Forestry,* **65**:621–624.

Stamp, L. Dudley, 1955. *Man and the Land.* Collins Clear Type Press, London and Glasgow.

Stone, C. D., 1974. *Should Trees Have Standing? Toward Legal Rights for Natural Objects.* William Kaufmann, Inc., Los Altos, CA. 102 pp.

Task Force Report, 1973. *The Use of Land: A Citizen's Policy Guide to Urban Growth.* Edited by William K. Reilly. The Rockefeller Brother's Fund, Thomas Y. Crowell Company, New York.

Thompson, D. L., 1972. *Politics, Policy, and Natural Resources.* Free Press, Macmillan Company, New York.

Twiss, R. H., 1969. "Conflicts in Forest Landscape Management—The Need for Forest Environmental Design." *Journal of Forestry,* **67**:19–23.

U.S. Department of Agriculture, 1960. *Soil Classification, a Comprehensive System, 7th approximation.* 265 pp., illus. Supplement issued in March 1967.

————, 1964. *The Principal Laws Relating to the Establishment and Administration of the National Forests and Other Forest Service Activities.* Agriculture Handbook 20.

————, 1965. *Land Resource Areas of the United States.* Agriculture Handbook 296.

————, Economic Research Service, 1968. *Major Uses of Land and Water in the United States with Special Reference to Agriculture.* Agricultural Economic Report 149. Data as of 1964.

U.S. Forest Service, 1973. *The Outlook for Timber in the United States.*

Worrell, A. C., 1970. *Principles of Forest Policy.* McGraw-Hill Book Company, New York.

Wagner, R. H., 1971. *Environment and Man.* W. W. Norton and Company, Inc., New York. 491 pp.

Wengert, Norman, 1962. "The Ideological Basis of Conservation and Natural Resources Policies and Programs." *The Annals of the American Academy of Political and Social Science,* **344**:65–75.

Wheatley, C. F., 1970. *Study of Land Acquisitions and Exchanges Related to Retention and Management or Disposition of Public Lands.* P.B. 194-448, U.S. Department of Commerce. Prepared for the Public Land Law Review Commission. Reproduced by National Technical Information Service, Springfield, VA.

Williams, E. T., 1961. "Trends in Forest Taxation." *National Tax Journal,* **14**(2):113–144.

Whyte, W. H., 1968. *The Last Landscape.* Doubleday & Company, Inc., Garden City, NY.

Zisman, S. B., and D. B. Ward, 1968. *Where Not to Build: A Guide for Open Space Planning.* U.S. Bureau of Land Management Technical Bulletin 1. 160 pp., illus.

Zivnuska, John, 1961. "The Multiple Problems of Multiple Use." *Journal of Forestry,* **59**:555–560.

Bibliography: Group 2

**Chapters 6 to 8: Planning Processes, Value Measurement
and Decision Making**

Abrams, Charles, 1965. *The City Is the Frontier.* Harper & Row, Publishers, Incorporated, New York. 394 pp.

Advisory Commission on Intergovernmental Relations, 1964. *Impact of Federal Urban Development Programs on Local Government Organization and Planning.* Committee on Government Operations. U.S. Government Printing Office, Washington, DC. 198 pp.

Alonzo, William, 1964. *Location and Land Use.* Harvard University Press, Cambridge, MA.

Anthony, R. N., 1965. *Planning and Control Systems: A Framework for Analysis.* Harvard Graduate School of Business Administration, Boston. 180 pp.

Appleby, P. H., 1945. *Big Democracy.* Alfred A. Knopf, Inc., New York.

Barlowe, Raleigh, 1972. *Land Resource Economics: The Economics of Real Property.* Prentice-Hall, Inc., Englewood Cliffs, NJ. 616 pp.

Battelle Columbus Laboratories, 1972. *Environmental Assessment for Effective Water Quality Management Planning.* Environmental Protection Agency, Washington, DC.

Bethune, J. E., and J. L. Clutter, 1969. *Allocating Funds to Timber Management Research.* Forest Science Monograph 16-1969.

Bosselman, Fred, and David Callies, 1972. *The Quiet Revolution in Land Use Control.* Prepared for the Council on Environmental Quality. U.S. Government Printing Office, Washington, DC. 327 pp. with appendixes.

Brahtz, J. F. Peel (ed.), 1972. *Coastal Zone Management: Multiple Use with Conservation.* University of California Engineering and Physical Sciences Extension Series. John Wiley & Sons, Inc., New York. 352 pp.

Brecher, Joseph F., 1971. "Environmental Litigation: Strengths and Weaknesses." *Environmental Affairs,* **1**(3):565–577.

Breese, Gerald, et al., 1965. *The Impact of Large Installations on Nearby Areas: Accelerated Urban Growth.* Sage Publications, Inc., Beverly Hills, CA. 632 pp.

Campbell, T. H., and R. O. Sylvester (eds.), 1968. *Water Resources Management and Public Policy.* Seventeen contributors. University of Washington Press, Seattle.

Chapin, R. Stuart, Jr., 1965. *Urban Land Use Planning,* 2d ed. University of Illinois Press, Urbana. 498 pp.

Chester County Water Resources Authority, 1968. *The Brandywine Plan.* Summary of the *Plan and Program for the Brandywine,* prepared by the Chester County Water Resources Authority, West Chester, PA.

Clawson, Marion, 1950. *The Western Livestock Industry.* McGraw-Hill Book Company, New York. 401 pp.

Coomber, N. H., and A. K. Biswas, 1973. *Evaluation of Environmental Intangibles.* Genera Press, Bronxville, NY. 77 pp.

Council on Environmental Quality, 1970. *First Annual Report.* Transmitted to the Congress, August 1970. U.S. Government Printing Office, Washington, DC. 326 pp.

Dana, S. T., 1956. *Forest and Range Policy: Its Development in the United States.* McGraw-Hill Book Company, New York.

David, Elizabeth L., 1968. "Lakeshore Property Values: A Guide to Public Investment in Recreation." *Water Resources Research,* **4**(4):697–707.

Davis, K. P., 1966. *Forest Management: Regulation and Valuation,* 2d ed. McGraw-Hill Book Company, New York. 519 pp.

————, 1970. "Land: The Common Denominator in Forest Resource Management; Emphasis on Urban Relationships." *Journal of Forestry,* **68**(10):628–631.

Davis, L. S., 1965. *The Economics of Wildfire Protection with Emphasis on Fuel Break Systems.* California Division of Forestry, Sacramento. 166 pp.

————, and W. R. Bentley, 1967. "The Separation of Facts and Values in Resource Policy Analysis." *Journal of Forestry,* **65**:612–620.

Dorfman, Robert (ed.), et al., 1965. *Measuring Benefits of Government Investments.* Studies of Government Finance. The Brookings Institution, Washington, DC.

Eckstein, Otto, 1961. *Water Resource Development: The Economics of Project Evaluation.* Harvard University Press, Cambridge, MA.

Enk, Gordon A., 1973. *Beyond NEPA: Criteria for Environmental Impact Statement.* The Institute on Man and Science, Rensselaerville, NY. 140 pp.

Environmental Protection Agency, 1971. "Requirements for Preparation, Adoption, and Submittal of Implementation Plans." *Federal Register* **36**(158) part II:154 86–15506.

Ewald, W. R., Jr. (ed.), 1968. *Environment and Policy: The Next Fifty Years.* Papers commissioned for the American Institute of Planners. Indiana University Press, Bloomington.

Flora, Donald F., 1964. "Uncertainty in Forest Investment Decisions." *Journal of Forestry,* **62**:376–380.

Frank, Bruno, 1942. *The Days of the King.* The Press of the Readers Club, New York. 236 pp.

Galbraith, J. K., 1967. *The New Industrial State,* Houghton Mifflin Company, Boston. 427 pp.

Gans, H. J., 1968. *People and Plans: Essays on Urban Problems and Solutions.* Basic Books, Inc., Publishers, New York. 395 pp.

Goodman, W. I., and E. C. Freund (eds.), 1968. *Principles and Practice of Urban Planning.* Published for the Institute for Training in Municipal Administration by the International City Manager's Association, Washington, DC.

Gosselink, J. G., E. P. Odum, and R. M. Pope, 1973. "The Value of the Tidal Marsh." Submitted for publication.

Gregory, G. Robinson, 1972. *Forest Resource Economics.* The Ronald Press Company, New York. 548 pp.

Guitar, Mary Anne, 1972. *Property Power.* Doubleday & Company, Inc., Garden City, NY. 322 pp.

Hall, O. F., 1962. *Evaluating Complex Investments in Forestry and Other Long-Term Enterprises.* Purdue University Agriculture Experiment Station Research Bulletin 752.

Hamill, Louis, 1968. "The Process of Making Good Decisions about the Use of the Environment of Man." *Natural Resources Journal,* **8**(2):279–301. University of New Mexico Law School.

Hammond, Richard J., 1966. "Convention and Limitation in Benefit-Cost Analysis." *Food Research Institute Papers Natural Resources Journal, School of Law, Univ. of New Mexico,* **6**:195–222.

Henderson, J. D., 1931. *Real Estate Appraising.* The Bankers Publishing Co., Boston.

Hendrick, B. J., 1937. *Bulwark of the Republic: A Biography of the Constitution.* Little, Brown and Company, Boston. 465 pp.

Holbrook, S. H., 1957. *Dreamers of the American Dream.* Doubleday & Company, Inc., Garden City, NY. 369 pp.

Howard, J. K., 1943. *Montana, High, Wide, and Handsome.* Yale University Press, New Haven, CO. 347 pp.

Hughes, J. M., 1968. "Wilderness and Economics." *Journal of Forestry,* **66**:855–858.

Krutilla, J. V., 1966. *Is Public Intervention in Water Resources Development Conducive to Economic Efficiency?* Reprint 56, Resources for the Future, Inc., Washington, DC.

Leak, W. B., 1964. *Estimating Maximum Allowable Yields by Linear Programming.* U.S. Forest Service Research Paper NE-17.

Leopold, Luna B., 1969. *Quantitative Comparison of Some Aesthetic Factors among Rivers.* U.S. Geological Survey Circular 620.

———, and Maura O'B. Marchand, 1968. "On the Quantitative Inventory of the Riverscape." *Water Resources Research,* **4**(4):709–717.

Lewis, P. H., Jr., and R. W. Oertel, 1964. *Landscape Planning for Regional Recreation.* Soil Conservation Society of America, Ankeny, IA.

Likert, Rensis, 1961. *New Patterns of Management.* McGraw-Hill Book Company, New York. 279 pp.

Lindblom, C. E., 1968. *The Policy-making Process.* Prentice-Hall, Inc., Englewood Cliffs, NJ. 122 pp.

———, 1965. *The Intelligence of Democracy: Decision-making through Mutual Adjustment.* The Free Press, New York. 352 pp.

Little, R. Burton, Jr., 1968. *Forest Landscape Description and Inventories: A Basis for Land Planning and Design.* Pacific Southwest Forest and Range Experiment Station, U.S. Forest Service, Berkeley, CA.

MacKaye, Benton, 1928. *The New Exploration: A Philosophy of Regional Planning.* Harcourt, Brace and Company, Inc., New York. Paperback reprint, with introduction by Lewis Mumford, University of Illinois Press, Urbana, 1962.

McConnen, R., M. Kirby, D. Navon, 1968. *A Planning-Programming-Budgeting System for National Forest Administration.* Pacific Southwest Forest and Range Experiment Station, U.S. Forest Service, Berkeley, CA.

McDonald, John, 1950, 1963. *Strategy in Poker, Business, and War.* W. W. Norton and Company, Inc., New York.

McHarg, Ian, 1969. *Design with Nature.* Natural History Press, Garden City, NY.

Novick, David (ed.), 1964. *Program Budgeting.* The Rand Corporation, U.S. Government Printing Office, Washington, DC. 236 pp.

O'Connell, P. F., and H. E. Brown, 1972. "Use of Production Functions to Evaluate Multiple Use Treatments on Forested Watersheds." *Water Resources Research,* **8**(5):1188–1198.

Odum, E. P., and H. T. Odum, 1972. "Natural Areas as Necessary Components of Man's Total Environment." *Transactions of 37th North American Wildlife Conference.* Wildlife Management Institute, Washington, DC.

Pearse, P. H., 1968. "A New Approach to the Evaluation of Non-Priced Recreational Resources." *Land Economics,* **44**(1):87–99, University of Wisconsin, Madison.

Peters, G. H., 1968. *Cost-Benefit Analysis and Public Expenditure,* 2d ed. Eaton Paper No. 8. Institute of Economic Affairs, London.

———, 1970. "Land Use Studies in Britain: A Review of Literature with Special Reference to Applications of Cost-Benefit Applications." *Journal of Agricultural Economics,* **21**(2):171–214.

President's Water Resources Council, 1962. *Policies, Standards, and Procedures in the Formulation, Evaluation, and Review of Plans for Use and Development of Water and Related Land Resources.* 87th Cong., 2d Sess., S.D. 97.

Prest, A. R., and R. Turvey, 1965. "Cost-Benefit Analysis: A Survey." *Economic Journal,* **75**(4).

Regional Science Research Institute, U.S. Geological Survey, 1968. *The Plan and Program for the Brandywine.* Institute for Environmental Studies, University of Pennsylvania, Philadelphia.

Rogers, Taliafero, Kostritsky, Lamb, Planning Consultants, 1964. *The Plan for Downtown Cincinnati.* City of Cincinnati.

Rothenberg, Jerome, 1967. *Economic Evaluation of Urban Renewal: Conceptual Foundation of Benefit-Cost Analysis.* Studies of Government Finance. The Brookings Institution, Washington, DC.

Rowen, H. S., 1968. "PPBS: What and Why." *Civil Service Journal,* January–March 1968, pp. 5–9.

Sax, J. L., 1971. *Defending the Environment: A Strategy for Citizen Action.* Alfred A. Knopf, Inc., New York. 252 pp.

Schiffman, Irving, 1970. *The Politics of Land-Use Planning and Zoning; an Annotated Bibliography.* Davis Institute of Governmental Affairs, University of California Environmental Quality Series, no. 1.

Scott, Mel, 1969. *American City Planning since 1890.* University of California Press. 745 pp.

Second Report on Physical Planning in the Netherlands, 1966. *Future Pattern of Development,* part II, condensed ed. Government Printing Office of the Netherlands, The Hague. 86 pp.

Sewell, W. R. D., John Davis, A. D. Scott, D. W. Ross, 1965. *Guide to Benefit-Cost Analysis.* Roger Duhamel, F.R.S.C., Queen's Printer and Controller of Stationery, Ottawa, Canada. 49 pp.

Simon, H. A., 1957. *Administrative Behavior,* 2d ed. The Macmillan Company, New York.

————, 1959. "Theories of Decision-Making in Economics and Behavioral Science." *The American Economic Review,* **49**:253–283.

————, 1960. *The New Science of Management Decision.* Harper & Row, Publishers, Inc., New York.

Simonds, John Ormsbee, 1961. *Landscape Architecture: The Shaping of Man's Natural Environment.* McGraw-Hill Company, New York.

Sinden, J. A., 1967. "The Evaluation of Extra-Market Benefits: A Critical Review." Review article no. 7. *World Agriculture and Rural Sociology,* **9**(4):1–16.

Society of American Foresters, 1969. "Sound Resource Decisions: What Kind of Foresters Will Be Needed?" Symposium of two articles and four discussion papers. *Journal of Forestry,* **67**:569–572.

Steffens, Lincoln, 1931. *The Autobiography of Lincoln Steffens.* Harcourt, Brace and Company, Inc., New York.

Stewart, G. A. (ed.), 1968. *Symposium on Land Evaluation.* Macmillan of Australia, Melbourne. 392 pp.

U.S. Bureau of the Budget, 1965. *Planning-Programming-Budgeting; Instructions for Systems Establishment as Directed by the President.* U.S. Bureau of the Budget Bulletin 66-3.

U.S. Congress, 1969. *The National Environmental Policy Act of 1969,* P.L. 91-190.

————, 1970. *The Environmental Quality Improvement Act of 1970,* P.L. 91-224.

U.S. Forest Service, 1968. *Planning-Programming-Budgeting-Allocation.* Report of Apr. 30, 1968. El Dorado National Forest, CA.

————, 1971. *Guide for Managing the National Forests in the Appalachians.*

————, 1971. *System for Managing the National Forests in the East.*

————, 1973. *The Outlook for Timber in the United States.*

————, 1973. *Roadless and Undeveloped Areas; Final Environmental Impact Statement.* 670 pp.

U.S. Water Resources Council, 1971. "Proposed Principles and Standards for Planning Water and Related Land Resources." *Federal Register,* **36**(245):24144–24194.

————, 1972. *Summary and Analysis of Public Response to the Proposed Principles and Standards for Planning Water and Related Land Resources and Draft Environmental Statement.* 135 pp.

————, 1973. "Water and Related Land Resources: Establishment of Principles and Standards." *Federal Register,* 38(174):24778–24869.

U.S. Water Resources Council, Policy and Procedures Committee, 1973. *Work Group Report, Part I (May 1973) and Part II (June 1973), on Principles and Standards.* U.S. Water Resources Council, 2120 L St., N.W., Washington, DC.

Vermont State Planning Office, 1971. *Vermont Interim Land Capability Plan.* Prepared for presentation to the State Environmental Board, Walter H. Blucher, general consultant.

Walker, R. G., 1961. "The Judgment Factor in Investment Decisions." *Harvard Business Review,* Capital Investment Series, 39(2):93–99.

Williams, T. H., and C. H. Griffin, 1967. *Management Information: A Quantitative Accent.* Richard D. Irwin, Inc. Homewood, IL.

Bibliography: Group 3

Chapters 9 to 12: Land Use in Action; Case Studies

Agarwal, S. K., 1971. *Economics of Land Consolidation in India.* S. Chand, New Delhi. 159 pp.

Agena, Kathleen (with Richard Spicer), 1972. "Tahoe." *ASPO, a Newsletter of the American Society of Planning Officials,* **38**(1):3–16.

Ames, L. W., 1972. "The Real Life Adventures of a Planning Agency; Protecting Lake Tahoe I." *California Journal,* **3**(1):12, 16–17.

Ayer, J. D., 1972. "A trip through the Fiscal Wilderness: Protecting Lake Tahoe." *California Journal,* **3**(1):13–15.

Barney, C. W., and R. E. Dils, 1972. *Bibliography of Clearcutting on Western Forests.* College of Forestry, Colorado State University. 65 pp.

Bohte, Hans-Günther, 1970. *Landeskultur und Verbesserung der Agrarstruktur in der Gesetzgebung.* Landschriftenverlag GmbH, Berlin-Bonn, Kurfürstenstrasse 53. Printed by Landwirtschaftsverlag, Hiltrup bei Münster. 313 pp.

Botz, Maxwell, J. D. Coons, R. R. Ream, 1972. *Report and Draft Environmental Statement for the Lake Tahoe Plan and Effectuating Ordinances.* Theodore J. Wirth and Associates, Billings, MT, and Chevy Chase, MD. 115 pp.

Brendt, Steven, 1971. "What's Going Wrong at Lake Tahoe." *Sierra Club Bulletin,* **56**(10):8–10, December 1971.

Brooks, Paul, 1967. "The Fight for America's Alps." *The Atlantic,* February 1967, pp. 87–90, 97–99.

Bundeskanzler Brandt, Bundesrepublik Deutschland, 1972. *Raumornungsbericht, 1972.* (Report on German land or space ordering.) Bonner Universitäts-Buchdruckerei, 53 Bonn 1. 193 pp.

Bundesministerium für Ernährung, Landwirtschaft und Forsten, 1968. *Das Dorf im Wandel.* Landwirtschaftsverlag GmbH, Hiltrup bei Münster (Westfalen). 124 pp., illus.

Burk, D. A., 1970. *The Clearcut Crisis: Controversy in the Bitterroot.* Foreword by Michael Frome. Jursnick Printing, Great Falls, MT. 152 pp., illus.

The Case for a Blue Ribbon Commission on timber management in the National Forests, n.d. (late 1970). Joint publication of the Rocky Mountain Chapter of the Sierra Club and the Western Regional Office of the Wilderness Society. No publisher given. 72 pp.

Citizens Review Committee, 1967. *Report of the Magruder Corridor Review Committee.* Presented to Secretary of Agriculture Orville L. Freeman, Apr. 17, 1967. Processed report made available to public.

Crafts, E. C., 1971. "Men and Events behind the Redwood National Park." *American Forests,* 77(5):20–28, 58.

Craig, J. B., 1971. "Montana's Select Committee." *American Forests,* 72(2):35–37, 48–49.

Davis, K. P., 1971. "A-B-C-s of Even-aged Management." *American Forests,* 7(8):19–21, 49–50.

——— (ed.), 1972. *Southern Forest Industry and the Environment.* Environmental Improvement Committee, Southeastern Technical Division, American Pulpwood Association. 80 pp.

Davis, R. G., 1970. *Regional Government for Lake Tahoe: A Case Study.* Institute of Governmental Affairs, University of California, Davis, Environmental Quality Series, no. 2.

Environmental Policy Division, Congressional Research Service, 1972. *Public Land Policy: Activities in the 92d Congress,* prepared by Elmer W. Shaw. U.S. Government Printing Office, Washington, DC. 26 pp.

———, 1972. *An Analysis of Forestry Issues in the First Session of the 92d Congress,* prepared by Elmer W. Shaw. U.S. Government Printing Office, Washington, DC. 64 pp.

Erz, Wolfgang, 1970. *Nature Conservation and Landscape Management in the Federal Republic of Germany—Dates, Facts, and Figures.* Association of German Commissioners for Nature Conservation and Landscape Management. 53 Bonn–Bad Godesberg, Heerstrasse 110.

Evans, D. J., 1966. *North Cascades National Recreation Area; Report and Recommendations.* Report by Governor Daniel J. Evans, state of Washington.

Federal Ministry of Food, Agriculture and Forestry, 1967. *Forestry and Wood Economy in the Federal Republic of Germany,* 5th ed. Published by the Land- und Hauswirtschaftlicher Auswertungs- und Informationsdienst e.V. (AID, 532), Bad Godesberg, Heerstrasse 124. 151 pp.

Hasel, K., 1971. *Waldwirtschaft und Umwelt: Eine Einführung in die Forstwirtschaftspolitik.* Paul Parey Verlag, Hamburg and Berlin.

Hottes, Karlheinz, Sürgen Blenk, und Uwe Meyer, 1973. *Die Flurbereinigung als Instrument aktiver Landschaftspflege.* Landswirtschaftsverlag GmbH, Hiltrup bei Münster.

House of Representatives Report 1870, 90th Cong. 2d Sess., 1968. *Report establishing the North Cascades National Park and Ross Lake National Recreation Area, et seq.* 22 pp.

Joglekar, N. M., 1962. *Report on Consolidation of Holdings in Madhya Pradesh (Pilot Survey 1956–57).* New Delhi Research Programmes Committee, Planning Commission. 100 pp.

Kenny, N. T., 1968. "New National Park Proposed, the Spectacular North Cascades." *National Geographic,* **133**(5):642–667.

Ministry of Agriculture and Fisheries, n.d. *Rural development in the Netherlands.* Government Service for Land and Water Use. 23 pp.

———, 1954. *Land Consolidation Act of 1954.* Government Service for Land and Water Use, Maliebaan 21, Utrecht, the Netherlands. 40 pp.

Molfenter, R., 1969. *Das Flurbereinigungsgesetz,* 4th ed. W. Kohlhammer, Deutscher Gemeindeverlag, Stuttgart.

Müller, Peter, 1964. "Recent Developments in Land Tenure and Land Policies in Germany." *Land Economics,* **10**(3):267–275.

Niemeier, Hans-Gerhart, with assistance by Gerhard Bensberg, 1967. *Landesplanungsrecht in N. W. Nordrhein-Westfalen, West Germany.* Verlag für Wirtschaft und Verwaltung, Hubert Wingen.

North Cascades Study Team, 1965. *The North Cascades; a Report to the Secretary of the Interior and the Secretary of Agriculture.* U.S. Government Printing Office, Washington, DC. 190 pp., illus.

Norton, Boyd, 1972. "The Oldest Established Perennially Debated Tree Fight in the West; the Magruder Corridor Issue." *Audubon,* **72**(4):61–69.

Parks, Edwards, and Kathleen Revis, 1961. "Washington Wilderness, the North Cascades." *National Geographic,* **119**(3):334–364.

Public Lands Subcommittee, 1972. *Clearcutting on Federal Timberlands.* Report to the Committee on Interior and Insular Affairs, U.S. Senate, 92d Cong., 2d Sess., March 1972. 13 pp.

Public Law 90-544, 90th Cong., S. 1321, Oct. 2, 1968. To establish the North Cascades National Park and Ross Lake and Lake Chelan National Recreation Areas, to designate the Pasayten Wilderness and to modify the Glacier Peak Wilderness, in the state of Washington, and for other purposes.

Report of the Federal Republic of Germany on the Human Environment, 1972. Prepared for United Nations Conference on Human Environment, Stockholm. Published by the Federal Minister of the Interior.

Report of the Lake Tahoe Joint Study Committee, March 1967. Prepared and printed by the committee. 56 pp.

Senate Report 700, 90th Cong., 1st Sess., Oct. 31, 1968. Report authorizing the establishment of the North Cascades National Park, the Ross Lake and Lake Chelan National Recreation Areas, designating the Pasayten Wilderness, and for other purposes. 42 pp.

Smith, R. M., n.d. (circa 1969). "Reconnaissance Report—Lake Tahoe Basin Area." Unpublished. 26 pp.

————, 1971. *Housing Study of the Lake Tahoe Basin.* Report prepared for the Tahoe Regional Planning Agency, April 1971.

Society of American Foresters, 1968. "Decision in the North Cascades." Five viewpoints: A. M. Roberts, J. H. Stone, J. M. Kauffmann, G. R. Staebler, W. R. Cotton, Jr. *Journal of Forestry,* **66**:521–546.

Southern Forest Resources Analysis Committee, 1969. *The South's Third Forest.* No publisher given. 111 pp.

Tahoe Regional Planning Agency, 1971. "Proposed Regional Plan, Lake Tahoe Region, California–Nevada." TRPA, May 1971. South Lake Tahoe, CA. Unpublished. 63 pp.

Tomlinson, O. A., and others, 1937. *Report of Committee, Northern Cascades Area Investigation.* National Park Service. 40 pp. (typed).

U.S. Forest Service, 1970. *Framework for the Future: Forest Service Objectives and Policy Guides.*

————, 1971. *National Forest Management in a Quality Environment: Timber Productivity.*

————, 1972. *National Forests in a Quality Environment: Action Plan.*

U.S. Forest Service Special Review Committee, 1970. *Even-Age Management on the Monongahela National Forest.* 39 pp., illus.

U.S. Forest Service Task Force, 1970. *Management Practices on the Bitterroot National Forest.* A Task Force Appraisal, May 1969–April 1970. 100 pp., illus.

University of Montana Select Committee, 1970. *Report on the Bitterroot National Forest.* Univ. of Montana. 33 pp.

Washington State Planning Council, 1940. *Cascades Mountains Study.* Washington State Report. 56 pp., illus.

Wirth, T. J., and Associates, 1972. *Report and Draft Environmental Impact Statement for the Lake Tahoe Plan and Effectuating Ordinances.* Theodore J. Wirth and Associates, Billings, MT, and Chevy Chase, MD. 115 pp.

Wood, Nancy, 1971. *Clearcut: The Deforestation of America.* Sierra Club, San Francisco.

Wyoming Joint Forest Study Team, 1971. *Forest Management in Wyoming.* Timber harvest and the environment on the Teton, Bridger, Wyoming, and Bighorn National Forests. U.S. Forest Service. 81 pp., illus.

INDEX